A Trenchard Brat

A Life in Aviation

To Des Longthorne

A Trenchard Brat

A Life in Aviation

by

**Flt. Lt. Frederick George Weston M.B.E.,
F.R.Ae.S. RAF(Rtd.)**

With Best Wishes

Fred Weston

13th Nov 2002

First published by Brewin Books Ltd.
Studley, Warwickshire B80 7LG in 1999.

© 1999: Flt. Lt. Frederick George Weston M.B.E.

British Library Cataloguing in Publication Data
A catalogue record for this book is available from
The British Library

ISBN: 1 85858 152 4

Typeset in Times
and made and printed in Great Britain
by Warwick Printing Company Limited,
Theatre Street, Warwick, Warwickshire CV34 4DR

ACKNOWLEDGEMENTS

The portrait of Lord Trenchard shown on the Frontispiece has been reproduced by kind permission of the Royal Air Force Club, Piccadilly, London.

Per Ardua ad Astra by Michael Donne and Sq/Ldr. Cynthia Fowler

The Turn of the Tide by Arthur Bryant

Memoirs of World War II by Winston S. Churchill

Courage in the Skies by Johnnie Johnson and P.B. Laddie Lucas

Ribbentrop by Michael Bloch

The Luftwaffe 1933–1945 by Prof. Wilkinson Murray

Pure Luck (Biography of Sir Thomas Sopwith) by A. Bramson

North American Indian Wars by Richard Dillon

I pay tribute to the loyal band of RAF "Cavemen" of the Propellor Repair Section with their proud Latinised motto "Ubendem Wemendem" whose untiring efforts in the Egyptan Tura Caves (No 111 M.U.) gave me such faithful support and thus ensured our highly successful contribution to the victorious North African Campaign in World War II.

For my family whose insistence and continuing encouragement caused this book to be written.

To my wife Pam for her support, encouragement, and able typing without which the book would never have been written

TABLE OF CONTENTS

Foreword

By Group Captain D.N. Williams O.B.E., B.Sc., C.Eng., F.R.Ae.S., R.A.F. Officer Commanding, R.A.F. Station Cosford

Throughout recent history many characters and events have shaped the Royal Air Force, none more so than Lord Trenchard. His vision and dedication as the Service emerged from the Royal Flying Corps during the First World War provided the foundation for the high regard in which the Royal Air Force is held today.

One of Lord Trenchard's many innovations was the apprenticeship scheme for aircraft technicians entering the newly formed Royal Air Force. He realised that the Royal Air Force could not rely on recruiting sufficient skilled tradesmen from civilian life with aircraft skills and this led to his pioneering the introduction of the scheme in 1920, at Royal Air Force Halton in Buckinghamshire. Entrants to the apprenticeship scheme became known as 'Trenchard Brats', a nickname they adopted with pride. From those early days to the present, Royal Air Force technical training has been regarded as a world leader and graduates have proved equal to this reputation. Their resourcefulness over many years has been backbone to the Royal Air Force's engineering maintenance capability, ensuring the serviceability and reliability of aircraft in both peacetime and war. To their great credit, many graduated into the commissioned flying and engineer branches of the Service and achieved great distinction. The development and design of many modern-day aircraft and equipment also bear witness to their outstanding achievements.

The author of this book, a retired RAF engineer officer, now 92 years old, is a product of the Trenchard apprenticeship scheme and is truly a Trenchard Brat emanating not from RAF Halton but from the No. 2 School of Technical Training at RAF Cranwell. Here in September 1923, along with Frank Whittle, the jet pioneer, he was one of a group of boys commencing their three years training in aeronautical engineering.

This book tells the story of his entire working life spent in aviation from the earliest types of aircraft to modern jets. It covers thirty long years in military aviation (RAF) and seventeen years in civil aviation. (de Havilland Company). The value of his apprenticeship training is evident from the services he has rendered to aviation throughout his long eventful life in which he has had innumerable exciting experiences all over the world, including the Middle East and Far East, South Africa and Europe.

The Royal Air Force apprenticeship scheme has been instrumental in ensuring that training needs were adapted to changes in technology, it has continued to faithfully serve the Royal Air Force and its legacy will continue for many years to come. The Royal Air Force still recognises the value of apprenticeship training and modern day recruits wishing to undergo aircraft technician training now follow a Modern Technical Apprenticeship. The raison d'être of the 'Trenchard Brat' remains with us ñ aircraft technical training has been designed to train our people for tomorrow's Royal Air Force by developing strong technical and military skills together with a fierce pride in the Service.

Portrait of Marshal of the Royal Air Force Lord Trenchard

Chapter 1

Birth, Boyhood and Background
Working Class Life in Pre World War I
England

The doctor spoke: 'I'm sorry but this baby has acute dysentery and will not live another twenty-four hours'. Turning to leave he said : 'I will not be calling again. You may call at the surgery for the death certificate'.

So has it been described to me by my mother, this episode in my young life as a baby of six months at death's door.

As was usual for poor families at that time, 1907, the year of my birth, the local doctor was called in only in extreme urgency, in desperation and as a last resort. He knew full well that his services could not be afforded by such a poverty stricken family, which was the reason why he uttered that apparently callous final instruction.

Fortunately for me my young and inexperienced mother, 20 years of age, had a very good neighbour next door. This lady was aware of my condition and knew the doctor was calling. As soon as she saw him leave she rushed round to my mother and asked her what had transpired with the doctor.

On hearing the news this good lady exclaimed: 'To hell with the doctor. We are not going to let this baby die. Have you any brandy?' Fortunately my father, in a surge of Christmas good cheer, had bought a bottle of Martells 3-star brandy which had lasted throughout the year – and this purchase became a habit each year afterwards. Thus my mother was able to produce the requested 'eau de vie' and I was spoon-fed with it, proving it really was 'eau de vie'! This may account for my favourite tipple in later years!

I was born in a humble terraced house in a run-down poor quarter of Old Portsmouth. The address was 11 Wilton Terrace, Upper Church Path, Landport. It no longer exists, following the German bombing blitz during the Battle of Britain. The ensuing reconstruction and redevelopment of Portsmouth after the Second World War eliminated this street layout.

My parents were poor working class like the majority of people in England at that time. My mother's maiden name was Flora Webber and her parents were upper working class, her father being a foreman shipwright in H.M. Portsmouth Dockyard. He was a member of the Order of Masons and in those Victorian times he was respected as a man of worthy and honourable status. He had re-married after his first wife died. All his children were borne by his first wife and thus the children were reared by a stepmother. This lady was a very severe Victorian martinet with very little sympathy or understanding of the youngsters who, consequently, all left home at the earliest possible moment.

To escape this unhappy environment my mother married young and hastily. Her young husband, whose parents owned a hotel near Fratton Bridge, died of consumption within a year of their marriage. A baby boy was born but he too died within a few months. Thus the young widow, whose married name was now Flora Spearing, returned to her parents' home at 127 New Road, Portsmouth. She then became an apprentice dressmaker in a well-known establishment in Southsea. She began taking piano lessons at the house of a young lady music teacher and there she met the teacher's brother, Henry George Weston, who became her second husband. They were married on 1st December 1906.

My father was born in London at 4 Ballantine Street, Wandsworth on 17th May 1884. His father was William Frederick Weston and his mother was Annie Amelia Weston nee Benstead. His father was a master baker with his own business in Wandsworth. Unfortunately he became an alcoholic and by his drinking habits he destroyed his business and his family. He became bankrupt and the family moved to Portsmouth where he had found a job as a baker's assistant in a small old-fashioned family bakery cum cake shop in Arundel Street. However his continued drinking finally ruined his life and he finished in the Portsmouth workhouse. I have vivid memories of visiting him on some Sunday afternoons carrying gifts of pipe tobacco for him. I entered a grey building like a prison. In fact it was opposite Portsmouth prison. Climbing stairs I entered a kind of huge dormitory where there were lines of beds similar to an army barrack room and dozens of men all dressed in a uniform thick rough grey cloth suiting. My grandfather with his prickly

My parents on Portsdown Hill, Portsmouth

ill-shaven chin would greet me and painfully kiss me whilst I would fearfully present my package and retreat as rapidly as possible, glad to escape from that morbid atmosphere.

My father had several brothers and sisters, none of whom were outstandingly successful in life with the exception of one older brother, Thomas, who had achieved some distinction in England in the horticultural world. Uncle Tom was born on December 12th 1877 and, like my father, spent his early days in Wandsworth, London and was taken to Portsmouth with the rest of the family. Tom became interested in horticulture at a very young age and built his first 'greenhouse' when in his early teens. He served an apprenticeship as a gardener on a large estate owned by a distinguished family in England. Later he became associated with many well-known nurseries and seed concerns, gradually becoming recognised as an authority on hybridisation of plants. He succeeded in producing by cross-breeding a number of new varieties of flowers such as carnations, sweet peas and other economic and ornamental plants and even introduced new varieties of potatoes. He was elected secretary of the British Sweet Pea Society and the British Carnation Society. The latter Society awarded him a special gold medal upon his resignation. He was a well-known horticultural writer, having contributed many articles to gardening journals and professional florists' magazines as well as special sections to the Encyclopaedia Britannica and a horticultural dictionary. He emigrated to the United States in 1921 and had a very distinguished career in the horticultural world in New York. He also had a regular gardening column in the New York Herald Tribune.

I was born on 13th October 1907. My father was employed at this time as a labourer on the L. and S.W. Railway and I believe he graduated to becoming a porter before leaving the Railways to become a self-taught watchmaker and jeweller employed in a small family jeweller's establishment in Russel Street. After a few years experience in this employment he decided to leave and set up his own business as a self-employed watchmaker and jeweller with premises in Fratton Road, Portsmouth. To have acquired such self-taught skills and embarked on such an enterprise with little or no capital or support was greatly commendable and required no small intelligence and considerable courage. This was an era when social security was an unknown term. For the working class there was no security except from their own efforts. The old-fashioned Workhouse was the penalty for those who failed to provide their own security. The Workhouse was the great dread of all the working class. Independence was the only way of life and was mandatory to all who wished to avoid the dreaded Workhouse. To maintain independence was the daily struggle and the jealous pride of all working class families.

To break out of the social level into which one was born was considered to be almost an impossibility. This was an era in which class distinction and class privilege were still the ruling social order. It was the universally accepted unwritten law that the class into which you were born was your ordained social status given by the Almighty. It was not a matter to question and few people did.

People who might aspire to improve their social status were viewed with suspicion and often hostility. It was described commonly as 'thinking above their station in life'. Against such possibilities many barriers had been erected and to climb these required exceptionally high levels of intelligence and character. Few people in the early years of this century achieved such levels.

It is fashionable in these days to claim that the poor working class of this country in the nineteenth and early twentieth centuries were supported by extensive charity networks mostly provided by the middle and upper classes. It is claimed that to a large extent these charities provided by private people furnished a level of assistance to the needy similar to that of the Social Security Services of modern times. This is totally untrue. A small number of charities certainly existed. But as previously mentioned the poor working class were jealous of their independence and it was considered degrading to ask for or accept charity. In any case the availability of charity assistance was so little and so limited that it would have been impossible to provide much assistance except for a very small number of people. I witnessed this when my mother needed some urgent hospital treatment for my young sister. It took my mother weeks of effort every day going round the town begging various sponsors for special coupons which, added together, would provide the necessary entitlement to the required treatment. Snobbery was accepted as a natural function for all classes including the working classes.

For most working class people unfortunate enough to need help from the local authorities controlling municipal charity the regulations were terrifying. The municipal charity was the workhouse. The applicants for the municipal charity were forced to exhaust their entire savings and to sell all their possessions including all their furniture until they were reduced to nothing in their house but the regulation one table and chairs. They were then eligible to apply for public assistance which was the workhouse. In the workhouse husband and wife were not permitted to be together. They were separated and forced to enter into prison-like institutions, one for males and another for females and children. It is not surprising that the greatest fear of the working class at this time was the workhouse and the loss of family and independence and the potential descent into the gloomy depths of official charity.

Against these odds my father made a success of his business and quickly gained a very favourable reputation in the neighbourhood and amongst his fellow tradesmen in their various businesses in Fratton Road. This was later to prove very fortunate both for my mother and for my father.

The premises which my father rented were in a row of Victorian properties in Fratton Road almost opposite Newcombe Road. They consisted of a large old three bedroom Victorian house, in which the sizeable ground floor front room had been converted to form a shop fronting directly onto the main road. A door in the rear of the shop gave into the living quarters. In the shop window area was my father's work bench and working items including a jeweller's lathe with some small display of watches etc. The shop window must have been a goodly size for I remember my father was persuaded to display the Portsmouth variety theatre weekly programme for which he received free tickets each week. Thus he was enabled to take his family occasionally to the local theatre in Lake Road – in the gallery! I shall never forget the first occasion in the evening, climbing the stairs inside the theatre and then entering the gallery at the back and looking down in fear, 'horror of horrors'! I was sure that I would fall down that dark precipice, so steep and deep, down to the seemingly bottomless pit.

We had a large garden at the rear of the house which adjoined, and was shared by a family in the next door shop. This was an old-fashioned family sweet shop run by a widow, Mrs. King, with three children of a similar age to myself. Mrs. King specialised in boiled sweets which she made herself in her kitchen. Many times I witnessed the making of them and marvelled at her skill in producing such wonderful skeins of hot shining sugary lengths which eventually were divided down into the delicious boiled sweets on display in her shop window. And she made toffee apples by the hundreds laid out in beautiful rows on trays like soldiers on parade. At the annual August Fair on Portsdown Hill Mrs. King would always have a stall and she would hire a horse and flat cart to take all her sweets and toffee apples to her stall there. All of us children were permitted to ride on the cart to the fair, which was a journey of 3 or 4 miles. Such a great adventure was so thrilling and such huge joy!

Further down the road from my Father's shop was the Globe cinema where we children often had a wonderful afternoon film show of Cowboys and Indians with a parting present of a small bag of sweets and an orange when we came out of the cinema. Next to the cinema was the Carnegie Public Library where I became a member at a very young age and marvelled at this splendid palace of thousands of exciting books all at my disposal – for a limited period of time. A little further on was the imposing and elegant St. Mary's Church with its magnificent clock tower. I shall never forget the profound impression I received when I first heard the mighty thunder but beautiful music of the church organ occasionally played during my confirmation class.

At this time cars and coaches were practically unknown and horses and carriages were commonplace. I remember it was the sport of little boys, myself included, to run behind the hackney carriages and secure a seat on the back beam, which joined the two back wheels. We would thus have a free ride hidden from the driver perched high in the front. This happy state of affairs lasted only until the carriage passed other boys on the pavement who, with children's mutual cruelty to each other, would call out to the cab driver 'Whip behind, Governor'. Then the cab driver, who carried a long horsewhip, would slash to the rear of his cab and dislodge his unwelcome passengers. Electric trams rumbled along rails laid in the middle of the cobbled road and most people rode bicycles. In fact, at the age of six, whilst running across the road, I was knocked down by a bicycle and suffered damage to my nose which in later life caused difficulties.

It is interesting to note that at this time occurred an event in my young life which

I so well remember, and which I now realise, looking back, was an astonishing link with the cruel, crude and primitive birth of the Mid-West of the United States of America as we now know it. The period I am referring to is, of course, the tremendous movement of American white settlers westwards around the middle of the 19th century, resulting in the building of the Union Pacific Railway which, crossing the Rocky Mountains, finally united the East and West. And the event which I remember was none other than Buffalo Bill's Circus which came to Portsmouth and set up on Southsea Common.

Buffalo Bill was an American hero and was known internationally for his tremendous exploits as an American frontiersman. A frontiersman was one of the early pioneers of the American settler movement westwards. These pioneers were in the vanguard of the white settlers and thus experienced all the difficulties and dangers from the Red Indian tribes who were being driven westwards. The frontiersmen were scouts and guides and often operated the crude wagon trains that were the only means of transportation at that time. They not only lived in constant danger from Indian attack but also existed in an environment of lawlessness where the gun was the law and men often survived only by their expertise with their guns.

Such a man was Buffalo Bill whose real name was Colonel William F. Cody. He had a remarkable career as a frontiersman from boyhood. His life span from 1845 until his death in 1917 covered a tremendous period of amazing feats. He gained his rank of Colonel from his valuable service to the American Army as a scout and guide during the many battles of the wars against the Red Indians. These wars were not finally terminated until the year 1890, only 17 years before I was born.

After the Wild West was subdued and pacified there was little work left for frontiersmen of Buffalo Bill's class. He hit on the idea of creating a Wild West show and became an actor playing himself as frontiersman. He gathered together a theatrical company and a number of Red Indians complete with all their war weapons, their exotic feathery regalia and war costumes, and their horses. He organised a complete show and drama, often with a mock attack on a full-scale stagecoach. This proved a tremendous success in the States so that he finally exported the idea to England, where it gained equal success. In England the show moved around the country as a Wild West circus.

So here in Portsmouth as a very small boy I was privileged to see Buffalo Bill's Circus making a promotional procession past my father's shop in Fratton Road. The road must have been closed to traffic because I remember a stage coach rumbling down the middle of the cobbled road with its team of horses, driver and guards. Circling the coach were the white men cowboys on horseback and riding on each side of the road in single file were the Red Indians, also mounted, some in their full-feathered regalia and others bare-chested with feathered headgear, proceeding at a trotting pace on each side of the stage coach. Whether it was the original Buffalo Bill himself I cannot be sure, but the circus procession certainly made a deep impression on this little boy. Indians and cowboys were the heart and soul of all boys' adventure stories at that time.

Another event in my young life that occurred about this time was a great Royal Review of His Majesty's Royal Navy in the Solent just off the Southsea shores. There was a grand sea-borne ceremonial inspection by King George V in the Royal Yacht, possibly as a propaganda exercise just prior to the outbreak of World War I in 1914. My mother and father took us to the Southsea sea-front to see this mighty Armada in all its colourful decoration and the event created a considerable national and international sensation. But it did not deter the Germans from their World War I ambitions in August 1914 led by their aggressive and contemptuous Kaiser Wilhelm II.

Chapter 2

World War I
Disaster for the Weston Family

My father was now making steady progress with his jewellery and watch-making business and the future looked rosy. Suddenly disaster struck. The 1914 war was declared, and Father, who had previously in his younger days volunteered to join the Territorial Army, was immediately called up. On August 4th 1914, the day war was declared, he received his Army instructions to report to Colchester Army Depot.

On arrival there he soon found himself made a member of the British Expeditionary Force and bound for the front line at Mons in Belgium. Here the British force was scornfully described by the German Kaiser Wilhelm as the 'Old Contemptibles' and he prophesied that the German invading army would soon prove their superiority by destroying the British Army.

The German army certainly showed its superiority. Up to a point. The British were forced to retreat rapidly from Mons to avoid being surrounded and destroyed. My father described to me how the retreat of the army from Mons involved marching day and night for a whole week until they finally arrived in the environs of Paris. Here they made a stand. During the retreat they had rest periods during the night of a few hours only on the floor of places like abandoned breweries or anywhere else large enough to give them shelter. They were forbidden to remove their boots because being so footsore they would never get them back on again.

Their rearguard was continuously harassed by the German cavalry, the dreaded Uhlan lancers. He said that after some days men began falling out by the roadside, no longer able to continue due to painful sore feet. If they were lying by the roadside when the German Uhlans appeared they were sometimes used as practice targets for their lance thrusts.

The Allies defence around Paris succeeded in stopping the German advance. The French rushed reserve troops to the Allied lines using all kinds of transport including taxis! The fighting was so close to the city that the Germans were able to train their big guns (nicknamed 'Big Berthas') on the city itself. The French commander of the Allied force, General Joffre, established a strong defence line on the River Marne and in the ensuing Battle of the Marne (September 5th-9th) Paris was saved.

The Allies resistance held. In fact, the Germans were forced to backtrack a little to the River Aisne. Here began the disastrous horrific trench warfare where human life was at its lowest value and sank to utter degradation and the sacrifices were completely futile. A whole generation of the young men of Europe was destroyed. In the trenches junior officers often had a life expectancy of a few days only.

My mother by this time had four children of whom I, at the age of seven, was the eldest and my brother Lesley, at 5 months, was the youngest. On the day of my father's departure we all prepared to escort him to Fratton Railway Station for this sad farewell. Just before we left the house my father, holding me close, said: –'Now son, don't forget you are head of the house while I'm away, so you must look after your mother!' We all trudged up to the station with my father. My mother was pushing a pram in which were my baby sister and brother. Having seen my father off, my mother, downhearted and in despair, could not face up to returning to our empty house. And so she walked us to the Southsea sea front and only returned to the house when we children were too tired to walk any further. Back at the house her lonely situation seemed to overwhelm her. Typical of the times, she had never had responsibilities outside of the household, and she had never been left alone. My father had always accepted all responsibility and made all decisions. Now here she was with four young children, a large house, the shop, and a watchmaker's business, of which she knew nothing. She could expect no help from her own family for she was not on good terms with her stepmother.

After our evening meal my mother announced to us that we would now all go to bed and we would all sleep in her bedroom. So up we went and, having settled the baby and my sister, my mother then instructed me (a seven year old!!) to assist her in moving a tall-boy chest of drawers into a position against the bedroom door. This manoeuvre seemed to help her to a greater sense of security against a possible intruder!

Our situation was indeed bleak, especially financially, for my father was called into the army as a private soldier with his pay the magnificent sum of one shilling a day. My mother would have an army allowance of a few shillings a week for the whole family. These rates had not been changed since Victorian times.

Coming down to breakfast the next morning we began the first dreadful day of our new unhappy changed life. My mother laid the table for breakfast - with a large tablecloth whose folds extended almost to the floor. Whilst my mother was in the kitchen preparing the food my baby sister, crawling around the floor of the dining-room, grabbed the table cloth fold and pulled the whole breakfast lay-out onto the floor. Bread, butter, sugar, milk, plates, teapot, cups, saucers, all went crashing onto the floor. A disastrous start to a gloomy day !

After breakfast my mother opened up the shop dreading the arrival of customers with difficult watch repair problems. The common belief and official opinion at the time was that the war would be over by Christmas. Thus my father, before leaving for the front, had asked my mother to keep the shop open as he thought he would return by Christmas. He had made an arrangement with his previous employer, Mr. Jones, whereby my mother could receive watch repairs at the shop and Jones would carry them out. Of course the war was not over by Christmas. In fact it went on for more than four years. As a consequence my father did not return as he expected and his plans to resume his business failed to materialise.

A never forgotten episode my young mind registered at this time occurred at night soon after the War was declared in 1914 and my father had departed. I had gone to bed and had been asleep some while when I was awakened by an unusual loud noise coming from the street. Getting out of bed and peering through the curtain I was amazed to see long lanes of hundreds of horses with mounted soldiers in khaki all clip-clopping along with horse teams pulling guns and wagons. The noise of so many horses' hooves and the bumping along of the gun carriages etc. on the street cobbles seemed to be like continuous thunder with tinkling rainfall. I presume it was a regiment of World War I Royal Artillery embarking for France.

Later in those war years I witnessed another spectacular event at night when again I was awakened by noise and excitement. This time my mother called me downstairs to see an amazing sight in the sky. It looked like a silver cigar seemingly floating along high in the heavens, an eerie ghostly cigar suspended in space. In fact it was a German Zeppelin which had been caught in the beams of the defence searchlights located around Portsmouth. Of course I did not realise its significance as aerial warfare had not yet become known to little boys of the 1914 era. Whether the Zeppelin had made or intended to make an attack on Portsmouth, I never knew but the moment when we saw it high above it looked a shining peaceful pretty picture.

My mother struggled along to run the shop as my father had wished but it was all too much with four young children and no help. In the end she was utterly confused and found herself in trouble with the authorities with a court summons for failing to pay her rates. It was at this point that the good relationship with the neighbouring tradesmen which had been established previously by my father, came to the rescue. The local butcher, Mr. Billing, who was on the town council, wishing to show appreciation of my father's sacrifice for the country, assumed protective care of our family and he paid the resulting fine. It should be remembered that at that time there was no conscription. All the members of the armed forces were volunteers. The carnage that ensued in the mud of Flanders finally required more 'cannon fodder' and in 1916 total conscription of the country's manpower was introduced. War widows and fatherless families became commonplace. With the killing of hundreds of thousands of men the wives at home lived in constant fear of the dreaded telegram or letter stating her man was killed, or missing, believed killed. She would receive a few personal possessions of her husband's and that was all she had left of her man.

It was inevitable that the shop arrangements my mother was endeavouring to carry out at the behest of my father must fail. And fail they did. The shop was closed down. My mother gave up the premises and moved to a rented terrace house in Stamford Street which was close by. My father spent his Christmas in the primitive trenches in France. His Christmas dinner was bully beef and hard Army ration biscuits, eaten while sitting in a muddy trench. In heavy rains these trenches would be like ditches, sometimes filled with water up to the soldiers' knees. It is a strange fact that the opposing lines of trenches were so close that on this Christmas day of 1914 a kind of unofficial truce occurred. Greetings were exchanged across No-man's Land and in some places even football matches were arranged. Later such fraternisation was forbidden.

As the Allies gained experience in this slogging static trench warfare so trench construction improved. Amenities were introduced such as deep dugouts where dry comparatively secure conditions could be organised for special purposes. One of these special purposes involved my father. His commanding officer discovered my father's watch repairing skills and set him up with a little bench deep down in a dugout. With some locally garnered tools my father then became the official dugout watch repairer. There were no watch repair facilities for the troops as far as the shells could reach so my father had a kind of underground monopoly in his local war zone..

Unfortunately twice in two years his dugout was demolished by a shell and he had to be dug out of the dugout. In spite of the terrible slaughter of millions of men my father managed to survive. He returned home in 1916, having completed his official term of service. Here again his good standing with his former butcher neighbour proved of tremendous value. With the aid of the butcher's influence as a councillor on the town council my father obtained a post as an instrument maker technician in H.M. Portsmouth Dockyard. Shortly afterwards national conscription was introduced by the War Minister, the famous Lord Kitchener. However my father's work in the Naval Dockyard was a reserved occupation. He was thus saved from returning to the trenches.

Nevertheless my father's health had been destroyed by his two years in the mud and water of the Flanders trenches. When he was later recommended for promotion in H.M. Dockyard to the status of an established permanent civil servant, with pension rights, it was discovered, at the mandatory medical examination that, due to his war service, he was suffering from tuberculosis, or consumption as it was called in those days. Thereby he lost his right to establishment and a Dockyard pension although he served in this post for thirty years after his rejection for establishment. When the war ended in 1918 he could have claimed compensation for the loss of his business due to his war service. For some reason, possibly because he did not become aware of the regulations until it was too late, he never made the necessary application. Unlike today when great publicity is given to the 'rights' of the public, in those days very little effort was made to acquaint the public of government benefits available. Thus my father after two years WWI war service served the British Government in H.M. Portsmouth Dockyard for more than thirty-three years and received not a penny pension. Nor did he receive a war pension since he was not invalided out of the Army. He never made a claim as would be the case today.

Meanwhile I made progress in my 'Board' School in Penhale Road which I attended from the age of five. Around the age of ten it seems I was perceived as a likely candidate for the Grammar School entrance examination, for which my school had a special preparatory class for selected pupils. To have a better chance of being selected my form master, Mr. Ward, suggested that I should attend a night-school class which he had organised. My father said he could not afford to pay the fee. My form master then permitted me to attend the night-school course free of charge. I was eventually selected for the grammar school class and after a year of hard work I succeeded in passing the grammar school entrance examination.

I can remember the full day of the examination so clearly. In a vast schoolroom were seated a huge number of boys with the invigilator moving between the spaced out desks. All so solemn and silent and a little awesome.

We stopped for lunch and I went home. My mother, who seemed to be desperately keen for me to pass this examination, greeted me when I arrived with the news that I was to have fish for lunch because she had read it was good for the brain! I returned after lunch and had only been seated a few minutes in the exam room when my mother appeared at the door. She held out my exam entrance card which I had forgotten to take with me after lunch. This had involved for her an anxious desperate tram ride of at least a mile! The invigilator calmed her fears and handed me the entrance card.

As a matter of fact I came out top of the pass list and I was thus entitled to be granted a free scholarship if my father should apply for this and if his financial circumstances warranted. Of course his financial circumstances certainly did qualify him for my grant, but whether to apply for me to continue my education for a further three years became a domestic debatable point. The family had now increased to six children and my parents were finding it difficult to manage on my father's meagre Dockyard pay. He augmented this in a small way by doing private watch repairs at home in the evenings and at weekends. However it became a constant strain to make ends meet and this often caused tension between my parents.

Thus my mother began to have second thoughts on this question of the grammar school offer. Normally boys of my class would, at the age of 14, leave school and, as errand boys or such like, start earning to help the family finances. This possible early financial help seemed enticing to my mother. At the same time she posed the question of whether it would be right or just for me to receive this privilege when there were five other children who would have to be considered. She rightly pointed out that not only would there be the loss of my contribution to the family exchequer over the three year period, but also there would be an additional financial burden in providing the support that would be necessary to sustain me at this higher education level.

However my father had a tremendous belief in education and the attainment of professional qualifications for success in life. He considered that, regardless of the financial pressure, this grammar school opportunity should not be missed. He agreed to the free scholarship for myself at Portsmouth Northern Grammar School (in those days called a Secondary School). In fact he was extremely interested in my schoolwork thereafter and often discussed with me the subjects which I was studying. In this way he endeavoured to improve his own education by reference to my schoolwork.

Grammar school boys – self on right front with George Short

Chapter 3

School Days

For me my new school life was a time of happiness and I was very proud to be a member of this elite minority of boys. I felt terribly superior as I walked along my working class street in my school cap with its distinctive badge. I enjoyed academic study and had a competitive urge to master the subject of whatever I was reading. Possibly my priggish superiority showed when walking down the street because, one afternoon returning from school, I was attacked by a gang of street boys throwing stones. I was so mad with anger at being so ill treated that I rushed at them intending to fight regardless of their number. To my surprise they turned and fled and, although I bolted after them and ran for some distance, I could not catch them. From that time on I had no more interference from these street boys.

Our street was a typical working class area with dreary rows of flat fronted uniform terraced houses inhabited by decent honest people mostly struggling to maintain a basic standard of living for their families. With these good people the front room looking onto the street was usually reserved as a kind of reception room and was only used when receiving visitors or guests. Here were usually installed the best pieces of furniture in the house including possibly a three-piece suite and a piano. On Sunday evenings the family might gather round the piano for a family singsong. It should be remembered that there was no radio and no television. Thus the family made their own entertainment.

Our house was like all the others in the street - a three up and three down. Unlike the others our front room was not reserved for visitors, nor did it have any furniture. It was reserved for my father who had his watchmaker's bench and lathe there and, as previously mentioned, supplemented his income by working in the evenings and at weekends. The house had no electricity supply and lighting downstairs was by gas - there was no lighting upstairs so there was a daily exercise of cleaning and filling portable paraffin oil lamps. In the living room and kitchen were old-fashioned cast-iron stoves comprising a fireplace cum oven positioned under a chimney flue with a wooden surround and mantelpiece. Adjoining the kitchen was a small scullery with a large kitchen sink over which was a cold water tap. There was no hot water nor of course was there any central heating. The trough-like sink was large because it had to be used for the weekly family clothes washing - this occurred every Monday - an all-day operation. In this scullery was a substantial open boiler with a wooden lid at working height, built into brickwork and heated from below by means of a small fireplace which was part of the boiler brickwork. On Monday morning early my mother filled the 'copper', as it was called, with cold water and lit the fire underneath. After some time the water would begin to boil. Meanwhile my mother had collected a mighty heap of washing from her numerous children and two adults and the house seemed to turn into a Chinese steam laundry. Every item of clothing would be subjected to soaking in the sink and rubbing with a bar of solid yellow soap onto a corrugated wooden board and would then be immersed with some blue substance, apparently designed to preserve the 'whiteness' of the white articles, and boiled up in the steaming 'copper' Clouds of steam wafted over the entire ground floor and in inclement weather damp clothes needing to be dried were hanging from every conceivable place of suspension. To assist in the boiling up process my mother used a long wooden batten with which she pressed and stirred around the clothes in the boiling water, thus providing more clouds of billowing steam. She then replaced the cover over the 'copper' to keep this gurgling witches brew under control.

Also located in the scullery was an old-fashioned mangle used for removing the excess water following the boiling process and prior to drying. This crude and fearsome machine consisted basically of two wooden parallel rollers each about two feet long and some five or six inches in diameter supported in a heavy mobile cast-iron frame on small wheels. The wooden rollers were rotated manually through heavy gearing by a large wheel to which was attached a wooden handle. The gap between the two rollers could be adjusted by a screw mechanism located at the top of the frame. Thus the pressure and space for the wet clothes being fed between the rollers could be varied according to the shape and size of the articles. The water drained into a bath on the floor. This 'mangling' process was obviously much quicker and more efficient if done by two people, one doing the wheel turning and the other feeding the clothes between the rollers. It was this dual operation which often proved dangerous. If the wheel turner was too enthusiastic in winding his wheel he could create a tricky situation for the clothes feeder. Many were the stories one heard of fingers and even arms being caught and crushed between the wooden rollers. In our family it was of course the older children who were enlisted as the wheel turners whilst my mother would do the clothes feeding operation. Needless to say there were often alarming and tense moments during this dual mangling operation but I cannot remember any serious mishaps such as I have mentioned previously.

The floor of the scullery was crudely made of rough red brick whose mortar joints had long given up the fight and had therefore accumulated dust and dirt. Every Saturday morning it fell to my lot amongst other tasks to scrub this ghastly floor on my hands and knees and rid the joints of their muddy linings. It was understandable that, with her eight children (eventually nine) and a husband to look after, my mother was forced to delegate some household chores to us children. One other daily task came my way and that was to go to the butcher's and buy our meat requirements. This had to be done in the morning before my departure to school. Obviously economy was all-important in my mother's budgeting. Thus she had discovered a cut-price butcher about a mile distant in the centre of the town. To this butcher I ran each morning and was back in time for school at nine o'clock. Maybe it was this healthy exercise which enabled my considerable athletic achievements in my future years. But more of that later in this tale of the Trenchard Brat. However at this time

I certainly had an urge to compete in athletics and I had a feeling that I had the ability to win at possibly a middle distance running event. This feeling surfaced when I saw in a sports shop window a poster advertising an Annual Sports Day on August Bank holiday at a local park and recreation ground. I badly wanted to enter in my age group half-mile race. I asked my mother if she would buy me a pair of tennis shoes (plimsolls we called them in those days) so that I could run in this event. I told her that I had seen just the very thing at three shillings in the local shoe shop. She was somewhat surprised at my idea and a little dubious but she said she would ask my father if he would agree. To my bitter disappointment the answer was negative. The family finances would not stand such excesses. And that was the end of my athletic aspirations for the next fifteen years. Fifteen years later I was an RAF champion, and a national champion, proving my hunch was justified.

We had a small garden at the back of the house, a rather forlorn barren plot of ground, which at some time might have been intended for a lawn. Our one and only lavatory was at the bottom of this garden. This rather primitive wooden convenience, which was scrubbed every week, was housed in a small brick shed with a rather dilapidated wooden door. There was no lighting. Thus, to use the lavatory, which was a water closet, one had to trundle through the house, through the scullery, out into the garden, down to the bottom of the garden, and wrestle with the leaning door. At night the user had to provide his own illumination in some form. Often matches! In the wintertime at night this was no enviable journey and was undertaken only by

Boyhood – the future author (first right, back row) and siblings at home in the garden

the brave. In fact the younger female members of the family needing to make the journey often begged for an escort!

In the summer time we played together in the garden - often playing cricket with a home made bat and stumps consisting of three chalked lines on the house wall. After work and having had his high tea my father would often join us for cricket to our great delight.

We had no bathroom so the weekly bath for all members of the family was undertaken in a large galvanised 'tin' tub in front of the fire. Of course the tub was of galvanised steel, not tin, but that was the name it was known by. Upstairs were three bedrooms and the largest one at the front of the house was occupied by my parents. The centre one was reserved for the four girls and the small one at the back was for the two boys, this being the child population at this time. As mentioned previously there was no bathroom so my parents room was equipped with a typical Victorian wash-basin stand with a pitcher jug for water. In the children's bedrooms there was no space for such luxury. The girls slept in two double beds which occupied nearly the whole of the room and the boys slept together in a double bed which also occupied most of the space in the small rear bedroom. As there was no lighting in the bedrooms the bedtime procession in the winter months was led by my mother carrying a paraffin lamp. Bedchambers of a basic utility type were available under each bed. We later moved house to a better class district where more spacious bedrooms and a bathroom were available and the older children began to leave home, myself to the RAF and my sister to nurses training accommodation.

Friday was my father's pay-day. He made this a very happy occasion for us all each week, arriving home in the evening with a large bag of coloured boiled sweets in all kinds of animal and fish shapes which he had purchased in Charlotte Street Market. These he would pour out in the middle of the table with all the brood of children standing round with gaping eyes and watering mouths. Each child would be allowed in turn to pick one shape until the heap was exhausted. We all then gathered up our spoils, found some container and jealously guarded them against prying eyes or unauthorised pickings by the other junior members of this considerable household population. This indeed was a characteristic of the children. Being so considerable in number, of similar age group and with the family resources so limited, it was obvious that those resources had to be rationed so that all would get a fair share. Needless to say, each child was on the constant watch that he or she was not being overlooked, or missing out, especially at meal times, and especially at tea time when everyone was limited to a defined number of slices of bread and jam. There was a constant check on individual consumption with often loud protestation if one child endeavoured to exceed the laid down consumption figure. Tea-time was a tiring ritual for my mother. She would stand at the table around which her brood of children would all be seated, and she would be constantly cutting and buttering the bread and spreading it with jam to provide innumerable slices that disappeared rapidly into the hungry young mouths.

Chapter 4

Life in Portsmouth Post World War One
Boy Entry into the Royal Air Force
Cranwell Apprentice

During this time occurred the world wide epidemic of a deadly strain of influenza. In England the disease was widespread and often proved fatal to those unfortunate enough to fall victim to it so that thousands of people died all over the country. I have a vivid recollection of the atmosphere of fear that seemed to reign everywhere in our street with neighbours daily discussing in hushed tones the news of the latest victims.

Shortly after this deadly outbreak my young sister Edna fell ill with pneumonia. She was only about three years old and the disease quickly developed into double pneumonia which in those days was considered to be terminal. The little girl slowly wasted away until she was little more than a skeleton with her bones almost protruding through the skin. As I have stated previously poor people had the greatest difficulty in finding the money to pay for a doctor's services and there was no National Health Service to provide help. My mother was completely distraught by her helplessness in this frightful situation and seemed to be possessed by some instinctive urge to protect her daughter's life by physically holding her. Thus she nursed my sister in her lap like a baby for hours on end. It was a pitiful sight in my parents' bedroom with my mother sitting rocking and crooning over what looked like a bag of bones in her lap.

My father saw this unhappy picture morning and night, day after day, until he could stand it no longer. He had visited his former watchmaker employer, Mr. Jones in Russel Street, to purchase some spares and noticed that a young doctor next to the shop had set up a new surgery. In his agony of mind he went into this new surgery and had an interview with the doctor - Doctor Hodge by name. My father told him that he had no money but that his daughter was dying and he implored the doctor to help him. I think the doctor must have been impressed by my father's tragic sincerity for he agreed to call regardless of fees. Doctor Hodge was only recently qualified and I think he must have considered this case as described by my father as a personal challenge to the accepted medical opinion. He quickly diagnosed double pneumonia and by all precedents there should have been no hope. Twice a day this doctor visited Edna and what treatment he applied I do not know but gradually she was pulled round and slowly retreated from death's door.

After three long months my sister finally left her sick bed. However the cruel passage of the disease had left her with very serious side effects. One of these affected her sight so that one eye was turned inwards. Another disastrous result was an infection in one of her ears. There was a constant discharge having an evil smell from the infected ear. As mentioned early on my mother had a most difficult time extending over several weeks begging coupons from various people which might permit the required hospital treatment. In fact, this ear infection troubled my sister for most of her life.

One amusing incident during the many visits of Doctor Hodge to our house happened when my father in his lunch hour was supervising the feeding from a large central stew-pot of the many hungry children sitting around the table downstairs. My mother was upstairs with my sister and the doctor. When he came down he popped his head into the lunch room with all the children gathered at the table and my father standing with ladle in hand.   Dr. Hodge said, smilingly, looking at the brood busy eating, 'Oh, Mr. Weston, you really have done your duty by the state!'

Here indeed was a case where middle class charity did show through. But my father's unusual and desperate action together with the medical challenge to the young doctor embarking on his new general practice career must have been factors which made the case exceptional.

And again, only my mother's extraordinary toughness and endurance brought my sister back to some degree of normal health. Having won through the battle to get the hospital treatment for the ear infection my mother then had an early morning 3-mile return journey, on foot, taking my sister in a push-chair to the hospital for the child's daily treatment. She then had to return home in time to prepare lunch for my father and the other children who were coming home from school. This lasted for several months.

It is interesting to record that Dr. Hodge wrote a paper for the B.M.A. journal on my sister's case and his treatment and experience of the patient he brought back from the dead, gaining a considerable reputation. He became a well-known doctor in Portsmouth and was very successful in later years.

By this time my parents had decided to leave Stamford Street with its antiquated outside garden toilet and its lack of bathroom and electric light. To find suitable alternative rented accommodation my mother began to peruse the 'Houses to Let' column in the small ads of the Portsmouth Evening News. Acting on the principle of the 'early bird catches the worm' I was sent each afternoon during my school summer holiday to the headquarters offices of the Portsmouth Evening News in Stanhope Road, off Commercial Road, next to the General Post Office where one could purchase a copy of the early edition of the Evening News.

I remember very well my daily urgent afternoon trips to join the awaiting crowd of eager customers at the Evening News offices because Stanhope Road is almost opposite the Town railway station. Next to the station was an intriguing small restaurant cum cook-shop with huge dishes of steaming hot faggots, potatoes and onions cooking on some form of cooker on full display in the shop window and giving off delicious odours to attract the attention of the ever-hungry small boy who, standing outside, would stare with longing gaze at these delicious smelling bubbling

Cranwell – attempt by experimental aircraft (Gloster II) to break the world speed record (1925)

Gloster II crashed landed at 280 mph at Cranwell

Lord Trenchard having retired from the RAF became the head of the Metropolitan Police.

Lord Trenchard as Chief of Air Staff with Senior Officers.

mouth watering faggots. A large notice in the shop window proclaimed that a substantial faggot meal could be obtained for the princely sum of 6d ($2^1/2$p. in today's money). I must admit that this attraction and its delicious smell would divert this schoolboy's attention, causing a slight delay in delivering the paper to my Mother for her eager search in the small ads.

Sadly to say no golden discovery resulted from my summer holiday urgent excursions to the Evening New Offices to bring the early edition. However my Mother's efforts were rewarded some time later when she did find a suitable terrace house with the necessary mod.cons. in the Copnor district. The house was located in Idsworth Road adjacent to Baffins Pond and the family duly took up residence there. After some two and a half years attending the Portsmouth Secondary (later Grammar) School I was entered for the annual combined entrance examination for Royal Navy Artificer apprentice and/or H.M. Dockyard apprentice. The R.N. Artificer selection was a highly prized opportunity for working class boys and in consequence there were very many candidates and comparatively few vacancies. To my delight I passed the entrance examination but to my disgust failed the medical examination on the grounds that my chest measurement was too small. Looking back now I am somewhat relieved that my future was destined for the air and not for the cold cruel sea.

Following this failure the school suggested to my father that the Royal Air Force, which had only recently been formed, might be an alternative answer. An RAF apprenticeship scheme, founded by Lord Trenchard, had just recently been started and the Headmaster suggested the medical examination standards might not be so high. My father, who had attached great hopes to my becoming an R.N. artificer, whose training he greatly admired, felt that this new proposal was a good second best. He gave me a serious lecture on how this new Service was based on new technology which would offer me a great opportunity in the future. He gave me this talk because he knew my great aspiration at that time was to become a schoolteacher and there was no hope whatever that he could finance such ambition. To the great delight of the headmaster of my school I passed the RAF Apprentice Entrance Examination top of the Portsmouth section candidates and in fact fourth in all the United Kingdom entry which totalled thousands of candidates. A total of six hundred boys was selected by the RAF to form a new apprentices entry at the RAF Apprentices Wing, Cranwell. As my school had forecast, the medical examination was not so strict.

Thus I became one of Lord Trenchard's Brats as we were called by the old timers of the RAF. But I was certainly in good company for amongst this gathering of boys at Cranwell in September 1923 was one boy who was to completely revolutionise world aviation. He was none other than Frank Whittle, later to become Sir Frank Whittle O.M., K.B.E., C.B., F.R.S., later to be the inventor of the jet engine and jet propulsion for aircraft. Many others of this Cranwell entry were to become distinguished high-ranking Royal Air Force officers. Certainly Lord Trenchard, by introducing this apprenticeship scheme, made a great contribution to the ensuing high quality of the technical standards of the Royal Air Force and was certainly a factor in our victory over Germany. In fact in post war years the RAF became admired and imitated by the whole world's air forces. And in the pre World War II years the quality of the RAF flying was considered to be the finest in the world. The Royal Air Force provided pilots that won the Schneider Cup, the world's greatest air speed competition and so set up world air speed records. Sir Winston Churchill acknowledged the prowess of the Royal Air Force in the Battle of Britain in his famous speech eulogising 'the Few' who had saved the country from the German invasion in 1940.

For this new entry of boys at Cranwell, all between 15 and 16 years old and all of a good secondary level of education, their introduction to life in the RAF came as a great shock. From their protected lives with easy-going decent family backgrounds they found themselves suddenly plunged into the highly militarised cold unfeeling harsh discipline of an intimidating organisation, from which there was to be no escape, for this was to be their home and way of life for the next three years.

They found themselves at the mercy of the old timer non commissioned ranks who had been transferred from the World War I British army to man the newly formed Royal Air Force which had only begun its life in 1918. These N.C.O.s were disinclined to view the apprentices with any favour for these boys were all of superior education to themselves and, as apprentices, they would certainly be trained for a future service level superior to their own. To humiliate, to insult, and to terrify the youngsters in their charge was considered to be normal routine and it was

Cranwell apprentices –
myself on right with George Short

Cranwell apprentices – self first right relaxing in Cranwell village

claimed that such methods would produce the necessary qualities of character. It certainly developed a hardness of character that could withstand such cruelly degrading treatment. This proved indeed useful for, on completion of their apprenticeship, the young men found, in their early years, the same kind of low grade N.C.O.s in the ranks of the normal service. Their three years of apprenticeship had taught them how to outwit these ill-intentioned bullies. The technical training, however, was excellent and of a very high order. Three times a week apprentices spent half a day at school studying academic subjects relevant to aeronautical engineering. The teachers in these subjects were very highly qualified and of exceptional standard. Examples of this were Mr. Pobjoy, teacher of mechanical drawing, who later became famous in the aeronautical world for his small engine designs and who founded his own engine manufacturing company and Fl/Lt. Comper, teacher of metallurgy, who became famous for his designs of very light aircraft which were later commercially manufactured in the Comper-Swift partnership.

One temporary avenue of escape from the tedious atmosphere of the barrack room was membership of the Cranwell Model Aeroplane Society. This society had been created for apprentices keen to extend their aeronautical knowledge and practice. Members were given guidance and instruction to enable them to design and construct their own models. The society was supported by the Service and encouraged by the Commanding Officer, Wing Commander Barton, who took a keen interest in the skilful models produced by the members. Frank Whittle became a stalwart of the Society. He could be found every evening and during leisure hours in the workshop which had been allocated to the society on the ground floor of the school building.

*Cranwell apprentice –
myself in parade uniform in my
final year at Cranwell*

Without doubt it was Whittle's enthusiastic dedication to aircraft model making in the society's workshop, which became one of the most important factors influencing his subsequent career. Long before his arrival at Cranwell he had been associated with his father's engineering work in Coventry and in Leamington Spa to where his family moved in 1916 and, from the age of ten, he had been taught workshop practice and the use of tools. The Model Aircraft Society gave him a valuable facility to extend his skills to aircraft structure design and construction in model form. In my own case I did not have the advantage of any previous experience in workshop practice. When I joined the RAF I had not the slightest idea of the use of tools or mechanical processes. In consequence the Society activities did not attract me and I never became a member. As mentioned previously my interest had been largely in academic study. My escape from the military atmosphere of Cranwell was by taking long walks in the Lincolnshire countryside and by weekend afternoon visits to the nearby Cranwell village teashop, where light-hearted gatherings of RAF apprentices were a regular weekly feature.

It is interesting to note that Whittle was born in the West Midlands and did most of his research and experimentation there. He was born on 1st June 1907 in the Earlsdon district of Coventry and he was educated at Leamington College to which he had won a scholarship. With the aid of private finance and with the approval of Air Ministry he managed to form his own company Power Jets. He was then associated with the engineering firm BTH at Rugby who undertook to build his first engine. They later moved the engine experimental test house to Lutterworth near Rugby. Further association was with the Rover car company. The final production and development of the Whittle invention was at Rolls Royce Derby.

Frank Whittle, inventor of the gas-turbine 'jet' engine, as a boy aircraft apprentice and member of the Model Aeroplane Club at RAF Cranwell 1925.

Chapter 5

Entry Into RAF Regular Men's Service Central Flying School, Upavon, and Wittering

My three years at Cranwell were dull and uneventful. I certainly did not enjoy them. Great excitement came at the end of the three years when the results of the final examinations were announced. On the results of the final examinations largely depended one's future rank on passing out into the regular Royal Air Force. The top five apprentices in the final examination were given cadetships for commissioned officer pilot training in the RAF Cadet College at Cranwell. Flying training was therefore central to the cadet curriculum and, to be accepted, it was necessary to pass a very strict comprehensive medical examination. Fortunately for Whittle, who was sixth in the final examinations, one of the top five candidates for cadetship failed the medical examination and, as a consequence, Whittle took his place. This was the second most important factor in shaping his career for it was his studies during his two years at Cranwell Cadet College that gave birth to his initial radical ideas of the gas turbine and jet propulsion. In fact his Cadet College fourth term science thesis was based on the idea of a power plant that was capable of aircraft operation at extremely high altitudes to generate speeds in the region of 500 miles per hour. At this time in the 1920s maximum aircraft speeds were around 150 miles per hour. Conventional piston engines could never produce enough economic power to operate aircraft at these high altitudes. The story of Whittle's future struggle to put his theories into practical application makes fascinating reading. It provides a profound study of how Government departments, bureaucracy, jealousy, ruthless commercial intrigue, Treasury niggardliness and competing personalities of people in high places can frustrate, impede and connive to deflect the progress and development of radical innovative schemes with which they disagree, or over which they aim to take control, or use for their own advantage. It is to the credit of the Royal Air Force that Whittle was perceived as a worthy and brilliant engineering genius and that they gave him the necessary help and support to enable him to succeed in spite of all the difficulties and obstructions he met along the way.

My own lack of enthusiasm for technical training was reflected in the comparatively poor results I obtained in the final examinations. I forget exactly how far down the list I was positioned but I passed out into the regular service with the humble rank of aircraftsman first class (AC1 in the official jargon) for which I received the grand sum of four shillings and sixpence (equivalent to about 22$\frac{1}{2}$p) per day. My introduction into the regular ranks of the Royal Air Force was unpromising and certainly did not augur well for my future. After passing out

Central Flying School – Avro 504K trainer aircraft with group of maintenance ground crew – with self in second from right in top row

ceremonials at Cranwell the whole apprentice entry left for their summer leave with instructions to proceed individually to their new RAF stations on the conclusion of their leave period in September 1926. This unusual instruction was due to the cessation of apprentice training in mechanical trades at Cranwell. In future Cranwell apprentice training would be for wireless (radio) trades. All mechanical trade training was to be concentrated at Halton.

My posting was to the RAF Central Flying School which was situated at that time at Upavon on the Salisbury Plain. The day before my leave expired I checked the train service from my home town, Portsmouth, to Upavon, which was only some 40 miles or so. There was no train service to Upavon! It was necessary to take a main line train to Salisbury, change to a local train to Ludgershall, and then hope there would be a bus service to Upavon village which was some 4 miles from Ludgershall. I was told that a train leaving Portsmouth at 2 p.m. the next day should get me to Upavon in ample time before midnight when my leave pass expired.

The next day, a Friday, bidding farewell to my parents at the station, I caught the 2 p.m. train, arrived in Salisbury around 4 p.m., and found to my horror that there was no local train to Ludgershall! Nor was there a bus service to anywhere near Upavon which was a considerable distance from Salisbury. I certainly did not have enough money to pay for a taxi over that distance and so, remembering the instruction received at Cranwell to report to the police in such kind of emergency, I went to the nearest Salisbury police station. The officers were very helpful and confirmed that there was no way I could get to Upavon that day. They then rang RAF Upavon and I reported my situation to the Duty Officer who instructed me to catch the first available train to Ludgershall the next morning. The Police kindly allowed me to sleep in one of the station cells and I caught the first train to Ludgershall the next morning. Having then walked with my heavy kit and luggage the four miles or so to the RAF station I reported in at the guardroom. I was immediately arrested by the RAF police for being AWOL (absent without leave)! I was then marched to the office of the station sergeant major complete with heavy suitcase and in my full back pack and marching webbing gear, which Cranwell had instructed us to wear. Standing rigidly to attention before the station sergeant major I was asked to explain why I had been absent for eleven hours!

Explaining the problem of the train service I informed the station S.M. that I had finally acted on the personal orders of the Station Duty Officer. Totally ignoring the legality of my obeying an officer's orders the S.M. proceeded to verbally destroy my character. He informed me that he was making a formal charge against me to be heard by my section officer on the following Monday. Meanwhile he placed me on 'open arrest' which meant I had to spend the weekend reporting to the guardroom at two-hour intervals during the day and attend staff parade in full marching order at 6 p.m. on Saturday and on Sunday. He then proceeded to analyse my general appearance in an extremely derogatory manner ending by ordering me to get a hair-cut immediately and to purchase a new pair of breeches from the clothing store as he considered mine too 'fancy'.

Come Monday I appeared before my section officer to answer the charge of A.W.O.L. He was an engineer officer commissioned from the ranks and unsure of himself. It was evident that, having heard my story, he was surprised that I was being charged when I had obviously obeyed an officer's orders. He was at a loss to know how to handle this case and, whilst I stood before him, he telephoned the Station Sergeant Major seeking his advice. The net result of this conversation was that I was pronounced guilty and given some restrictive punishment which involved a few more days attending staff parade in the evening in full marching kit. In addition I was penalised one day's Royal Warrant which in effect meant that King George V would get one extra day of my service for nothing! A most depressing start to my career in the Royal Air Force!

The Station Sergeant Major was of the class of non-commissioned officers I had met at Cranwell, a First World War Army's gift to the newborn RAF I soon found that the S.M. dominated the whole station and in the short life of the RAF had already earned himself a reputation associated with illegitimacy - he was known in the ranks as 'Joe the B...d'. The ranks in which I found myself consisted mostly of tough uncouth WW1 'old sweats', somewhat brutal and crude in outlook, people with whom I could have little in common. When on parade with Joe out in front barking at them I was astonished to hear around me such obscene insults muttered sotto voce and directed at the S.M. and his family.

Three months after my arrival the Central Flying School was moved from Upavon to Wittering near Stamford. I was sent there with an advance party to make the necessary preparations for the arrival of the main body of the school.

The aircraft used for instruction in the early days were ancient Avro 504 fitted with a peculiar French designed rotary engine named Gnome Monosoupape, probably designed around 1914. Instead of the conventional engine design with the crankshaft rotating driving the propeller, in this engine the crankshaft was fixed and the whole engine with the propeller attached revolved around the crankshaft. It was a radial engine with its 7 cylinders in a circle whirling around the static crankshaft. The centrifugal forces generated by this whirling mass were one of the hazards in the control of this aircraft.

Another difficulty with this engine was that it had no carburettor and thus no throttle. Petrol was fed by pump and jet system via the crankshaft bore into the crankcase and so found its way into the cylinders via the pistons similar to the two-stroke engine. Because there was no throttle the engine could not be controlled in the conventional manner by graduated throttle control and thus there was only limited power control with two engine throttle positions – 'flat out' or 'stop'. To control the engine during the taxiing on the ground the pilot had to cut the ignition 'in' and 'out' at short intervals. He did this with a thumb switch located on top of the control column. Pressing the 'blip switch' down with his thumb the pilot cut the engine. If he forgot to release his thumb he would lose his engine. There was no self-starter! If this happened when flying with no engine and no means of starting it again the situation would necessitate urgent optimistic search for an open piece of ground below on which to make a forced landing.

The aeroplane of course was a biplane constructed of a wooden frame covered with Irish linen which was painted with cellulose dope to tighten the fabric to the frame. The wings were held together with wires and struts - in fact it was a mass of 'sticks and strings' very similar to those peculiar aircraft that were portrayed in that famous humorous film 'Those magnificent men and their flying machines'. The aeroplane had no brakes, either in the air or on the ground, so that steering while taxiing was a very precarious business especially as there was no engine control except 'on' and 'off'. Collisions with other aircraft on the ground or with hangar walls were quite common. In fact during the early days of WWI British aircraft killed more pilots than did the Germans.

To assist the pilot when taxiing the two ground crew would station themselves one on each wing tip and, by running with the aircraft and pulling on the wing tip, they would help to maintain direction as indicated by the pilot. If the pilot was of a nervous disposition or perhaps had some antipathy to the ground crew he might over 'blip' his engine so that the aircraft would gather an excessive speed on the ground and the poor sprinting wing tip ground crew would cling on, with their feet sometimes lifted off the ground.

After their aircraft had taken off the ground crew would remain on the tarmac whilst the instruction flight was in progress and, as soon as the machine landed, it was their job to run out onto the aerodrome to meet the aircraft and once again assist in the taxiing process. The earlier models had a long wooden arm shaped like a huge hockey stick attached to the undercarriage and protruding forward to stop the plane tipping up on its nose if the pilot made a bad landing. Attached to the underneath of each of the wing tips of the bottom mainplanes was a school headmaster's cane bent round to form a U-shape and designed to prevent damage to the wings if inadvertently touching the ground on landing or taxiing. The undercarriage was a somewhat crude structure with a system designed to take the landing shocks. It consisted of lengths of rubber elastic cord securing the wheel axles to the undercarriage struts. Flying and navigation instruments consisted only of a small compass, an air-speed indicator and an instrument indicating the attitude of the aeroplane relative to the horizon. There were also an engine revolution indicator and an oil pressure gauge.

There was no radio so that communication between instructor and pupil was by means of a speaking tube. This consisted of a piece of flexible metal tubing, similar to domestic gas piping, which ran between the two cockpits, one end of which was connected to a small metal funnel-like mouthpiece fixed to the dash-board edge into which the instructor could speak. The other end in the pupil's cockpit had a detachable rubber connection to which could be attached a small flexible Y-tube running to ear diaphragms in the pupil's flying helmet, similar to a doctor's stethoscope. This system was duplicated from the pupil's cockpit to the instructor and the instructor also had the 'doctor's' listening device in his flying helmet so that the pupil could speak to the instructor. Needless to say speech was hardly 'loud and clear' with the tremendous roar of the engine and the whirling propeller noise enveloping the open cockpits.

Communication between aircraft in the air was difficult and of course had to be visual. I did a considerable amount of flying with my flight commander. When leading formation flying with other aircraft he would give me verbally his required formation order such as 'turn left' or 'turn right' and I would thrust my left or right arm out of the cockpit to indicate to the other aircraft around us - just like signalling on a bicycle! Although our cruising speed was only about 65 or 70 miles an hour the strain on one's arm in the slipstream was quite severe. Another hazard in formation flying with our ancient aircraft was due to the engine occasionally shedding one of its cylinders in flight. The engine immediately lost all power which would act like a sudden brake so that the formation would tend to run into each other resulting in complete chaos, with the stricken aircraft diving down violently to maintain flying speed. Later models of this aircraft had conventional engines with throttle control, which were British design 'Lynx' manufactured by Armstrong Siddeley. These were much more reliable, better controlled, and in consequence taxiing and control of the aeroplane in flight was much easier.

I became very keen on flying and had ambitions to become a pilot myself. The instructor who regularly flew my aircraft, which by now was the more advanced type, 504K, knew this and was always encouraging. Whenever convenient I was invited to fly with him or one of his pupils. One day the instructor landed with his pupil and as usual my ground crew colleague and I met the aircraft. The aircraft stopped taxiing and, with the engine still running, the instructor got down and told the pupil he could now go off on a solo flight. Turning to me the instructor asked me if I would like to fly with this pupil. I immediately agreed and he then ordered the pupil to move from the rear cockpit, which was the normal pupil's position, to the front cockpit.

With the engine still running, the pupil climbed down wearing his seat parachute, which had just recently been introduced into the service. He mounted the lower wing to enter the front cockpit. The top wing of this biplane passed over the front cockpit and the narrow space between the two made entry into the cockpit a little difficult, even more so when wearing the recently introduced seat parachute. It involved wriggling one's body (which faced rearwards) through the gap into the cockpit. This pupil was a huge international rugby player, Flying Officer Beamish by name, later a senior officer in WW2. Because of his size his entry into the front cockpit needed greater wriggling and, unbeknown to him, his parachute, whilst he was descending into the cockpit, touched the dashboard and moved the engine petrol feed lever to the 'off' position. We had just enough petrol in the engine and pipeline to permit us to take off. When we got to about 300 feet the engine cut dead. Fortunately for me my pupil pilot was a very intelligent person and, instead of trying to get back to the aerodrome, which would have been fatal due to lack of height and speed for we would certainly have stalled and plunged into the ground, he did the right thing. He kept straight on to make a landing as best as he could on whatever ground was in front of him! This happened to be a small field of ripe barley!

We had just enough height to clear a few small trees growing in the aerodrome boundary hedge when we flopped down and ploughed into the barley. It was August time so the barley was fully grown to a height of around five or six feet but the field, typical of English fields of those days, was very small. With our 'string-bag' aeroplane, full of wires and with a fixed undercarriage, we cut through the barley like a combine harvester. With no brakes to control our progress I saw a plantation of trees on the far side coming towards us at a disconcerting rate and I speculated whether we would hit the trees or possibly turn over in trying to avoid them.

However the barley must have had a braking effect on the aeroplane because we managed to slow down enough to be able to turn just before we reached the far boundary. The barley and the wing-tip cane supported our wing tip so that we did not 'dig-in' due to the somewhat urgent violent turn we made. The aeroplane then came to a standstill and I heard the pilot shout 'What the hell's going on?'

I stood up on my seat and, leaning over to the front cockpit, looked over the pupil's shoulder and luckily spotted straight away that the petrol cock was turned to the 'off' position. Having pointed this out, the pupil asked me if we could re-start the engine. This was a good question because with no engine self-starter the only way to start the engine was by violently pulling the propeller round by hand. Furthermore with no brakes and no chocks to block the wheels if the engine was started the aeroplane could immediately tend to move forward onto the person starting it! However, ensuring the throttle lever was set well back and the ignition switches were off I climbed out and went round to the front of the aircraft and tugged the unwieldy propeller through a couple of revolutions to prime the cylinders with fuel. Then, calling to the pupil to turn the ignition switches 'on' I gave a huge tug and 'Eureka!' I was lucky enough to get the engine started at the first go. Jumping out of the way of the whirling propeller I ran back to my cockpit and climbed in. The pilot then opened up and we began to move off, back to the spot where we landed which would give us the optimum position for take-off against the wind direction.

So once again we traversed the field of barley mowing down sheaths in our progress towards the take-off point. Turning into wind the pilot then opened up and we tore through the barley once more, hoping to lift off. Just before the far hedge arrived we rose in the air and had just enough height to do a circuit of the aerodrome before coming in to land, for by this time the pupil had had enough excitement for the day and it was lunchtime anyway!

When we taxied in with our undercarriage full of sheaves of barley we found that everyone had gone to lunch. So we dumped the aeroplane and went off to lunch ourselves. It was somewhat surprising that no one had spotted us go down into the adjoining field - or maybe they had, but seeing us take off again they had taken no action. However, coming back after lunch, I had only been in the hangar a few minutes when there were urgent cries for my presence in the Flight Office. I was informed that the Chief Flying Instructor wished to see me urgently. Making my way to Headquarters I met the C.F.I. who, after questioning, took me along to the Commanding Officer who asked, 'Were you flying in aircraft no. ...?' When I answered in the affirmative he went on 'Did you have a forced landing in a barley field?' When I again answered in the affirmative he then said, 'Well, why didn't you report it?' I told him that everyone had gone to lunch and I had only just returned from lunch myself when I was called. He then told me that he had had an irate farmer on the phone who claimed that we had practically ruined his ripe crop of barley. The C.O. asked me to write a detailed report of my part in the episode and I presume the poor farmer was eventually compensated by the government for our ill treatment of his field of barley.

One other flying incident I remember during my stay at the Central Flying School concerned the introduction of a new type of personal safety gear called 'Sutton harness' which would permit the aeroplane to be inverted without the pilot and passenger falling out. This new harness arrived as a package for the 504K aircraft and had to be fitted to the aeroplane seats by the ground crew. The fitting of the harness involved drilling of the structure and attachment of various links of the harness by nuts and bolts passed through the drilled structure. When I informed the instructor pilot of my aircraft that the aeroplane was ready for air test he suggested to me that, as I had fitted the harness, perhaps I would like to fly with him on the air test so that I could test the passenger seat harness. I agreed and we both climbed into the aircraft, buckled ourselves in with the new harness and off we went.

Climbing to around seven or eight thousand feet we did a few manoeuvres and then came the crunch-test when the pilot told me that he was about to turn the aircraft upside down. Down went one wing, up came the other, and we rolled over to the inverted position when, Horror upon Horror!, I felt myself falling. All kinds of frightful thoughts flashed through my mind. Had I made a mess of the fitment? Had a bolt fractured or the drilled structure fractured? I fell only three or four inches but in that short space of time I died several times.

When we resumed level flight and finally landed my pilot laughingly asked me if I had experienced the awful fright of falling out of the aeroplane. Hearing my reply he confessed he had had the same experience. It was entirely due to our inexperience with this type of harness which had shoulder straps. We learnt later that, to secure oneself firmly to the cockpit seat, it was necessary to depress each of one's shoulders whilst tightening each shoulder strap. By that means the slack in these straps was taken up and there could be no body movement downwards when inverted.

An SE5 aircraft similar to the WWI machine (Government surplus) which
F/O Batchy Atcherley bought and flew

Chapter 6

Flying at Central Flying School, Wittering C.F.S. Pilots' contribution to the Schneider Cup Air Race

By this time, 1928, the 'old sweats' of WW1 had largely disappeared, having mostly completed their terms of service. More 'Trenchard Brats' from the Halton Apprentices School were emerging to join the regular RAF units and a new recruitment scheme training younger direct entry mechanics resulted in raising the general tone of the Service and increasing the interest and enthusiasm emanating from the younger population.

The standards of education and background for the direct entry mechanics training were much lower than the Halton Apprentices Scheme and recruitment of course was widespread over the whole United Kingdom. In consequence there appeared in our ranks young men from remote, little known villages of England, Ireland, Scotland and Wales, a truly highly cosmopolitan mixture with some very strange dialects and varied and unusual characters. For instance, in my barrack room, in which some thirty men lived, were two young Irishmen who were great friends. Each Friday, pay day, after work, these two made a regular visit by the primitive local bus service to Stamford town which was about four or five miles from our camp at Wittering. They then made their way from the bus terminus in the town square to their regular pub in one of Stamford's side streets some half-mile distant. Here they installed themselves at the public bar counter and consumed many pints. They remained there the entire evening. Then, at closing time, which in those days was 10 p.m., they quaffed their last order and moved outside; there they fought each other until one or the other collapsed on the pavement. The victor would assist his fallen friend onto his feet and, supporting each other, together they found their way back to the town square to catch the last bus to camp. A clean-up and straighten-up during the bus ride would permit them to book in at the guard room without awkward questions and so wend their way to bed; another happy outing to remember.

Another interesting feature of this young RAF was our uniform which was influenced by the ancient cavalry traditions of the British Army. The birth of the flying service originated under the control of Army officers who viewed the new-fangled flying machine as 'cavalry of the air' to assist the cavalry on the ground. Thus our uniform of those early times was designed to give the appearance not of airmen, but rather of horsemen. Our walking out ceremonial parade uniform was flared riding breeches and putties wound from the ankles to meet the breeches at the knee. We had to carry a cane with this walking-out uniform so that we had the appearance of jockeys on holiday! The officially issued puttees were of very rough blue serge of inferior design which did not improve one's appearance. Officialdom permitted all ranks to provide their own bought puttees so that elegant expensive Foxes puttees were commonly worn. This, coupled with the fact that all ranks were permitted to have the flares of their riding breeches shaped by the Station tailor to their individual taste, gave rise to a considerable variety of exotic shapes. Officers' dress for formal parades consisted of elegant riding breeches with highly polished black jack-boots and they carried a walking stick. They had the appearance of stud farm owners going to the races.

Fortunately the 'cavalry of the air' were permitted to wear ordinary slacks when at work. The lower ranks wore overalls of the boiler-suit type over their uniform when working. When flying aircrew wore 'Sidcott' suits which were fur-lined thick cloth overalls and flying gloves or gauntlets over separate inner silk gloves. It should be remembered that the aircraft of this era had open cockpits with no heating whatever so that flying at altitude, especially in winter, was a chilly business. The aircraft had no windscreen wipers so that when flying in the rain, as one often did, in order to get any forward vision, one had to peer round the side of the windscreen, wiping one's goggles whilst facing into the hurricane of the slipstream. As there were no navigational aids pilots going on a cross-country flight sometimes used a 'Baedeker' railway guide. Consulting the 'Baedeker' they could select a railway line going in the direction of their destination. They could then fly along the line and if by chance they got lost en route they would then fly down level with the nearest station platform where they could read the name of the place. Night flying in those early days was a joke by modern standards; we simply placed a line of buckets with paraffin and a rag on each side of the grass landing strip. The rag which we ignited, formed a lane of flaming paraffin in anticipation of an aircraft landing.

The pilot instructors of the Central Flying School at Wittering were a band of young daredevils but they were very competent pilots. Many of them became famous for their flying skills, for instance in major international air races such as the Schneider Cup etc. Many of them achieved very high rank and became great leaders in WW2. One in particular was already well known for his daredevil escapades. He was Flying Officer Atcherley (later Air Marshal in WW2) who was better known in the Service as 'Batchy' Atcherley. I was present at a 'clothing' parade at the clothing store at Wittering when 'Batchy' Atcherley was supposed to be present as the officer in charge or 'witnessing' officer to see that correct procedures were carried out. He was absent so the 'clothing' parade carried on without him. Suddenly, very low over the heads of the lined up ranks of the parade appeared an aircraft descending to land on the adjoining grass aerodrome. The Avro 504K biplane aircraft was so low that the pupil pilot could clearly be seen in one cockpit. The other cockpit was empty and 'Batchy' could be seen sitting on the leading edge of the lower mainplane clutching a strut between his legs which were dangling down in front of him! He waved as he passed over our heads. We later heard the sequel to this episode when 'Batchy' was hauled up before the Commanding Officer for being absent from the clothing parade and for dangerous flying. The ancient string-bag 504K aeroplane in which he was flying was so underpowered that in strong winds, particularly in winter-time, it could often be seen flying backwards relative to the ground. This was due, of course, to the fact that the aeroplane's forward speed was less than the head-on wind speed. So the aeroplane had the necessary airlift to remain airborne but was being pushed backwards by the superior wind force.

In winter time when it had been snowing I once witnessed 'Batchy' load his aeroplane with snowballs and then, taking off and flying low round the hangar tarmac, he put the aircraft in a steep banking turn, at the same time hurling snowballs at the ground crew below. After he had been with us for some time he bought an old Farnborough ex-WW1 S.E.5. aeroplane. This machine was a small 1914-18 war single seater fighter which 'Batchy' picked up for a few pounds at a Government surplus auction. He managed to fly this antique to Wittering and it was completely overhauled by volunteers in their spare time. When the reconditioning work was completed and it had been successfully air-tested 'Batchy' decided to fly it the following weekend to his father's estate. He persuaded his brother who was also in the RAF at a station nearby to join him in this air trip to their home. The only problem was that the aeroplane had only a single seat cockpit.

'Batchy' suggested to his brother that one way round the problem would be for the latter to be strapped on top of the fuselage at the tail and adjacent to the rudder whilst 'Batchy' would fly the aeroplane. His brother agreed to try it and he was duly tied down on top of the rear end of the fuselage. They took off in a trial flight during which the brother indicated in no uncertain manner his violent dislike of his precarious situation. When they had landed and taxied to the hangar his brother was released. After a further conference they finally decided that the only solution to their transport problem was for both of them to sit in the single cockpit. 'Batchy' sat in the cockpit seat with his feet working the rudder bar and his brother sat in his lap with the control column ('joystick') between their legs and operated by his brother. A kind of 'dual' control. The idea was successful and they made it home.

Incidentally 'Batchy' Atcherley was a member of the RAF High Speed Flight team that won the Schneider Cup Race for Britain in September 1929. 'Batchy', by now promoted to Flight Lieutenant, established a 100-kilometre closed circuit speed record of 331.32 m.p.h., in a Supermarine S6. A few days later a World Absolute Speed record was established by the RAF (Squadron Leader A.H. Orlebar) at 357.75 m.p.h., also in a Supermarine S6.

The Schneider Cup air race for seaplane aircraft had seized the British public imagination during the 1920's although it was originally the idea of a Frenchman, Jacques Schneider. In the early days of aviation Schneider argued that with so much of the earth's surface covered by water in the oceans, seas, lakes, rivers etc. it was logical that the development of future air transport must be with seaplanes. To this end he provided a great impetus in 1912 by successfully inaugurating an international air race for seaplanes under his own name.

Schneider had laid down in the race rules that any competitor winning three times

Schneider Cup Race – the Supermarine 5 which won the race at Venice on 26th September 1927 flown by Fl/Lt. Webster of the RAF High Speed Flight

Schneider Cup Race – The Supermarine S6B which won the race at Colshot on 13th September 1931 flown by Fl/Lt. J. N. Boothman

in five years would be considered the final victor and permanent holder of the Cup. This caused tremendous public excitement especially when Italy had won the race twice in consecutive years and then the British RAF high speed flight had won twice in the following years.

The history of the race illustrates the remarkable development of aviation from its early days when the race was first won in 1913 at an average speed of 45 m.p.h. to the final Schneider Cup race won in 1931 by the RAF high speed flight (Flight Lieutenant Boothman) at a speed of 310 m.p.h.

However our winning entry in 1931 was not achieved without considerable difficulty caused by objections from all sides including the Labour Government on the grounds that the country was in no state to support such side-show activities. This negative attitude caused a great outcry from the public, the aircraft industry and from the media. The public outcry was so great that the Government finally made a concession that if financial support from the private sector could be organised then permission would be granted for the RAF to compete.

The financial support demanded by the Government did indeed arrive from a public spirited benefactor, Lady Houston. Her gift to the nation permitted the Government to give the necessary approval for the RAF to enter the 1931 Race with the resulting victory for our country.

The nation gained greatly from this RAF Schneider Cup victory in many ways, not least from the international recognition of our leadership in aviation technology. Unfortunately this was to be sacrificed on the altar of appeasement in the following years.

And it should be realised that this RAF triumph was even more notable since we had just passed through an era where our Service had been subjected to serious attempts by the Royal Navy and the Army to eliminate the RAF entirely as an independent force.

Our country owes a great debt to the aircraft designer R.J. Mitchell who was responsible for the design of the all three victorious aircraft beginning with the Supermarine S5, then the Supermarine S6 and finally the Supermarine S6B. This was the foundation for the eventual design of the Spitfire fighter aircraft which provided such valuable performance against the German Luftwaffe in the Battle of Britain.

Furthermore the power plants of the victorious aircraft of the second and final race were both Rolls Royce 'R' engines , firstly of 1900 h.p. which Rolls Royce finally boosted by modification to 2350 h.p. for the final race and ultimately to 2550 h.p. to give our country the World's Speed Record of 407.5 m.p.h. This 'R' engine became the basic design for the famous Rolls Royce Merlin engine which powered the Spitfire and in its many modified forms powered many other British aircraft right throughout World War 2.

Thus it may be said that Britain's triumph in the Schneider Cup Race provided one of the foundation stones for our victory over Nazi Germany and certainly the ubiquitous Rolls Royce Merlin engine was a large factor in our final air superiority over the Luftwaffe.

A Vickers Vimy visits Wittering. It was this type that in 1919 was the first aircraft to fly the Atlantic Ocean non-stop piloted by Messrs. Alcock and Brown

It was not recognised at the time but the generosity of the great patriot Lady Houston virtually changed the course of the future history of the free world. The triumph of the RAF in the Battle of Britain foiled the plans of Hitler to make his German 'master race' the rulers of Europe and eventually the controllers of the whole world. This is no exaggeration for the defeat of Great Britain was considered to be a fundamental and final step by the Nazis. Hitler considered our country was the only real obstacle to his ambition. He viewed America militarily at this time with contempt and possibly he had some justification for although America had the tremendous infrastructure and huge industrial capacity it had no military strength since the American public believed their country could never be attacked or invaded. Furthermore following the Vietnam war disasters the American military were viewed by the American public with critical condemnation amounting almost to contempt. Thus there was no public support to provide finances to modernise or expand their Army. Their Navy escaped this condemnation but the Japanese later demonstrated the Navy's vulnerability at Pearl Harbour in December 1942.

Chapter 7

Iraq – My Ambition but Failure to become an RAF Pilot

As previously mentioned I was at this time extremely keen on flying and my great ambition was to be officially accepted for a full-time pilot's course. There was for me one possible avenue open by competitive selection and that was for training as a pilot with the rank of sergeant, known as the Sergeant Pilot's course. If one was fortunate enough to be selected for this year long course and if one succeeded in completing the course then there was automatic promotion to the rank of sergeant with further advanced operational flying training.

The instructor pilot on my aircraft knew of my ambition and he gave me his support so that I was formally recommended for selection. To assist in the favourable consideration of his recommendation of the course he arranged for me to take a Link trainer test.

The Link trainer was an American designed machine to provide simulated flying on the ground in a test room. It could provide all the controls etc. of a conventional aircraft and these were connected to measuring systems which could provide an indication of the suitability or otherwise of the candidate under test. It also provided a means of administering a shock test whilst handling the controls in the form of an unexpected sudden loud siren scream under one's seat. The reaction to this shock treatment was measured to determine the suitability of a candidate to handle a crisis. It would appear that my test results were favourable and the Commanding Officer of the station forwarded my recommendation to the Command Headquarters.

After a successful interview with the Air Officer Commanding at Inland Command Headquarters at Bentley Priory near Stanmore I was placed on the selection list and had only one more hurdle to pass which was the final pilot's medical examination. Then Disaster struck. The annual overseas posting list was promulgated and I was on it – posted to Iraq in October! The year was 1929.

This new posting was not entirely unexpected for most people of my background were due to appear on the overseas posting list around this time. I thought it a little unfortunate when everything seemed set for my pilot's course. But I considered that my selection for the pilot's course would follow me through and I would probably have my course at an overseas flying training school.

October arrived and after a departure leave spent at home I finally travelled to Southampton and boarded the awaiting troopship, S.S. Somersetshire of the Bibby Shipping Line. Some 1500 other young men were my fellow passengers soon to be transported to guard the outposts of the British Empire. My ill luck continued to haunt me for, no sooner was I on board viewing the primitive accommodation with some slight apprehension and disgust, when I was informed that I was to take over immediately the duties of armed guard on the top boat deck.

A rifle was thrust into my hands and I ascended the various decks to the boat deck, weaving my way through the forest of hanging hammocks. There, playing the soldier sentry with gun on shoulder, I looked down on the quayside and, to my dismay and chagrin, spied my parents, who had made the journey from Portsmouth to bid me farewell, standing there in pouring rain. There was nothing I could do to meet them for I could not desert my post! We could only call to each other until the ship's gangways were drawn up and the troopship moved out with the band playing patriotic farewell music. I was not in the mood to appreciate their musical efforts.

The troopship moved down the Solent towards the open sea amid rising stormy waves and high winds. Just prior to gaining the English Channel we began executing a peculiar circling manoeuvre which I later was informed was necessary to 'box' or check the ship's compass. That completed, we headed down the English Channel southwards towards our first port of call which would be Port Said in Egypt. Meanwhile the stormy weather persisted and winds rose higher and higher until we were steaming along the Channel in a 60-mile an hour gale.

The troopship, although a 30,000 ton steamer, was thrown around rolling and dipping to the great discomfort of all on board. In those days ships' stabilisers were unheard of and our engine power was marine coal-burning steam engines, thumping away and producing a continuous vibration underfoot and a filthy smoky atmosphere overhead on deck.

Needless to say that very soon the 'land-lubber' troop passengers succumbed to the exaggerated movements of the ship and the distracting vibration underfoot. The latrines and toilets were completely inadequate for this mass of humanity suffering the horrors of seasickness. The ship was ploughing into the high waves and shipping water, some of which was finding its way below, and, there it was adding to the ghastly overflowing drains exuding rivers of filth and the contents of thousands of stomachs, since it was too dangerous to go on top deck.

Being relieved of my sentry duty I had a meal and wondered at the misery around me since I had not yet experienced any queasiness in the abdominal regions. Ten o'clock in the evening and the hour of 'lights out' approached so I decided it was time to prepare for my first ever experience of going to bed in a swinging hammock surrounded by a multitude of other hammocks.

Having prepared my slithering pendulum nocturnal couch for my night's rest I paid my last visit to the nearest latrine and there occurred my downfall. The horror of the rolling waves of filth swishing from side to side in the toilet together with the sight of the agony of the suffering people present was too much to resist and I immediately joined the suffering majority, no longer wondering at the misery around me.

As the ship steamed out of the Channel southwards the weather improved and the punishing rolling and pitching lessened but it was some two days or more before the majority of people recovered from their unpleasant experience. We had some ten days or so sailing to Port Said. Our time was spent in various activities including attending lectures by the military doctors on board on the precautions we should take to avoid the many dangerous tropical diseases which could so easily attack the unwary. Other lectures were on the subject of respect for the customs and religion of the local population and on life in the tropics with regard to the effects of the climate and protection from the sun during one's various daily activities. For most of the day, however, the majority of the men were lying on the top deck either reading or indulging in the game of 'housey housey' or bingo as it is called these days.

Arrived at Port Said the contingent for Egypt disembarked but we unfortunates destined for Iraq or the Far East were now subjected to the unpleasant experience of 'coaling' our ship. This involved a day long loading of coal to replenish the fuel stocks for the ship's steam engines and resulted in an atmosphere of horrible black coal dust which permeated the whole ship throughout the day. There was no escape anywhere. We were anchored offshore and a constant stream of small rowboats (bumboats) with all kinds of Egyptian wares were peddled by unsavoury looking Arabs.

The coaling process completed we again set sail heading into the Suez Canal and down the Red Sea. The further we progressed south the higher the temperature rose and the troops suffered their first experience of the relentless tropical sun. Eventually we arrived at Aden where we moored again quayside and off loaded a contingent for this barren featureless Protectorate. Continuing on our way we turned north sailing up the Persian Gulf towards our next port of call, Basrah in Southern Iraq which was to be my destination. Here the Iraq contingent disembarked. Close to the quayside was the Iraqi railway, and on the nearest line was a tremendous length of cattle trucks which had been prepared for the carriage of the RAF contingent. This crowd was due to be transported to Baghdad en route to its final destination which was to be RAF Station Hinaidi situated about 15 miles from Baghdad city. Prior to embarkation in this long line of cattle trucks the RAF personnel were allocated to duty teams that were to perform various functions during the long journey of approx. five hundred tedious miles across the Iraqi desert. One of these functions was the brewing up of tea at approximately 4 hourly stops in the desert. The members of each tea team were provided with the necessary buckets and rations with instructions that, as soon as the train stopped, wherever it might be, they were to run forward to the engine, collect boiling water and do the necessary brewing of the tea for their truck. Another team was instructed to fetch rolls of sacking, wooden stakes and shovels and proceed to a suitable distance from the train where they had to dig trenches and erect suitable screens with their stakes to provide earth closets. A short time before the train departed from each stop these closet teams, of which I was a member, had to fill in the trenches and collect the screens and stakes. The journey was indeed tedious, the train travelled at a very slow pace and, in consequence, took a tremendous time to cover the distance – in fact, if I remember correctly, it was two days and one night.

Our desert journey in a cattle truck from Basra to Baghdad in Iraq. Breakfast in the desert.

Halfway on the journey we met a similar train going in the opposite direction, full of the RAF contingent that had completed their two-year tour of duty at Hinaidi. The two trains stopped to greet each other and, amid cries of 'You're going the wrong way!' our own train continued on our journey north.

These cattle trucks were all metal, including the floor, and there were no amenities and no windows. At night we slept on the metallic floor with a blanket, with the noise of the wheels pounding our ears. The vibration was such that it was a considered opinion of the occupants that our truck was fitted with square wheels!

Arrived in Baghdad main station we disembarked with our kit and were taken by lorry to Hinaidi cantonment. Hinaidi, at that time, was a huge enclosed area in the desert comprising a bomber squadron and it's aerodrome, a huge maintenance unit, a very large military hospital and a large contingent of RAF armoured cars. These were Rolls Royce cars, the chassis of which had been fitted with an armour plated enclosed body which carried a mounted machine gun and forward vision slits for the driver. These were used to afford protection to weekly convoys run by the Nairn Company across the desert from Baghdad to Beirut. Also within the cantonment was a huge barracks area for Iraqi native levy troops. These native soldiers were equipped by the British to provide guards etc. for the various installations and technical units. The whole cantonment was surrounded by a raised dried mud barricade known as the 'bund'.

One unfortunate incident occurred around the time when we arrived at Hinaidi and that concerned a very good friend of mine with whom I had been at Cranwell and who was a newcomer like us. In spite of the warnings mentioned previously by the doctors on the troopship concerning the dangers of drinking refreshments from dubious sources my friend, Tucker by name, had bought a bottle of lemonade on Basrah quayside from an itinerant Arab. This resulted in him being a victim to typhoid which developed rapidly and he was admitted to the cantonment hospital. Here he sank rapidly until his life was in danger for in those days we had no antibiotics. He was put into isolation and was only just rescued from death's door by careful nursing. After three months he was sent back to England, a shadow of his former self.

I was posted to the engineering depot and my home became a barrack room constructed of dried mud walls at least 18 inches thick and a flat mud roof. There were some 30 men in each of these barrack rooms and, suspended from the ceiling, were a number of electric fans which were operated at full blast in the summer when temperatures would often be of the order of 120-125 degrees F. in the shade. At these times one could burn one's hands on the metal doorknobs. Our bathrooms were showers in a separate block. Permanent residents in the bath block were nests of hornets. Between the barrack rooms were irrigation ditches in which hundreds of frogs would chant and croak in the evenings. The purpose of these frogs was to consume the mosquito larvae. Unfortunately their consumption rate was quite inadequate and in consequence from sundown onwards we were constantly attacked by armies of voracious mosquitoes. We all slept with mosquito nets draped over our beds. It was quite surprising how clever the mosquito hordes were in finding the slightest break in the netting.

My work was in the aero-engine overhaul workshop where I was concerned with highly technical processes relating to the re-conditioning of Bristol Pegasus and Napier Lion aero-engines. I pursued my application for a pilot's course and to my great disappointment I was told that on changing commands overseas one had to start from the beginning again. I submitted my application and, in contrast to the U.K. procedures, the first phase was a medical examination. I duly reported to the medical officer who was a young recently qualified doctor from Dublin University. His Irish brogue was so strong that, to his annoyance, I had difficulty in understanding him and thus the atmosphere became strained and unhelpful.

The lung test consisted of a U-tube of mercury to one side of which was attached a rubber tube with a glass mouthpiece through which the candidate was instructed to blow in order to maintain a pressure on the mercury column and thus lift the other side column in the U-tube until it reached a defined mark. The test was to hold this column steady at this mark for a minimum of 55 seconds. The mouthpiece was designed with a crosspiece so that one's tongue could not be entered into the mouthpiece orifice and thus hold the column steady. Unfortunately during this test my heartbeat began to affect the level of the mercury, causing it to fluctuate up and down and I was thus rejected on the grounds that my lung condition was not suitable. The irony of this medical rejection is that two years later I was an international 10,000 metres champion of Egypt and RAF cross-country champion of the Middle

East. In addition I won many events including setting a record for the half mile in Egypt and a 6 1/4-mile road race. I question whether that lung test which I failed told the correct story. In fact later I learned that candidates in the know would, some weeks prior to the medical test, go to the sick quarters where they were instructed in methods of passing this test; they then practised this technique at the clinic for some time until they were proficient in this test. With hindsight, perhaps it was for the best that I failed, for I most certainly would have become an experienced pilot by 1940 and possibly would have been a leader in the Battle of Britain. The majority of these leaders were killed during this time. However I made up my mind that the RAF would not stop me from flying and I resolved that at the first opportunity I would go for a private pilot's licence. The successful accomplishment of this ambition I record later in these memoirs.

My disappointment at this rejection and the consequent loss of the opportunity for pilot training was intense. I experienced a very severe adverse reaction and vowed to myself that I would no longer strive or make efforts to advance my RAF career. On the contrary I decided that I would use my time to make a study of a subject which was directly opposed to my aeronautical career. That subject was music and in particular the study of the violin.

It so happened that one of my minor voluntary activities was playing the cornet in the station military band. The band had various engagements outside the normal military duties and one of these was to play at the very exclusive Alwyah Social Club in Baghdad. The occasion was the annual garden party celebrating King George V's birthday. Also playing at the club that day was the Club resident orchestra which was led by a very highly talented Russian virtuoso violinist. In the interval I engaged this Russian in conversation and expressed my interest in the violin and my wish to pursue a serious study of the instrument. The Russian violinist told me that he was giving lessons and, included amongst his pupils, was the son of the King of Iraq. Noting my sincerity, the Russian made me an offer. He said he would give me an audition and, if he was satisfied, he agreed to give tuition at a very nominal fee provided I was willing to undertake a minimum of two hours practice a day. Needless to say, I accepted this offer and, transporting myself to Baghdad on my rather ancient motorcycle with my violin strapped to my back, I had my audition at his flat in Baghdad. The Russian was rather critical of my technique but said that, provided I was willing to start from scratch, he would give me instruction twice a week. I naturally agreed and, following his directions, I purchased the necessary violin study books which he had prescribed.

I conscientiously pursued my studies with this Russian for some two years. As time went on I discovered that he was a graduate of the highly reputed St. Petersburg Conservatoire. He had commenced his studies at the age of four in this highly specialised school in which the study of music formed the main part of the general school curriculum for all pupils extending over many years. In his own class was the future world famous concert virtuoso violinist, Jascha Heifetz, who later escaped the Russian Red Revolution and eventually found his way to America, making his home in San Francisco. My tutor, having married a banker's daughter, was in considerable danger of his life. They both escaped south and settled in Baghdad.

I studied conscientiously with two hours daily practice during the week and four hours or sometimes six on Saturdays and Sundays. I was fortunate that the padre of the Congregational Chapel in the cantonment permitted me to use the chapel premises for my practice sessions. This obviated the nuisance it might have caused for the outside world in having to listen to the efforts of a pupil violinist.

My violin became my greatest source of comfort in this period of mental agony and deep hurt that I suffered following my rejection and the consequential destruction of my burning ambition to become an RAF pilot. It seemed to me that, although the bottom of my world had fallen out, my violin, my everlasting constant soul-mate, spoke sweet words of comfort and gave me profound sympathy. This great empathy has remained with me all my life and my violin has been my never failing refuge in any situation of stress or unhappiness.

IRAQ AND THE MIDDLE EAST

Chapter 8

Life in Iraq

My hobby interests apart from music centred on motorcycles and motor cycle exploration trips across the Iraqi desert to various places of interest. Having very little money one's choice of machine was limited to second-hand ancient models which had been handed down year after year to each succeeding new set of arrivals from U.K. My first machine was indeed an ancient relic which in England would have been considered a valuable antique suitable for a museum. It was a 1914 $2^1/_4$ horsepower Douglas with an air-cooled engine with twin cylinders horizontally opposed. It had a rubber belt drive to the rear wheel and three gears which were operated by a hand lever.

With this machine I covered many miles on the only made-up road to Baghdad, both for my music lessons and for evening visits to the Baghdad Y.M.C.A. The Y.M.C.A. was a very pleasant place sited on the banks of the River Tigris just on the

My ancient Douglas belt drive motorcycle outside our mud hut bungalow at Hinaidi

Life in the Iraqi desert (Hinaidi). My native servant Abdul and self

outskirts of Baghdad. It was also interesting since it provided visitors with lodging and thus one met all kinds of unusual travellers, such as missionaries of various nationalities, oil company officials and Middle East desert explorers etc. On Sunday evenings a Church service was held in the main lounge, for which I played my violin accompanied on the piano by the Matron of Hinaidi RAF hospital.

These evening excursions by motorcycle to the Y.M.C.A. in Baghdad formed a very pleasant break from the exhausting daytime heat of the desert at Hinaidi. The cool balmy evening air providing soothing relief as it rushed past one's face accompanied by the throb of the little motor-cycle engine gave a feeling of joyous exhilaration. On the journey back to the cantonment the desert silence, broken by the urgent beat of the industrious little motor propelling one homewards, was sometimes overwhelmed by raucous croaking where a regiment of frogs had gathered in the adjoining irrigation ditches which ran along each side of the road. In the winter rains this dirt road became a quagmire so that the journey became somewhat hazardous; one had a nervous feeling of riding in masses of slippery brown margarine.

My close friend Phillips was also an enthusiastic motor cyclist and he, too, acquired a machine. We rode together in the evenings and we always travelled together on our desert adventures. One such desert trip was to a primitive small town called Hillah where some American missionaries we had met at the Y.M.C.A. had set up a small mission just outside the town.

These American missionaries were very brave people for the Hillah district was a centre of fanatic Muslims. Originally it was the site of the capital of the Babylonian civilisation and the famous hanging gardens of Babylon were built there some three or four thousand years ago. There was now very little evidence of what was once a powerful Persian Empire. After a variety of conquests by the Persians followed by the Arabs and the Turks the remnants of this civilisation had all but disappeared. The present Islamic population was fanatically opposed to all Christians. When the Americans arrived no Arab would allow his property to be rented to them. This was on the grounds that the Christians would defile and foul up for ever any Muslim building in which they might be permitted to live. In consequence the Americans were forced to build their own accommodation, during which time they lived precariously under canvas on a site well outside the town. Eventually they established a small chapel, a school and a small clinic in the face of much obstruction and enmity.

Hillah was between 70 and 80 miles south of Baghdad. No road existed between the two so that one had to navigate over a wide expanse of desert using, as a guide, the tracks left in the sand by other vehicles which had passed that way. Travelling thus on a motorcycle required great care. One needed to anticipate where the way ahead might be in deep loose sand which could cause a tumble. Sometimes a wadi or ditch might suddenly materialise immediately ahead in what falsely appeared to be a clear stretch of sand stretching far into the distance.

On these expeditions Phillips and I agreed to ride several hundred yards apart, one ahead of the other, so as to avoid the unpleasant clouds of sand thrown up by the rear wheel of the leading machine. On this particular expedition to Hillah, at the invitation of the American missionaries, we spent an interesting weekend with them and on the Sunday set off on our return journey across the desert. After some twenty miles or so I unfortunately ploughed into a stretch of very deep loose sand, lost control, and the front wheel dug into the sand, sending me over the handlebars. The motorcycle fell on top of me and my left leg was locked between the engine and the front wheel, preventing me from rising.

As I said previously, the engine was a horizontally opposed twin cylinder. As I went down and the motorcycle fell on my leg, the left cylinder sparking plug cut into the calf of my left leg but the right cylinder continued firing. Thus I was being burnt by the very hot cylinder, electrocuted by the sparking plug which had entered my calf, and held down by the acute angle of the front wheel locking my leg to the engine.

Collecting my wits after the shock, in my prone position I found the control to stop the engine running but found it impossible to rise. My sun helmet had of course come off so there was I, held down in the sand with the midday sun blazing down on my head in a temperature of some 120 degrees Fahrenheit in the shade – but there was no shade. Probably the temperature was more in the region of 160 deg. F.!

After what seemed an eternity lying there, I spotted in the distance a model T Ford car loaded with Arabs inside and outside heading in my direction. They were travelling on a course about 50 yards away from where I was lying so that, when they were parallel with me, I screamed out at the top of my voice. They stopped and several of them ran towards me and, seeing my plight, immediately attempted to lift the machine from my leg by taking hold of the engine. They probably had never seen or handled a motorcycle so they had no idea that the engine would be extremely hot.

Typical Iraqi desert tramway (1930) from Nedjaf to Kujah

In consequence they lifted the machine but burnt their fingers, dropped the motorcycle in shock, but freed my leg. I stood up, retrieved my sun helmet, picked up the motorcycle, started the engine which fortunately had not been damaged, mounted and rode off with out a word of thanks to the Arabs who had rescued me! I suppose I was still in shock and not capable of thinking clearly.

My friend Phillips, who was riding ahead, was totally unaware of the mishap and in consequence was some half mile or so in the distance. My leg was somewhat burnt and damaged and needed urgent attention. Phillips had the first aid kit so I went flat out to catch him. When I arrived I stopped him. Together we gave first aid treatment to my injured calf which had rather a nasty hole in it, due to the sparking plug which had penetrated it. There was a somewhat blackened area around the hole where the skin had been burnt.

We passed through Baghdad and made our way back to Hinaidi, parked our motor cycles and had our evening meal. Feeling a little 'under the weather', I went to bed early and, on waking next morning, I felt worse. However I was anxious not to prejudice our hard-won official permission to undertake our motor-cycle desert excursions so I did not report sick and, by doing so, reveal my mishap in the desert. Halfway through the morning I had to leave the workshops and return to my bungalow for I was feeling very ill indeed. By the afternoon I was vomiting, perspiring badly and in a fever. As I was no longer capable of movement my bungalow friends reported my condition and an ambulance was called; I was transported 'hors de combat' to the Hinaidi Hospital. By this time I was semi-conscious with sunstroke and knew little of what was happening. Coming to later I was somewhat delirious but found myself in a large hospital ward that seemed to be full of men in a similar or worse condition. In fact, some were at death's door, with the hospital staff desperately trying to save lives by improvising cooling systems to bring down the patients' critical body temperature. One small room had been set aside and a lorry radiator had been mounted at the bed end. This was fed with iced water with an electrically driven fan mounted in front to drive air cooled by the radiator onto the naked patient, who received the full benefit of the cooled air.

It should be remembered that, at this time, air conditioning had not yet been invented and, in fact, refrigerators were unknown in Europe. In Iraq there only existed ice-chests, wooden boxes in which were placed large blocks of ice – manufactured in a Baghdad factory from River Tigris water – deadly if drunk by Europeans.

Patients in a critical condition were moved to the radiator cold-air room but of course the availability of that treatment was completely inadequate. All up and down my ward were people with temperatures of around 104 deg.F. or more which, in England, could have been fatal. One or two patients would occasionally seem to go over the top and get out of bed. They would rush out of the ward through side doors onto the lawn outside and into the glaring sun to be struck down quickly.

My own temperature was around the 104 deg. figure and it was some ten days before I was considered to be recovering. During this time the hospital staff concentrating on treating the sun-stroke condition were unaware of my damaged leg. One day they discovered me in the bathroom endeavouring to clean up my wound. The duty nurse was very upset and railed at me for not informing them, for by this time the leg looked a real black mess As stated previously there were no such things as antibiotics in those days so that, in such very hot climates, skin healing was a very slow business. In fact the doctor attending my case threatened me at one stage that, if my leg did not begin to heal, he would graft skin from my behind! During those long weeks on my back I had, for the first time in my life, an awareness of the value of good health and fitness. I remember so well my feeling of tremendous envy of those people I could hear outside who were lucky enough to be fit and well. I had a great longing to once again be able to be freely moving in the world outside of my 'prison ward' and durance vile.

However I finally returned, full of joy, to my dried mud bungalow home. I was so happy to be once more amongst my fellow men and to pursue those activities that had been so suddenly cut short. Having by now saved a few more pennies I was able to consider up-grading my ancient and primitive motor-cycle. By so doing I would have greater security for my various activities, especially the adventurous expeditions which I so much enjoyed in the company of my friend Phillips. An opportunity had just arisen at that time to do precisely that. Another friend with a far superior motor-cycle and sidecar outfit had now finished his tour of duty in Iraq and was due for the 'boat', either home or to some other station in India or Egypt. His machine was an aristocrat compared with mine and he was very proud and jealous of its well-being and anxious that the future owner should treat it properly when he finally sold it.

My improved desert transport – a P and M sloper chain driven motor cycle

Iraq Desert expedition with my sidecar outfit and friend

Apparently he had confidence in myself from his knowledge of my care for my own motor-cycle so he let me have it although there was quite a number of potential buyers. The machine was of course of ancient design, known as a P and M 'sloper', due to the fact that the engine formed the sloping forward part of the motor-cycle frame. The top of the sloping single cylinder was bolted to the forward end of the top horizontal frame member and the bottom crankcase was bolted to the lower frame member, thus completing the cycle frame. The engine was a long-stroke 'thumper' giving an aristocratic slow beat instead of the fussy rattle of my previous power unit. It was a larger engine, being 350 cc. and thus more powerful. The great advantage for desert travel, however, was the fact that it was a sidecar outfit, which permitted greater loads to be carried and, even more important, it gave greater stability in difficult conditions. And of course the transmission system was the more modern chain and sprocket drive instead of my previous rubber belt drive. This gave greater confidence in the reliability of the machine to bring you 'home'. There were no garages in the desert. If you were unfortunate enough to break down you were on your own!! And the sun and thirst could kill you.

After something like another year of activities on our motor-cycles Phillips and I became even more ambitious in our mobility standards and decided to acquire four wheels. We had discovered that in the bazaars of Baghdad was an Arab who owned a sort of Government surplus goods yard from which one could purchase all kinds of ex-Government machinery including motor-cars, motor-cycles, various types of weapons, shot guns etc.

The pair of us descended into the Bazaars of Baghdad and, wandering through the crowded passageways of the bustling noisy market place, we eventually located the Government surplus compound. This was presided over by a big fat Arab in his galabiyah' or 'night-shirt' gown, crowned with his Arab style head-dress, shuffling in leather sandals and wearing his leather waist-belt and money pouch. His beady eyes and evil grin warned us to beware in our proposed dealings with him. In his yard he had a number of decrepit vehicles including some ambulances, vans, three ton lorries and a few passenger cars, but in the midst of these wrecks was a large hooded car of ancient vintage but in reasonable condition. It was an American Willys 'Whippet' car of probably around 1914 design with a capacious body and large engine of possibly some 3.5 litres. Surprisingly the wheels were wooden but were clad in reasonable tyres. Instead of the wheels being all metal as in the modern design they consisted of a metal hub from which protruded a series of wooden spokes which then terminated in a steel rim plus rubber tyres. This feature was to prove a problem later as you will see. The car was probably a Turkish Army staff car from the 1914-18 World War I but there was no way possible to confirm this because such things as log books, licences or insurance were unknown in these regions at that time. And such things were not on the minds of these two young British members of the ruling 'Raj' military class. We found the engine actually started and seemed able to continue running long enough perhaps to get the thing back to Hinaidi – providing we knew how to drive it! The brakes worked and the car actually moved when the clutch was depressed and the gear was engaged.

Now we were really interested with visions of ourselves in this, by our standards, enormous American luxury car promenading before the gaze of our friends like some bloated capitalists. After considerable haggling with the Arab owner we agreed to buy the car for the magnificent sum of the equivalent of £25 in Iraqi money. We each paid half of the purchase price so becoming co-owners of this American Willys Whippet at the knock-down price of £12.50 each. Then arose the problem of how to get it back to Hinaidi since neither of us had ever driven a car in our lives. Phillips nominated myself as the most likely to get the thing back without too much hassle since he knew that I had done a considerable amount of reading of automobile magazines and had studied the theoretical driving of motor cars if only in written articles. He considered this sufficient know-how to have me in the driving seat. Being rather proud of my theoretical knowledge I accepted the challenge but with considerable secret misgivings.

Fortunately there was an exit at the rear of the compound premises which gave onto a reasonable size street which would lead us into the main thoroughfare of Baghdad complete with trams, traffic, donkeys, carts and humans etc. The Arab gave us sufficient petrol and oil to accomplish our journey and we boarded our purchase – with considerable trepidation let it be said. I pressed my foot on the clutch pedal for I knew that was the key to the whole thing! I knew that as long as I kept my foot on the clutch pedal and my hand on the hand brake I was perfectly safe. I then gingerly engaged bottom gear of this three-geared mechanism and the car shot forward and stalled with my foot now frozen on the brake pedal. Slowly recovering from this initial shock life returned to my right foot and I was able to release the brake and with my left foot once again apply pressure to the clutch pedal. The car of course had no self-starter system so Phillips undertook the hazardous winding-up process with the long starting handle. Once again the engine started and with Phillips on board I again gingerly let out the clutch and we moved off. Slowly I negotiated the yard exit and then, with my heart in my mouth, I guided this dreaded vehicle without mishap, in bottom gear and with engine racing, never daring to change up to a higher gear. On arriving at the main street I dodged the donkeys and the trams and the odd camel or two at around 7 or 8 miles an hour with the engine revving noisily, until, in the open country, my courage began to return and in spite of the dreaded double-declutching routine I succeeded in changing up to the second gear. We were then really bowling along bravely although my foot was hovering in a nervous twitter over the brake pedal most of the time.

However we duly arrived in one piece at the Hinaidi cantonment where we slowly wended our way to our Depot garage. Then came the tricky question of getting into the open air garage The entrance to this garage was unfortunately located off the road and adjacent to an irrigation ditch. One had to turn off the road, enter a small side road and do a U-turn to enter the garage. My theoretical expertise did not extend to accomplishing the necessary complete U- turn in one movement so that there arose the new problem of reversing in the narrow space available. Nothing daunted by this time I engaged reverse gear and shot backwards straight into the irrigation ditch! Fortunately the ditch was not deep and interested spectators laughingly lent a hand to push the car out

Luckily the car was not damaged and was safely parked in one of the garage bays. Then commenced the second phase of this new enterprising hopeful venture into the desert motoring world. Both Phillips and myself were aero-engine technicians working in the aero-engine overhaul workshops in the Depot. The acquisition of this unusual automobile presented an exciting challenge to us: a technical challenge which we both relished. It was a challenge to embark on even more daring desert expeditions with the car extending our range of operation and permitting us to carry much greater loads such as blankets, tinned food supplies, beer, water, fuel etc.

One mandatory condition for desert travel in those days was that one's vehicle must be 100% reliable, as mentioned previously, for not only were there no garages in the desert, but one could not expect any help, even in any centres of civilisation which might exist en route. Motor cars were few and far between. In fact one's life might depend on the machine. We therefore decided that to obtain the necessary reliability we required we would need to strip the motor car down to its bare frame and recondition everything including the engine.

We obtained official permission from the authorities to make use of the aero-engine workshops in non-working hours and this proved a great boon for, with this concession, we had considerable technical facilities at our disposal. We then began taking the whole motor car to pieces. And when I say to pieces that indeed was the operative word for we stripped the car down to the bare chassis. In those early days of motor car design the whole structure was based on a strong rigid steel beam frame chassis to which everything else was bolted, including the body or carriage work.

My upgraded desert travel in a 1916 American Willys Whippet ex Turkish Army staff car with wooden wheels together with my partner Phillips and his brother

Nowadays tremendous economy in weight has been achieved by doing away with this heavy steel frame. The necessary strength is obtained by using thin pressed steel panels which together provide their own inbuilt rigidity.

But for us with our 1914 designed car we were very happy because all the parts were bolted on and they could therefore be taken off and reconditioned. So we finally had the unusual spectacle of our motorcar reduced to one steel girder frame on the ground with everything else removed. The engine we transported to the workshops and stripped down to all its many bits and pieces and we rebuilt it with new main bearings, big-ends, piston rings etc.

The bodywork was inspected and rust etc., removed and checked for wear and tear. The wheels we removed, cleaned out the hub bearings and re-assembled with fresh grease. The wooden spokes were in good condition but somewhat loose in their housings. We could do nothing to rectify that and this defeat would prove to be a severe handicap on our future excursions in the desert. The transmission was removed, cleaned, and checked with the gearbox which we stripped down, cleaned and re-assembled. All was found to be in reasonable condition, fortunately,

After three months hard work we began the re-assembly of the car. The old fashioned semi-elliptic leaf springs were attached to the steel beam girder and the rear axle and wheels attached to the springs. Then the engine was built into the forward bay between the girders and the gearbox and transmission attached to the engine and connected to the universal gear driving the half shafts and so to the wheels. The steering gear was assembled and 'Lo and behold!' we had a working bare chassis that we could drive and steer – that is if we had anything to sit on! This little problem we overcame by attaching two soapboxes where the front seats should be. We did this because we wished to test the viability of the working parts prior to re-assembling all the body work and lighting etc. to the chassis. In addition we thought it a good idea to have an engine 'running-in' period without the weight of the carriage-work.

We then hit on the idea of a running-in exercise driving our bare chassis complete with soap-box seats on a short trip across the desert to Ctesiphon Arch which was situated on a flat plain area some 40 miles or so south from Hinaidi. This trip would be avoiding all civilisation and thus free of traffic so that I could improve my limited driving skills. Our engine started and ran sweetly and there were no squeaks or rumbles from the transmission or rear axle, or even the wheels – although we discovered that the wheels began to squeak somewhat when the temperature rose and the wooden spokes shrank and loosened in their housings. There was nothing we could do about that except – another discovery! – we could pour water on the spokes and that made the wood expand and the squeaks stopped. Later we found that when in the desert about every 50 miles or so of travelling the spokes would set up a noisy cacophony and we would then stop, pour water on the wheel hubs and we could then do another 50 miles before we had to repeat this exercise. The critical part was to ensure we had sufficient water with us for our own drinking needs and for the wheels on our planned trip.

Ctesiphon Arch is the largest brick-built archway in the world and is a relic of the ancient Royal City of Ctesiphon, capital of the Parthian and later the Persian Empire of the period of the 2nd century B.C. to the 3rd century A.D. It is an impressive sight, covering a very great area rising to some 150 feet at its apex. Here we arrived after a gentle uneventful journey across the desert, by which time I had gained the courage to change up to top gear so that no longer did the engine have to complain in loud terms about overworking in low gear.

When we arrived at this ancient Ctesiphon Arch we felt truly exhilarated that the car was performing so well and that all our work of the last three months had now proved to be successful. Our joyous mood on this trip then led to the idea of some celebratory prank. After some thought we decided to remove our soap-box seats, start the car and fix the steering in full lock so that the car would run round in a continuous circle with us sitting on our soap-boxes in the centre of the circle. This was possible because the old design of cars had a hand throttle on the steering wheel as well as a foot pedal accelerator. Thus one could set the hand throttle to have the engine running continuously at any setting required. So there we were in the desert, miles from any civilisation, with our bare chassis running round us continuously at around 10 miles an hour. We just loved it! and we were so thrilled we just sat there laughing our heads off – and of course we were assisting in the running-in process. After possibly half an hour of this mad hilarity we ran after the car and stopped it. We once again secured our soapboxes on board and made our way back to Hinaidi, proud of our new possession and full of plans for our future adventures.

Having eventually attached the bodywork to the chassis and completed the remainder of the fitments such as the lighting system, which was acetylene gas, and the running boards etc. we began using the car for our local running. As I had now graduated from a theoretical expert driver to a successful practical driver it was time to give Phillips driving lessons so that he could take over as driver No. 2 when necessary. This done successfully, we began planning our next expedition. As previously mentioned there was a weekly mail desert convoy run by the Nairn Company which travelled across the wide bare desert expanse between Baghdad and Beirut on the Mediterranean coast. This convoy was escorted by RAF armoured cars whose drivers brought back stories of a huge lake and plantations of date palms and cotton fields in an area of the River Euphrates some 100 miles west of Baghdad by the name of Habbaniyah. We decided this was to be the object of our next visit.

By this time we had become even more ambitious in our excursions and, having heard that it was possible to shoot sand grouse and pigeons in this area, we decided to acquire shot guns. This we did by once again visiting our fat old Arab friend in the Baghdad bazaar. He had a stock of these guns which were the weapons with which the RAF equipped their locally recruited Iraqi Levies. How our Arab friend acquired these guns we did not enquire but for a comparatively paltry sum we each equipped ourselves with 12-bore shot guns. We then found that we could purchase as much ammunition as we wanted from an up-market French owned department store in Baghdad with no questions asked. Again no thought arose in the minds of these two young members of the ruling Raj military class on the subject of gun licences, or ammunition permits and certainly not for a moment was there any consideration of hunting licences or even driving licences.

It may be interesting to consider why we British were there at all, and especially why the RAF had such a prominent presence in Iraq. In actual fact we in the RAF were part of a unique, revolutionary experiment by the British government to use military air power to provide control of a country instead of the conventional garrison of military ground forces and sea power which had always been used in the past. By the Treaty of Versailles the Middle East, formerly part of the Turkish Empire, was divided into a number of countries, all under the protection and tutelage of either France or Great Britain. Iraq become a Protectorate of Britain who undertook, amongst other responsibilities, the internal and external defence of the country until such time as Iraq could organise its own defence forces.

However the World War I had put a tremendous strain on the economy of the United Kingdom. In the post WW1 years the Government was already having great difficulty in finding the enormous sums of money required to provide for the upkeep, administration, and control of the mighty British Empire and all its colonies, let alone the new Protectorates. Therefore Ministers were searching anxiously in the economy for possible savings to reduce national expenditure.

The Chief of Staff of the newly formed Royal Air Force in 1918 was Air Marshal Trenchard, later Lord Trenchard, who had radical ideas on the uses of military air power. He persuaded Winston Churchill who was the Air Minister at that time that tremendous savings could be made by using RAF air power to provide the necessary defences of the British Protectorates instead of the vastly more expensive military ground and naval sea forces used in the past. Churchill finally persuaded the Government which agreed, as an experiment, to sanction control and garrisoning of Iraq by air power. The reasoning was based on the facts that the Air Force could move much more rapidly to any trouble spots. It would operate with a smaller force which could fly over adverse terrain such as mountains etc. and could obtain much more rapid results with far fewer casualties and at greatly reduced costs.

So here we were, part of a great unprecedented experiment in the use of air power in international policing and military control. It is somewhat ironic to me nowadays that the modern media and the Western Governments all scream abuse at Saddam Hussein for his cruelty in bombing the Kurdish rebels of Northern Iraq. When I was in Iraq in the 1930s we regularly bombed the Kurds. Admitted we dropped polite warnings in Arabic on the target villages three or four days before the delivery of our bombs. These kind warnings stated that the inhabitants had been naughty people shielding their insurrection leader and we were going to bomb their village so they should move out to a place of safety. The Kurdish leader of these revolts was Molla Ahmed Barzani who was a fanatic Kurdish nationalist from the village of Barzan in Northern Iraq. The rebellion was put down with the aid of Iraqi troops and Barzani fled into hiding in various mountain villages

Our intelligence would locate the village shielding him and it was generally for this reason that they were punished. To-day it is an interesting feature of current Kurdish operations in Northern Iraq that the political party, the Kurdistan Democratic Party (K.D.P.), which is now supported by Saddam Hussein is headed by Massoud Barzani, the grandson of Molla Ahmed Barzani whom we used to bomb. His grandson has been more successful up to present times as he is now in control of the whole of Northern Iraq thanks to the support of Saddam Hussein. This is causing a serious problem for America and her Allies since this area was supposed to be a 'Safe Zone'.

One can imagine that the Kurds of the 1920's and 1930s were not exactly pleased about our air activity at that time. If one of our bomber aircraft was unfortunate enough to have to force land in the Kurdish mountainous country the aircrew might expect a rather antagonistic reception if they were unlucky enough to be captured. In fact the prevailing story of past encounters gave gory details of how the captured aircrew were given considerably rough treatment by the Kurdish tribesmen who then handed over the helpless prisoners to the women of the tribe. These ladies gave the prisoners their own special torture treatment, finally cutting off their privates and sewing them up in the prisoners mouths. This prospect of course was somewhat daunting to the aircrew since aircraft engines of those days were not noted for their reliability. But in order to alleviate to some degree the aircrew anxiety the British Government had agreed that all aircrew should be provided with a small certificate which guaranteed that the British Embassy would pay £5000 to any Iraqi who would assist any member of an aircrew to safety. The certificate was known as a 'goolie chit'.

Chapter 9

Adventures in the Iraqi Desert

Now equipped with our shotguns and with a plentiful supply of ammunition we began to plan our proposed hunting trip to Lake Habbaniyah. Official sanction for the trip obtained, together with the grant of a week's local leave, we arranged with the cookhouse caterer to provide us with an issue of rations of the official hard tack including tins of Maconochies stew. Maconochies was a basic ingredient of all Iraqi RAF menus and hard Army biscuits were a substitute for bread when in the desert.

We loaded up with spare four gallon tins of petrol, several four gallon tins of water, blankets and sleeping bags, our paraffin Primus stove cooker, a tin of paraffin for the cooker, tools and engine spares, guns and ammunition, first aid kit, and canvas cooler water carrier bags which were slung on the outside of the car. These canvas water carriers provided a good cold water drink due to the water seeping through the canvas being cooled by the evaporation process which extracted heat from the remainder of the water – in technical terms, the latent heat of vaporisation.

So off we started, full of joyous anticipation of our new adventure into the Iraqi desert. We drove through Baghdad and headed out west into the desert where, after some two hours travelling, we ran into stony desert which consisted of fairly compact sand covered with a layer of stones of various sizes. This led down eventually to plantations lining the banks of the River Euphrates. Crossing the Euphrates at Fallujah Bridge we passed through Fallujah which is a small desert township on the banks of the Euphrates. We carried on westwards to Ramadi which was at that time a staging post for the Nairn Company weekly transport desert convoy and which provided the regular service across the desert from Baghdad to Beirut. The River turns westwards at Fallujah so that we were now following the course of the River. Ramadi is on the west bank of the River. Here were very pleasant plantations of date palms and small fields of cotton adjoining the banks of the river.

We found a so-called Rest-house which was a sort of concrete hut which had been built, I presume, by the Nairn Company to provide a sheltered stopping place for their convoy of passengers. We installed ourselves in our desert home and the news quickly spread to the local Arabs in the riverside village. Soon we had interested Arab spectators, mostly children, come to gaze at the white intruders and to speculate on their unusual activities.

We gathered information from our visitors that Lake Habbaniyah was about ten miles or so south of Ramadi. We decided to explore the lake area and so headed in that direction. Arriving at the lakeside, we found it not very impressive in scenery and shallow for some way, but very suitable for a cooling swim in the desert heat. We undressed and waded out into the lake. Very soon we had another crowd of Arab spectators, mostly children again, who had heard the news of the unusual spectacle of two pale faced white-skinned naked creatures from the outer world who were disporting themselves in the lake. There were great chortlings of amusement and wide-eyed wonder at our activities in the water.

Refreshed and dressed again, we drove back to our concrete shelter. Having purchased some fresh vegetables en route, we made preparations for our evening meal. It was accepted wisdom in Iraq that the addition of a few fresh vegetables to the tinned Maconochies made a very tasty stew. Whilst we were so engaged we had another Arab visitor, this time an elderly grey-beard. This old Arab spoke a few words of English and said that he had heard from the children that we had shotguns amongst our possessions. He said that if we perhaps wished to shoot some pigeons in the riverside plantations he could guide us to some very likely spots where we should get a plentiful bag. He offered his services for the following day for the equivalent of a few pence. We accepted his offer and arranged that he would call for us at 9 o'clock the following morning. Having cooked our meal of garnished tinned Maconochies stew on our Primus stove we relaxed on the sandy floor in front of our concrete hut as we ate our delicious meal – or so it seemed to us in that isolated desert spot. I suppose after a strenuous day travelling in the desert and swimming in such an unusual lake the alfresco meal in the cool of the evening was a wonderful contrast. It is remarkable to me after sixty-five years have passed that I can remember so clearly that lovely evening and almost taste and savour that delightful stew dish which gave us such pleasure.

Little did we realise that this remote and primitive spot in the desert was to be, in a few years time, the site of a great new British RAF cantonment, which would replace the old site at Hinaidi. This was probably done as a political move in order that the British presence would not be so obvious to anti-British nationalist Iraqis around Baghdad. What is more, it was to be the scene of an amazing British feat of arms by the RAF against overwhelming odds. In 1941 an Iraqi Army officer, Rashid

Our desert expedition residence Easter 1932

Trouble in the Iraq desert on a YMCA organised 'package' tour

Ali El Galani, organised a military coup in Baghdad which ousted the reigning five-year-old young King and his 5-year-old government.   Setting up a military dictatorship which was pro-German and supported the Axis, he made contact with the French Vichy Government forces in Syria. His object was to eject the British from Iraq and he hoped to obtain the help of the Vichy French forces and the German Luftwaffe who were about to establish bases in Syria. The Germans planned to establish a fighting force which would attack our supply bases in Palestine and threaten the rear of the British forces in Egypt and the Western Desert.

Not only was this a serious threat to the British position in Iraq, but it would have also constituted a danger to Britain's oil supplies from the Middle East. Furthermore it was a planned German threat to our base in Egypt. The Vichy French agreed to help but advised Rashid Ali to await the arrival of the German Luftwaffe and the establishment of their bases in Syria. However the success of Rashid Ali's military coup in Baghdad and the promise of help from Syria overcame caution and Rashid Ali in May 1941 decided to attack the RAF cantonment at Habbaniyah.

The former RAF No. 70 bomber squadron originally located at Hinaidi had been moved to Egypt but now, due to the Iraqi crisis, had been moved back to Shaibah to support the Iraqi British base. The flying unit at Habbaniyah was now No. 4 Flying School equipped with very ancient pre-war bi-plane aircraft used for instruction such as the wooden Oxford trainer and the bi-plane fighters Audax and Gladiator. These few pre-war aircraft were later assisted by six ancient Gladiators flown in from Egypt. The Habbaniyah ground forces consisted of 300 troops (King's Own Royal

Regiment) flown in from India which, with the small force of native Iraqi levies, were the entire defences in the RAF Habbaniyah cantonment. Habbaniyah had no tanks, no field guns but they had 18 armoured cars which, as mentioned previously, were armoured bodies on ancient Rolls Royce chassis

Rashid Ali moved 9000 Iraqi Army troops with artillery to lay siege to the RAF base. They positioned themselves on high ground overlooking Habbaniyah and were thus able to fire directly into the cantonment. The RAF Officer Commanding the cantonment ordered the Flying School to put every aircraft in the Flying School, no matter how old, into the air. The ancient Audaxes and Gladiators together with Oxford twin-engined trainers were flown by the School instructors and senior pupils to form a ground strafing attack force which made life uncomfortable for the Iraqis in their defenceless open positions. Meanwhile urgent requests for help brought limited reinforcements of Wellington bombers from Nos. 37 and 70 Squadrons located at the RAF base at Shaibah in southern Iraq. Further assistance came from a few Fleet Air Arm Swordfish aircraft from the aircraft carrier Hermes, located in the Persian Gulf. The flying school personnel with the assistance of the Wellington bombers succeeded in destroying the morale of the Iraqi army artillery gun crews so that, as soon as the attacking aircraft appeared overhead, the gun crews disappeared rapidly.

After days of continuous bombardment from the air, the besieging Iraqi Army lost heart and decided to call it quits. To the amazement of everybody in the cantonment the Iraqi troops began to withdraw and retreated back to Baghdad. Here they were eventually defeated by a British column from Syria and another column which moved up from the south assisted by a campaign of continuous air attacks by the RAF. The King and his government were restored to power and there was no further trouble in Iraq. Syria was invaded by a combined British and Free French force who took control of the country and the Germans abandoned any idea of advancing through this area. Eventually the British cleared the whole area of Vichy and German forces.

To return to the tale of our own pre-war private shooting party, the elderly Arab guide turned up the next morning as arranged. Off we went on foot with our shotguns and plenty of cartridges. We headed into some fairly dense date-palm plantations and soon our guide indicated to us to be prepared for immediate action as we were near an area with plentiful pigeons. And, indeed, he was right, for pigeons began to appear in and around the date-palm tops. We duly blazed away at these fleeting targets with no success. Having wandered around the plantation, again with no success, we lost heart and gave up. We then headed back towards our rest house and, as we got near, we saw in the distance a horseman galloping madly towards us. As he got nearer we could see that he was an Arab with galabiyah flying in the wind and obviously heading straight for us. He had a little boy mounted behind him. He pulled up in front of us and shouted some incomprehensible Arabic in a very aggressive tone. On asking our guide what the shouting was about, we were told that the Arab claimed that we had shot his son, now mounted behind him.

Our guide said that the boy had climbed up into the top foliage of one of the palms to pick dates where he had received wounds in his arm from our shooting.

We expressed astonishment for we had seen no boy in the treetops, nor had we heard any cries. However, to prove the truth of this story, the Arab told the boy to get down from the horse and show us his arm. We were invited to feel this little ten-year-old boy's arm and, sure enough, one could feel the pellets under the skin. We asked our guide what we should do to settle this matter and he suggested that we give the father the equivalent of half a crown (12p). This we did and, to our great relief and surprise, the father was quite happy to accept this arrangement. He thanked us profusely before galloping off with his son. We had no further ambitions that day to demonstrate our lack of hunting

Desert hunting expedition in our Willys Whippet

skill but we made a further plan with our guide for the next morning. He said we could try another venue which would also provide good shooting.

After an afternoon swim in Lake Habbaniyah we returned to the rest house and amused ourselves with organising scorpions in single combat contests. We did this by building a circular arena about 18 inches in diameter with a perimeter of raised sand to form an enclosure. The sand wall we doused with paraffin which was from our fuel for the Primus cooker and hurricane lamps. We found a couple of desert scorpions which we placed in the arena. The paraffin-soaked sand walls provided barriers the scorpions would not cross. By confrontation and provocation the two scorpions with their poisonous tails raised would eventually attack each other using their powerful claws. The ensuing fight proved to be entertaining to the two spectators.

The next day our Arab guide arrived as planned and again we set off on foot but in a direction opposite to that of yesterday. For this we were indeed thankful as we rather wished to avoid any further meeting with the injured boy or his father. Soon we entered a dense date-palm plantation with little space between the trees. We followed a track which had a very uneven surface, often with large tree roots above ground so creating obstacles across the path.

Penetrating some distance into the plantation our guide gave us a signal warning us to be prepared to shoot. We both cocked our shotguns and in proper cautionary mode we moved forward with our gun barrels lowered, pointing at the ground. Suddenly I stumbled on one of the palm-tree roots on the path and I must have had my finger on the trigger because the gun went off. The shot landed close behind the feet of our Arab guide who was walking ahead of us. The old man leapt into the air and then, without a word, took off, running at a smart pace.

We never saw him again. That incident, for which we were thankful we had not another wounded victim on our hands, seemed to completely undermine our confidence. We lost our enthusiasm for any further hunting exploits in the Habbaniyah desert. So ended our expedition with shotguns and henceforth we gave up all further ambition to become intrepid huntsmen in the wilderness of the Iraqi desert.

However we made quite a number of expeditions, some of weekend duration and a few more extended, on local leave. Those made on local leave were subject to approval by the authorities and one of the conditions laid down for approval was that we should report in to a police or military unit at sundown if we proposed to travel to remote areas. In this way a radio check could be made on our safety.

One curious incident I can recall on one of these local leave expeditions involved the Iraqi Desert Camel Police. These Bedouin police were located in remote desert fortified posts similar to the French Foreign Legion in North Africa. They travelled on high-speed racing camels which were capable of short sprint speeds up to 30 miles per hour. Their function was to patrol the desert areas in order to guard against Bedouin robbers and evil-doers. They were fierce savage-looking Arabs of dark skin and dark plaited hair which was covered with grease probably of a type of margarine or ghee.

It so happened that on this particular trip heading to a remote place of interest which, I think, was Ur of the Chaldees to the south-east of Hillah(Babylon). Sundown arrived and we were still in the desert miles from anywhere. We spotted in the distance one of these Camel Police posts and decided to report into this place. This proved to be quite an experience for we were most hospitably welcomed by the officer in charge who provided us with accommodation for the night. The single storey barracks were built in a circle round an open area which provided a

Our night stop in the desert with the Iraqi Desert Police

kind of parade ground. The whole unit was encircled with a strong high palisade through which there was only one entrance. This was closed after sunset by large heavy double doors.

We were invited by the officer to join their communal evening meal. In accepting we had some reservations but diplomacy dictated that we should participate. We were led to the centre of the open area parade ground and there, gathered in a circle, round a huge stew-pot, was a small group of Bedouin police. This was the garrison of the post, all sitting on the sand floor. Each in turn around the circle dipped his hand into the pot and removed some piece, possibly gazelle meat. We joined the circle and partook of the meal which proved to be quite tasty. Afterwards Phillips and I, wishing to reciprocate the kindness of our Bedouin host, presented him with two tins of our Maconochies stew. He promptly opened up the tins, tipped the contents into the sand, and thanked us profusely for the empty tins which he said were highly valued! The reason, of course, he tipped the contents out, was because he was fearful that the stew might contain pork which their religion forbade them to eat.

One of our favourite relaxations in the Hinaidi cantonment was swimming in the magnificent full Olympic size Cantonment swimming pool. In such a hot climate swimming was naturally a generally favourite sport. A grand annual swimming championship sports programme was arranged by the RAF authorities and I became very interested in developing my aquatic skills. It so happened that at this time the American swimmer Johnny Weissmuller had come to world prominence by creating world records with his invention of the fast American swimming crawl and his swimming performances as the star hero in Holly wood films depicting life in the African jungle living as Tarzan amongst an ape population, He had written a book giving a very clear and interesting exposition of his theory and practice in the development of his crawl technique, A friend and I bought the book between us and began a very serious study and practice of the American crawl. We both became very proficient high speed free style swimmers.

In the Hinaidi swimming world there was great propaganda for the Royal Life Saving Society and people were encouraged to enter for the various level certificates including the ultimate 'gold' certificate. My friend and I, having developed our speed swimming, decided to train for the 'gold' life-saving certificate which required some fairly sophisticated tests including diving from 50 feet to simulate rescuing a person who had fallen or jumped into a river from a high bridge. The tests also included 'dummy' rescuing of a person in the deep end of a pool who imitated a panic stricken drowning person who would attempt to clutch you and drag you under. One had to demonstrate the technique of releasing oneself from the victim and bringing him in to safety.

The dive from 50 feet was for me the most frightening of the various tests. I had never dived from such a height and I wondered if my nerve would fail when I climbed up to the topmost diving board with which our swimming pool was equipped. Once one climbed to that height all eyes in the pool were trained on one as a potential star performer or potential 'flop'. To avoid this possible nerve failure before a large audience I decided I would try myself out on a quiet Sunday morning before breakfast when hardly a soul was about. I climbed to the top diving board fifty feet above the pool and looked down. Indeed it was truly daunting. The pool looked so small from this height that I felt that I might miss the water altogether and hit the side. There was only one redeeming feature and that was that the pool was almost completely free of any other swimmers so that at least I could avoid injuring someone by hitting them on my descent into the water. Advancing to the front edge of the diving board without looking down I thought 'Quick! This is it! Do or die! And get it over with…' I lifted my arms forwards and sprang upwards and outwards towards the far end of the pool as I had been instructed. I descended what seemed forever but I entered the water in a perfect dive travelling along the bottom at what seemed a tremendous pace. But, joy of joy, I had done it. I swam rapidly to the side and raced up to the 50 feet diving board again and in I went – some half dozen times, cementing my confidence so that the height no longer held any fears for me. Shortly after I took my examination tests and passed to obtain my 'gold' certificate.

Chapter 10

Egypt – 45 Squadron, Helwan

The normal tour of duty at this time for RAF personnel in Iraq was two years. However, various interests I had developed plus my extra pay entitlement for service in Iraq persuaded me to volunteer to serve an additional year. My three years having been completed in 1932, I was now due to join the annual elite group on the train journey going south (the 'right' way) and thus would have the privilege of informing the passing newcomers train that they were going the 'wrong' way.

To my joy my posting notice informed me that my next tour of duty would be in Egypt. Egypt was considered to be a 'golden' posting and highly preferable to the alternatives of India or the Far East. Having shed my various possessions including my car half share I joined the lorry loads of departing 'old sweats'. We drove into Baghdad Railway main station and, boarding our cattle trucks, we made the miserable return desert journey to Basra. Here we embarked on the awaiting troopship. This troopship was of course on its outward bound circular tour to India and would eventually return to the United Kingdom. So those people destined for Egypt sailed via India, actually Karachi, now in Pakistan. At Karachi all disembarked whilst the ship was turned around and prepared for the return journey to England. Having spent a few pleasant days in Karachi the contingent for Egypt re-embarked together with the people for U.K. Sailing via Aden we arrived at Port Said where the Egypt contingent disembarked.

My posting detail in Egypt was to Number 45 Squadron which was located at Helwan, some 25 miles south of Cairo and situated on the banks of the River Nile. This squadron was equipped with Fairey IIIF light bomber aircraft and had a history of considerable achievements. When I arrived the squadron had just completed, in 1931, the very difficult task of locating and establishing staging posts with re-fuelling facilities along the length of the African continent from Cairo to the Cape. This exercise was designed for the use of the eventual Imperial Airways commercial aircraft flying on this route. In 1926 the RAF pioneered the first flight from Cairo to the Cape using Fairey IIID aircraft. On the return journey via Cairo they arrived back in England on 27th May 1926 having established the viability of an air route to be operated by Imperial Airways. Following this exercise it was then 45 Squadron's task to fill in the essential details. This involved flying over wild jungle country and often landing in very difficult terrain to survey with the object of establishing the required staging posts. The re-fuelling facilities were created by setting up stacks of four-gallon tins of petrol which were fed into 50-gallon bowsers used for re-fuelling the aircraft by means of hand pumps.

By the time of my arrival in the squadron the aircraft had suffered tremendous wear and tear and the engines were much the worse for wear. They were water-cooled 12 cylinder Napier Lion engines and the cylinder water jackets were now badly corroded internally so that occasionally the corrosion would penetrate right through the metal and the cylinder jacket would then spring a water leak. If this occurred in flight, which was often the case, then the engine would lose its water coolant and a dangerous rise in engine temperature would result. As soon as the pilot saw the engine temperature begin to rise on his temperature gauge he knew he had to make a forced landing rapidly, regardless of the type of country over which he was flying. If he failed to land he would lose all his water coolant, the engine would overheat and seize up, and he would stand a good chance of a crash landing. Sometimes this could happen over African jungle country full of wild animals, especially elephants who could make a mess of an aeroplane if they happened to be in an aggressive mood.

This type of crisis became well known in the squadron and an emergency first-aid system had been developed. Every aircraft going off on an operational flight would carry a stock of Wrigleys chewing gum and, immediately any engine temperature rise was observed, the pilot would begin to search for a possible site to force land. Meanwhile the crew would begin chewing the Wrigleys gum as fast as possible during the descent. On landing the sticky gum would be plugged into the perforated water jacket, the water tank topped up with the reserve water always carried, and the aeroplane would take off again, hoping to reach a safe base for assistance before any further trouble developed.

I had an interesting experience during my stay with 45 Squadron. There was no education officer attached to the squadron and it was decided to fill this gap by calling for a suitably qualified person to volunteer to undertake the duties of an education officer. This involved taking charge of a small school building with a library and arranging courses of instruction. These courses were designed to the education standards required for various Service promotion examinations. I volunteered and was accepted for this work which was additional to my normal daily squadron technical duties. It was done mainly in the evenings. The small addition to my basic pay was very welcome but it also permitted me to use the school study facilities since I was studying at that time for a higher education service examination of the level of a Science B.Sc. It was an interesting experience for I found myself for example teaching Higher Mathematics etc. to senior N.C.O.s who were my bosses during my daytime squadron duties.

I also arranged elementary 3 Rs type of courses for junior rank people taking promotion examinations. At this particular level I had a very satisfying experience of successfully tutoring a very difficult problem pupil. In the class for the promotion examination to corporal was one of the squadron cooks. He was a married man living with his wife in the squadron official married quarters.

He had sat this examination several times and had failed each time, always in the Arithmetic paper. In consequence he could never be promoted. His frustration in being passed over for promotion year after year had resulted in his taking to drink. His drunken sessions resulted in domestic violence as a result of which the Commanding Officer had a constant problem of dealing with complaints from the injured wife. Apparently the man, when on duty, was an efficient and valued cook and the C.O. was reluctant to lose his services.

In class I soon saw that the cook was struggling, trying to keep up with the rest of the class. Finally he came to me after class and admitted his difficulty. He asked me if I would be kind enough to give him private coaching in his married quarters with the promise of a first class supper to follow! I agreed and for the next few months I spent a couple of evenings a week at his house, helping him to master the intricacies of simple Arithmetic. Came the promotion examination and, to the squadron's amazement, and to my own pride, the cook passed with flying colours. He was promoted to corporal shortly afterwards. The C.O. sent for me and, congratulating me on the success of my classes, told me how relieved he was that his married quarter's problem was solved. It was all quiet on the domestic front.

During my stay in 45 Squadron another incident occurred which was to bring to light my latent athletic talents. In the squadron Wednesday afternoons were set aside for sports activity, but I was no sportsman. One Wednesday afternoon, lying on my bed, reading, I was insultingly challenged by one of the squadron pilots, chasing up laggards like myself, to join him on a cross country training run. Rising to the challenge I changed into running kit and off we went. Following him I ploughed through the deep sand across the aerodrome and beyond and managed to keep up with this very experienced cross-country runner. He seemed to be impressed by my endurance and on the return section of this run gave me encouragement when I was really suffering and was ready to collapse. However I made it back to the quarters but then experienced such agonies of stiffness that I could hardly walk. My entire muscular system seized up, having been so cruelly treated by such unusual violent exercise. At teatime I was like a board and walked like an automaton. I could barely sit.

However it would appear that my performance had indeed impressed this squadron cross-country expert. He persuaded me to take up serious training. A few weeks later was the Squadron annual Sports Day and I had my first athletic success, winning the one-mile track race and the two miles walking race. Enrolled in the squadron cross-country team, entered in the RAF Middle East cross-country championship, I contributed to the squadron team's success in winning the cup. I came in fourth, behind our team leader who was third. He was delighted that his discovery of this sports laggard had proved such a valuable find for his squadron team.

Flying with 45 Squadron in their tired old Fairey IIIF aircraft was extremely interesting and many times I had magnificent views of the Nile Valley from thousands of feet up. It was a wonderful experience, flying down the Nile and over the ancient Pyramids which are grouped together on the river bank. Somehow, looking down from the aircraft on these magnificent monuments which are four thousand years old gave one a feeling of being in a celestial presence, visiting man's earthly tributes to the Gods. This aerial view of the Nile Valley also brought home to one how fragile were the two green strips each side of the Nile that constituted the heart of Egypt, set in a vast ocean of sand. Little did I realise that, a few years later, I would return to Egypt and, as an Engineer Officer, plan and develop modern high precision aero workshops in the sites of the ancient Pharaohs where their stonemasons had quarried the stone to build their wondrous pyramids.

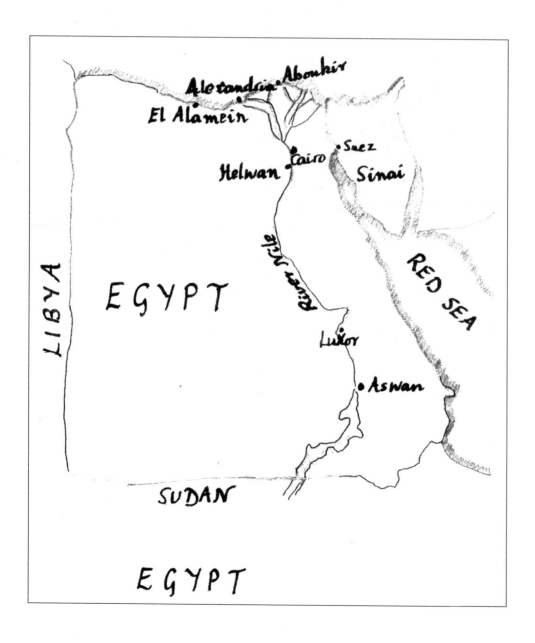

Chapter 11

Lower Egypt – the RAF Depot at Aboukir

After some months I applied for a transfer to the RAF Engineering Depot at Aboukir on the Mediterranean coast near Alexandria. My aim was to be in an environment which would facilitate my private engineering studies for a civilian professional qualification examination for which I proposed to sit in the near future. My good standing with the C.O. ensured that this request was granted and, in fact, the C.O. himself flew me up to Aboukir in one of the squadron aircraft. I felt greatly honoured although too shy to express myself. This officer became a famous air marshal in WW2.

At the Aboukir depot I was once more concerned with aero-engine overhauls and testing. This move was to have a profound effect on the future course of my life. Very soon I was once again involved with the athletic element on the RAF Aboukir station and I took up distance running quite seriously. I won the RAF Middle East cross-country championship and in the annual RAF station sports I won the one mile and the three mile events. This brought me to the notice of a world famous athlete.

At this time (1934) at RAF Aboukir there had just recently arrived a notable athlete, Flight Lieutenant Dickens, who held the world record for the 200 metres and had been captain of the British Olympic team at Los Angeles in 1932. He organised a RAF Aboukir one mile medley team comprising four people, two (of which he was one) running 220 yards, one a quarter of a mile and one half a mile. I was the half miler. Obviously this was the most critical leg of the race for one could gain or lose the most distance in the half-mile.

Dickens entered this team in every major athletics sports event in Egypt including the Middle East British Army championship and the Egyptian Army championship. We won every event we entered, so that we became famed throughout the whole of the Middle East. I suppose Dickens' fame had a lot to do with the team's renown. I remember in one championship event in Cairo the team was entered in an open invitation medley mile and was flown down from Aboukir the day before the event. We were lodged at RAF Heliopolis and Dickens, as team Captain, warned us to have an early night with a good night's sleep to be fit for the next day's event. Hildred, our second leg 220 yards team man, suggested to me that a supper in Cairo would be more pleasant than going to bed early. I agreed.

In the evening we journeyed into Cairo by the Heliopolis Brown Tram and had an excellent meal in a fashionable restaurant. Relaxed, with a liqueur brandy following our meal, Hildred, who seemed to know his way around Cairo, suggested we visit a pleasant house he knew where one could get a drink and meet German ladies. These ladies were apparently housewives who earned pocket money on the side and, as

The author, National Champion of Egypt (10,000 metres) and RAF Middle East cross-country Champion, with some trophies

Hildred carefully explained, the acceptance of their services was not mandatory. Needless to say I fell in with his suggestion and we soon found ourselves in a pleasant well-appointed flat, sitting at ease, supplied with drinks and engaged in pleasant conversation with several agreeable ladies.

As the evening progressed and the drinks followed suit, the inevitable temptation triumphed. We eventually paid our way and at midnight returned by taxi to Heliopolis, in my own case full of remorse. Not only full of remorse, I was also full of fear for the consequences that might follow such stupidity. However, RAF Heliopolis provided a permanent all-night First Aid clinic for such occasions and we headed for the treatment. Never had I experienced such painful and ruthless treatment. The pain was so intense that I passed out and eventually woke and found myself sitting in a comfortable armchair, also provided for these occasions. And so to bed, as Pepys might say.

The next morning, visiting the toilet for the first time, the intense pain returned. I could hardly walk and, with a tremendously guilty conscience, joined the athletics team to be transported to the sports ground. Fortunately, my event in the sports programme was not until 3 o'clock in the afternoon so that I was able to spend most of the available time in the competitors' tent on my back with my feet up and supported. As the time for the event approached, I began to take cautious exercise, but still found it painful to move. I wondered how on earth I could possibly run two laps of the track at speed when I could hardly walk.

The British High Commissioner was present with many important people in the Royal Box at this championship. I dreaded the prospect of letting the team down in front of these celebrities. Came the call for the one-mile medley open event. The most dangerous rival team was a Greek Club. Their half miler in this event was an Egyptian club member named Sadek who had held the championship of Egypt for 5000 metres. The event opened with the first leg of 220 yards, followed by the second leg of a quarter of a mile, followed by myself doing the half-mile and, as we hoped, handing over, in the lead, to Hildred, who did the final 220 yards.

Dickens did the first 220 yards and gave a comfortable lead to the quarter mile man who, for some reason, could not produce his usual form, so that when he handed over the baton to me for the half mile leg, I found myself with some 30 yards deficit behind Sadek who was streaking ahead. This deficit of 30 yards was a serious handicap but somehow the sight of Sadek ahead with this advantage, made me very angry and the adrenaline began to flow. Slowly but surely I began to overhaul the Egyptian so that by the completion of the first lap I was only five yards behind him. Halfway round the second lap I was at his shoulder and then began my usual technique of lengthening my stride. I passed him with about 200 yards to go and, finally sprinting ahead, to hand over the baton to Hildred, who, as I said before, was running the final 220 yards. I had given Hildred some 20 yards advantage so that he was able to comfortably cruise home, in fact occasionally looking over his shoulder to ensure that he preserved his lead. The team was summoned to the Royal Box and presented to the High Commissioner who seemed mightily pleased that we had beaten the Greeks and their Egyptian champion. I was told that my half-mile had been timed, unofficially, and was an Egyptian record for that distance. At another international championship in Cairo I again bettered the Egyptian half-mile record with a time of 1 minute 59 seconds. I think that the world record at this time (1934) was around one minute 51 seconds.

Media publicity concerning our team's performance at the various championships attracted the attention of the athletics club coach of the Italian University in Alexandria. I received a letter from the university, inviting me to meet their coach and to use their club facilities for training. They brought to my notice that the university club possessed a 400-metre Olympic cinder track which was the only cinder track in Egypt. A very modern gymnasium was sited at the track and the coach was a well-known and very reputable professional with a very fine international record.

The university had only recently been built for the 30,000 strong Italian community of Alexandria. Mussolini had donated the necessary finances as a part of his political strategy to encourage the active resistance of Italian communities resident in Egypt and other former British colonies or Protectorates. Later Hitler developed the same political strategy; it was called the 'Fifth Column'. In Egypt at this time the British viewed the Italian activities with a certain amount of suspicion and wary caution. The Italian colonies in North Africa were being militarised by Mussolini. Libya, Egypt's next door neighbour, was viewed with particular attention. As a precaution the RAF moved their fighter squadrons into the desert to patrol the frontier with Libya. The British suspicion and caution was later justified when Italy in 1938 invaded Abyssinia, treating the unfortunate natives with ruthless cruelty. An interesting feature of Mussolini's initiative in Egypt was that he attempted to kill two birds with one stone, for he tried to win over the considerable Maltese community in Egypt by offering them equal free university education in his new Alexandria university

Meanwhile, at RAF Aboukir, Flt. Lt. Dickens called on me one day in the aero engine workshops and told me he had also received a letter from the Italian university inviting him to use their club's training facilities. He asked me if I was agreeable to accept the invitation; if so he proposed to request official permission from the Commanding Officer. Really we were justified in seeking to accept the Italian invitation, seeing that the RAF provided no facilities whatever except at the annual Sports Day when a track was marked out with chalk on the grass football pitch. No training or coaching facilities were provided and the Authorities seemed to have no interest in personal athletics achievement. In fact, my immediate superiors in the workshops complained bitterly regarding my various periods of absence when I was competing in outside Championship events. My training was done in my own time in the evenings and at weekends.

At Flt. Lt. Dickens' interview with the Commanding Officer the C.O. considered the question of official approval was too political for him to decide and referred the matter to RAF Middle East Headquarters in Cairo. The Headquarters replied that provisional approval would be given subject to each of us taking out private insurance in the sum of £1000 to cover any possible injury or mishap. This we did and we then accepted the Italian offer. Dickens had a small car and twice a week in the evenings we journeyed together to Alexandria where we joined the Italian athletes at their 400 metre cinder track. The Italian coach took over our training on the floodlit track and in my case I entered a strenuous and tough regime. Often the coach ordered me to run ten laps or more against a relay of Italian middle distance men who set a punishing pace. In addition the coach would increase the pressure by instructing me that, at any point in the ten laps paced by relays of runners, he would blow a whistle and I would have to sprint with the pace man until he blew another whistle when I could resume the normal pace. Such cruel treatment undoubtedly increased one's endurance and speed.

After some six weeks or so of attendance at the Italian club we were approached by the coach with the suggestion that we competed as members of the Italian team in the Annual Alexandria Inter-Club Championship. This was held on a Sunday morning in the Alexandria City Stadium. Since the Italians had been so generous to us we felt morally obliged to agree. Thus I found myself competing one Sunday morning in Alexandria as a member of the Italian University athletics team and wearing Mussolini's Fascist clutch of arrows insignia on my running vest. We were competing against clubs of various nationalities including Arab, French, Greek, Maltese and Israelis. I won the 5000 metres event and thus became Champion of Alexandria in this class.

After some time we were again approached by the Italian coach, suggesting that we joined the university club team which would be competing in the National Championships to be held in Cairo. It was suggested that Dickens should represent the Italians in the 200 metres event whilst I would be running in the 10,000 metres race. Naturally we agreed, for we could not represent the RAF since the Egyptian Athletic Association rules insisted that a National Championship competitor should be a member of a club affiliated to the National Athletic Association. The RAF Middle East had no athletic club and was certainly not affiliated. At the championship in Cairo Dickens won his event quite easily and became champion of Egypt in the 200 metre class amid much excited Italian cheering from the huge Italian crowd in the spectators stands. Some two hours later competitors for the 10,000-metre event were called to the starting line and I found myself in the company of my old rival Abousbah of the Egyptian Army Kings Bodyguard who held the 10,000 metre Egyptian championship.

The pistol sounded and off we went with the daunting prospect of 25 laps of the 400-metre track. Soon Abousbah and I were well ahead of the main body of runners. Following my usual technique in such a race I allowed Abousbah to lead with myself at his shoulder. So together we reeled off the laps and, for a student of racial physiology, it would have presented an interesting sight for we were of the same height and identical physique that is to say lithe, long legged, slim built but the one difference was one was jet black and the other white. Came the bell sounding the last lap and still we were together with the rest of the field a long way behind. We both lengthened our stride and, as we entered the last 200 metres, we both began to accelerate to a sprint. The finishing tape came into view and the crowds in the stands were screaming. We both broke the tape together and there arose an almighty uproar from the stands. Pandemonium broke out on the track with Italian officials screeching and racing round to the judges.

A broadcast announcement was made over the Tannoy. To my amazement Abousbah had been disqualified and the race was awarded to me. When I enquired from the officials what was the reason for this extraordinary decision I was told that, in the opinion of the judges, Abousbah had committed a foul in the final run-in to the finishing line by deliberately extending his bent arms outwards, making an obstruction which, in their opinion, prevented me passing him in the time available to the finishing line.

I must confess that this explanation of events was not in accordance with my own impression but maybe the tremendous concentrated effort to overtake had dulled my perception. However what followed the announcement was practically a riot in the stands. The Egyptian Arab contingent began attacking the Italian spectators and benches and seating were torn up by the crowds to be used as weapons and missiles. I had no wish to linger in this dangerous environment especially as I was a subject of the dispute. I decided to get myself out of the stadium as quickly as possible so that I never saw the outcome of this fracas. I was later officially notified that I was Champion of Egypt in the 10,000-metre class.

Various unusual incidents occurred during my athletics career in Egypt. I remember one very vividly in which I was a member of the RAF Aboukir team competing in the annual Egyptian Army championships in Cairo. Dickens, our captain, had entered me in the one mile open event and, for some reason, my black rival, Abousbah, was not competing in this event. In consequence I had no serious competition in the race. By the third lap I was well ahead of the field when suddenly from the crowd of Egyptian soldiers lining the track came loud and continuous hissing. With a shock I realised I was surrounded by an environment of enmity and hate. I won the race but was rather glad to rejoin my friends in the RAF team.

Another incident of a more unusual nature occurred at Aboukir. An annual six and a half mile inter squadron road race was organised to start at Victoria College which was about half way between Alexandria and Aboukir. Hundreds of competitors from the RAF station Aboukir were transported to the college for the start of the race. An ambulance was provided to follow the competitors because past experience had shown that some inexperienced runners developed painful foot blisters which burst during the race and in consequence they were incapacitated and unable to continue.

At the start I, and two or three more experienced runners, raced ahead at sprinting speed for about half a mile to get clear of the crowd. We then settled down to a more normal pace suited to the six-mile distance remaining. Very soon I took the lead and gradually drew ahead until I was running completely alone. I reached the finishing line some half mile or so ahead of the nearest competitor. In fact, I established a new record for this race and I broke my own record in the following year's race. It so happened that, that afternoon, due to reasons which I will explain later, I had an appointment in Alexandria. To keep this appointment it was necessary that I caught the 4 o'clock train from Aboukir village. When I arrived at the race finishing line it was half past three and I had half an hour to catch my train. Without bothering to stop at the race finishing line or to speak to the officials, I continued running to my billet which was about half a mile away. Rapidly showering and dressing, I then ran about three-quarters of a mile to Aboukir station and caught the 4 o'clock train. The railway track followed a line parallel and close to the road. A straggling number of runners in the race could still be seen on the road from the carriage window. An RAF passenger sitting opposite me and watching the runners through the carriage window remarked 'I wonder who won the road race?' I answered 'I did!' The RAF passengers looked at me with unbelieving suspicion. They perhaps thought they had a madman in their midst. I made my Alexandria appointment on time that afternoon.

My last major event was a disaster and a great humiliation. Following so many past victories I had become over-confident with little respect for the competition. The Annual Army Middle East Championships were held that year in the Alexandria Stadium and I was entered in the Open One-Mile event. Following my usual race technique of staying at the shoulder of the leader until half way round the last lap when I would take over by lengthening my stride, I was soon well in front. When some 60 or 70 yards from the finishing line, instead of beginning my usual sprint to the tape I began thinking 'No, I will finish in style without the ugly facial grimace of strained effort. My fiancée and her sister in the stands will see me finish in a graceful run-in.' That vainglorious idiocy resulted in my giving the opportunity to a little Army opponent to catch and overtake me just before the tape where there was no possibility to retrieve the situation. I was runner-up but my pride was shattered and I was ashamed that my conceit had let down my friends in the RAF Aboukir band who were playing on this occasion. They told me afterwards they were laying bets on my winning this race.

Chapter 12

My Marriage and Return to England (1936)
No.101 Light Bomber Squadron, Bicester

As mentioned in the previous chapter, my move to Aboukir not only resulted in outstanding athletic achievements, but also brought about extraordinary events leading to my first marriage. An RAF friend at Aboukir was to be married to a young Egyptian lady whose family was resident in Alexandria. My friend asked me to be his best man and I duly attended him on this happy occasion. I was introduced to the bridesmaids, among whom was a cousin of the bride, Rose Sadek by name. She was the daughter of a wealthy merchant family in Alexandria and, with the assistance of the wife of my friend, we met covertly and developed a serious friendship, unbeknown to the Sadek family. Rose was strictly controlled by her family, as were all Egyptian girls of good family, and was not allowed the freedom to mix outside her own family.

The Sadek family, originally from Lebanon, were Christian Maronites. Their religion is basically a Lebanese form of Roman Catholicism. The family was strictly religious and Rose herself was a devoted daughter whose life seemed to be dedicated to the Church. She spent a considerable amount of her time attending the Cathedral in the centre of Alexandria which was quite close to the Sadek residence. In fact I was told that Rose had such great devotion to the Church that she had serious intentions of joining an order of Catholic nuns. Her father, originally from a village in the mountains overlooking Beirut, had, as a young man, emigrated to Egypt. In Alexandria he set up a bespoke furniture business which proved to be very successful and, with the assistance of his two sons, the business developed to a considerable size, employing a number of people. At this time, Sadek Senior had retired from the business and the two brothers, Max and Peter, had taken control. The brothers were also very successful and had expanded the business into other fields such as ship re-fitting, providing high class panelling for top grade cabin accommodation and public rooms.

Following a year of secret assignations and correspondence, I proposed marriage and Rose accepted. But of course, as stated above, she was subject to her family's approval. This was unlikely, on several grounds. Not least was religion for I was not a Catholic and, furthermore, our social status was widely different. Obviously we were from completely different racial origins and with different cultures. Nevertheless Rose raised the question with her family and, as expected, received a completely negative answer.

On the morning of the day of the Victoria College to Aboukir Road Race which was described in the previous chapter I was at work when I received a message from the gate police, saying that a lady was there, wishing to speak to me. I went along to the main gate entrance and there was Rose who calmly informed me that she had left her parents home and had no intention of returning unless she received the family's permission for our engagement. To say I was stunned would be an understatement. The complications in my dilemma seemed overwhelming for it was obvious that this crisis had to be handled immediately. I had the commitment that afternoon as leader of my squadron team to run in the road race. If I failed to appear in the race my reputation in the squadron would be destroyed for ever.

After some desperate thinking I fortunately hit on a solution which would at least give me time to honour my obligations to the RAF and then to meet Rose to decide what we should do in this crisis. I knew that Rose had some very close Maltese girl friends whose parents were wealthy merchants in the armoury and gunsmith business in Alexandria. The father was a member of the Knights of St. John chivalry order and was an important businessman in Alexandria society. He was a close friend of the Sadeks who had a great respect for him.

I suggested to Rose that she should return to Alexandria and go to her Maltese friends, tell them what had happened and seek their advice. I promised that immediately the race was over I would come to Alexandria and meet her at the Maltese family's home. We could then decide what we should do after receiving the advice of her friends. This explains the urgency following the road race which I have described in the previous chapter. As it turned out, the suggested arrangement proved to be a most fortunate solution. Rose's Maltese friends were kindness itself and gave Rose comfort and shelter pending my arrival. I met the parents and they, having questioned my intentions, volunteered to act as intermediaries with the Sadek family. They persuaded the Sadeks to accept the situation in principle and the Sadek family agreed subject to investigations on my family and my background in England. Rose returned to her family home and I was invited to visit her at home on Sundays. A detective agency in England was engaged by the Sadeks, unbeknown to me, to make a report on my family and myself. Apparently this proved to be satisfactory and approval of our engagement was given.

We were married on 21st August 1935 at a British Military Roman Catholic Church in a camp near Alexandria. The Sadek family were in attendance and my RAF Aboukir friend was my best man. Following a small reception at the Sadek apartment in Alexandria Rose and I embarked that evening on a French Messageries Maritimes ship sailing from Alexandria to Beirut in the Lebanon, at that time a part of Syria. We spent our honeymoon at the country home of the Sadeks, situated in the hills overlooking the city.

Returning to Egypt we took an apartment in Aboukir village which was convenient to my work at the RAF Depot. Here we set up a comfortable home where we stayed until May 1936 when my overseas tour of duty was completed and I was posted back to the United Kingdom. I arranged with the Authorities for permission to travel independently of the RAF and at our own expense. Thus we had a very pleasant journey by sea through the Mediterranean calling at various ports. Arriving back in England we stayed a short while with my parents in Portsmouth. After a pleasant three months leave I was informed that my posting was to RAF Bicester. There I joined No. 101 Light Bomber Squadron in August 1936.

This was a time when the British Government had at last woken up to the dangers threatened by Hitler's Nazi Germany. Germany had, contrary to the Treaty of Versailles, surreptitiously developed the Luftwaffe over several years to an overwhelming strength. The Nazis had then carried out a policy of conquest and had already invaded several European countries. The British Government decided to expand the Royal Air Force as rapidly as possible to try and catch up with the German Luftwaffe. One method of expansion was at this time planned on the basis of existing experienced squadrons receiving inexperienced additional personnel. These people who would be trained 'on the job' over a period, usually, of some six months or until they were considered capable of flying and operating independently in the planned role. The parent squadron would then 'give birth' to a new squadron in the same role as the parent. The new squadron would be staffed mainly by the personnel who had just been trained by the parent squadron. The new squadron would be equipped with the same type of aircraft as the parent squadron.

In the case of No. 101 Squadron, which I had just joined, we were operating a twin-engined light bomber, the Bolton and Paul Overstrand aircraft which was a bi-plane and was the first RAF bomber to be fitted with a power-operated turret in the nose of the aircraft. Its turret armament was a single .303 Lewis gun. It was a slow and unwieldy aircraft and only lasted in service until 1938. Its power plants were two Bristol Pegasus engines each developing 580 h.p. It was replaced by the Bristol Blenheim with power plant of two 840 h.p. Bristol Mercury VIII engines The maximum speed was 260 m.p.h. at 15,000 ft.

I can remember one squadron flying incident which I witnessed at Bicester. A sergeant pilot had just joined us for training in preparation for the birth of a new squadron. After some instruction on the Overstrand aircraft he was cleared to go solo and duly taxied out across the grass aerodrome. He lined up the aircraft and set what he thought were his flaps for take-off, opened the throttle wide and went roaring across the aerodrome, gathering speed as he headed towards the aerodrome perimeter but, as he progressed to take-off speed, so the aeroplane slowly sank towards the ground and ended the run on its belly. The flap control and the retracting undercarriage control were very close together and he had operated the wrong one. The hydraulic undercarriage retracting system once operated was irreversible as the unfortunate sergeant discovered as he hurtled forward and slowly descended towards the ground. Sliding along the grass at high speed on his belly, he had plenty of time to consider this problem, fortunately without any dire results to himself, although the aeroplane suffered a little from its unusual landing pattern.

Prior to the Overstrand No. 101 Squadron was equipped with the Sidestrand which was also a twin-engined Boulton and Paul aircraft powered by two Bristol

Jupiter 460 h.p. engines. The Sidestrand was a lighter less powerful aircraft than the Overstrand but it had much greater manoeuvrability and gained a tremendous reputation for its qualities as a stable aircraft, thus permitting No. 101 Squadron to achieve high bombing and gunnery accuracy. In fact 101 Squadron established RAF accuracy records in the annual inter-squadron bombing competitions at Catfoss.

Squadron bombing practice at Bicester was carried out using the camera obscura technique. The camera was located on the roof of the squadron headquarters building and pilots did their practice runs at varying altitudes with the simulated bomb attack being recorded on the cameras down below. Practice for bombing attacks against shipping was of course necessary and the Royal Navy was approached by RAF Bomber Command for assistance and in particular to provide target craft. This the Royal Navy refused on the grounds that no RAF aircraft could possibly sink one of their fighting ships. Thus they considered our request for practice facilities was a negative exercise and a waste of time and would serve no useful purpose.

World War 2 very soon proved how wrong they were! It should be remembered that the Battle of Britain was not won by the Royal Navy but by the Royal Air Force. In fact the great fighting ships of the Royal Navy were ordered to keep clear of the action which was largely over the English Channel and Southern England. The Straits of Dover ceased to become a British Naval Barrier. It was considered by the Admiralty to be too risky to endanger our battleships from German air attack and, by risking our capital ships, we could possibly have lost control of our sea routes which were our lifelines. Thus all Royal Navy capital ships were moved to the Orkneys 600 miles away from the battle zone. The only R.N. ships in the Channel were destroyers and light craft. An interesting fact not very well known or publicised by the Authorities is that, if the results of the RAF sea mine laying campaign at enemy ports and river estuaries are added to the results of the actual RAF attacks on enemy shipping, then the total would show that the RAF sank more surface ships in WW2 than the Royal Navy! Another interesting fact is that in July 1943 during the battle of the Atlantic 37 German U-boats (submarines) were sunk. Of this total 3 were sunk by air action. When, later, the Royal Navy reluctantly admitted that air attack could destroy their surface fighting ships they resorted to a change of policy in post WW2 by hiding under the sea in submarines which eventually became the Trident atomic submarine force. The only R.N. surface ships are carriers which act as porters, carrying the fighting aircraft to the war zone to let them do the fighting whilst the carriers stand well back out of the actual fighting area. The development of rocket guided missiles is permitting a new naval combat technique where surface ships are used for stand-off launching platforms for these precision guided missiles.

It can be said that the final nail was driven into sea power's coffin by the RAF during WW2 by the campaign to sink the mighty German battleship the 'Tirpitz'. The Tirpitz was perhaps the most powerful warship in the world. It was the sister ship of the mighty 'Bismarck' which was sunk by the R.N. assisted by Torpedo bombers in May 1941. It had a displacement of 42,900 tons, heavier than the largest Royal Navy battleship and was ultra sophisticated with the latest technology. The

Tirpitz was the most heavily armoured battleship in the world. Its extraordinary weight of armour was specifically designed to make the ship invulnerable against air and sea attack. An armoured steel belt 12.6 inches thick was welded to the hull plates to give protection from torpedoes 8 feet below the water line and 8 feet above the water line. The 3 inch steel deck had a supplementary armoured area 5.7 inches thick welded above the ship's magazines. Its colossal armament consisted of eight 15 inch guns twelve 5.9 inch guns, sixteen 4.1 inch anti-aircraft guns, sixteen 37mm. anti-aircraft and fifty-eight 20mm. anti-aircraft guns. For sea attack it had eight 21 inch torpedo tubes.

In spite of this tremendous aggressive power the Tirpitz never entered into the Atlantic battle area. Nevertheless her very existence, lying in one or the other of the Norwegian fjords constituted a threat which could be directed into the Battle of the Atlantic or against the northern sea route used by the Allies to supply equipment to the Russians. It thus tied up a certain amount of Allied defences and required constant vigilance. Repeated air and sea attacks causing repairable damage to the Tirpitz occurred during a period of two years from 1942 to 1944, none succeeded in sinking the ship. However an RAF attack in September 1944 of 38 Lancasters from a base in Archangel (Russia) carrying 12,000 lb. 'tall-boy' bombs and special 500 lb. 'walking' mines caused such serious damage that the Germans decided to move the ship to a safer base in Tromps Fjord, some 200 miles south where the required extensive repairs might be carried out, sufficient to preserve the battleship as a continuing threat. However, on 12th November 1944, the RAF completed the end of the sea power story by a raid of 29 Lancasters from Lossiemouth, Scotland carrying 'tall-boy' bombs, three of which scored direct hits on the Tirpitz which, together with the effect of near misses, caused the battleship to capsize with her superstructure embedded in the mud at the bottom of the fjord. Of her crew of 1500 men half were killed or drowned. Never again would such battleships be built. Air power had established its superiority. Russia too learned this lesson when Allied air power in the Berlin air-lift frustrated their planned blockade of Berlin.

After the defeat of the Allies in France and the evacuation of the British Forces from Dunkirk between May 27th and June 4th 1940 without their heavy armaments, tanks etc. Britain was lying practically naked militarily. We expected a German invasion attempt at any time after Dunkirk. But the Germans realised that they must obtain air superiority before they could launch their invasion forces across the English Channel. Thus commenced the Battle of Britain on 10th July 1940 when the German Air Force (Luftwaffe) attempted to crush the Royal Air Force. This mighty air battle lasted for two months and ended on 15th September 1940 with the victory of the Royal Air Force. The German Air Force retreated with their tail between their legs. Hitler was thereby frustrated; he could not launch his invasion attempt because his Air Force had not delivered the promised victory. He cancelled the planned operation for 1940 and never again was the operation attempted. Hitler vented his frustration by ordering his Luftwaffe to carry out heavy bombing attacks on London, hoping to destroy the British capital city.

Never was a truer word spoken than when Churchill in his famous speech following the Battle of Britain, reporting the victory of the RAF to Parliament said *'Never in the field of human conflict has so much been owed by so many to so few'*. Indeed all the free peoples of the world owe their present freedom to the victory of the RAF. And that includes the people of the United States of America. If we had lost the Battle of Britain our country would most likely have been overwhelmed. The American people firmly believe the conventional wisdom that it was America that rescued Britain from defeat in WW2 whereas in fact it was the victory of the Battle of Britain that originally prevented the Nazi domination of the whole world. Another belief in American conventional wisdom is that the military might of the American armed forces won WW2 whereas in fact it was the mighty Russian armies who really won WW2. The bravery and endurance of the Russian soldiers necessitated the bulk of the German forces being deployed on the Eastern front. It was the Russian Army who broke the back of the German military machine and slowly bled their armies to death. . On the Eastern front the German army deployed 200 divisions whereas on the Western front they deployed only 49 (later 59) divisions. The greatest contribution by the Allies to the final victory was through air power – air attacks on factories, communications etc. No less a witness to the truth of this statement on the Russian army contribution to the Allied victory is P.M. Winston Churchill when he stated in a message to Russia's Stalin on 27th September 1944 :-

'..........*I shall take occasion to repeat tomorrow in the House of Commons what I have said before – that it is the Russian Army that tore the guts out of the German military machine and is at the present moment holding far the larger portion of the enemy on its front'*.

At the outbreak of WW2 on 3rd September 1939 the small American army was completely inadequate and poorly trained by modern warfare standards.. Their training and preparation for modern warfare was pathetic. The general American public was not interested in national defence because it was considered unnecessary since they believed no other country could ever attack them. The general attitude of the Americans at this time was that 'it is a European war so let the Europeans get on with it. We are making a nice fast buck from it and we prefer to stay that way'. As stated above, following the collapse of France and the evacuation of the British army less their armament from Dunkirk, we had an urgent need of replacement of all types of weapons. To reinforce the output of our own factories we bought American weaponry for cash until our available liquid assets were exhausted and we could no longer pay for these vital supplies. The American Ambassador in London at this time was Kennedy, grandfather of the future famous President. The Ambassador had a reputation for being very sharp commercially. In his reports to the President and the American people following Dunkirk he literally wrote us off and predicted that Hitler would soon invade and that we stood little chance of defeating the Germans. He advised America on the basis that giving credit to us was like giving credit to a dead man. Following this advice a minority in Congress proposed that we should pay by handing over our colonies in the West Indies etc. This we refused to do and fortunately a Congress majority was satisfied with the concession that America could use the colonies to establish military bases as required. Finally, in 1941, President Roosevelt was successful in establishing the generous Lease-Lend system which ensured our much needed supplies throughout the duration of the war. This public lack of interest was reflected in Congress in 1940 when the Conscription Act was due for renewed approval. Renewal was won by a majority of only a single vote. If this one vote majority had not been obtained America would have had, by modern war standards, practically no army at all! The Japanese forced them to change their minds.

Again, in spite of over two years in which America was standing on the sidelines with the opportunity to study and to take note of WW2 lessons available in modern warfare, the Japanese were able to put the greater part of the American Navy out of action at Pearl Harbour. By so doing, they forced America to fight in WW2. The low standard of American army training was evident in the 'Torch' invasion of North Africa. Their soldiers addressed their officers by their Christian names and the junior officers often failed to carry out their orders, so exposing their men to unnecessary dangers. In consequence, when the 1st U.S. Armoured Division met General Rommel's Afrika Korps panzers face to face, for the first time, at the Kasserine Pass in Tunisia, they were routed and the majority of the Americans were taken prisoner. The Germans continued their advance northwards towards the Tunisian coast with the object of cutting the communications between Montgomery's Eighth Army now in Tunisia and the 'Torch' invasion forces. They had the misfortune to meet a British 26th Armoured Brigade and the guns of the 17th and 21st Lancers together with an infantry detachment of the U.S. 9th Division. The German advance came to a halt. A fierce fight over two days in the mountains of central Tunisia resulted in the complete defeat of the Germans who withdrew back to their own lines. The American Army prisoners were rescued.

As regards the U.S. Army Air Force their faith in their Flying Fortress aircraft and their policy of unprotected mass formations was misplaced. After they entered WW2 it took them many months in England following a complete change of policy before they dropped a single bomb on the Germans in Germany. They fondly believed their Flying Fortress aircraft were so well armed and their flying tactical 'packed formations' were so strong that they did not need the support of fighter aircraft cover. The German Luftwaffe fighters very quickly disillusioned them on their first sorties. Their losses to the German fighters were unacceptably heavy so that they were forced to abandon their unescorted policy. They only flew unescorted sorties over France until long range fighter protection was available. This was sometimes provided by RAF Spitfires and Hurricanes. As their fighters at this time had a very limited range, so consequently were their bombing targets. Thus they could not reach targets in Germany until long after their entry into WW2, in fact they did not drop a bomb on Germany until late 1943. Later, urgent fighter aircraft design and development permitted much longer ranges. Only with the arrival of the long range Mustang fighter and the P47D Thunderbolt aircraft could the American bombers penetrate deep into Germany. In fact the first U.S. Army Air Force attack on Berlin was not until 4th March 1944. However it must be said that once the American Air Force had established their daylight bombing strategy of attacks on German industrial targets they made a tremendous impact on the successful outcome on the Western European front. In fact the Allies contribution to winning WW2 was considerable through air power. Once the Americans had learned their modern air-war lessons and developed their long range fighter cover permitting their high altitude daylight attacks on the Ruhr plus our night attacks on military centres the Russian task of breaking the German armies became much easier.

Further examples of air power in World War 2 were demonstrated by the German Air Force in Hitler's successful invasion of Greece and then the invasion and capture of Crete. Crete was a unique operation where, for the first time in the history of the world, an invasion and conquest of a land was executed solely from the air. The German 11th Air Corps was an elite body of young men, highly specialised and forming an extremely well-trained parachute army. However the brave and resolute defence by the British in Crete resulted in the tremendous losses of the elite German parachute army who sacrificed their lives for the Fatherland. They gained their victory in spite of 28,600 British troops on the ground and tanks and artillery on the three Crete aerodromes. But the German losses were so great that the parachute army was never again operational. Hitler decided he could not accept such losses. Provisioning and reinforcement of the Crete forces by sea was prevented by the German Air Force and many Royal Navy ships were sunk or damaged in the Cythera strait to the north of Crete with the result that R.N. patrolling of the north coast of Crete was limited to night time only. Admiral Cunningham, the Commander in Chief of the Royal Navy in the Eastern Mediterranean, received a lesson in air power which he never forgot. From that time on he was constantly badgering the RAF for air cover and considered that he should have had priority over everyone else including the 8th Army in the Western Desert. Such was the reversal of the Royal Navy strategic wisdom. The superiority of air power over sea power was demonstrated on 11th November 1940 in the attack by the Fleet Air Arm on the Italian Navy in Taranto harbour when 21 obsolescent 'string-bag' Swordfish aircraft from the carrier 'Illustrious' sank or put out of action 3 battleships and damaged a cruiser whilst bombarding shore installations. The main destruction was done by aerial torpedoes carried by 11 of the Swordfish whilst 6 aircraft carried bombs and 4 carried flares to illuminate the target.

Only two aircraft were lost and this victory resulted in a shattering blow which shifted the entire balance of sea power in favour of the British in the Eastern Mediterranean area. It gives a vivid example of air power if a comparison is made between the action by Admiral Jellicoe's famous R.N. Grand Fleet which attacked the Germans in the Battle of Jutland in WW1 resulting in 6000 Royal Navy casualties and the Taranto air attack where only 40 aircrew in 21 ancient aircraft destroyed half the Italian Navy with only four casualties.

The prime example of air power against sea power of course occurred early one

Sunday morning in late December 1941 when a comparatively few Japanese aircraft destroyed or damaged three quarters of the U.S.A. Pacific fleet putting a considerable number of the ships on the bottom of Pearl Harbour, not to mention the destruction wrought on adjoining airfields.

The Japanese later demonstrated to the Royal Navy how wrong their pre-war policy was when Japanese aircraft sank two of the mightiest British warships defending Singapore. H.M.S. 'Prince of Wales' and H.M.S. 'Repulse' were sunk in a matter of four hours or so. These powerful modern capital ships went under very quickly together with all their crews off Malaya on 10th December 1941 during the Japanese invasion of Malaya and the eventual capture of Singapore. Of the 3000 or more officers and men of these ships some 2000 were saved by their accompanying destroyers. Admiral Tom King, the Flag Officer with this R.N. force, completely ignored air protection and paid the price with his life and that of some one thousand of his crews.

It is interesting to record confirmation of this previous arrogant and ignorant Royal Navy attitude to the RAF by no less a person than Winston Churchill. When Prime Minister in 1940 he minuted a note to the Admiralty recalling their previous attitude, extracts from which concerned Royal Navy operations in the Mediterranean:-

Prime Minister to First Sea Lord (15th Nov. 1940).......... *'Warships are meant to go under fire. Our position would have been very different if I had been assisted in my wish in October of last year to reconstruct the Royal Sovereign class with heavy anti-aircraft armour on their decks at a cost to their speed through bulging. The difficulties which were presented at every stage were such as to destroy the proposal and we are no further on than we were a year ago. If we had the Royal Sovereign armoured and their guns cocked up, or some of them, we could assault the Italian coasts by bombardment with comparative impunity. The various Boards of Admiralty which preceded the war altogether underrated the danger of air attack and authorised sweeping statements to Parliament on the ability of ships of war to cope with it. Now there is a tendency to the other extreme........'*

The above lack of co-operation between the Royal Navy and the Royal Air Force is only one of many such similar incidents which happened at this time. In the difficult period of world depression from 1929 to 1932 there had to be severe financial stringency by the British Government. The Navy and the Army put tremendous pressure on the Government to maintain their own financial vote levels at the expense of the junior RAF service. In fact the senior services made a concerted effort to persuade the government to abolish the independent Royal Air Force altogether. They proposed that each of their services should have its own Air arm which would be under their sole control. Fortunately for the future of the RAF and of our country, Air Marshal, later Lord Trenchard, the Chief of the Air Staff of the Royal Air Force at that time was a great leader and a tough fighter. He fought his corner for the RAF against the power of the senior services and he won through although only very meagre financial support was available. Another factor was that

Britain was at that time passing through a period of pacifism and the people wanted peace almost at any price. The popular attitude was 'We will not fight a war for far-off countries that we know nothing about.'

Appeasement was the dominating political thought in the Western Allies governments in spite of the very obvious aggressive German military operations. This philosophy of appeasement was particularly evident in Britain at this time and was the policy advocated by the aristocracy and the upper class who generally held the seats of power. They feared the Russian International Communism threats of spreading world-wide class revolution and thus endangering their privileged position and their great wealth. They viewed the German Nazi thugs as a bulwark defence against any Communist Russian encroachment into Western Europe. In fact there were many who went out of their way to be friendly with Hitler and who later would have welcomed an alliance with the German Nazis. Such people included the former King (Edward VIII), when Duke of Windsor and his wife the Duchess of Windsor who was very friendly with the Nazi German Ambassador, Ribbentrop. On May 29th 1999 British Television (Channel 4) in their programme 'Edward VIII Traitor King' claimed that the Duke of Windsor encouraged Hitler who indicated in correspondence that he would restore the exiled king to the throne following a successful invasion of England. However it must be said that when Hitler's malignant objectives were finally understood by the British public, by the aristocracy and by the upper classes, appeasement was abandoned completely and utterly and in its place intense patriotic endeavour and undying determination to defeat the German thugs became the national spirit in the face of all adversity and however seemingly hopeless our cause until the final victory.

To return to the previously mentioned pre-war RAF problem of bombing practice on sea targets, it was decided that the RAF would provide their own sea targets. To this end power boats were provided and an RAF sea target section was set up. This was located in Bridlington harbour on the Yorkshire coast and a summer-tented camp was organised on a local aerodrome. Squadrons moved into the summer camp for a short period of training. The power boats left the Bridlington harbour each morning and headed out into the North Sea towing their targets and thus providing bombing practice on moving sea targets. I believe the results obtained were not very impressive! In fact it is true to say that RAF bombing techniques and bombing accuracy at this time were very poor. This was due to two factors:- Poor navigation to find the target resulting from lack of good navigation aids. In consequence, in the early years of WW2 only a very small percentage of a bomber force would find a target and the few that found the target would often obtain poor results due to lack of high quality bomb-aiming equipment and the high quality of German defences and their fighter aircraft. Post war analysis of Bomber Command bombing results at this time stated that aircrews reporting successful attack were often some five miles away from the target. The only casualties were often a few cows in open fields.

However the invention of the navigational aid 'GEE' and later navigational and

'OBOE' with improved bomb-aiming equipment which were introduced into Bomber Command in 1942 plus the inauguration of the Pathfinder force, which innovation under Group Captain, later Air Vice Marshal, Bennett, revolutionised target location, completely reversed the previous poor results obtained by Bomber Command attacks. The later introduction and development of indicator target bombs added even further improvement to RAF bomber force attacks. Further navigational aids were introduced later which made a tremendous improvement in bombing accuracy and in addition new developments in electronic aerial warfare were introduced which aimed to jam and confuse the German flak gun defences on the ground. My youngest brother William (Bill) in Bomber Command eventually became involved in these electronic special operations, He had volunteered for the RAF in 1941 but was rejected on the grounds that he was working at that time for the Airspeed Company manufacturing the Oxford aircraft and was thus in a reserved occupation. However he overcame this problem by resigning from Airspeed and volunteering for aircrew in 1942. This time he was accepted and trained as a radio operator and air gunner in Bomber Command. He did a full operational tour (30 bomber operations plus in his case four extra) in 1944 with No. 625 Squadron which was in No. 14 Bomber Group. In accordance with bomber command regulations he had exceeded the permitted maximum tour of operations and he was grounded. However he became bored and seized the opportunity to resume flying when volunteers were called for to participate in Special Operations. These Special Operations involved flying in elderly bomber aircraft carrying tremendous electrical generating plant plus powerful electronic signal producing equipment which could generate beams which could be directed towards the German ground defences resulting in jamming and confusing their gun aiming systems. For this operation over the Ruhr etc. he was a member of No. 233 Squadron flying in ancient Liberator aircraft. These jamming operations were no sinecure, in fact they were dangerous, more dangerous than the actual bombing operation, since they had to sit over the target for the whole bombing operation and could only leave when the last bomber had departed. Only then could they find their way back to base. Their return journey in slow aircraft was full of hazards because the whole German Luftwaffe would have been alerted and would be looking for them ready to shoot them down. They survived often by dodging from one cloud cover to another, so hiding from the pursuing German fighter aircraft.

To return to my pre-war posting to No. 101 Squadron at Bicester, this required revolutionary changes in our domestic arrangements. I was fortunate in finding a pleasant three-bedroom newly-built semi-detached house just outside Bicester and my wife and I settled down to our new English way of life. This was a revolutionary change for Rose whose whole life in Egypt had been one where servants were employed in the house. To her credit she very quickly adjusted to the chores associated with settling into a newly-built house with a husband who was in no financial position to provide a servant or even a part-time daily help.

It is interesting to look back at this somewhat unusual event of my arrival in this

My brother Bill – Bomber Command

conservative little country town of Bicester with a foreign wife from the Middle East, seeking to set up home in the midst of these rural people. It should be remembered that in these pre World War 2 days in Britain international air travel for the masses had not yet arrived. People in rural districts such as Bicester rarely travelled far and very few indeed had ever travelled abroad. There was no television to bring knowledge of the people of other countries. The break-up of the British Empire had not yet occurred and in consequence there was no large movement of ex-colonial people who settled in our country after the war, thus resulting in a multi-racial society.

In our initial exploration of Bicester to find a place in which to live we put up in a bed and breakfast arrangement in a dairy run by a cattle farmer's wife in the town centre. This lady was sweetness itself and so kind to us young innocents lost in a strange new world. When she learned of our desire to find rented accommodation she told us of a local builder who had just completed a small row of houses built as a speculation for rent. The houses were just outside the town and on the road to the RAF Bicester station. It was ideal from my point of view. She volunteered to contact the builder on our behalf and duly arranged an interview for us. When the builder saw my wife was a foreigner from Egypt he expressed concern, stating bluntly that he had invested a lot of money in these brand new houses and he wanted them maintained properly to sustain their value. He intimated that he had doubts about letting to a foreigner. When we informed our good dairy landlady of the result of our interview she immediately took up our case and so kindly vouched for us that the builder agreed to let us the house.

Then followed a tremendous amount of work for us as we settled in. As with all newly-built houses, there were many tasks such as staining and varnishing floors, putting up curtains, shelves etc., and of course establishing a garden from the builders yard that greeted us at the back of the house. In consequence we had very little contact with the locals, apart from our dairy friend. Our neighbours were unknown to us and never spoke. However Rose's family in Egypt was very curious to know how she was faring in this strange land. To satisfy their curiosity we had several visits from various members of her family. One of these was her mother, a truly matriarchal, dictatorial type. She was typically a portly, dour, censorious family head with a very jaundiced eye and authoritarian attitude. By this time I had acquired a car, a brand new Vauxhall 10 hp. for the mighty sum of £100 and Rose and I drove down to London to meet her. Driving back through the beautiful spring countryside her only remark was a critical 'Why is so much countryside wasted when it could be ploughed up and produce crops?' The beauty of our pleasant green countryside seemed to have completely passed her by.

The Commanding Officer of RAF Bicester must have been informed of my musical activities during my past service for I was called up to Headquarters where he interviewed me to confirm my musical experience. He asked me if I would undertake to organise a small station orchestra primarily to play at an approaching annual Station children's Christmas party and later for station dances. He said that

No. 101 Squadron Bicester 1936 Dance Band. The author (trumpeter) is in front row second from left

there was a drum set available as well as some instruments and a piano, and he would give any assistance that might be needed. He told me that there were several people on the Station, both RAF and civilian, who were instrumentalists and willing to join in such an orchestra. I agreed to undertake the project and a notice was promulgated calling for volunteers. In due course I had eight or nine people playing different instruments, with whom I was able to organise a small orchestra with two saxophones, two trumpets, a euphonium for bass, two violins, a banjo, drums and a pianist. I performed as one of the trumpeters and I played the violin for waltzes, tangos, and romantic stuff. In the short time available before Christmas we practised together very conscientiously so that, on the day of the children's party, we were able to give quite a good performance which was widely acclaimed and greatly appreciated by the large gathering of children and their parents. These families were both RAF Bicester personnel and station civilian employees, and a whole afternoon was given over to their entertainment with generous refreshments and free gifts all at the expense of RAF Bicester. From that time we performed regularly for Station dances which were organised in the NAAFI building.

In September 1937 I was selected for advanced technical training at RAF Henlow Technical Training School. Here I was to follow a 12 months course designed to broaden the responsibilities of aero-engine specialists such as myself to cover maintenance of aircraft airframes in addition to that of engines. Following successful completion of the course I would be classified as Fitter I. Likewise a similar course was designed for selected airframe specialists to cover engine maintenance as well as their responsibilities for airframes.   These technical specialists would thus not only provide an economic source of highly trained aircraft maintenance technicians but also in an emergency expansion would provide a fertile field for the recruitment of Squadron engineer officers.

I found a very pleasant 3-bedroom house to rent in Hitchin which is near Henlow and my wife and I set up home there. By this time the political tension in Britain was rapidly increasing with the inflammatory speeches of Hitler and the aggressive actions of the German military. In spite of a considerable element of pacifism in the British political spectrum the Government redoubled its efforts in the expansion of our military defences. The RAF began an increased programme of expansion and there was beginning to be a certain atmosphere of apprehension that Germany had evil designs in Europe. They had developed tremendous military strength whilst we had completely neglected our defences and were pitifully unprepared. Winston Churchill, long since relegated to the political wilderness, made periodic powerful speeches condemning the policy of appeasement that was being pursued by the Governments of Britain and France. He issued many warnings of the terrible growing national dangers from the developing Nazi Germans military ambitions.

On the successful completion of my year long technical course at Henlow I was promoted to the rank of sergeant technician and posted in September 1938 to No. 63 Squadron at Upwood near Cambridge. No. 63 Squadron was a light bomber squadron equipped at that time with Fairey Battle aircraft powered by a Rolls Royce Merlin I engine, and later by the Merlin II engine. It was a three-seater single engine monoplane capable of carrying a 1000 lb.(454 kg.) bomb load a maximum distance of 1000 miles (1609 km.) at a speed of 200 m.p.h.(322 km/hr.) It had a maximum speed of 241 m.p.h. at 13,000 ft. The Battle had accommodation for a crew of three comprising pilot, bomb-aimer-observer and radio operator cum gunner. It was the first all metal aircraft with light alloy stressed skin and was a revolutionary step forward in design from the old linen-covered 'sticks and strings' type which had held sway since the original airframe invention of the Wright Brothers in 1903. Due to the urgent expansion of the aircraft industry it was also the first aircraft production Government contract to be awarded to a 'civilian' non-specialist aircraft firm, namely the Austin Motor Company.

The Fairey Battle was a robust aeroplane which replaced the biplanes Hawker Hart and Hawker Audax. However it was never a really successful aircraft and, although at the outbreak of World War II it formed part of the Advanced Air Striking Force in Belgium, its war record was deplorable and Squadron losses were very heavy. For example at the conclusion of the 'phoney' war period 32 Battles in a raid attempted to halt the advancing German invaders in Belgium. 13 of these were shot down and all the others were damaged. Another terrible example occurred on 12th May 1940 when five Battles of No. 12 Squadron attacking vital road bridges over the Albert Canal were all lost. On 14th May another tremendous loss took place when 35 out of 63 Battles failed to return from attacks against bridges and troop concentrations. These losses marked the end of the Battles career as a day bomber. Henceforth they were mostly used for training purposes or target towing.

To return to my own experiences following the completion of my engineering course at Henlow, when I arrived in my car at the No. 63 Squadron gates guardroom at Upwood, to my amazement I was told to report immediately to the RAF sick quarters clinic for inoculation for overseas service. At the clinic, whilst I was being given the jabs for tetanus, typhoid etc. I was informed that the Squadron was under orders for an immediate posting to Belgium as part of the Advanced Striking Force if Mr. Chamberlain, the Prime Minister, was unsuccessful in his peace mission to Hitler. These talks were taking place at that very moment in Germany.

Chapter 13

Return to Egypt
British Military Mission with the Egyptian Air Force 1939-42

'Peace in Our Time', so said the elderly gentleman with the umbrella as he disembarked from the aeroplane at London Airport and waved a piece of paper in the air. It was Mr. Neville Chamberlain, Prime Minister of Great Britain, who was speaking this highly public pronouncement which echoed round the world – and he looked pleased with himself. He was just returning from Munich in Germany after the so-called Munich Conference in September 1938. Hitler had dictated his humiliating terms in exchange for the piece of paper which was the agreement Mr. Chamberlain was now so happily waving in the air. Hitler promised Chamberlain to be a good boy henceforth providing he was allowed to invade Czechoslovakia and annex it in to the ever expanding German Master Race Empire. Chamberlain had been treated with contempt by Hitler at Munich and, unknown to the Englishman, he had been hoodwinked as Poland and France would discover at a later date.

But also, unknown to Mr. Chamberlain of course, he had just changed my life. Although that piece of paper he waved in the air was false it did provide me with a change of destination from one which Hitler and his hordes would soon have made extremely dangerous for me. Instead, my changed destination would be one where even greater danger would come at a later date. I could in the meantime relax and enjoy life, thinking I could see a peaceful future once again. That future proved to be far from peaceful, in fact exceedingly precarious, thanks to the activities of an unfriendly German, General Rommel by name, and his Afrika Korps.

As reported in the previous chapter unsuspecting Freddy arrived at the Camp gates and from that moment my feet never touched the ground. Reporting to the squadron hangar I found the aircraft were already armed and 'bombed-up' and the aircrew were sleeping in the hangars. As you may imagine we in No. 63 Squadron followed the news of Mr. Chamberlain's efforts in Munich with very keen interest and with tremendous anxiety because we knew our under-powered slow-flying out-dated aircraft ('Fairey Battles') and unreliable engines (Rolls Royce Merlin 1's full of bugs which Rolls had had no time to eliminate) would be no match for the German Luftwaffe whose remarkable aircraft performance we had also studied. A most joyous party was held when Mr. Chamberlain waved his piece of paper in the air and said 'Peace in our Time'. As I have written in the previous chapter the Fairey Battle aircraft were still the front line advanced strike force in Belgium when World War Two finally broke out a year later. It is sad to reiterate that they were massacred by the German Luftwaffe.

So our lives in the Squadron reverted to a more normal vein and I had a trip to the de Havilland Aircraft factory where I did a short specialist course studying the manufacture, operation and maintenance of the latest sophisticated variable pitch aircraft propellers. This was to prove a valuable engineering asset in my later involvement in the Desert War in Egypt. On my return from de Havillands there was an announcement of the requirement by Air Ministry for a specialist aircraft engineer to be a member of an air component team for a British Military Mission to the Egyptian Government. I volunteered for this post and was selected to be a member of this mission. This involved being seconded from the Royal Air Force to the British Military Mission with Corps Diplomatique privileges. This secondment was a 3-year contract to the Egyptian Government and I was attached to the newly created Royal Egyptian Air Force. It was with feelings of great pleasure that I handed over all my RAF responsibilities and, in civilian clothes, called at the Egyptian Embassy in London who provided me with a large sum of money for my passage and for my family's passage to Egypt and for my first Egyptian salary. I was informed that I could proceed to Egypt to join the Mission already there by any route I might choose and in my own time. Such freedom of action I had never experienced in my life and I was really thrilled with the prospect before me of such a free and easy way of life in the future. Well! Of course Hitler had to go and spoil it all for me! But I am jumping the gun!

I decided to take the Egyptians at their word and so, in January 1939, I meandered leisurely across France staying a few days in Paris and doing the night spots. Then, arriving in Marseilles, I booked a sea passage with the French Line Messageries Maritimes to Alexandria in Egypt. Here I stayed a couple of days and finally headed by train for Cairo where I was to join the Mission. Actually the Air side of the mission was located at Heliopolis about 12 miles from Cairo on Almaza aerodrome already occupied by the Egyptian Air Force and an Egyptian Flying Club. The airfield was all sand with no runways and no control tower – a 'hit or miss' organisation. Three Egyptian Air Force Units had just been formed and located here with a supporting workshop for repair and overhaul of the engines and aircraft. One unit was an elementary Flying School with 200 Egyptian cadets learning to fly. Next door to the School of Flying was an operational Communications Squadron equipped with British 'Lysander' aircraft which were a specialist communication type with remarkable ability to operate from very small fields having very short landing and take-off requirements. A third unit was a specialist Kings Flight which contained the royal passenger type aircraft reserved solely for use of the King of Egypt and his family and entourage.

Reporting to the Chief of the Mission (Air) I was informed that my responsibilities would be as Technical Adviser to the Flying School equipped with 52 very modern (for their time) British trainer aircraft named the Miles Magister. This aircraft was quite extraordinary, being a monoplane constructed entirely of wood. Even the 'skin' or covering of the mainplanes and fuselage was of thin flexible plywood. This was to prove a problem later since the hot-climate wood boring insects like termites for example, just loved to board this aeroplane and so, undetected, could undermine the structural strength. It was manufactured by the Miles Aircraft Company located near Reading. In addition to the Miles Magisters were a few of the old fashioned de Havilland Gipsy Moths which were biplanes of course. I was warned that my position with the Egyptians was in a purely advisory capacity and that I would have no executive authority whatever. I could give no orders or direction.

The British Mission (Air) consisted of the Mission Chief (Air) who was a Group Captain, the Senior Adviser (a Wing Commander), 12 RAF flying instructors and 4 engineers (one for each unit and one for the Workshops). I was informed that I would be in a position of great delicacy where I would be required to supervise the technical maintenance of the entire aircraft of the School, but I would have no executive authority whatever. My responsibility would be limited to offering advice and guidance to the Egyptians who could accept or ignore it as they wished. Needless to say this arrangement required great diplomacy particularly where one was dealing with Egyptians who were often anti-British and sometimes evil-minded. Having settled into a small family hotel in Heliopolis my first task was to have myself measured up by an Egyptian military tailor who in two or three days made my Egyptian uniforms. I was then permitted to appear in my new uniform in my new status as the technical 'Oracle' in the new Flying School. The School aircraft, being new, gave very little trouble and the Egyptian engineers had been well trained in England in the Miles factory so that operations of flying instruction for the cadets proceeded quite smoothly. Nevertheless I soon found the situation very stressful. I had been used to a position of authority in the RAF in England where I could give instructions which were mandatory and orders which would be carried out without question.

Here in the Egyptian Air Force I soon found that, whilst I was viewed with respect by the majority as some sort of Colonial 'Mastermind', there was amongst the Egyptian engineers an element whose attitude and ambition was to undermine the status and technical reputation of the hated Colonial supervisor. My advice and statements were sometimes questioned and criticised by such people who had no background of experience and thus could not appreciate that there might be technical ways and methods which might differ from or not be included in their official handbooks.

However, in spite of occasional difficulties with the anti-British element I was successful in establishing a good rapport with both my Egyptian and British colleagues. The Egyptian flying Cadets were young men of around 18-19 years of age who were mostly the sons of Egyptian aristocracy or wealthy landowners etc. Egyptian society at that time was dominated by an extreme feudal system. The wealth and ownership of the land was in the hands of a privileged class who were a minority of only about 5% of the total population. A small group of civil servants etc. formed what might be termed a middle class whilst around 90% of the population were agricultural peasants, most of whom could neither read nor write. These peasants (fellaheen) were extremely poor, terribly primitive, full of disease and living almost in slavery conditions. About 98% of them suffered from the disease of bilharzia, caused by standing in the mud of irrigation ditches.

My relationship with the cadets was on a very good footing. Part of my work was to give lectures to them on the theory of flight and the design and construction of the aircraft and their engines. In return they often instructed me in the Arabic language and thus I got to know them quite well. Part of my responsibilities was to arrange for an air-test after the completion of periodic inspections or repair work on the aircraft. To this end I was allotted one of the British pilot instructors as a test pilot. Bill Brooks did all my air-tests and he and I always flew together whenever an air-test was required. He very soon realised that I was mad on flying and began to allow me to handle the controls without actually giving me forbidden flying instructions except for an occasional acid comment such as Get your b….y nose up' or 'What the hell are you doing with your left wing down there?' I had some natural talent in handling the aircraft and began to perform the complete manoeuvres of basic flying. Bill seemed to be impressed with my efforts and decided to let me advance to the more difficult stages of a pilot's training such as making mock forced landings in the desert miles away from the aerodrome. Again, without being given any formal instruction, I would be happily flying along enjoying the wonderful panoramic view over miles of the Egyptian desert when without any warning I would suddenly find myself without engine power. Bill had cut my engine and then shouted 'Now get down there into that little flat space and don't overshoot!'

One day, after we had just done another air-test flight, to my surprise Bill said to me 'Why don't you get a private pilot's licence by taking the exam and flying test over at the Egyptian Flying Club?' Bill saw that I was a little taken aback by this, as I thought, somewhat audacious suggestion, especially as I explained to him that like all Service people I had no financial reserves to pay for expensive flying lessons. Bill scoffed at this, saying I was good enough to take the test without a prolonged flying course. He said 'I'll tell you what! You'll have to take the test in the Club's dual control Tiger Moth aircraft so tomorrow I'll give you half an hour in one of our own Tiger Moths and I'll give you a letter of introduction to the Chief Flying Instructor of the Egyptian Flying Club and he will fix you up for the test at the Club flying their Tiger Moth'. I had my half hour with Bill in the Tiger Moth getting the feel of the controls and learning the lay-out of the Tiger Moth cockpit.

And so, the next day, a little apprehensively, I went along that afternoon to the Egyptian Flying Club and met the Chief Flying Instructor to whom I presented Bill's letter of introduction. I was wearing just my shirt and shorts as usual in the summer heat so that my uniform dress was the same as a qualified pilot's who, in those days, only wore his pilot's brevet (wings) on his tunic. When a pilot was not wearing his jacket his shirt carried no distinguishing brevet. Later on this was changed and pilots in summer uniform wore their flying brevet on their shirts as well as their tunics. So on this occasion the Chief Flying Instructor could not tell from my uniform whether or not I was a pilot. I do not know what Bill had written in his letter of introduction but certainly on my part there was no intention to deceive the Egyptian Chief Flying

Instructor. The latter jumped to the wrong conclusion that I was a qualified military pilot wanting a civil pilot's licence for some private purpose – perhaps of flying friends or relatives in a civil aircraft. To be eligible for the flying test one had to complete a minimum of three hours flying solo in a civil aircraft. The Egyptian instructor ordered a Club Tiger Moth to be wheeled out and said he would have to check me prior to giving me authority to hire Club aircraft for completion of the necessary three hours solo flying to qualify for the licence test.

Private Pilot's Licence (1940)

We both donned our flying helmets and climbed into the Tiger Moth and the instructor told me to take off and do a circuit of the aerodrome and then to make a landing.

Off we went and I climbed the aircraft to about 1000 feet, circled the aerodrome with its huge expanse of sand, throttled back, dipped the nose and glided towards the sand. The sand came rushing up towards us and looking down I levelled the aircraft at about ten feet above the ground. I lifted the nose slightly, gradually stalled the aircraft, and we sank gently down onto the sand making a perfect three point landing (the two wheels and the tail coming down together). Lucky me!!

The instructor said 'Do that again!' and I opened the throttle and away we went tearing through the sand and lifting off smoothly into the climb. Up we went again to around 1000 feet into a constant smooth banking turn, looking down all the time to pick my landing approach path as we circled the aerodrome. A final turn into my approach path, throttle back and a silent peaceful glide towards the sand which again came rushing up towards us. Eyes glued over the side to judge my height – 50 feet, 40 feet, 30 feet, 20 feet, 10 feet – that's it! – level out gently! Float along with the sand rushing underneath, sinking, gently back with the stick, lift the nose, stall – and there we were settling smoothly on the sand, another perfect 3-pointer: How lucky can you get, Freddy?!!

We came to a stop not far from the hangars and to my startled surprise the instructor said 'Do you wish to go solo?' This was the crunch moment I had to face up to although I could hardly believe my ears. In a kind of wonderment I murmured 'Yes!' The instructor climbed out clutching his cushion which, being a shortish chap, he used to give himself a better view forward. Still thinking he was dealing with an experienced qualified pilot he said to me in a semi-apologetic tone, producing a small yellow airsock streamer 'Do you mind if I tie this on your wing strut? It is required by the regulations for unlicensed pilots flying solo in civil aircraft.' It was a sort of L-plate system similar to that used on cars but instead of a plate they used a streamer. As you may imagine I raised no objection! I thought to myself 'You could put one on each side and I would have no objection seeing that I ought to tell you that I have never been solo in an aeroplane in my whole life and I'm feeling a bit chicken'. But I didn't tell him that and he waved me off.

I opened the throttle and the Tiger Moth began moving. Incredible! The thing was obeying me! – little me sitting in this cockpit was controlling this aeroplane all by myself! I taxied back to take-off position into wind on the aerodrome sand and opened up the engine to full take-off throttle and away we went. Stick forward gently to lift the tail out of the sand and so we gathered speed hurtling through the sand. After about a hundred yards or so with stick control centred we began to gently lift. Stick gently back to lift the nose and Whoopee! we were airborne! How easy! the thing flew itself!

Climbing gently and turning once again into my now familiar 1000 feet circuit I looked down and saw the instructor standing near the hangar looking up and watching. With a little shock I suddenly realised the implications of the situation into which I had got myself. I had to get this aeroplane and myself back down on the ground without damaging either of us! If I failed then the whole story would be out and – even worse – I might kill myself or smash the aeroplane and land myself with some terrible financial liability.

And so I climbed higher, thinking of the best way of tackling the problem. I decided I wanted the instructor to give up watching me in case I made a bad landing. I thought if I continued climbing he would probably get tired of watching and go back to his office. And so I climbed and climbed in continuous circuits of the aerodrome until I was at about 7000 feet and some considerable time had elapsed. I thought, 'This is ridiculous. I've got to face up to it! And I've got to get this thing down without breaking it! ' And so, instructor or no instructor, I throttled back the engine and put the nose down, losing height slowly. As I circled the aerodrome in a continuous banking turn I decided that, in case the instructor was still watching, I would make my approach and landing on the far side of the aerodrome as far away as possible from the hangar and the instructor who would not be able to see too much if I made a bad landing.

Actually the approach was familiar territory to me because it was over the hangars of the Egyptian Air Force Flying School where I had flown quite a number of times with Bill Brooks breathing down my neck with caustic comments. After the long descent and setting the aeroplane in its final approach with a check on my airspeed the roofs of the Flying School began to appear underneath and once again the sand began to rush up towards me. Steady! Down! Down! 30 feet! 20 feet! 10 feet! Gently level! Glide! Hold it! Don't let it sink! Nose up slightly! Wow! We're down! No damage! No worries! As we rushed through the sand I felt like screaming with joy. I was so happy. I immediately slammed the throttle wide open and the aircraft leapt forward to another take-off. I was determined to repeat this wonderful exhilarating experience and show the instructor how good I was by landing closer to his side of the aerodrome.

I did this 'circuit and bump' routine for some half an hour and finally taxied the aircraft back to the hangar and handed it over to the ground staff. I saw the instructor who said he would authorise me to hire the Club aircraft to fly solo any time I wished. He signed my logbook to that effect.

Oh heavenly joy! I had made it! I was so pleased with myself. From then on for some three weeks I would go to the Flying Club about twice a week. I would do about half an hour or so practice flying with constant good landings and no worries. Thus I was building up my solo hours in preparation for my final licence exam and flying test.

And then – 'Disaster!' One afternoon I went along to the Club for my usual practice 'Circuit and Bumps' flights and, instead of my first landing being the normal smooth three-pointer I hit the ground with a thump, the aircraft jumped up in the air about 8 or 9 feet, came down with a thump a second time and leap-frogged three or four more times until we finally subsided on the sand, running forward in the normal way. I was panic-stricken for I knew that kind of 'kangaroo' landing would put considerable strain on the undercarriage structure and could cause serious damage if repeated a number of times. But perhaps it was a one-off mistake, I thought, and if I was a little more careful it would not happen again.

And so – off I went again, up and round the circuit as quickly as possible and into the approach to prove I could still land as well as ever! Up came the sand towards me, faster it seemed than before. Bang! we hit the ground and there we were with the aircraft once again buck-jumping across the aerodrome. Horror! 'What am I doing wrong?!' I cut short my practice session and taxied into the hangar thinking I had better put a stop to this before I damaged the aeroplane. I could not seek the advice of the instructor since that would probably reveal my dubious position and he would certainly specify dual-control instruction flights which I could not afford financially. But if I continued to make mistakes it might result in discovery of the deception and involve my friend Bill Brooks in serious trouble; not to mention the damage I might do to my own person.

Leaving the Club I decided to go immediately to Bill Brooks and seek his advice. Bill was at home and I told him my story. I asked him if he could possibly come to the Club with me next time I flew and watch my landings. It was not a very sensible suggestion and Bill did not want to know! I could see he did not want to be involved at all. I think possibly he had a sudden realisation of the trouble that might arise for him if I had an accident. And so I was on my own! 'You've got a problem, Freddy, and you have got to solve it yourself!' Over-confidence had got me into this mess and I had to find the solution myself.

That night and several nights following I was lying sleepless in bed deeply worried, churning over and over again the problem of what I was doing wrong to cause my bad landings, and dreading the possibility of the eventual exposure of my bogus flying status and likely financial penalties, not to mention possible repercussions for Bill Brooks and my own service career.

Finally I decided to get hold of a copy of the voluminous RAF Flying Training Manual which I knew my flying colleagues had, and study it to see if I could find the answer to my problem. For days on end I read the Manual – from cover to cover! – and came to a conclusion which I would try out on my next practice flight. In many years of RAF experience, particularly in the first three years when I was at the RAF Central Flying School, I had witnessed several accidents where pupils had killed themselves by stalling into the ground on the approach, due to their approach speed being marginal, so that if the wind dropped at a moment in their approach they would lose lift and stall into the ground. This phenomenon was engraved in my mind and when I began flying solo I vowed to myself that I would never commit this error. Reading the manual I came to the conclusion that I must have allowed this vow to have caused a gradual increase in my approach speed on each practice until my approach speed was too high. Thus, after levelling out and lifting the nose to stall the aircraft to land, I had too much speed on. When I hit the ground the aircraft still had lift and would thus soar back into the air, stalling again and hitting the ground, repeating the process several times so making 'kangaroo' landings.

I resolved, come what may, even if I killed myself on my next flight, I would reduce my approach speed and see what happened! Eureka! It worked! On my next practice flight I reduced the approach speed from around 55 miles per hour to around 45 m.p.h. and made a perfect landing. From that time onwards I never looked back! Guaranteed perfect landings every time!

After more practice flights I completed the required 3 hours solo flying and submitted myself for the Licence examination and flying test. The Egyptian examiner gave me an oral examination in Air Navigation regulations etc and then instructed me to take an aircraft to around 2000 feet and perform various manoeuvres including 8 'figure of 8' tight turns and precision landing on a defined spot in the centre of the aerodrome. He fitted a barograph instrument into the aircraft which registered any deviation from the line of flight in the banking turns on a print-out. Thus any skidding or sliding, side slipping downwards, or lifting above the level line of the turn was registered. I succeeded in all the tests, the examiner was satisfied with the barograph readings – and there I was – a proud qualified private pilot! I flew a number of times after I had my licence, particularly in a small de Havilland monoplane called the Moth Minor. I did this particularly when I wanted to impress a girl friend by flying round her chimney pot in Heliopolis! But it was an expensive hobby and I felt I had answered the challenge. My later involvement in World War 2 finally put an end to my days as a private pilot. But forever after I had a feeling of distinction in that I was one of the few people in the world who had become a licensed pilot without any proper flying lessons or formal instruction at a flying school.

Now to return a little in time to the moment of the announcement of my secondment to the Land of the Pharaohs which was January 1939. My wife Rose, whose parents were living in Alexandria, was naturally very pleased and, very soon after, she returned to Egypt with our two sons Max and Peter. The family stayed with her parents in their flat in Alexandria pending my arrival.

Following my installation in my new British Military Mission post in Heliopolis my family moved down to Heliopolis to join me. We set up home in a delightful furnished flat on the ground floor in a new modern luxury block quite close to Almaza aerodrome. I acquired a large American family saloon car and, now enjoying full Egyptian Diplomatic status, my car carried C.D. plates. I paid no Egyptian taxes whatever and that included my petrol purchases. My petrol cost about 5p. a gallon paid for on a monthly credit account to the Shell Company!

Chapter 14

Romantic Adventures in Egypt

Life went along very smoothly and comfortably. My wife made friends with a young Polish couple who lived in the flat on the same floor and adjoining our own flat. The husband was a lawyer with a practice in Cairo and his young and pretty wife had only recently arrived from Poland. On returning from playing tennis one afternoon I found this lady having tea with my wife and thereafter she became a regular visitor to our flat.

An official car called at the flat each morning to take me to my office at the aerodrome and I began to notice that the Polish girl next door always came on to her veranda as I was leaving. An affair developed very soon after with romantic assignations in the desert around Heliopolis. This liaison continued for several months until one morning in the post I found a bombshell! The Polish lawyer next door had written me a letter and, to my horror, invited me to meet him at a stated rendezvous to discuss the future of his wife who, he said, had confessed to him our liaison. What is more he said that she had declared that she loved me and had no further interest in their marriage! He suggested in his letter that I should take over his wife or he would send her back to Poland! This shattering shock caused all kinds of lurid imaginings in my mind and I wondered if my life might be in danger if I agreed to accept the invitation to meet him at the stated rendezvous. I was in such a state of anxiety that I confided in Bill Brooks and sought his advice. He suggested the best thing would be to meet the man and clear the air by categorically stating I had no intention of changing my present married status – nor did I intend to commit bigamy or set up a harem!

Somewhat apprehensively I went to the suggested rendezvous with the irate husband. He told me his story in a sort of restrained and resigned manner. I told him I was happily married and had no intention of a divorce. He then told me had beaten his wife and now intended to throw her out by sending her back to Poland. Whether he did or not I never knew because very soon after this episode Hitler invaded Poland and World War 2 was declared. This changed everything.

The resulting change for the members of the British Military Mission was profound. Those members who had their wives and families with them were ordered to send them back to the U.K. for security for the families and freedom of action for the men. In my own case my family returned to my wife's parents in Alexandria and I gave up our flat. I found myself a small unpretentious two bedroom bachelor type of flat in Heliopolis centre. Life then continued on a changed basis – going about armed and on the 'qui-vive'. Weekends I travelled by car using the new desert route across the desert from Cairo to Alexandria to visit my family residing in Alexandria. This was a 160 mile journey on a narrow recently constructed tarmac road which went directly in a straight line across the desert with, at that time, nothing but deep sand each side of the solitary road. It had been built to improve military communication across the desert to the Eastern frontier following the threat by Mussolini to Egypt's Eastern frontiers from the Italian colony of Libya.

Working as I was in a purely Muslim Government Military Service organisation my routines and calendar had of necessity to be in harmony with the Muslims. Their holy day was Friday, thus my weekend was from Thursday lunchtime to Sunday morning when we resumed work. One week-end returning by car from Alexandria on the desert road in the late afternoon I saw ahead of me a car parked on the edge of the road, obviously broken down. The driver was standing by the car hoping for help to come along. As I drew closer I recognised the driver as one of the Egyptian Air Force cadets in the Almaza Flying School.

I pulled up behind the car and the young man, recognising me, explained that his car had a serious problem beyond roadside repair possibilities and asked me to call at the first possible garage in the Cairo area which was some 60 or 70 miles further on. I agreed to do this and he then said that he had his sister with him in the car. He asked me to give her a lift to their home in Heliopolis as it was dangerous for her to be stranded in the desert with him. This was true for this new road penetrating deep into the desert had attracted the attention of prowling Bedouin robbers and there had been several reports of motorists unfortunate enough to break down being murdered. I naturally agreed with his request and the young lady installed herself on the back seat of my car.

Thinking to relieve the monotony of this somewhat boring journey for my Muslim lady passenger I switched on my car radio to the local Arabic music programme. After a while the young lady spoke from the back of the car and said that unless the Arabic programme was my choice she would prefer to listen to the European programme. Surprised, I immediately switched over the radio realising that my ideas concerning young Egyptian Muslim ladies were not altogether accurate. This girl was no shy shrinking nervous female temporarily in transit from her confined cloistered world of the Muslim harem, having little or no contact with the outside world. She was obviously a very well educated and sophisticated modern young woman.

We began to talk and of course it was difficult with her in the back of the car and the noise of our passage and so she suggested that she should come and sit in the front passenger's seat. I stopped and she transferred to sit beside me and so began an animated conversation which lasted until we reached a garage on the outskirts of Cairo. Here she arranged with the breakdown service to send a rescue truck for her brother stranded in the desert. We continued on our journey to Heliopolis where she told me she lived with her father and her brother and older sister. Her father was a notable of Egypt and was a friend of the King and, although we arranged to meet again, she warned me that she had to be extremely careful not to be seen in my company by any of her family or relatives, or by any Egyptian who might know her.

We met again shortly afterwards in a delightful and exclusive riverside open-air cafe restaurant on the outskirts of Cairo on the bank of the River Nile where we had tea in a secluded and relaxed atmosphere. And so began a long, intense, passionate romance fraught with danger, fear and anxiety, sometimes with despair, but always compensated by the profound love which developed between us. Her family, she told me, was of Turkish origin as were most of the leaders and top level functionaries in the Egyptian Establishment. The King was a descendant of the Khedive Mohammed Ali, the Turkish general who founded this dynasty in the 19th century and he was surrounded by an aristocracy, all of Turkish origin. She spoke several languages fluently and her English was faultless and without an accent. Educated to high school level she had been married at an early age, as was the Egyptian custom. Her husband, she told me, was a doctor studying in London for his F.R.C.S. qualification. He had already sat the examination of the Royal College of Surgeons and failed three years running. He was continuing his stay in London until such time as he obtained his qualification. Hence her unusual situation of living with her father.

For an Egyptian lady, she enjoyed great freedom and independence in her life style but always had to be home by early evening. This was naturally a difficulty in our affair which developed at a tremendous rate so that we saw each other almost daily. In spite of the family insisting that she return home by the early evening she managed by devious means to sometimes accompany me on nocturnal excursions to various social functions. Once we attended a ball together in evening dress at Shepherds Hotel in Cairo. Shepherds of course was the very select top grade hotel in Cairo and at that time the well-known rendezvous of the English military society. When I asked her how she managed to leave her house at night in evening dress when she should have been in bed at home she told me that she had bribed her maidservant and the family lodge keeper at the house gates. Her maidservant had taken her evening dress during the day to the lodge gatekeeper who hid it in the lodge. She had bid her father goodnight! and waited in her bedroom until her father retired which he usually did quite early. She had then crept down silently into the garden and changed her dress in the gate lodge – et voila! On her return the lodge keeper let her in and back to bed!

One unforgettable occasion we even went off on a weekend trip together. I met her early on a Thursday afternoon and we drove 150 miles across the desert from Heliopolis to the Red Sea where we stayed in a delightful small holiday village on the seashore just south of Suez. We spent the whole weekend swimming and sunbathing on the warm sands and returned on Saturday afternoon. She told me that she accomplished this extraordinarily adventurous expedition by seeking the connivance of a close female family friend or relative who wrote and invited her to spend a fictitious weekend with her. It would appear that the Egyptian male dominance over the females was undermined by a sort of secret female mutual aid system which could always be called upon to provide cover, support and protection when needed.

As a result of our trip to the Red Sea I contracted malaria. I had already had a bout of malaria in 1934 when with the RAF at Aboukir near Alexandria so I suppose I was vulnerable to the bite of the mosquitoes of Suez. However my shivering fever fits only came on in the afternoons and I was reluctant to see the doctor for that would mean I would go into the military hospital and thus it would be impossible to see my lady friend. Hoping this thing would go away by itself I carried on my usual routine except that I passed out on my bed in the afternoons with my lady-friend holding my hand and innumerable blankets piled high on me whilst I shivered lying on the bed. This situation continued for about ten days or so until one morning at the aerodrome I was ground testing an aircraft. Sitting in the cockpit with my feet and hands on the aircraft controls a shivering fit suddenly descended on me. In this condition it is impossible to control any of one's limbs or muscles and so the whole aircraft began to shake.

One of the Mission pilot instructors happened to be passing and, noticing the peculiar movements of the aircraft, jumped up, peered into the cockpit and saw the obvious. He reported his observations to our Senior Air Adviser who ordered him to take me immediately to the doctor at the RAF station in Heliopolis. Here I was put to bed in their sick quarters and the doctor told me I had an attack of a malignant type of malaria. When he heard how long it had been going on he said that I was lucky because this type of malaria attacked the heart and I could have dropped down dead at any time. However, I recovered, and life was resumed once again as before.

My domestic day to day life in my flat ran very smoothly and comfortably and this was entirely due to Mohammed who was my Sudanese servant. Mohammed did everything needed in the flat including the cooking, cleaning, laundry, shopping and was at my bedside first thing in the morning with my early morning tea. He retired to his quarters on the apartment block roof after he had served dinner in the evening. He was jet black, very quiet and unassuming, but extremely efficient in all departments of his work. His cooking was excellent and his knowledge of the whole range of English gastronomy was impressive. He could produce anything from the humble Lancashire hotpot to the most sophisticated Christmas dinner of roast turkey or pheasant with all the correct trimmings. He had an excellent knowledge of all varieties of dishes which could constitute the courses of a formal dinner including delicate savouries. His laundering was superb and my tropical style summer uniforms, lightly starched, always looked extremely smart. His method of ironing, which he did in the afternoon in my sitting room because the kitchen was too small, was curious to say the least and perhaps would shock an English housewife. In those days electric irons had not yet arrived in Egypt and Mohammed, like all ironers, had well proven equipment which had been used since time immemorial. This consisted of a huge heavy metal container in the shape of a flat iron. Inside this heavy flat iron was a live fire consisting of red-hot charcoal lumps.

He would set up his ironing board in the sitting room whilst I usually had an hour or so's 'siesta'. He would place a jug of cold water on an adjoining table with a drinking glass handy. Taking say my shirt for ironing he would lay it out ready then, taking a mouthful of water from the glass and filling his cheeks, he would blow the water out in a fine spray and proceed to iron, repeating the process as necessary! The result was a very smartly ironed shirt! I never pondered on the question of the Sudanese saliva content, thus avoiding any anxiety on this subject.

He assumed a kind of protective 'father-figure' to me – his 'master'- and was very conscientious in seeing I kept up my correct routines and appointments. One morning I awoke a little earlier than usual and, feeling under my pillow where I usually kept a handkerchief, my fingers encountered some hard object. Lifting the pillow I found to my astonishment a bunch of rusty long nails tied together. Calling Mohammed from the kitchen I demanded to know the meaning of this peculiar discovery. At first he denied all knowledge of the matter but under pressure from myself he finally confessed that he had put them there. I demanded to know why he had done this. In great embarrassment he told me he had done it to protect me. He said that he knew that the lady friend who visited the flat frequently was Moslem and had very powerful friends. He said I would be in considerable danger if this relationship continued and he had been very worried about it. Finally he had decided to consult a witch doctor and seek his advice as to what action he might take to protect me.

Mohammed said that the witch doctor had communicated with his various media and had then given him the final solution to his problem. The witch doctor had told him that I was under a spell of an infatuation in which my lady friend held me bound and the only way to save me from the terrible consequences that might ensue would be to break this spell! Breaking the lady's spell could only be brought about by penetrating my mind with the witch doctor's own spell. This would destroy the attraction and admiration I felt for the lady and thus release me from the infatuation. On payment of the prescribed fee the witch doctor produced the nails and into the nails he introduced his spell. He tied these nails into a bunch and told Mohammed to place them under my pillow in a position immediately below my head. The nails would drive the spell by magic into my head and completely destroy my regard for the lady. I was somewhat perturbed that Mohammed had taken such an active interest in my private life but at the same time was sympathetic and a little gratified by the good-will which had motivated this extraordinary exercise. I assured Mohammed that I did not need the witch doctor's spells and forbade any further such activities for my protection.

By this time the affair had indeed become very serious and marriage and ways and means of achieving this became a constant subject of discussion between us. The obvious difficulties on both sides seemed insurmountable and often led to tensions and unhappiness. Then the inevitable finally happened and the relationship was discovered by her family. We met for the last time in Heliopolis and she told me she had been banished to Alexandria by her father. She said that her father had made an arrangement with her aunt, her father's sister, living in Alexandria, whereby she would reside with her aunt and be under her supervision. She gave me her aunt's telephone number and address and said that she would communicate when it was possible. She warned me that I was known and that I should be very careful.

The move took place and before very long I received a letter giving me unbelievable news. The Egyptian female mutual protection secret society which I have previously described in these memoirs was once again working. My lady-friend had confided the whole story to her aunt in Alexandria who, seeing it was a serious affair with marriage as an objective, had given full support. I was invited to meet my friend at a hotel in Alexandria the following weekend. This I did and for several months, I spent my Muslim weekend journeying 160 miles across the desert from Cairo to Alexandria every Thursday afternoon returning to Heliopolis on Saturday night or early Sunday morning in time for Sunday morning duty. Ironically I was now repeating the same journey as I had done in the days when I visited my wife some two years previously.

One day, after my friend's departure to Alexandria I was approached at the aerodrome by her brother who, as I said previously, was a cadet pupil pilot at the Flying School. During our conversation he asked me if I would like to visit a well-known high-class pedigree Arab horse stud farm in the locality. He told me this stud farm was owned by a friend and famous for its valuable pure-bred bloodstock horses. Such a visit sounded extremely interesting and I readily agreed to meet him the following Saturday morning early. When we arrived at the farm we found several other young Arab friends there and we were invited to join them for breakfast in the substantial farmhouse. We were overlooking a sort of open quadrangle and very soon a number of horses were brought into the arena saddled and ready for riding. I was invited to join the party for a ride around the farm. I had never ridden a horse except for sitting on a mountain pony in the Kurdistan mountains of Northern Iraq, so I had no idea of horsemanship. But I was not going to lose face by admitting this. After all I was English and had therefore to put on a show in front of these Egyptians! I was given a horse which, unknown to me, was a thoroughbred fiery Arab stallion with a mind of its own and a cantankerous character. I mounted and, thinking I should be firm with the reins to control the horse, I gripped them and immediately the horse reared up in the air on its hind legs, its front legs pawing the air like a circus act. We descended to the ground and my companions advised me to be more gentle with the reins.

So off we went – a party of about five or six horses walking sedately down an avenue lined with trees in an extensive plantation. I was in the lead and after a while I suddenly became aware that I was on my own. The others had disappeared into the plantation without a word. Not relishing the idea of riding alone further into unknown country I decided to turn back to the farmhouse. By this time my horse knew that this human on his back was clueless. I turned the horse and it immediately decided to take over. The next thing I knew we were at a stretch gallop. The horse had taken charge and we were going 'hell for leather' down the avenue towards the house and back to the stables. How I remained in the saddle I'll never know. The horse had sensed that its rider was without any know-how! And could this thoroughbred gallop! We literally flew towards the house! I was hanging on like grim death.

Arriving at the quadrangle in front of the house we were going at such a speed that the horse could not stop or turn. So at high speed we entered a fairly narrow pathway which extended right round the square farmhouse and back to the quadrangle. On the first 90-degree sharp turn we brushed one side and I lost one stirrup but remained in the saddle. We then negotiated the other right angle turn and by the time we arrived back in the quadrangle we had lost a fair amount of speed but I was still in the saddle. It was here that the situation became very dangerous, not only for me, but for the other members of the party in the plantation. A most horrendous development of this wild careering stallion's intentions became evident. In the party of horses which had entered the plantation of trees was a mare girl-friend whose scent my stallion had picked up. My horse, still going at a gallop, dashed straight into the plantation and I found myself, still on its back, crouching low with tree boughs sweeping at high speed over my head.

We went straight for the party of horses in the plantation. Before the Egyptians could move their horses out of the way my stallion rushed straight at the mare, reared up on top of her and came down with his front legs missing the Egyptian on her back by inches. The tremendous blow on the back of the mare cut her back open with a gash possibly some 18 inches long and blood was pouring from the wound. By this time the noise and commotion had alerted the stable lads who came running to catch the stallion. They arrived at the scene to grab my horse and I then dismounted calmly and with the true British stiff upper lip I apologised to the astounded Egyptians! They gathered round me with a certain amount of astonished semi-admiring respect that I had come through that ordeal in one piece unscathed and my composure indicated complete 'sang-froid'! Little did they know of my weakness at the knees. Their trick had rebounded on them and they realised that they were lucky not to have a fatality to one of their own party.

Needless to say after that episode I did no more riding! Later in the morning the Egyptians invited me to see one of their stable lads ride my stallion and, if I had seen this demonstration before my invitation to ride, I certainly would never have agreed to ride the animal. The stable lad mounted and at first the horse refused to move. It pawed and dug its forefeet into the ground and only when the jockey lashed it violently with his whip did the horse move. It shot off like a rocket into an immediate stretch gallop at a colossal speed which to me was frightening. However the rider gained control and his mastery of the fiery animal was admirable. But it raised in my mind the question whether there had been any intention on the part of the Egyptians to involve me in an accident whereby I could have been severely injured or possibly lost my life. On my return to Heliopolis I was determined I would never again be caught out by my ignorance of horse riding and I took riding lessons at a local riding school.

As mentioned previously, almost every weekend I journeyed to Alexandria and met my lady friend. She was now pressing me to take action with my wife's family to obtain a divorce and I finally agreed to do this. In those days of course divorce was not as easy as it is to day. Furthermore my wife was a Catholic and so was her family and of course for practising Catholics there is no divorce. I approached my wife's brother Max Sadek who was the head of my wife's family, her father having died. We arranged a meeting at which I stated my position and asked for their co-operation in arranging a divorce. I received a point-blank refusal. Conveying the negative news to my lady-friend caused an unhappy reaction but worse was to follow. Shortly after this came the news that her husband had passed his F.R.C.S. examination in London and would be returning to Egypt in the near future. With that news she decided that it would be better for all concerned that our affair should end and that she should resign herself to a future with her Egyptian husband. No amount of argument from my side would persuade her to change her mind and to my great sorrow the affair came to an end. Repeated phone calls, pleading, in my misery, for a change of heart, came to nothing. Now, looking back, I know that it turned out for the best in the long run. It was a mad infatuation that could not succeed. For one thing my financial situation at that time would never have been sufficient to support her at a level that would have brought her happiness. Furthermore life in England would have been hard for her; she was used to servants and a personal maid.

Meanwhile my work with the Egyptian Air Force Flying School proceeded reasonably smoothly in spite of the inherent difficulties and antipathies that existed. In February 1940 after I had been with the School for just over a year I was asked by the Mission Senior Air Adviser to accept a move from the School to take over the responsibilities of adviser to the King's Flight. This unit was commanded by an Egyptian officer who was notoriously known to the Mission members for being extremely anti-British and uncooperative and critical of members of the British Military Mission. The previous Mission adviser to the Kings Flight had had considerable difficulty with this Egyptian commanding officer and had been the subject of severe criticism and finally an adverse report by the Egyptian. This had resulted in the unfortunate Mission member finally being sent back to England under a cloud and relieved of his Mission duties.

The Senior Mission Adviser saw my hesitation and evident reluctance to take on the proposed new role. I said that judging by what had happened to the previous British adviser my future career in the RAF could be at considerable risk if I moved into that anti-British situation. It was well known that the King of Egypt himself was very anti-British and pro-Italy. He favoured our Axis enemies with whom we were at war and with whom we were fighting in the desert on the Egyptian frontier. My senior said that if I took on this role of adviser to the King's Flight he would guarantee that, whatever happened, it would not have any adverse effect on my RAF career. On that understanding I agreed to accept the changeover.

The next day I went over to the Royal Flight hangars which were on the same aerodrome as the Egyptian Flying School. The Flight was very well organised. The Egyptian C.O. was an extremely intelligent officer and had good training and experience with the RAF in England. The administration offices in the hangar were well run and the C.O.'s office could only be approached through the office of his adjutant. Thus I reported my presence to the adjutant and asked to present myself to the C.O. himself. The adjutant went into the C.O. and quickly returned saying that they had received no official communication from the Chief of the Mission concerning my appointment to this Egyptian unit and, until such a communication was received, my presence could not be officially recognised. However I would be permitted the use of an office in the hangar which had been allotted to the previous adviser. I immediately reported this contretemps to the senior air adviser who acknowledged that nothing official had been done to inform the Egyptian C.O. of my appointment and he agreed that the Egyptian officer could rightly claim he was carrying out correct procedure, much to the embarrassment of the British. He promised that he would communicate with the Chief of the Mission and get the necessary official notification sent to the C. O. of the King's Flight.

Following this setback my routine every morning for some three weeks was to report to the adjutant asking if he had received the necessary paperwork. Each day I received a negative. I was thus forced to confine myself to the allotted adviser's office doing nothing, not daring to make any contact with the Egyptian technical personnel in the hangar. To have done so could have possibly provoked a row with the anti-British Squadron Commander. Finally, early one morning just after I had arrived, an Egyptian N.C.O. rushed into my office and somewhat agitatedly said the C.O. wanted to see me urgently. Donning my cap I went along to the adjutant's office and he immediately ushered me into the C.O.'s office and then retired. The C.O., sitting at his desk looking extremely worried, said somewhat solemnly: 'What we want is co-operation!' 'Hypocrite!' I thought. 'You, who deliberately obstructed me for some three weeks from having any contact with yourself and your organisation, are now telling me I should give you co-operation!' Naturally, I kept my thoughts to myself and merely said that I was at his service, and would be happy to co-operate when and where I might be of assistance.

The C.O. then told me in a somewhat nervous manner that the King had given instructions through the Palace Staff that two of the Royal aircraft were to fly down to Luxor early the next day. They were to pick up the King and his family together with his entourage and return with them to Cairo. The two aircraft nominated were the latest additions to the Royal Flight. They were twin-engined passenger aircraft named Percival Q6 fitted out with special luxury cabins and the latest de Havilland Gipsy 6-cylinder engines driving recently invented variable pitch propellers. In fact for that period in time the aircraft were extremely sophisticated and built to the most up-to-date standards of technology. The C.O. said one aircraft was perfectly serviceable and would be available as required in the morning. The other had technical problems which made it unserviceable and his technical staff were unable to locate or correct the fault. He asked me to assist his staff as time was running out to get this aircraft ready for the morning. He intimated that if the aeroplane did not arrive at Luxor the next day there would be tremendous trouble for all concerned. The King was noted for his evil character and his cruel callous treatment of his underlings. I promised to do my best!

Moving into the hangar for the first time I spoke with the senior Egyptian technician who told me that the aeroplane was suffering from severe vibration, the cause of which they were unable to establish. On ground testing the aircraft on the tarmac apron I soon diagnosed that the source of the vibration was lack of synchronisation of the two engine revolutions at equal throttle openings. This was due to an incorrect setting of the governor controlling one of the variable pitch propellers. Thanks to the previously mentioned variable propeller course I had had at de Havillands factory when in England I was able to adjust the governor and luckily obtained perfect synchronisation quite quickly.

I reported to the C.O. that the aircraft was now serviceable and explained what had occurred. I said the aeroplane now needed an air-test before going back into service. The C.O. said he would air-test it himself immediately and, glaring at me once again, he said rather harshly 'You will fly with me on the air-test!'

This ultimatum put me in a very difficult position because a British Mission order had been made that no Mission members except flying instructors were to fly with an Egyptian military pilot because our insurance did not cover this situation. On the other hand this Egyptian pilot had a moral right to expect me to fly with him on this air-test for it was my work and adjustments on the aircraft which were being air-tested. If I pleaded Mission rules and regulations and refused to fly with him I knew my future standing with this Egyptian would be somewhat jeopardised and I could probably expect a difficult relationship such as my British predecessor had experienced. On the other hand what would be my position in the British Military Mission if it became known I had disobeyed the Mission standing order and agreed to fly with this Egyptian pilot? These thoughts flashed through my mind as the C.O. waited for my reply and then, thinking – 'To hell with the consequences – I have to achieve a working relationship with this man and make a possible success of this difficult task', – I said I would be happy to fly with him on the air-test.

The C.O. ordered the plane to be prepared for air-test and we both boarded the machine and went up front to the flight deck where I occupied the second pilot's seat. Engines started, tested, we taxied out into the sand, positioned for take-off and away we went. We did about half an hour's testing, climbing to several thousand feet, and executing various manoeuvres, designed to prove the aircraft performance in various attitudes. We then returned to the aerodrome, landed, and taxied up to the King's Flight hangar.

By this time the word had gone round the squadron that this newly arrived Englishman had carried out work on one of the King's aircraft to rectify a serious fault and that he was now flying with the C.O. air-testing the machine. In consequence, when we taxied up to the apron in front of the hangar, there was, in typical Egyptian style, practically the whole squadron personnel waiting on the tarmac, including all the Egyptian officers curious to know and to witness the C.O.'s reaction when he returned from the air-test. The C.O. descended from the plane and I followed. Walking towards the group of his officers, when he was near enough for them to hear, he turned round to me and ostentatiously shook hands saying 'The aircraft has never flown better since it was new.' From that time onwards I was treated by all the Egyptian Squadron including the C.O. with great respect. In fact the C.O. invited me to parade early each morning with him on the tarmac apron as he watched the Squadron personnel preparing the aircraft for his officer pilots to carry out their various flying activities such as training flights or scheduled duty flights etc.

And thus began a strange relationship between this Egyptian C.O. and myself. We engaged in quite frank and friendly discussions quite often unconnected with aviation matters. He was very intelligent and amongst other things was a Bridge playing champion of Egypt. He was an unusual Egyptian in that he was quite honest and freely spoke his mind and in no way attempted to hide his political or other views on life in general. He freely admitted to me that he hated the British as a colonial nation who, he claimed, were imposing on Egypt a regime which was quite unsuited to the requirements and social conditions of that country. Furthermore, whilst he obviously respected my professionalism which had rescued his career in the Royal Palace service, he had no hesitation in letting me know that I was included in his antipathy to all things British. Little did I suspect that all around me was being hatched a conspiracy of these Egyptian officers which would eventually result in a revolution and the downfall of the King and the feudal system of Egypt. At the time of that episode of the air-test with the Egyptian C.O. I was puzzled as to why he walked to within hearing distance of his officers and he then had ostentatiously shaken hands with me and in a loud voice so that his staff could hear he had said 'The aeroplane has never flown better since it was new'. Looking back on it I now realise he was making a sort of public announcement that I was not to be molested and that I was to be considered a useful (but unknowing) friend to their cause.

In late May 1940, after several months of uneventful work with this Egyptian Squadron, I was with the C.O. doing the usual early morning walk-about amidst the activities on the tarmac apron when the C.O. suddenly turned to me and, without blinking an eyelid and in a matter-of-fact voice, said 'I will have you in prison in about 3 weeks time!' Somewhat surprised, I said I did not understand his meaning. He then said 'Haven't you heard the news? The French have surrendered to the Germans and the British have been defeated and driven out of France. The British are now trying to evacuate their forces at Dunkirk!' He said that he estimated that the Germans would invade Britain almost immediately and that the British would surrender within two to three weeks. The Egyptians, he said, would throw the British out and the British Military Mission members would be imprisoned! He said this with a certain amount of relish but with no real animosity and we continued our walk-about in the normal way without my having expressed any reaction to these alarming statements at all.

The quoted three weeks passed by without incident and the C.O. spoke no more of my impending imprisonment. I presume he was awaiting the anticipated German invasion of Britain and his prophesied British surrender. Time went by and it became obvious that his heart's desire was not to be achieved and regretfully he resumed our previous relationship. However some other Egyptian officers in our circle had other ideas which culminated in one of the Squadron aircraft being stolen in an attempt to join the Vichy French and the Germans in Syria. Unbeknown to me I was right in the middle of a conspiracy of officers whose aim was to throw the British out of Egypt and to join the Axis forces. Secret approaches to Germany and Italy were made by contact with Axis legations in neutral capitals.

At this time of unsettled conditions in Egypt the Egyptian Air Force had introduced in this Squadron a duty ground crew which was always on stand-by after working hours and throughout each night. In addition the Mission always had one member on duty in the Almaza Aerodrome Headquarters during non-working hours and throughout the night. A certain well-known, very senior Egyptian army general appeared late one evening in the Aerodrome Headquarters. He was the veteran nationalist political leader Aziz Ali El Masr who was a member of a conspiracy of military officers whose aim was anti-British and against the existing Egyptian government who were considered to be too conciliatory to the British. This officers' conspiracy considered that with the British defeats by the Germans in Europe and in the desert the time was ripe for rebellion to throw the British out of Egypt. He was with one of the junior officer squadron pilots of the King's Flight and informed the British Mission duty officer that the King of Egypt had ordered that this Army general was to be flown in one of the King's Flight aircraft to the frontier on an urgent mission! The junior King's Flight officer with him was to fly the aircraft and they had what appeared to be supporting documents to that effect. The British officer, believing this to be a genuine situation, allowed the junior squadron officer to instruct the duty ground crew to open up the hangar and move one of the aircraft – a very ancient twin-engine Avro Anson passenger plane – out of the hangar and prepare it for immediate take-off. The Egyptian General and the junior King's Flight pilot hoped to fly to Beirut to make contact with a German mission located there.

The ground crew did as instructed but, as they were not familiar with this type of aircraft, they were unaware that, before starting the engines, it was necessary to turn on an oil control cock on each engine to allow the necessary oil feed, and they failed to do so. In consequence they started up the engines and the pilot and general climbed in, took off, and flew for some ten minutes or so when both engines seized due to lack of oil feed. The pilot then successfully made a forced landing in a cotton plantation along the side of the River Nile. The general abandoned the aircraft and made off rapidly to the nearest village where he found the local police station and informed the police sergeant in charge of what had happened. He said he was on an urgent mission ordered by the King of Egypt and showed him his false papers to prove it. The general then commandeered the police car and drove himself to Cairo where he went straight to the apartment of an Egyptian night club dance-girl he knew in the native quarter of the city. He persuaded this girl to conceal him in her flat pending such time as he could arrange an escape out of the country.

The next day the news of this farcical escapade spread like wildfire throughout Egypt for it could not be concealed from the press since the forced down Egyptian Air Force plane was on view in the middle of a cotton field for all to see. The Egyptian police and the army were hot on the trail of the general and the junior officer pilot was in custody. He had confessed his involvement in a plot masterminded by the Egyptian army general who was well known for his extremely anti-British opinions. The General's scheme was to steal the aircraft and fly eastwards across the Sinai over Israel and Lebanon and land in Syria, hopefully Damascus, where they intended to desert to the Vichy French and their German allies. Every day following this episode there were headlines in the newspapers giving news of the progress of the intense searches which were being made over the whole of Cairo for the renegade general. The authorities were certain that the general was holed up somewhere in the city and thus every sector was being meticulously combed by the police and the army, the progress of the search being given great publicity by the press. After about three weeks the nerve of the young Egyptian dancer concealing the general broke down under the constant tension caused by the press publicity and she betrayed the general to the police who moved in rapidly and the general was apprehended.

The public soon lost interest in these extraordinary events but soon after this the press seized on another remarkable and unbelievably hilarious episode which had occurred in Cairo city centre. All kinds of criminals, pickpockets, thieves and ne'er-do-wells swarmed around the city centre and its adjoining poor areas which included extensive red-light districts. One notorious haunt of con-men and criminal gangs was the main railway station in the centre of the city. Here a well known ploy by Arab con-men was to await the arrival at the main station of trains coming from the provincial rural districts and accost obvious peasants getting off the train with the object of robbing them if possible. Such visitors could easily be picked out from the passengers descending from the train by their dress and general appearance and of course by their air of bewilderment and uncertainty in this great metropolis.

One day one such arriving provincial train was surveyed by the observers of a con-gang and an obvious 'fellaheen' peasant country yokel was spotted and accosted. He was a very simple rustic illiterate as were about 85% of the population. He had at that time never ventured beyond the bounds of his primitive village. He thus fell for the smooth talk of the con-men and freely confided that he had saved up some considerable sum of money which he was carrying with him and had come to the big city to make his fortune. The con-men told the peasant he was lucky to have made their acquaintance since they knew all the ways and means of obtaining the objective that the peasant desired. They invited the fellaheen to have a coffee with them in a nearby cafe. Here they propounded to him a money-making scheme which they said could make his fortune in a very short time. They took him over to the Brown Train terminal in the centre square, Midan al Mahatta, which is the heart of the city and throbbing with life day and night.

The Brown Train system connects Heliopolis to Cairo over a distance of 8 or 9 miles. Its huge trams consisting of several long carriages arrive and depart every 10 minutes or so and carry huge numbers of people on each journey. The peasant was thus able to witness masses of people disgorging from these trams and the con-men pointed out the conductor with his large leather pouch collecting the fare money.

They said that it was possible to buy one of these Brown Trams and they were agents in a position to sell one to him. They said that if he wished they would send for their lawyer who would prepare a proper contract of sale. All the peasant had to do was select one of the trams and note its number and their lawyer would quote that number in the contract. The price, they said, was several hundred pounds in equivalent Egyptian currency. This happened to be the amount which the peasant had told the con-men he had brought with him. The peasant agreed with this proposition and the so-called 'lawyer' was sent for. The 'lawyer' was of course another member of the gang. The paper work was completed and the peasant handed over his money. He was then escorted back to the terminal and the group awaited the arrival of the Brown Tram numbered as in the contract. The tram arrived and the con-men bade the peasant farewell and disappeared while he boarded his tram. Sitting happily through the half hour or so journey to Heliopolis he watched the conductor collecting his fares. Approaching the terminal he observed with satisfaction how the conductor's leather pouch was now bulging with coins. Arrived at the terminal the passengers dismounted but our peasant remained seated in his carriage. The conductor came along and said this was the terminal and everyone must get off the tram. The peasant replied that there was no need for the conductor or himself to get off – the conductor could hand over his takings direct on the spot, as he was the new owner.

The conductor, thinking the peasant was having some practical joke, told him not to be stupid and ordered him off the tram. The peasant refused to move and demanded the money. By this time the conductor saw that this was a serious matter and he called the police. The police arrested the peasant, took him back to Cairo, and there he told his story which was soon broadcast nation-wide by the press. The aftermath was almost as curious for the poor peasant who was now destitute and at the mercy of any schemer who might think of ways of making money out of his plight. I witnessed one such scheme in which an enterprising character set up a small marquee in the very square of the city centre adjacent to the Brown Tram terminal where the peasant had 'bought' the tram. He had a large notice attached to the entrance of the marquee inviting the public, for a small fee, to come in and see the man who bought the Brown Tram! Needless to say, the police never succeeded in prosecuting the gang nor in getting the peasant's money back for him.

Chapter 15

1942 – Commissioned and Recalled to the Royal Air Force, Middle East

Towards the end of my contractual stay with the Egyptian Air Force another incident involving the Kings Percival Q6 aircraft occurred. Once again two aircraft had been ordered to pick up the King and his family at Luxor. One of these aircraft developed engine trouble en route and made a forced landing in the desert some hundred miles or so south of Cairo. The pilot informed us of his plight by radio and I was flown immediately by a British pilot to the stricken plane to assess the situation. Checking the defective engine I found a cylinder head had lifted slightly and further investigation revealed that the piston of that cylinder was damaged. I decided I could fix this engine in situ in the desert and I sent the British pilot back to Almaza for spares including a new piston and piston rings. Meanwhile another plane had been flown to the King to replace the defective aircraft.

The British pilot returned with the spares for me and also bringing a reserve pilot to fly the grounded aircraft back to base. I duly fixed the engine and flew with it back to Heliopolis where it resumed normal service. Then ensued at high level an almighty row. On learning of the Royal Q6 aircraft's forced landing the angry king ordered a formal enquiry into the incident. The court of enquiry was convened entirely with Egyptian officers and with no British representation whatever. Following the court's deliberation a report was issued absolving the Egyptians from any responsibility for this incident. The report concluded with damning criticism of the aircraft and the British aircraft engine manufacturers, laying the blame for the incident entirely on the poor quality of the aeroplane and passing derogatory remarks on British aeronautical engineers in general and on the British Mission in particular.

This verdict was of course ridiculous, and caused an immediate negative reaction from the Chief of the British Military Mission. Pressure was brought to bear via the British ambassadorial authorities to declare the Court of Enquiry invalid as no British representative had been present to give evidence. A new Court of Enquiry was convened in which a British Military Mission adviser was included with the Egyptian officers. I was called as a technical specialist witness. By this time I had made my own investigation into the background cause of the engine failure. This particular aircraft was, of course, of the pre-war design whereby the tail, when not in the flying attitude, rested on a tail wheel on the ground. This resulted in the aircraft when on the ground being at a fairly acute inclined angle to the horizontal which could cause the de Havilland Queen 30 in-line engines with inverted cylinder design to drain their oil towards the rear of the engine. In fact, if the aircraft was not flown for several days, oil would drain rearwards into the rear cylinder and gradually fill the combustion space above the rear piston. If nothing was done to relieve this excess oil in the combustion space of the rear cylinder, damage would be done to that cylinder and piston on next starting up. The power developed by the other five cylinders would cause 'hydraulicing' in the rear cylinder due to the incompressibility of the oil filling the cylinder combustion space. The 'hydraulicing' pressure would be transmitted through the oil to the cylinder head securing studs and nuts so loosening them slightly. Vibration from operation of the engine over a period of time would further loosen the cylinder head nuts and so produce failure by lifting that cylinder head. This was the series of events which caused the desert forced landing. The piston of the engine was also damaged by the 'hydraulicing' pressure.

Thus a mandatory pre-flight operation in the daily maintenance schedule called for removal of the sparking plugs of the rear cylinder to permit the excess oil to drain off before starting the engine. In this case under enquiry I found that the aircraft had been parked in the hangar without having been flown for some days and the mandatory oil draining operation had not been carried out prior to starting the engine for the flight to Luxor. At the court of enquiry I was able to demolish the Egyptian claim against the manufacturers by providing the court with irrefutable evidence that the damage to the engine was caused by omission of the oil draining operation by the Egyptian ground crew prior to the flight. In my evidence I gave the court a scientific explanation of how the 'hydraulicing' train of events in the engine would finally have resulted in the engine failure which actually happened in the desert. This evidence was accepted in a final court report laying blame fairly and squarely on the Egyptians and was confirmed by both sides at top levels.

I was congratulated by the senior British Air Advisor on my contribution to the enquiry and shortly afterwards was recommended for commissioning. My 3-year contract with the Egyptian Government was coming to an end and, in view of the desperate British situation in the Middle East War, the British Government refused to renew my contract to the Egyptians. At the same time I was commissioned as an Engineer Officer on 17th January 1942 and recalled into the RAF in February 1942. My commissioning and recall to the RAF brought about another revolutionary change to my outlook on life in general. In a similar way to my initial reactions when I was seconded from the RAF to the British Military Mission I again had feelings of being released from a kind of bondage. Indeed this feeling was justified and understandable if one realises the power of the structure of class-ridden English society and the tremendous class distinction that existed up to the early years of World War 2. When I joined the Service in 1923 as a boy apprentice the English class system was still at its most powerful. All classes viewed the services' rankers as the lowest social level. I was trained only to obey, without any right to have any individuality or claim as a thinking person. My time in the British Military Mission had brought some considerable change to the conditions in this lower level status but the class barrier still existed, particularly on the British side. However my commission changed all that! – suddenly I became an English gentleman with freedom to act and think as a responsible person. I felt as if I had climbed over a tremendous wall or barrier into a new world of freedom which had previously been forbidden territory. I was now a Flying Officer Engineer!

This happy feeling of freedom and status was further enhanced when I reported to the RAF Headquarters Middle East who referred me to the Engineering 206 Group Headquarters which was sited at Heliopolis. What a happy coincidence! with my flat just round the corner! The senior Engineer Officer, to my great surprise, said that they had been waiting for me and that two extremely urgent engineering tasks needed to be carried out with the utmost speed. He explained that the German Afrika Korps under General Rommel had air superiority at this time. Over a period of three weeks with nightly 'carpet bombing' the Luftwaffe had recently completely destroyed our main Technical Depot located at Ismailia on the Suez Canal. The whole lot had gone up in flames. This Depot had provided the main technical support and also had held the major bulk of spares stores for the Desert Air Force. Replacement of these technical services in the shortest possible time was an extremely urgent requirement.

I was invited to select whichever task I preferred to undertake. One task was concerned with the repair and overhaul of damaged aircraft structures, particularly salvaged crashed aircraft. The other was the repair and overhaul of the huge metal propellers salvaged from crashed and shot-down aircraft in the Western desert battle area. This involved high precision engineering technology and heat treatment for restoration of the metal blade shapes and the overhaul of the variable pitch mechanism. Heat treatment of the duralumin metal blades would be necessary to work the metal and would require the construction of massive high precision heating systems to obtain temperatures of up to 1000 degrees centigrade. Precision accuracy during the 10-hour sustained heating within a tolerance of only 2 degrees C. above or below the temperature was required to work the metal. Any heating of the metal outside these limits would destroy the strength of the propeller blades.

The airframe task would be located on an aerodrome at Helwan which was about 25 miles south of Cairo. The propeller task would be located in some extraordinary man-made caves at Tura which the ancient Pharaohs had created some 5000 years ago. The caves had been excavated in the side of an extensive limestone mountain range running parallel with and adjacent to the River Nile. They were located about 15 miles south of Cairo and had been cut to provide the stone to build the Pyramids.

As I have previously related I had some specialist knowledge of and experience with variable pitch propellers and the precision engineering aspects of the propeller task appealed to me. I therefore selected the task of setting up the propeller factory. The Headquarters Senior Engineer then gave me the 'downside' of the task I had selected. He said there were none of the specialist tools required for this task available from the RAF Middle East resources and that only a very small RAF skeleton manpower would be allocated. He said that there was no possibility whatever of getting any specialist equipment from the U.K. for two reasons. One was the U.K. at this time had its own problems with threatened invasion and air attack from the Germans. The U.K. had indicated very forcefully that they were not in a position to help. Secondly the Mediterranean Sea was now closed to any British passage due of course to German and Italian air superiority giving them control of the shipping lanes. Any supplies from the U.K. had to come via the Cape in South Africa and the sea voyage took 3 months. Finally, he said that there was no heat treatment plant available from the RAF. I would be required to provide a suitable system from local resources. Likewise I would have to recruit and train local Egyptian labour to supplement the skeleton RAF manpower.

For the tooling and equipment required I was authorised to seek assistance and if necessary commandeer supplies from any technical organisation in Egypt, civilian or military. For this purpose I was allocated a staff car and driver so that I could go anywhere I thought likely to have such equipment. For what I could not obtain by these means I was authorised to arrange design and local manufacture in the workshops which had been set up in the valley below the caves mentioned previously. For the manpower I would have a skeleton staff of RAF technical personnel comprising about a dozen people and I was authorised to recruit Egyptian civilian labour to augment this initial nucleus. The allotted RAF people had some experience in this type of engineering and would train the Egyptians in the various technical operations required. In the event the scale of the operation developed tremendously so that at the height of the factory production I had a staff of 50 RAF technical personnel and 300 Egyptian civilian mechanics.

My first visit was to the caves in which the factory was to be sited. There were 21 caves cut into the mountainside at a height of about 600-700 feet above the level of the valley below. These caves of limestone had been created some 4000 to 5000 years previously by Pharaonic stonemasons cutting into the mountain to provide stone for building the famous pyramids. For my purpose I had been allocated two adjoining caves cut parallel to each other and running into the mountain interior for some 500 or 600 feet. The entrance to each of these caves was tremendous being about 70 feet high and possibly 100 feet or more wide, giving into caverns of varying width averaging around some 60 feet or more with a roof height of some 30 feet. Thus I had a tremendous floor space in which to position large size machinery and massive workbenches. The larger of my two caves, Bore K, had a working floor space of 12,785 square feet while the other, Bore L, provided 9,580 square feet.

Arriving on my first visit and entering the caves thousands of bats flew out in startled whirling noisy confusion. The floors of the two caves were covered in rock rubble to a depth of some three or four feet resulting from thousands of years of loose rock fragments falling from the ceilings. So the first job was to get the RAF works and building people to make a thorough testing of the cave ceilings to locate loose rock and make them safe, and then to whitewash all the rock walls to give better light reflection. A small power station had been built in the valley below and electric supply cables ran up the mountain to give the cave workshops lighting of a high standard. This of course was needed all day and also all night, as we would be working the heat treatment section twenty-four hours a day – in three 8-hour shifts.

Of the 21 caves two or three were used as warehouses to safeguard the Pharaonic treasures removed from the Cairo museum. This was to prevent possible damage by German bombing attacks to the priceless gold etc artefacts such as those recovered from the tomb of Tutankhamun. Another huge cave, possibly two or three times the size of my cave, was already set up for aircraft engine overhaul. The largest cave of all, which we called the Cathedral Cave, was really an amazing sight when one passed through the huge entrance. The cave was so vast, both width wise and in depth, that the roof of the cave needed support. This support had been provided by the ancient Egyptian stonemasons leaving integral pillars joining the roof and floor which were of the necessary diameter and at the correct intervals, all according to calculated designs of the Pharaohs' architects. Thus when entering one had an impression of a medieval European cathedral with lines of enormous pillars stretching far into the vast interior. This cave was used for the RAF storage of overhauled and new aero engines and large-scale machinery generally. Another cave adjoining was set up as a workshop for repair and overhaul of radio and radar equipment. Several caves were used for general bulk stores, for technical spares, general equipment and materials, and replacement tyres for the whole of the desert Air Force vehicles and aircraft etc. Another huge cave had been set up as a general engineering workshop equipped with sophisticated machinery capable of major metal machining operations.

Following my departure from the Egyptian Air Force and whilst I was touring Egypt to commandeer tooling for my new task there occurred another farcical anti-British episode. Again the King gave vent to his anti-British animosity. Like the thinking of the Egyptian officers' conspiracy, the King considered that the difficulties of the British with Rommel's Afrika Korps in the Western Desert plus the resounding defeats already suffered by the British at the hands of the Germans in Europe and the Japanese in the Far East together presented an excellent opportunity to openly defy the British. The rise of anti-British feeling and openly and publicly demonstrated expressions of support by the Egyptian public for the Axis, particularly for Italy, gave considerable anxiety to the British authorities in Egypt. They felt that the support base for the British 8th Army and Desert Air Force was in danger.

The Government of the day was pressurised by the King to change the Foreign Minister following Farouk's anger that he had not been consulted about Egypt's break with the French Vichy Government. This political move had resulted from British influence and the King was determined to counteract such pressures. The King's ultimatum to the Government resulted in its resignation. The British Authorities had plenty of evidence of the King's involvement with the Axis powers. The British decided that the security of their base was in jeopardy. With the resignation of the Government the British advised the King to accept a new Wafdist Government headed by Mustapha Nahas Pasha who was a well-known enemy of the King. The King refused this advice and ordered the Abdin Palace gates to be closed and locked so that the British Ambassador, Sir Miles Lampson, could not enter. On 4th February 1942 Sir Miles Lampson (later Lord Killearn) then arranged for the British Army to position four tanks immediately in front of the Abdin Palace gates in

Abdin Square and then issued an ultimatum to the King that if he did not open up and receive him one of the tanks would smash down the gates and he would enter the Palace escorted by British troops and three tanks. The Palace gates were opened. Abdin Palace was surrounded by British troops and the British Ambassador, Sir Miles Lampson, entered the Palace accompanied by the British Commander in Chief of the Royal Navy and the military Commander of the British garrison. Sir Miles Lampson issued an ultimatum to the King in which he would be forced to abdicate if he did not agree to appoint Nahas Pasha as leader of a pro-British Government. The King capitulated and appointed Nahas who was leader of the Government for the remainder of the War years and was fully co-operative with the British during this period.

The Egyptian officers' conspiracy to oust the British and their own King, previously mentioned in these memoirs, was put on 'hold' following the entry of America into WW2 which occurred in 1941. Likewise at the same time the King abandoned his ideas of ridding himself of his hated British masters.

Chapter 16

No. 111 Maintenance Unit in the Pharaonic Tura Caves

Battle of Alamein. Defeat and Retreat of Rommel and his Afrika Korps

To get my two caves into operation it was necessary first of all to clear a considerable depth of rock rubble from the cave floors. This rubble consisted of loose rock which had fallen from the roofs and walls over the course of thousands of years of their existence. This task of clearing the rubble was done by hiring some 200 local donkeys fitted with straw panniers and complete with little Arab girls who with their stout canes guided their charges up the mountain path into the caves. There they filled their panniers on the donkeys' backs with loose rock picked up by hand and led them down the mountain where they off-loaded the stone to form the foundation for a ramp road which was finally constructed from the valley to the cave entrances. This permitted heavy lorry traffic to drive up to the caves and in fact to drive into the caves to pick up finished equipment etc. In clearing the rubble from my cave (Bore K) an interesting discovery was unearthed. This was a mummy of a young Egyptian female. Thinking that this might be of interest to the curators of the Cairo museum I reported this matter to them by telephone and they collected the mummy. They promised to inform me of their findings, which they did. I was visited by a Museum curator who said that the mummy was probably some 2000 years old. It was a young girl about 15 or 16 years old who had been murdered probably by her own family possibly for breaching the family honour by having an illicit affair. The body was mummified by the family, this being an important feature of their religion at that time. They believed that without this the girl's spirit would have had no resting-place and would have haunted the family for evermore.

I took the opportunity of this Museum expert's visit to get him to translate some hieroglyphics which were carved into the rock at head height at the entrance of one of my caves. He said it was carved by the Pharaonic stonemasons cutting the stone of this cave some 5000 years previously and was in fact a warning notice to all unauthorised personnel or loafers that they should take note that the foreman in charge of the stonemasons working in this cave was a tyrant and a fierce disciplinarian and would impose severe punishment on any intruders.

To set up this factory to undertake the various technical processes I needed a variety of specialised equipment. This included 50-ton hydraulic presses that could be used for straightening the thick solid metal propeller blades. On a fighter aircraft crashing into the ground it was usually the propeller which first hit the ground and received the full impact shock. Thus the salvaged propellers which would be received by us would be looking like huge bent-up scrap corkscrews. These bent-up blades would have to be first heated to a temperature of 385 degrees C. to soften the metal and make it workable. This process was called 'annealing'. Then would begin a process of straightening the bent blades using high power presses. After straightening the blades the designed angle of the blade would have to be restored by twisting the metal blade to give the correct pitch. This would be done using twisting machines and measurement by accurate templates at defined stations along the full length of the blades, each station having a different angle. The angle of the blade at each station along the length of the blade had to be of an extremely high precision, the tolerance being only a minute fraction of one degree. Otherwise the propeller would develop vibration in operation.

I decided to investigate the possibility that the Egyptian State railways' workshops might have the type of hydraulic power presses that I needed. I called at the Railway Headquarters and had an interview with the Chief Engineer. At that time in Egypt all the Government organisations such as the Railways etc. had English heads of their main departments. Thus I had a sympathetic hearing from the English Chief Engineer who, when he heard my story, told me that he had just the type of hydraulic press I required. He said that just prior to the outbreak of war he had provisioned 6 new vertical 50-ton hydraulic presses from England and they were still in his store unused. He said I could have them and I gave him a piece of paper on which the British Government promised to pay the Egyptian Railways their original purchase price. Whether this promise was fulfilled or not I shall never know.

I travelled far and wide over the country calling at likely firms where I might pick up tools and called at various RAF stations to investigate their tool stores to commandeer anything that might be suitable, sometimes incurring the resentment of senior officers who viewed the intrusion of this junior officer with some disgust. But I had carte blanche authority from the highest level. For the heat treatment plant that was required I decided to enlist the help of top level metallurgists at Cairo University. I had an interview with the professor who was head of the metallurgy department there. Again I was fortunate for the professor was English and entirely co-operative. Having explained the operations and the factors and conditions that could appertain in the caves the professor and his staff designed a heat treatment plant that could be manufactured in our own cave workshops and which would be suitable for operation inside the cave. The system was based on what is known as the salt-bath system whereby sodium nitrate salt crystals plus another type of crystal are heated in a large steel bath of sufficient size to accommodate the material i.e. the propeller blade to be treated. The bath in this case was about 12 feet long and some 3 feet deep designed to contain 4000 lbs. of salts. The required crystal salts were not available from RAF sources so, by searching in the Cairo Arab bazaars, we eventually located an Egyptian chemical supplier who could provide the necessary chemicals. We also located an Arab foundry which could cast suitable duralumin ingots from which we could machine Merlin engine piston replacement spares unavailable from our own stores. Our salt bath was designed to be encased in a brick construction which formed an enclosed firebrick furnace beneath it. Heat was supplied by a diesel oil burner fed by gravity from an oil tank located at a suitable height to give the necessary flow. The University also supplied the design drawings for the burner which was manufactured in our own workshops, as was the steel tank. The 4000 lbs. of salts I managed to purchase from an Arab firm in the Cairo market as mentioned above. I sited this system in the cave entrance hall to lessen fire risks and had a chimney pipe leading to the outside of the cave to carry away any smoke or fumes.

Over the bath was constructed a travelling electric winch which transported a steel cradle carrying the propeller blades to be treated. This permitted the cradle to be gently lowered into the molten salts. The salts required 48 hours of continuous heating to become molten and then had the appearance of water. But a splash from this liquid which was at 385 deg. C. would burn right through the flesh. Alongside this salt bath was another similar sized steel bath containing hot water which was heated to boiling point in the same manner. This hot water bath was used to quench out and so restore the hardness of the blades after the required ten-hour high temperature heat soak. This process was called 'normalising'. It was at boiling point to prevent cracking of the metal in the quenching process which had to be carried out within a mandatory few seconds to get the correct hardness value for the finished blades. Hence the electric travelling winch. After this it was necessary to check that the treatment had been successful and the correct strength and hardness value had been restored. This was done by a special machine which carried out what was known as the Brinell hardness test. This consisted of a vertical hydraulic ram forcing a hardened steel ball under a standard load into the metal to be tested and then measuring the depth of penetration.

One night, after about a year's service operating 24 hours a day by three eight hour shifts, our home made salt-bath gave us a fright. Round about midnight the operators of the night shift monitoring the bath temperatures noticed a sudden temperature drop and the next moment a stream of liquid salt, just like a volcano lava flow, began to trickle out from the furnace below the bath. To the horror of the night staff the lava flow reached the wooden forms which were provided for the comfort of the recording team, and immediately the forms set on fire. So we had a fire in the cave. The furnace had burnt a hole in the bottom of the salt-bath. The fire alarm was raised by phone and the fire-fighting team alerted who soon had the fire under control. We were out of heat treatment production for a few days whilst our workshops produced another salt-bath of a thicker gauge steel. We had no further trouble after that as I made an order that the bath had to be renewed every 12 months of use.

These various repair and overhaul technical services were needed to salvage damaged or crashed aircraft for the Desert Air Force. New aircraft to replace those that were shot down or damaged in combat were not available at that time. The fighting zone had moved quite near to the Cairo area and so we were able to send flat-top low loader transport into the desert at night to pick up any crashed aircraft that could be salvaged. These were brought back to Helwan where they were stripped down and the various components such as engines, propellers, radios etc. were sent to our Cave workshops for processing. The airframes were rebuilt by cannibalisation etc. and eventually from these components a salvaged aircraft was produced to go back into combat service. In this way the combat strength of the Desert Air Force was maintained whilst Rommel's Luftwaffe strength was gradually eroded away because Hitler diverted all available air support to the German invasion of Russia. The RAF desert force also began to receive supplies of American aircraft so that gradually the German air superiority was reversed and Rommel began to suffer from RAF air attacks on his communications, tanks, water and fuel supplies etc.

To return to the cave story: – having cleared the cave rock rubble, and whitewashed the walls and roof, the floor was then concreted and the lighting installed. Then followed the installation of the machinery, which involved bolting down the hydraulic presses etc. The twisting machines which were needed to twist the thick metal blades we designed and manufactured ourselves using 10-ton lorry car jacks operated by hand. The blade was held in two steel boxes, one of which was fixed and the other able to swivel by the thrust of the lorry jack. These also had to be bolted into the cave floor.

The integrated propeller motor systems which actuated the blade turning mechanisms and so changed the pitch of the propellers during flight also needed servicing, overhaul and repair facilities. There were different motor designs depending on the manufacturer. They came under two main headings, one operated hydraulically by oil under very high pressure, the other operated electrically by an electric motor housed in the propeller hub. In the aircraft the setting of the engine revolutions was done manually with the throttle by the pilot whilst the propeller pitch setting was varied automatically in accordance with the engine revolutions by means of a governor unit actuated by fly weights driven from the engine and thus responsive to the engine revolutions. The variable pitch of the propeller acted somewhat as an automatic gearbox on a car. When the aircraft was climbing and the engine was thus heavily loaded the revolutions and thus the power output were maintained by the governor unit automatically changing the pitch of the propeller to a finer angle thereby reducing the load on the engine.

When the various overhaul operations had been completed and the propeller finally reassembled ready for service it had to be statically balanced to a very fine degree. The slightest imbalance would result in serious vibration in flight. The operation of balancing such awkward mechanisms some 15 feet or more in diameter and weighing several hundred pounds required special facilities. In the cave was an alcove which had been cut out of the cave wall, forming a fairly large side enclosure. In the stone floor of this chamber I had a pit cut to a depth of about 8 or 9 feet and some 10 feet in length. This pit allowed the propeller to be mounted vertically on steel knife-edge supports which were positioned on the edge of the pit. It could thus be rotated on a steel mandrel or bar which was passed through the hub in the same way, as it would be mounted on the shaft of the aircraft engine. By turning the propeller by hand in the pit the balancing operations could be carried out by the operator at floor level. This balancing operation was so delicate that the slightest draught of air would affect the readings. To solve this problem I had a huge curtain made which would close off the open end of the alcove. The curtain was mounted on rails and so could be operated to open or close the alcove as required.

The preparation of the caves and the collection and installation of the equipment and tooling had taken two months from mid February 1942 to mid April. Then came the moment to put it all into operation. This was done by moving a small RAF technical unit in Heliopolis which had been doing light superficial work on propellers. This unit consisted of 12 mechanics headed by a flight sergeant. The unit formed the nucleus of my organisation. In six weeks we had the whole operation up and running. As the operation developed successfully so I was granted authority to increase my manpower until finally at the height of production, as I have previously stated, I had 50 RAF technical personnel and some 300 Egyptian personnel. We were then producing more than 200 propellers a month. During some 2 years and 7 months of my service with this operation we never had a failure or a reject from any aircraft using our products. From the commencement of operations to the date of my departure from this post we had a total production of 5,858 propellers and 5,355 constant speed control units. We were supplying the Desert Air Force, the forces in Abyssinia and Eritrea, Iraq and the forces in Lebanon and Syria.

The Egyptian personnel were mostly low-grade mechanics whom we recruited from the surrounding villages. The test for recruitment of these Egyptians was a simple knowledge of the use of basic tools and ability to read measurements in the metric system. These people were mostly peasant class and arrived at work each day dressed in their fellaheen galabiyahs which of course are long loose garments, something like cotton nightshirts. Their clothing was invariably full of lice in the seams and they often had lice in their hair and sometimes skin disease. I therefore had a problem controlling their hygiene and protecting my British RAF personnel from suffering adversely from their contact with the Egyptians. To assist in this control and administration of the Egyptians I recruited an educated Egyptian who was a graduate of Cairo University. I made him an overseer of the Egyptian personnel and issued all my directions and instructions for them through him. This overseer, a youngish man living in Cairo, was a Copt, that is to say an Egyptian Christian whereas of course all the remainder of the Egyptian mechanics were Moslems. They held him in great respect because, being Christian, he was considered to be one of us RAF boss Christians and therefore a man of great authority. He was a man of great honesty and sincerity with remarkable diplomatic skills so that, during the whole of my period of service in charge of this very large organisation, I had not a single problem with the diverse Egyptian workers nor with my British RAF contingent.

To overcome the lice problem I had built, on a level area of rock just outside the cave entrances, a bath-house of corrugated iron fitted up with a line of showers supplied by disinfectant water from a large overhead tank. The Egyptians were paid weekly at a table which was sited alongside the bathhouse. To draw their pay they had to strip off and pass through the bathhouse naked. Their clothes were treated in a fumigation process during their passage through the bathhouse. Thus, on that one pay-day each week, they would go home with money in their pockets and free of their itchy unwelcome guests.

To employ this crude labour successfully on such high precision engineering work the jobs were broken down and divided into small undemanding tasks which were repetitive. Thus the Egyptian could be taught his little piece of work in which he became adept by constant repetition. My RAF personnel I was forced to employ as supervisors only. Some of them enjoyed having this type of responsibility whilst a few resented it, being of a character that was fearful of carrying responsibilities, specially as they had been given neither the pay nor the status usually associated with such responsibility. As our production developed and grew, so of course the number of our expensive high precision measuring tools such as micrometers, verniers etc. increased. One day my senior N.C.O. came to me complaining that he had the responsibility of the safe-keeping of this large inventory of expensive tools which were in constant use by the Egyptian labour and that he had no secure safe storage to house such things. I agreed he had a valid case and promised to get a proper storeroom built inside the cave which could be secured with lock and key.

I should mention here that the work processes required movement of the various components from one cave into the other, and there was no communicating passage. Thus the work had to be transported from the first cave out into the open and then into the second cave. This was dangerous since such high precision components could be adversely affected by passing through an atmosphere which was often full of dust and sand. In addition time was lost in the work process due to loading and to the transportation. This was a constant source of annoyance to me.

Finally, I asked authority to cut an intercommunicating passage through the rock wall separating the two caves. This would reduce the transportation time and keep the work under cover. The rock wall was some thirty feet thick. My request was turned down by the authorities on the grounds of wartime economy. I resigned myself to this irritating handicap. However I pursued my promise to my N.C.O. and requested authority to have a secure lock-up store built inside the cave for the safe keeping of my valuable inventory. This was immediately granted and about three weeks later an elderly Arab dressed in peasant galabiyah with a young boy assistant arrived at my office. He said he had been sent to me to build the storeroom which I had requested. I asked him what material he was going to use to build this storeroom. He replied that he would build it of stone which he would cut from the rock outside my cave. In a moment of heaven-sent inspiration I saw this as an opportunity to achieve my dream of an interconnecting passage through the cave wall. I therefore told the old man to cut his stone from my cave wall. This he agreed to do. I then told him of my wish to have a passage right through the wall. To my amazement he said he could accomplish this quite easily! Here was an old man prepared to cut a roadway through a 30 or so feet thick stone wall all by himself in the comparatively short time allocated for building my store and with only hand tools – no mechanical appliances or power tools whatever!

Watching the old man working on the stone wall I soon learned how this amazing feat could be achieved! He was using the same stone cutting technique that the ancient Egyptian Pharaohs' stonemasons used 5000 years ago. This old man was cutting huge blocks of stone from the wall of my cave using a simple tool like an adze axe with its blade at right angles to the shaft. By means of this tool he would cut a shallow groove in a line around the periphery of the block of stone he planned to cut. He would then cut a series of wedge-shaped slots into the rock, each slot about 3 or 4 inches wide and 6 or 7 inches deep at about 18-inch intervals along the lines he had just grooved. Into these slots he would drive wedge-shaped pieces of wood shaped to fit into the slots. His young assistant would then bring buckets of water which he would pour onto the wooden wedges whilst the old man with his adze head would drive the expanding wedges down into their slots. Suddenly there would be an almighty crack and the block would crack apart from the solid wall. The water caused swelling of the wooden wedges which exerted simultaneous expansion pressure along the entire line of the cut. Et voila! a huge slab of stone would split off from the main body of rock. I was witnessing a live demonstration of how the Pyramids were supplied with stone.

As mentioned the caves we were in had been cut by the Pharaohs' stonemasons in exactly this same way 5000 years before to provide the blocks of limestone used to build the famous Egyptian pyramids. This was confirmed to me most dramatically when I was re-visiting Egypt with my wife Pam some 50 years later. Sailing down the Nile and visiting Upper Egypt we visited the site of a one-time Pharaonic quarry where the ancient Egyptians had cut their famous one-piece massive granite obelisks. There on the face of arock ledge was an uncompleted obelisk which had been abandoned due to cracking of the stone during the cutting operation. And there was the line of wedge slots in preparation for cutting another slab with one of the slots still holding a wooden wedge!

In those ancient days the River Nile had the habit of changing its course occasionally and at one time flowed in the valley some 400 or 500 feet below our caves. Now the valley was a sandy dried riverbed where my RAF men were living in tents. Over the passage of thousands of years the River Nile has changed its course many times. It is now flowing several kilometres away from the caves but 5000 years ago it flowed in the valley below. The stonemasons would cut the blocks and wait for the annual flooding of the Nile when the blocks could be levered onto barges on the river when it rose, level with the mouth of the caves. The barges would then be floated down the Nile to the site of the Pyramid building operations and levered off for the builders to use. The annual Nile flooding was caused by the melting snows in the mountains around the upper reaches of the river. Nowadays of course the water levels are controlled by the huge modern dams which have been constructed to form tremendous reservoirs.

My stonemason, using this same technique, would divide the huge cut blocks into smaller blocks. These he would then trim with his adze to give regular faces to build my store walls and – Hey Presto! in a few weeks I had my store and my intercommunicating passage! A visiting Staff Officer from the Engineering Headquarters which had been involved in the rejection of my original request for the interconnecting passage laughingly congratulated me on the cunning that had successfully by-passed their rejection with no official sanction.

It is interesting to record that the site of these caves close to the eastern bank of the River Nile was exactly opposite the site of the ancient Pharaonic city of Memphis on the West bank where the first stepped Sakkara Pyramids were built. Memphis was the capital of Northern Egypt (North Delta area) about 3000 B.C. In the religion of those ancient times it was also believed by the ancient Egyptians to be the seat of their God Ptak whom they considered to be the creator of the whole world and who was famous as a great craftsman and artisan who had also created their many other Gods. So perhaps it could be considered appropriate that, in their caves which they had cut into the hillside so long ago, we RAF engineers of this modern age should be installing high-grade workshops with skilful craftsmen and artisans performing feats of precision engineering. It is a strange and possibly unique phenomenon that we British people were co-opting the technology of the ancient Pharaohs to assist us in defeating the evil plans of Hitler.

We had been in production only some couple of months when the British Eighth Army in the desert suffered very serious setbacks. General Rommel with the German Afrika Korps very cleverly outwitted the British forces by outflanking movements in the desert, and forced the Eighth Army into an alarming retreat, abandoning many of their heavy weapons, tanks etc. Rommel then captured our fortress at Tobruk which we had held against all odds for a couple of years, and took 30,000 British troops prisoner. The Germans drove the British before them and it looked very likely that Rommel might overwhelm the British defences and conquer Egypt. As the Germans advanced to the Egyptian frontier and into Egypt itself absolute panic seized the Egyptian population. What was worse, the British authorities in the Cairo and the Middle East Headquarters went into an almighty flap and confusion reigned. Preparations were made by the British to evacuate Egypt and move to Palestine (now Israel). Huge bonfires were lit in the grounds of the British Embassy in Cairo to burn all their secret documents to prevent them falling into the hands of the Germans. Diplomats and foreign embassies all began making plans to pack up and evacuate to either Palestine or the Sudan.

The confusion gradually reached me in the caves. I began receiving urgent and often conflicting cabled instructions to prepare to evacuate the entire unit by train to Palestine. The defences of the RAF depot including the caves were practically nil. If I remember correctly we had only about a dozen rifles all told so that if we were overrun before we could organise the unit onto a train we would stand no chance whatever. With the state of panic that existed in Cairo I doubt whether there would have been a train available anyway. I then received more cabled instructions to prepare to lay explosives in all my heavy machinery so that it could be blown up when the word was given and I was ordered to suspend production. The next day I received a further cabled instruction countermanding the previous instruction and ordering production to be resumed.

In view of the conflicting instructions and the chaos and turmoil that existed everywhere I decided that perhaps it would be a good idea to acquaint my parents with the possibility that events might adversely affect my future. I have never been a good correspondent so they were never unduly worried when there were long gaps between my communications. For that reason I thought I should take the opportunity, while it still existed, of letting them know that the next communication gap might be due to unfortunate circumstances over which I would have no control. In fact I wrote saying amongst other things that, if they did not hear from me in the next three months, I might be a prisoner of war. I advised them that after three months without news they should contact Air Ministry in London who might be able to inform them of any untoward change in my circumstances. My young sister who was living at home at that time told me, when I eventually returned to England, that, like all war-time service mail, my letters were processed to reduce their size and thus postal bulk so that my parents got my sister to read their letters. She said that large pieces of the letter were often censored out but she has no recollection of such a letter arriving at that time.

Fortunately the disastrous situation which had been considered a possibility did not arise. The British were able to form and hold a defence line at El Alamein on a narrow strip between the sea and the Quattara depression, a huge impenetrable salt marsh and quicksand area 134 feet below sea level. An Australian Army veteran division, which was resting in Palestine (Israel) after long service fighting in the Western Desert, was brought rapidly back to Egypt by train to reinforce the defence line. These tough fighters, together with British and Indian divisions, held off the Germans who were somewhat exhausted by their long fighting 1000 mile advance along the North coast of Africa from Tunis. In addition the increasing superiority of our air strength permitted the RAF Desert Air Force to attack his Panzer units and disrupt his supplies of petrol and water, thus making life generally very uncomfortable for the German invaders. On top of this was the wonderful uplifting of the British Eighth Army morale caused by the arrival of General Montgomery who destroyed the myth of the invincibility of General Rommel and the Afrika Korps. Conditions in Egypt slowly returned to a more normal routine so that, although Rommel gathered his strength to attack the British in the first battle of Alamein in June, he was repulsed and our line held. Finally reinforcements and equipment arrived from the U.K. which permitted General Montgomery, leading the revived Eighth Army to achieve the great victory of the second Battle of Alamein.

During this time my Cave workshops developed at a tremendous pace and production soared. Our reputation grew as a remarkable and unusual unit in an unlikely environment. The uniqueness of this Tura Cave's Engineering Depot became known in Allied military circles so that nearly all visiting V.I.P.s from

My brother Leslie and self relaxing after the Battle of Alamein

By the River Nile April 1943, Fl/Lt. Powell and the author. Fl/Lt. Powell died the following year

England were conducted on tours round the caves. These visitors included Winston Churchill, Prime Minister of England. Churchill decided to visit Egypt in August 1942 just before the Battle of Alamein to restore British military morale there following our series of defeats by Rommel. He insisted on official visits to all key British units which included the Caves at Tura. He arrived in my cave on 22nd August 1942 at 7.15 in the morning complete with a high powered entourage. He made a detailed tour of my caves, showing great interest in a huge blackboard which I had erected in a prominent elevated position on the cave wall floodlit by electric spot lamps. On this blackboard I had designed the vertical and horizontal axes of a huge graph which showed production against days of the month. Each month an ideal curve was drawn to show the desired target output for that month and then for each day the actual production curve was drawn so that everyone could see and compare at a glance how near we were to the required output. In the U.K. it became a daily feature of the wartime newspapers and the media to have a headline 'Target for To-night' referring to RAF bombing targets in Germany. My blackboard was headed in big letters 'Target for the Month'. Churchill saw the connection and was rather tickled by the idea. He then asked that all my RAF personnel should stop work and assemble outside the cave where he wished to address them. This was done, our people forming a ring around him and his entourage, which incidentally also included General Alexander who had just been made Commander in Chief of all the Allied forces in the Middle East and also included Air Marshall Tedder who later became deputy Supreme Commander to Eisenhower for the D-day invasion of France. Among the many V.I.P.s touring the Middle East who visited these caves at different times were Lord Trenchard, the Duke of Gloucester, King Peter of Yugoslavia, General Eaker (American Commander in Chief of Mediterranean Forces), Prince Bernhardt of the Netherlands, husband of Queen Wilhelmina and many others. My younger brother Leslie was also one of my many visitors. Leslie was in a British Army unit of the Royal Engineers in the Middle East, training for amphibious operations somewhere around the Suez area. He unfortunately contracted a severe attack of amoebic dysentery and, after leaving the military hospital, was given local convalescent leave which he spent with me in Heliopolis. I was thus able to take him with me to the cave workshops. Unfortunately he later had a serious relapse and was invalided back to the U.K.

Churchill gave a sort of pep talk to my RAF people praising their endurance in the adversities we had suffered recently. He said that their efforts would not be in vain because he was here now to change things and to ensure that the British forces in the desert would now get everything they needed to secure a victory under their new Commander, General Montgomery, who had just arrived in the desert. As I mentioned previously, General Montgomery did indeed secure that victory over Rommel at the Battle of Alamein and that proved to be the turning point of WW2. I was proud of my workshop's contribution to the victory that the RAF had helped to achieve through their air superiority. In the 1943 New Year's Honours List I was awarded the M.B.E., (Member of the Order of the British Empire). This unexpected honour came as a most pleasant surprise. At the same time I felt a touch of regret that my RAF personnel could not also be included and honoured for their successful work under very trying conditions. I considered that I owed my success in this project to their loyal conscientious application to demanding tasks for which most of them had no experience and very little training. On top of this they were working in an artificial environment in the Cave workshops where they never saw daylight and, worse still, they never saw the results of their labours in a completed aircraft or in any aircraft flying operation. And of course they were thousands of miles from home living in primitive conditions under canvas.

With these thoughts I pondered how I might in some small way recognise the contribution of my RAF personnel and give them some pleasurable memory of this occasion. I hit on the idea of organising some sort of communal outing for the whole of my British staff. I finally decided to take them all on a river trip down the Nile for about an hour and a half's run to a very pleasant green parkland picnic area at a barrage across the Nile which controlled the flow of the river. I approached the Depot Commanding Officer with my proposal and got his approval on condition that his Depot Adjutant should be a member of our party – which I presume was to keep an eye on the party from the discipline point of view. I then hired for the day a river ferry and crew that would comfortably take 50 or more people. In the depot was a small dance band group and I persuaded them to accompany us. Finally we organised beer etc. estimated to last us the day and food to provide a slap-up meal in the afternoon as we were sailing back from the barrage. So there we were, with live music and plenty of food and drink, cruising down the Nile in a really jolly atmosphere. It proved to be a most successful occasion which everyone enjoyed.

However, already this episode in my career was approaching its termination. Following the victory at El Alamein of course the tension in Egypt and the constant pressures of the past months subsided considerably. The requirements from my workshops were considerably reduced but suddenly there came an unexpected call on my manpower. An amphibious invasion of French North Africa (code-named 'Torch') by a combined American and British force under General Eisenhower had been carried out in November 1942. This combined force succeeded in establishing themselves in Oran, Casablanca and Algiers but were very soon in difficulties. The inexperience of the Americans in modern warfare at this time, particularly in amphibious operations, plus the inexperience of their commander, Eisenhower, who had held only staff appointments throughout his military career, showed up. Even such simple operations as their ship loading were not given proper planning supervision so that, at the moment when their invasion force went ashore, they found that equipment and supplies they needed immediately had been loaded in the bottom holds instead of the top ones where they could have been off-loaded at once. Sometimes equipment was landed on the wrong beaches leaving troops without their vehicles or their gear. So it sometimes took days to get at the stores or vehicles they needed. It was only due to the half-hearted opposition of the French and, in some cases, no opposition at all, that the invasion was able to make successful progress.

This delay gave the Germans time to get over the surprise attack and they very quickly organised counter attacks, flying reinforcements into Tunisia and carrying out heavy bombing attacks across the Mediterranean from Sicily using the Luftwaffe air forces which Hitler diverted from the Russian front.

In addition the American Air Force in the past had had no call for overseas operations and thus their maintenance and overhaul was based on technical support from their aircraft manufacturers' factories in the States. Their engineering staff had no organisation for the major repair or overhaul of their aircraft or its equipment when on an overseas operation. In the States if serious repair or overhaul work was needed the manufacturer took over. In the 'Torch' invasion that policy proved disastrous. If an aircraft engine developed a serious fault the engine was changed for a new one and the old one was thrown into the nearest ditch. Likewise with propellers and any major component – all were scrapped if defective. Thus, with the limited availability of new engines, propellers and spares generally in North Africa, the American Air Force there very soon had an enormous unserviceability factor with little prospect of getting supplies from the States. The invasion force was therefore at the mercy of the German Luftwaffe. In the comparatively short space of a few weeks the unserviceability factor was so high that a considerable number of their aircraft were grounded.

The combined forces were subject to massive air attacks from the German and Italian Air Forces flying from Italy and Sicily. These attacks became quite serious and the American Air Force supporting the invasion forces was in considerable difficulty, due to lack of replacement aircraft, spares etc. as mentioned above. I received instructions from our headquarters that I was to assist the Americans by sending a contingent of my key technical personnel to French North Africa to provide a technical service to form part of an engineering unit which was to be set up in the American zone similar to our own in the caves. In reluctant compliance I sent some of my best people who had been with me from the beginning and whom I never saw again. However it must be said that although the Americans were inexperienced they were fast learners, In particular we owe a tremendous debt to General Eisenhower for his great leadership talents and for his remarkable diplomatic skills. This fortunate feature was early demonstrated in the 'Torch' invasion of North Africa. Eisenhower very cleverly persuaded Admiral Darlan, the Vichy French Defence Minister, who was on an official visit to the colony, to defect to the Allies in North Africa. More than this he was successful in getting Admiral Darlan to bring pressure on the Vichy French leaders in North Africa to remain neutral and not attack the invading Allied forces. This was a tremendous advantage to the Allied forces in French North Africa since their long lines of communication and supply would be free from attack. In return for this arrangement with Darlan Eisenhower agreed to make him head of all civic affairs in the French North African colonies. Darlan was assassinated a few weeks later.

Eisenhower's talents as a clever diplomat and leader, already displayed to the Allies advantage in North Africa, was to prove again a vital asset when he was later

Supreme Commander of the 'Overlord' invasion of Normandy. In the handling of all the powerful disparate political and military factors concerning America and Great Britain and the various countries of the British Empire he showed amazing skill and diplomacy. By his great leadership talents he welded together the mightiest military invasion force in the history of the world and contributed to the defeat of one of the greatest military nations of the world.

From that time onwards I seemed to enter into a state of depression. I suppose the victory of El Alamein and the resulting relaxation of pressure caused a reaction. The adrenaline had stopped flowing and after more than three years of high tension living perhaps I was more tired than I realised. I pondered on the problem and tried to find a reason for my unhappy lack of interest in life in general. I had read somewhere that decaying teeth and gum pyorrhoea over the course of time could cause poisoning of the system. I thought perhaps this might be my trouble so I had an appointment with the young RAF dentist who had been attached to our unit. On examination of my dental condition he told me that I had a certain amount of decay in some of my top back teeth and there was a small amount of gum pyorrhoea. Stupidly, perhaps due to my depressed condition, I told this young dentist to take all the top teeth out. I thought that having a top and bottom denture of complete false teeth would be a good idea with no more tooth decay, no more toothache, no more fillings etc.

The dentist agreed to do as I requested although a more experienced dentist would probably have advised me that such extreme measures were not necessary and the teeth could have been saved. I was advised by a dentist friend later that the pyorrhoea could easily have been cured. My young dentist then told me he could not possibly take all my top teeth out at once because he had no anaesthetic equipment. He proposed to take out three teeth at a time with intervals of three weeks between extractions, using some drug the name of which I have forgotten. I can only remember that after each session I felt much pain and misery. One afternoon, after the third session, I came back to my office in the cave feeling terrible. I developed a shivering feeling of coldness and my Flight Sergeant was most concerned. He volunteered to go down to his tent in the valley below and bring me one of his heavy jackets as I had only a light drill summer jacket. He returned with his jacket, put it on my desk and resumed his work in the workshop. I put the jacket around my shoulders, feeling grateful for his kindness. Then, looking down, I saw, lumbering slowly across my desktop, a hug red bug!

Whilst I was somewhat taken aback by this unwelcome visitor I was not entirely shocked for bugs, lice and fleas were a common feature of life for my men in their tented living quarters in the sand of the valley below the caves. In fact, every Saturday morning was an official de-lousing time, when all the RAF personnel living in tents would take action to rid themselves of their loathsome companions. Those people lucky enough to have a real metal RAF issue bed would use blow lamps, running over all the joints and crevasses in the bed frame to burn up the eggs, bugs and lice that colonised these places. Those who were not privileged to possess a proper bed, and that was most of the lower ranks, for beds were in very short supply, would construct for themselves suitable sleeping accommodation from wooden boxes or other material which they obtained from the N.A.A.F.I. or other sources. These makeshift beds were burnt each week on a bonfire.

Our uniform in the summer was naturally shirt, shorts and woollen stockings. A walk from the tented area in the valley up to the caves would be sufficient to guarantee picking up one or two fleas in one's stockings. I had great trouble getting rid of fleas which invaded my car parked outside the cave. Other visitors of a more serious type frequented the tented area. An example of this was an amusing incident which occurred one night to our unit Adjutant, a Flight Lieutenant. He had had a jolly evening in our temporary mess bar and, a little the worse for wear, flopped onto his bed in his tent and, removing his top denture and dropping it in the sand, fell asleep. On waking the next morning he found his denture had been stolen and demolished by rats seeking to devour the bits of food sticking to it.

In late October 1944, having completed nearly five years service in Egypt, I was informed that I was posted back to the U.K. Sadly I relinquished my duties in the caves and wound up the tenancy of my flat, settled my affairs in Heliopolis and bade farewell to Mohammed, my manservant. On 1st November 1944, my kit and I were transported by lorry to a camp in the desert located some distance from Suez. This was a sort of holding centre or transit camp for RAF officers awaiting passage by sea in troopships. It was an entirely tented camp located in the open desert with a temporary hut arrangement for a mess, consisting of a bar and dining room. I found some 200 Australian Air Force officers in residence there when I arrived. They also had completed their tour of duty in the Middle East and were awaiting passage back to their own country. In fact, they had done almost twice their official tour of overseas duty, due of course to the exigencies of the Western Desert war and, finally, the Battle of Alamein. Furthermore I gathered they had been in these primitive camp conditions for some time awaiting a troopship to take them back to Australia.

In consequence these Australian officers were in a somewhat rebellious and bellicose mood. The Camp Commandant was an ambitious RAF Squadron Leader of Scottish Jewish origin who unfortunately had no idea of how to handle such a delicate psychological situation of irate Aussie officers and he was not popular with the Aussies. He was determined to make a name for himself in his role as Commandant and had successfully obtained authority for a permanent building to be erected in the Camp to be used as an Officers Mess.

Soon after I arrived the permanent building work was completed. This project being the pride and joy of the Camp Commandant, he gave instructions that his photograph was to be put up centrally on a notice board in the entrance hall, immediately facing the entrance, so that this was the first thing that one saw on entering the building. At lunch time on the official opening day of this new Mess the Australian officer contingent arrived and, seeing the photograph of the Commandant prominently displayed in the entrance hall, took umbrage at this egoistic gesture. They took down the photograph and tore it into little pieces which they deposited on the floor immediately below the notice board. They then stuck a penny stamp with

Egyptian Desert transit camp awaiting troopship to UK. Self on right

the King of England's head on it in the centre of the space where the photograph had been. When the Commandant arrived at the Mess for lunch he was of course furious. He declared publicly in the Mess that he knew it was the Australians who had done this 'shocking' deed and he would punish them. He then gave orders that the Mess bar must ration them to only one pint of beer that evening. To the Australian Air Force personnel such an order was sheer cruelty and not to be tolerated.

As a kind of camp celebration for the great event of the opening of the new Officers' Mess a dance had been organised, to be held in the only other permanent building in the camp. This was the N.A.A.F.I. The Commandant had of course supported this venture and had given approval to invitations being issued to the British nurses in a military hospital on the Suez Canal. Transport was provided for them and the Commandant had agreed to attend in his official capacity to present the prizes for various fun dances. The Australian officers had been banned from attending this celebration and had been confined to their tents. They knew of course that the Commandant would be attending the dance and had therefore together concocted a scheme to avenge themselves for the indignity they had suffered. In the evening they waited for him, keeping watch for his arrival in his huge Humber staff car. The Commandant duly arrived in the Humber which he parked outside the N.A.A.F.I. building. He then went into the dance, of course leaving his car unattended. In the darkness a long line of some hundred or so Australian officers crept up to the Humber staff car, climbed in, and urinated! Some urinated in the front section and some in the rear until the whole car was awash back and front in a nauseous evil smelling sea of urine.

The Commandant was somewhat displeased when he came out from the dance and found himself paddling in urine. Once again he vented his displeasure on the Australian officers, this time ordering them to be rationed to one pint of beer and confined to their tents in the evenings for 14 days. By this time tension in the camp had mounted to a very high pitch and I began to feel very uncomfortable, praying that my troopship would arrive soon so that I could turn my back on this unhappy paranoid atmosphere. I somehow thought it preferable to risk meeting up with some unfriendly German submarine on the high seas than to have to brave the dangers of these irate tough Australians in this desert camp.

About a week later, one very dark night, after the official camp 'lights out' had shut down the generators and thus extinguished all camp lighting the Australian officers moved silently to the area where the Commandant had his tent. Then, forming a huge circle surrounding the tent, they began circling it, chanting some peculiar Australian dirge. The Commandant was in his tent but took no notice whatever of the chorus of Australians until finally some idiot amongst them threw some burning material onto the tent which immediately caught fire and burned fiercely in the very dry climate. The Australians scattered in the darkness and the Commandant ran out of his burning tent which could not be saved. In the pitch-black darkness of the night nothing could be seen of the escaping mob.

The sequel to this shocking and deplorable situation I will never know because almost immediately following this episode I received my posting orders to join troopship HMT 'Orantes' sailing from Suez for Liverpool on 13th November 1944. My happy relief at turning my back on the sordid atmosphere of the transit camp then gave way to a certain amount of speculation when I was on board the troopship which was carrying several thousand troops returning to the U.K. It was a kind of fatalistic speculation on our chances of meeting up against German mines or German submarines on our long sea voyage through the Mediterranean and the Bay of Biscay, skirting the English Channel and then continuing up the West coast of England through the St. George's Channel and the Irish Sea to good old Blighty shores at Liverpool. We were lucky for we met no German submarines as the Germans at that moment were rather pre-occupied by the Allied invasion following D-Day in Normandy. However, in our journey we did meet up with one floating German mine as we were leaving the Bay of Biscay area and skirting the French coast. Fortunately our destroyer escort spotted it and we took avoiding action. We were then entertained to an afternoon of target shooting by our destroyers. We slowed and they circled the mine with sharpshooters, peppering it to destroy it. We arrived safely at Liverpool docks on 4th December 1944 after some two weeks sailing in dangerous waters. And so ended just under 5 years in the Land of the Pharaohs. Including my first tour of Egypt from October 1932 to June 1936 I had passed nearly nine years living in the valley of the Nile.

The Nile excursion – some of my men with self seated at the table with friends

Chapter 17

Return to England
Derwent V Jet Engine Overhaul Workshop
Project at St. Athan

In view of the fact that I had been nearly five years on overseas service without a break I was granted one month's leave. This I spent with my parents in Portsmouth during which time I received official instructions to report, on the conclusion of my leave, to Oxford University where an RAF Engineering Group Headquarters was in residence.

On New Year's Day 1945 I reported to 43 Group, RAF Maintenance Command and to my disgust, found the Headquarters, located in one of the Colleges, practically deserted except for a very young lady who was the duty W.A.A.F. officer. She kindly told me I had been demoted from acting Flight Lieutenant to Flying Officer with effect from 1st November 1944 when I vacated my post in Egypt and that I was now posted to the No. 49 Maintenance Unit (M.U.) at Faygate near Horsham. The following day on reporting there I found this to be a specialised unit which provided engineer officer inspectors who were on call to proceed to the site of any RAF aircraft which had crashed or been shot down. The inspector's function was first, to arrange for the removal of any bombs, explosives or weapons and all removable valuables such as watches, radio equipment etc. He then made a survey of the aircraft to determine the extent of any damage, and then arranged for an appropriate repair or write-off destination. Finally he would survey the location of the aircraft as regards movement and transportation from its crash or landing site to determine what manpower and type of transportation would be required to salvage the aircraft.

After a few weeks on this type of work I was asked to take charge of a small engineering maintenance detachment which was part of 49 M.U. but located at Redhill aerodrome, near London. This proved to be very interesting because it was located directly below the path of the German V1 and V2 bombs. In fact I believe it was probably on the Germans list of targets because a V2 rocket dropped very close to us; so close in fact that all the windows of my living quarters were smashed. After about six weeks or so turning aircraft out from periodic servicing the Commanding Officer at Faygate called me in and asked me if I would establish a new small specialised Engineering unit at Lasham aerodrome which is near Basingstoke. The C.O. said this unit was needed urgently to provide technical support for RAF fighter aircraft shot up in support operations for the invasion forces in France. The idea was that if the aircraft received bullet hole damage in low level combat strafing the

Germans it could fly back to England, landing on our aerodrome, and we would repair the damage. The aircraft could then go back into combat service with its squadron.

This system proved very successful and we were able to return quite a number of aircraft to squadron service after a few days work at our unit. A considerable number of my mechanics were W.A.A.F.s – young girls who had been trained by the RAF as engine or airframe mechanics. They proved to be very good and reliable technicians. One interesting aspect of this operation was concerned with the return of the finished aircraft after our repairs. The pilot that flew the damaged aircraft into my unit would of course not wait around but return to his squadron. When the aircraft repairs were completed it was necessary to arrange for it to be flown back to its squadron for further combat duty. In order not to divert fighter pilots from squadron operations a system was devised whereby one could ring up a special transport corps of women pilots. These ladies formed a pool of experienced ferry pilots who would be flown to various units needing a ferry pilot. They arrived in a transport aircraft and dropped off to take over the ferrying job. They were competent to fly any type of RAF aircraft including the most up-to-date and the most powerful fighters capable of speeds around 400 miles per hour or more.

I shall always remember one particular day we had just completed the repair of bullet holes in the tail of an all powerful rocket-firing Hawker Typhoon fighter aircraft with its 2200 horsepower engine able to fly at more than 400 m.p.h. I rang up the ferry pool of the Auxiliary Transport organisation requesting a ferry pilot to be made available to deliver this 'state of the art' latest fighter to its parent squadron. Very soon a transport aircraft landed near us and out jumped an elderly lady with all her flying gear plus seat parachute. She came over to my office and introduced herself as the ferry pilot to fly my Typhoon fighter to its home squadron. Whilst completing the paper work to hand over the aircraft to this lady we exchanged friendly conversation and, to my amazement, I discovered she was a 55 year old grandmother. After we had provided her with a cup of tea she went over to the relatively huge powerful fighter aircraft and had to be lifted up by my mechanics to get her foot on the step to get into the aircraft! But Boy! Did she know what she had to do! I'll say! Wham! everything executed in highly professional manner – engine started with ease and with a great roar ground tested, ready for take-off. Chocks away! and away indeed she went with a terrific roar and was airborne and out of sight within minutes!

Victory over Germany finally came with Hitler's suicide and the surrender of all the German armed forces facing the Allies and including the German navy. Victory of the Allies in Europe was officially declared on VE day 9th May 1945. On this day I allowed my entire staff at Lasham to take the day off so that they might participate in the tremendous celebrations that were being held nation-wide on this historic day and particularly in London. I remained at the unit to 'hold the fort', speculating on the wild parties that the radio news broadcasts were reporting and wondering what I was missing.

The requirement for my technical unit no longer existed and soon after we closed down. I was then posted to another specialised technical unit No. 218 M.U. at Colerne near Bath. Here I was given the task of designing and installing systems for incorporating electronic RAF navigation radar black boxes into captured German transport aircraft to enable them to be employed on RAF operations. During this time I was once again promoted to Flight Lieutenant but this time in substantive rank and not 'acting' as in my Egyptian post. Completing my work at Colerne I spent some time at a further couple of Maintenance Units until finally I was posted on 30th May 1946 to the large engineering depot, 32 M.U., at St. Athan near Cardiff in South Wales.

This Maintenance Unit consisted of large workshops and hangars carrying out complete overhauls and major repairs to a variety of aircraft. One huge workshop was concerned with the overhaul of the Rolls Royce Merlin aero engine. The wartime organisation for this Merlin engine establishment was still in operation. This meant that instead of the RAF Engine establishment at St. Athan being controlled by RAF Headquarters Maintenance Command the technical control was directly by Rolls Royce at Derby. As Officer in charge of this Merlin establishment I had to report directly to Rolls Royce. This cut out several layers of RAF authorities and was designed to speed up production and improve engine output. In consequence I had to attend a monthly production meeting at Rolls Royce Derby where my unit's production performance would be examined by the Rolls Royce hierarchy. Questions would be asked and explanations demanded if the production target figure of engine output had not been achieved. Various difficulties could cause embarrassing situations in which I sometimes found myself. It might be a bottle-neck resulting from a shortage of vital spare parts or a fall in manpower due to sickness or other

Meteor Jet fighter arriving for overhaul

Rolls Royce Derwent V jet engine test bench

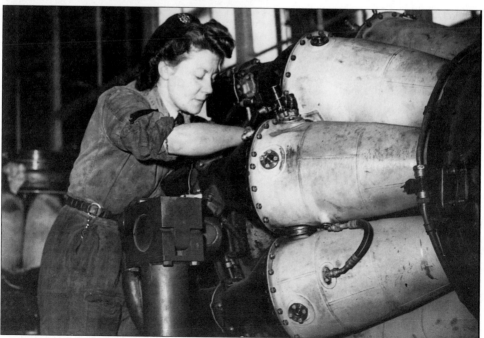

A WAAF mechanic working on the Rolls Royce Derwent V jet engine

reasons. Another reason was of an unusual local character. Due to the geographic situation in South Wales posting to RAF St. Athan was most Welshmen's greatest desire. There were in my workshop personnel a number of Welshmen from the Welsh valleys who had achieved this happy ambition by means of a 'compassionate posting'. This was an RAF system whereby an airman could apply for a desired posting if he could establish that there were important family sociological reasons that required his presence in the vicinity of his family. These Welsh valley personnel would receive their periodic 48-hour week-end pass, which permitted them to leave the unit on Friday evening. On Saturday morning some of them would sometimes go to their local doctor and for the fee of 2/6 (12$\frac{1}{2}$p.) would be provided with a doctor's certificate stating that they were unfit for travel. In consequence on Monday morning on my round of the shop-floor checking progress I would find here and there work at a standstill due to the absence of the operator from the Welsh valleys. On Tuesday morning the missing operator would appear fully fit and well – but my production target would be suffering.

After some time dealing with the production of the Merlin piston engines I was given a most interesting project where once again I had a free hand and large responsibilities. I was asked to create a comprehensive jet engine overhaul organisation together with a jet engine test plant. The initial plan was to be based on the overhaul and testing of the Rolls Royce Derwent V jet engine, two of these being the power plants for the Gloster Mark 4 'Meteor' jet fighter aircraft. At that time the only existing jet engine overhaul organisation was at the Rolls Royce factory in Derby. So to Derby I went, to study the Rolls Royce Derwent jet engine and its overhaul techniques, which would be the subject engine in the St. Athan overhaul system. Here I spent some six weeks on their factory floor actually working on their engines and assisting in the engine testing in their test-houses. I found this to be the best way of acquainting myself with all the details of overhaul of the jet engines and their tooling requirements. Having pumped myself full of this specialised information I was co-opted to the staff engineers department at 43 Group Headquarters which was now located at Stanmore in North London. Here I had work to do on all the necessary planning and the provisioning of the specialised equipment and the test bench which would be required at St. Athan. It must be remembered that at this time in 1946 we in post-war Britain were suffering from an acute shortage of everything including food. The post-war shortages in some cases were worse than the wartime shortages. And this particularly applied to construction materials such as steel. The whole nation was in a mad rush to rebuild the economy and to change over from production on a war basis to peace-time manufacture in order to take advantage of the tremendous export opportunities that now existed, particularly in the motor car industry. So steel was rationed by the Ministry of Production and I needed steel in some quantity to build the test-bed and housing at St. Athan.

In consultation with Rolls Royce we worked out a design for the jet test section and the quantity of steel that would be needed. An application for steel was made to the Ministry and following an interview I had in Whitehall we were granted the necessary

The Author

The Author with his father

permit for our requirement. Having completed the planning work I returned to St. Athan to await the arrival of the tooling and test equipment and to supervise the establishment of the jet engine overhaul workshops and the construction of the jet engine test-house and test-bed. A contract had been placed with Rolls Royce to provide the necessary skilled labour to build the test-bed and install the system in our test-house. Basically the system consisted of a mobile cradle carrying the jet engine arranged so that the thrust from the jet would tend to drive the sliding cradle up against a pressure pad which would transmit this pressure hydraulically to a pressure gauge in the control cabin. The pressure gauge would be calibrated in pounds thrust giving a read-out of the engine power being developed by the engine on test.

One problem that had to be solved in the jet engine test-house was how to dispose of the jet stream efflux when the engine was running. The efflux consisted of very high temperature gases which were the result of the combustion of the paraffin type fuel and hot air being driven rearwards at high temperatures and tremendous pressures and velocity. This constituted a seriously dangerous area and of course an extremely dangerous environment. The problem was solved by manufacturing a long tail pipe which was the diameter of the engine jet-pipe. This tail-pipe was about 30 feet long and carried the jet efflux from the engine jet-pipe through a hole we knocked in the test-house wall to the outside and away to waste ground.

Once the test-house, test-bed and the various controls and measuring systems were completed a test engine, to be used as a calibration power plant, was received from Rolls Royce. This jet engine had been tested by Rolls-Royce and thus all its functional parameters such as thrust, temperatures, pressures, etc., were known and could be used as a measure of the performance of our own test system. The engine was installed and the controls connected up to the control cabin, a Rolls-Royce engineer being present to certify its performance on our test-bed. I shall always remember the anxious moment when we were gathered in the control cabin and the engine starting procedure was set in motion. Would it start? Would it blow up? Would it give the power readings on the instrumentation of the control panel? Would it catch fire? Was the efflux tail pipe secure?! These anxious speculations were not unfounded because Rolls-Royce themselves had had many difficulties and upsets in the development of their jet engine overhaul programme. In fact they had one fatality in their jet engine test-house. At the time of this accident the jet efflux tail-pipe which extended through to the outside area had been designed to allow an air-gap between the jet engine pipe and the efflux tail-pipe to permit air cooling of the jet-stream. One tester inspecting the jet engine whilst it was running had failed to button up his dust-coat. As he worked close to the tail-pipe the tremendous suction caused by the air drawn through the gap into the tail-pipe caught one flap of his coat, spun him round out of control and sucked him into the tail-pipe, from which he emerged with his face burned away and so severely burned generally that he died very soon afterwards. The tail-pipe design was then modified to reduce the air-gap so that the gap would be too small to permit the entry of a human body.

The starter motor whirled and whirled, it seemed forever! Then Woof!! She was away! Screaming as the revolutions mounted, screaming to the warming-up regime and then settling, still screaming, at a constant r.p.m. With ear mufflers on we moved into the test-house to check over the jet engine as it was running to make sure that nothing was wrong with the installation. Then back to the control cabin to commence the calibration, testing through the entire operational regimes. Perfect!! With a tremendous sigh of relief I was able to report to the authorities that our jet engine testing system had passed all the testing requirements and had been certified by Rolls Royce.

During this time I was also setting up the jet engine overhaul workshops. This required the installation of various component test rigs and of an extremely sensitive electronic balancing rig which was necessary to obtain perfect static and dynamic balance of the compressor rotor and turbine shaft assembly. When all this was completed I was requested to write a technical official RAF manual which would give the whole overhaul procedure in detail, to be used in the training of jet engine overhaul mechanics of the future.

Chapter 18

Staff Post in Air Ministry London and my Divorce

Personal Staff Officer to Director General of Technical Services

Shortly after the completion of the St. Athan assignment I was posted to the Air Ministry as a staff officer in the RAF Technical Planning Directorate of the Ministry. On 7th February 1949 I arrived at Princes House, Kingsway, London. Here was located the Government Directorate whose responsibility was the formation of policy and direction of the technical services for the RAF I was allotted the staff appointment of Tech. Plans 3 and a squadron leader and myself constituted a team to study specialist technical requirements that could be needed in the RAF ten years hence.

When I joined the Directorate the emergency Berlin airlift was in full swing at a very high intensity, requiring exceptional technical support and resources. To help provide these exceptional requirements we were required to give assistance to the operational units. The airlift had commenced in the previous June 1948 when the Russians had blockaded all land and water access routes to Berlin. These routes all had to pass through Russian controlled areas of Germany.

The Russians were quite confident that they could block any Allied surface access to Berlin by force if necessary. This Russian confidence was possibly justified for the Allies had carried out an enormous demobilisation of their armed forces following the ending of hostilities against the Germans and against the Japanese. The Russians had maintained their military war strengths and they did not believe the two million people in the Allied controlled sectors of a huge city such as Berlin with all its requirements of food, fuel, etc. could be supplied by air transport. They were quite prepared to provoke a World War 3 which they believed they could win.

However, to the amazement of the Russians, the Allied Air Forces combined together with all available civil air transport and provided the famous Airlift which developed to such efficiency that Berlin was supplied daily with enough to sustain the city during its long siege.

In fact, at the height of the Airlift in May 1949, 2000 tons of food, coal etc. was delivered daily. To accomplish this tremendous task aircraft were taking off day and night in Allied territory at the continuous rate of one every minute. Total deliveries of food, coal and general supplies amounted to 2,325,000 tons which were carried in 276,926 sorties.

Thus airpower had achieved another remarkable contribution to world peace by defeating the evil intentions of the Russians, The Berlin Airlift ended in May 1949 when the Russians lifted their blockade. However the Allies continued their Airlift until 30th September 1949 to ensure a build-up of adequate reserves.

After the excitement of the Berlin Airlift my first task was to carry out research and write a paper on the specialised technical equipment that would be needed to make operational squadrons completely air-mobile. Up to that time operational squadrons on the move were only partially air-mobile. The aircrew could be moved in the squadron aircraft, but the ground crew and their tools and equipment had to be moved by road transport. With the development of modern aircraft the requirements of specialised equipment had grown tremendously. In addition the huge increase in the size of modern aircraft, especially transport aircraft, called for very large inspection platforms and ladders. Sometimes, for instance, rudders of transport aircraft might be some 30 feet above ground level. With the planned objective of making all operational squadrons completely air-mobile the first requirement was specialised military transport aircraft that could uplift the entire ground-crew and all their equipment, plus all the fundamentals to provide the administrative back-up. Secondly, the specialised tooling and equipment such as platforms and ladders etc. had to be designed to fit into the transport aircraft.

My task was first to discover what capacity could be available in the military transport of ten years hence and then to consider the design of maintenance equipment that could be carried within this projected capacity. I found this work extremely interesting, involving liaison with other Government departments and many visits to manufacturers.

Of course my own personal way of life changed considerably following my move to London. As a staff officer in the London Air Ministry I was not a member of any unit or operational squadron and thus I had no mess or RAF sleeping quarters. I was expected to find my own accommodation for which I received an additional allowance to my normal pay. In addition staff officers in the Ministry did not wear uniform except when visiting RAF stations on official duty. One was expected to wear a dark city type suit and a bowler hat which were the standard 'uniform'. This together with a rolled umbrella completed the 'city gent' disguise. I believe the idea behind this dress convention was based on security whilst travelling to and from the Ministry. For the first few months I stayed at the flat of a friend in Hatch End in North London but I found the travelling times a nuisance. Finally I discovered that there was a specialised RAF unit at Kidbrook in South East London which accepted 'guest officers' from Air Ministry and provided them with accommodation if they had a vacancy. I contacted the Commanding Officer of this unit and was fortunate to be accepted as a resident paying guest. This change of my circumstances was to have a profound effect on my whole future life for, in travelling to and fro from Kidbrook to my office in London, I eventually met my future wife Pam.

Working in the heart of London with all its adult education facilities I decided to take the opportunity to make a serious study of the French language. I had a typical English schoolboy's knowledge of French grammar but my ear had been very much attuned to French pronunciation as my first wife and her brothers were educated in French and spoke French fluently. For the first year I enrolled for a night-school course at the Regent Street Polytechnic and made rapid progress. I took the City and Guilds Certificate and passed quite comfortably. The second year I decided to go for a degree in the French language and enrolled for the inter-degree course at a Poly in the Camden Town area. In addition, to concentrate my studies I enrolled at Princeton College in Holborn to take the examination for membership of the Institute of Linguists. This was a professional qualification for which I failed the first year. I re-sat the exam. in the second year and was successful. To obtain conversational practice I joined the London Linguists Club whose premises were near Hyde Park Corner. Here one could join in conversational groups in the language one was studying. It was a club rule that one could open conversation with any other club member without introduction if the subject was language study. I often passed my Saturday afternoons in this way, and again this was to prove a very significant factor affecting my future life.

Whilst I was working at the Ministry in early 1951 a visitor was escorted to my office, who handed me an official looking letter. He turned out to be a solicitor's clerk representing a firm of solicitors in Portsmouth. These people were acting for my wife's family and the letter handed to me suggested a divorce to be arranged by myself as the 'guilty' partner, in return for which they undertook to make no financial claims whatever. They would make no maintenance claim provided I agreed the two children were to be in the sole custody of my wife and I would have no access whatever. After serious consideration I decided that the two children would have a much better future with my wife's family than that which I could provide. In fact this proved correct for they were both educated at Downside and both had very successful careers. The solicitors proposed a meeting at their offices in Portsmouth which I attended and accepted the conditions. I found myself a solicitor in Holborn who proved to be very efficient. I duly arranged the necessary evidence to prove my 'guilt' and whole thing went through very smoothly. I was officially divorced on 18th December 1951.

My daily routine at this time during my stay at the RAF Kidbrook Mess was to have breakfast in the Mess and then catch the train running into Kidbrook Station which was just outside the Mess. In fact, through the Mess window, we could see the train approach the station, and we would then run to catch it. This got me into London in time to be in my office by 9.30 a.m. There were several RAF staff officers lodging at Kidbrook so that each morning there would be the comical sight of several bowler hatted 'city gents' complete with rolled umbrellas running like fury out of this RAF Officers Mess to pile into the crowded train for Charing Cross. I went to night-school straight from my office round about 6 p.m. and after two or three hours at school I would catch a return train from Charing Cross Station in the Strand.

The French inter-degree class teacher at Camden Town Polytech was a grammar school master about my own age and after class we would often have a quiet drink together at a local pub. After one Friday evening class which finished at 9 p.m. we had our usual drink and I then decided to have supper at Lyons Corner House in the Strand and catch the last train from Charing Cross instead of going straight back to Kidbrook. The last train to Kidbrook was around midnight and did not stop at Kidbrook so I had to alight at Blackheath, the station before Kidbrook. From Blackheath station to get to Kidbrook one had to walk across Blackheath common which at that hour was pitch black, unlit and very solitary. As I set out across the common I became aware of a young lady nearby heading in the same direction. It was evident we were going to the same place and we were the only human beings in evidence for miles around so we naturally spoke. We soon discovered we had a mutual interest in the French language for this young lady had only recently obtained an M.A. degree in the French and German modern languages at Edinburgh University. Due to our interesting conversation, we seemed to arrive very quickly at Kidbrook Park Road, in which we both lived. My mess was to the right and the young lady's house was to the left and so, wishing my companion a very good night I turned on my heel and departed to my mess.

The next morning when I awoke I recalled our meeting and pleasant companionship across Blackheath common in the dark hours of the early morning and I derided myself for not attempting to further the acquaintance by some kind of invitation to meet again. I thought 'What a fool! I met a very pleasant young lady with similar tastes to myself and I simply said 'good-night' and turned my back on her without asking if she would like to have dinner sometime or go to a show or even for a walk!!' Full of regrets and hoping that perhaps one day we might meet again on my daily journeys into London the memory gradually faded. Later in this story I will relate how three years later we did meet again in quite different and unusual circumstances.

After just over a year in my post of Technical Plans 3 I was asked if I would take on a much higher level post as personal staff officer to the Director General who was supreme head of the RAF Technical Services Air Ministry Directorate. The Director General was at that time Air Vice Marshal Pidcock who controlled four Directorates covering every aspect of the RAF technical services including technical officers' training and their careers. The whole of these Directorates' work requiring the Director General's approval was passed through my hands prior to presentation to him. I found myself in a vast new world operating in a capacity for which I had neither training nor experience. Moreover the RAF had just recently entered into the realms of nuclear war. In consequence, airborne nuclear weapons, fitment, maintenance and storage together with specialised university nuclear physics courses for engineer officers and ground staff handling the bomb, became a responsibility of the Director General. This, coupled with a delicate problem of personalities in the Director General's office made life somewhat difficult.

In the D.G.'s outer office was myself as P.S.O. (Personal Staff Officer) covering

Air Vice Marshall Pidcock, Director General of RAF Technical Services at Air Ministry

all the RAF technical aspects of the D.G.'s work and also a P.A.(Personal Assistant) who was a Ministry lady civil servant covering all his secretarial work. This lady and the D.G. had been working together for some considerable time before I arrived and their relationship had become a subject of speculation in the Ministry. To complicate matters further the lady in question had allowed her close relationship with the D.G. to go to her head so that she had an unenviable reputation in the Directorate of 'wearing her master's cloak'.

My own work consisted of receiving the various papers and studies forwarded from the four Directorates to the D.G. After digesting their contents I would then collate and flag for ease of reference all the referred publications, bibliography, papers, or other references quoted in the work being submitted to the D.G. As I shared an office with the lady P.A. I was consequently within earshot of occasional episodes which were not part of the official day's work. In addition I felt that my presence in the office was to some degree resented by the lady and my every move was reported to the D.G., particularly if it could be criticised. Obviously in my early days in this post such occasions for criticism did arise and I felt the full weight of the Air Vice Marshal's stringent authority. And indeed he was a strict disciplinarian with a very strong character. Thanks to the lady P.A. I once received such a dressing down that I feared he might throw me through his office window. As we were five floors high, level with the top of the theatre opposite in Kingsway and with only the roof pigeons as our neighbours, this feeling was quite alarming. But nevertheless it was an extraordinary experience from which I benefited in many ways, if only in learning to absorb and retain what I read! I certainly learnt to think and to think logically and to express my thoughts concisely and clearly. I am happy to relate that in spite of my early fumbling I achieved a good relationship with the D.G. and was successful in earning his respect and commendation. One of several important assignments for which I was responsible during my tenure of this post was organising a top level conference at RAF station Halton, near Wendover, of all the Commanders in Chief of the RAF Bomber, Fighter, Coastal and Maintenance Commands. The conference was convened to discuss the proposed restructuring of the Technical Services of the RAF

At this time whilst still at the Air Ministry I began to have ambitions to continue my RAF staff career following my Air Ministry tour of duty. I hoped to achieve this by obtaining a staff appointment in the Western European Union (W.E.U.) headquarters which were located in Paris. I felt that if I could obtain a reasonably high qualification in the French language it would improve my chances of being selected for a post in the W.E.U. headquarters. It was for this reason that I was pursuing a very strenuous programme of French language study at various London night schools.

However my plans for my future were changed when Air Vice Marshal Pidcock was retired and A.V. M. Bilney took over the post as Director General of RAF Technical Services. For some three months I worked with Bilney to assist him in the introduction to his new post and he then informed me that my tour of duty at Air

Ministry was now completed and I could choose any station in the U.K. to which I would wish to be posted. I chose Hendon in North London as I wished to continue my French language studies at my London night school.

I arrived at the RAF station in Hendon in August 1951 and took over the post of Station Engineer Officer responsible for some fifty aircraft flying Air Ministry V.I.P.s around Europe. Soon after my arrival I received a letter from Air Ministry stating that my existing commission was confirmed but my promotion ceiling would be limited to squadron leader and my retirement would be at the age of 55 years. However if I did not accept this offer I would be permitted to retire at the age of 46 having completed 30 years service – which is exactly what I did. I rejected the idea of a future career in the Service of just over a further ten years with no prospect of promotion beyond Squadron Leader. I mentally rejected this ruling limiting my career prospects to a maximum ceiling only one step above my existing rank. Such a prospect was monotonous and boring and I decided that after 30 years service and before it was too late I would taste life in the outside civilian world and take my chance at the age of 46, come what may! By my decision to leave the service I met my wife and have a happy family life. I have been able again to successfully overcome challenges in many parts of the world. In partnership with my wife I have achieved a comfortable and secure financial position far superior to that which I could have expected from remaining in the service. And I have moved in both technical and social levels superior to what I could have expected had I remained in the Service.

During the last couple of months of my Royal Air Force service I witnessed a tragic accident which gave me considerable concern, not only for the death of a personal friend, which was devastating, but also with regard to my technical responsibilities as the Engineer Officer at Hendon. My unfortunate friend was one of our few station pilots with a 'green ticket' which at that time meant he was qualified for all weather instrument flying. This was a very important qualification at Hendon because the station was situated in a kind of saucer or basin surrounded by a very dense built-up area comprising many thousands of houses, all polluting the atmosphere with coal fires for central heating had not yet arrived in England and coal fires were almost universal. Due to its position in the saucer it was subject to low-lying smog and fog which often persisted throughout the morning. The demands on our aircraft by Air Ministry V.I.P.s and others were sometimes of an urgent nature so that the aircraft would be forced to take off in bad visibility in which only 'green ticket' pilots were qualified to operate.

One morning a particularly dense fog overhung the aerodrome and my friend was detailed to fly some V.I.P.s to Germany. He took off in one of our very ancient Anson aircraft in nil visibility and had gained height to around 2000 feet when one engine failed. The failed engine shed a cylinder which dropped into a householder's garden in Edgware. No-one was injured but my friend knew that this ancient Anson aircraft could not maintain height on the remaining one engine. He immediately radio-ed emergency 'Mayday' and asked permission to land at Northolt aerodrome which was only two or three miles as the crow flies. Unfortunately the fog conditions were extensive over the whole area and our pilot's request to land at Northolt was refused by air traffic control on the grounds of danger to the densely built-up area surrounding Northolt. Instead he was directed to attempt to fly to Luton airport which had no surrounding densely built-up area. However Luton was a considerable distance away and the Anson was slowly losing height so that it was doubtful whether he could make it. He was in constant communication with our own control tower who sent an urgent message for the Station Commander advising him of the crisis. The C.O. rushed up to the control tower and spoke to the Anson. He then sent for me to see if anything could be done to help. It was a dreadful experience for both of us to be talking to the doomed pilot as the aircraft slowly lost height in its endeavour to reach Luton airport. Fog covered the whole of the area so that the pilot was flying 'blind'. He almost made it to the airport but by the sheerest bad luck when over Luton Hoo Park, just adjacent to Luton airport, he collided with the top of a very tall tree and went straight in nose first. The machine immediately burst into flames. As soon as we lost communication the C.O. and I rushed down from the control tower and into his staff car. We headed out to Luton and arrived at Luton Hoo to see the aircraft still burning in a huge pit that the aircraft had made. It was a horrible, shattering sight for which we could do nothing. The police and fire-fighters were in charge and doing their best but the situation was beyond help.

As I said previously I was very worried that the engine failure might have been caused by a technicality for which I could be held responsible. However the defective cylinder with its piston which had fallen into the garden at Edgware was handed into the police who passed it back to Hendon. The defective Cheetah engine with its missing cylinder and piston was passed back to the manufacturers, Armstrong Siddeley, for a report to the official enquiry. To my great relief Armstrong Siddeley reported that the engine failure was due to a collapsed piston in the fractured cylinder due to material fatigue which was a defect known to the manufacturer. Why a modification to the piston had not been introduced I will never know. Perhaps the Authorities considered that such an obsolete aircraft was due to be scrapped and did not warrant such expenditure.

This unhappy event brought sadness to the closing days of my Service life. About a week before my retirement the C.O. of Hendon sent for me. He said that he had just heard that I was about to retire at the comparatively young age of forty five and a half. Then the following conversation took place:-

C.O. How long have you been in the Service?

Self. Thirty years.

C.O. What! You are going to throw over thirty years' service. Have you got a job to go to?

Self. No, Sir.

C.O. Then why are you sacrificing thirty years for a sheer gamble?

Self. Because the whole of my adult life has been spent in the RAF way of life and I would like to experience civil life before I am too old to get a job.

C.O. What kind of a job do you hope to get?

Self. I am a qualified aeronautical ground engineer. I hope to get something in Civil Aviation.

C.O. Have you any contacts?

Self. No, Sir.

C.O. I would like to help you. I tell you what! It is against RAF Kings Rules and Regulations to give references but you go and tell my adjutant to type out what you might wish to put into a reference that will assist you in getting a job and tell him to bring it to me and I will sign it.

Self. That should be a great help. Many thanks indeed, Sir.

Chapter 19

My Retirement from the RAF
I join the de Havilland Engine Company, Leavesden

On my last night the Officers' Mess dined me 'out' and I gave a farewell speech after dinner. Armed with my C.O.'s reference in the year 1953 I left my Service life forever and went back to the place from where I had started my RAF service as a boy apprentice at Cranwell at the age of just under 16 in 1923. My father having recently died I went back to my widowed mother's home in Portsmouth to face my new world of civilian life. The first few weeks at home passed something like a dream. I somehow could not come to terms with the fact that I no longer had Service responsibilities. I would wake up in the mornings and anxiously start wondering if I should be attending some parade or some meeting or carrying out some duty or other. I took myself for long walks along the sea-front and got bored for I met only elderly pensioners doing the same thing and I began to realise that people of my age or younger were all busy somewhere doing a job of some kind. With that realisation I decided it was about time that I started looking for a job. So I began to read the job vacancy columns of the newspapers. One day I saw that the de Havilland Engine Company was advertising for service engineers. I wrote applying for such a job but got no reply nor even an acknowledgement of my letter. This experience was a little depressing and I thought that perhaps I should look for any other job that might be going.

A week or so later I saw that the same Company was advertising for technical authors for their publishing department. Having had quite a lot of experience writing technical reports and actually having written the RAF repair manual for Rolls Royce Derwent jet engine overhaul, I thought I would have a go at this job seeing that the de Havilland Engine Company was not interested in my engineering qualifications. I had a reply to my letter of application almost by return and I was invited for an interview in London at the de Havilland Engine Co. offices in Stag Lane, Burnt Oak, near Hendon. There I met the head of the Publishing Department and after the interview I was informed that I certainly would be offered the job but there were several more applicants to be interviewed before the formal official offer could be made. To cut a long story short, I joined the de Havilland Engine Company as a technical author and wrote a manual for them on testing their engines. The de Havilland Engine Company Service Engineers Department discovered my presence in the Company, apologised for their lack of response to my first application and, after some four months, I transferred to the Engineers.

This transfer in January 1954 when I became a new member of the de Havilland Engine Company Service Department at Leavesden resulted in a revolutionary change to my whole life. Very soon after my arrival at Leavesden which is near Watford I was informed by the assistant manager that my first appointment would be in Jakarta, capital of Indonesia. I had not the faintest idea where Jakarta was, it being a re-named city in one of those re-named third world countries which, in the post war years, had gained their independence. I soon found out that the former name was Batavia but even then I had only a vague idea that Batavia was in the former Dutch East Indies.

Seeing my bewildered reaction, the assistant manager advised me to take a look at an up-to-date map of the Far East. He then went on to brief me on my new appointment. He said that the Company had just recently sold 14 de Havilland Heron 17-seater aircraft to the newly nationalised Indonesian airline. The airline was called 'Garuda', the name of a mythical bird, which is the country's national symbol, an all-powerful protective bird and part of the Indonesian religion. These new de Havilland Heron aircraft were now used by 'Garuda' airways as a scheduled interior service 'island hopping' between the numerous islands which constitute the archipelago of Indonesia. Java is one of the largest islands, about 600 miles long and averaging around 100 miles wide, covering some 51,000 square miles. It is one of the most densely populated islands in the world with a population at that time of some 90 million people. Now it has a population of 107 million. Most are Muslims and at that time it was a Communist state. Its western island neighbour is Sumatra which is the largest island in the archipelago but not nearly so developed or so densely populated. At the eastern tip of Java, separated by a narrow channel, is the internationally well-known small island of Bali.

De Havilland Heron aircraft as operated by Garuda Indonesian Airways

The D.H. 114 Heron aircraft used by Garuda for the 'Island Hopping' service was a development of a scaled up design from the original successful D.H. Dove aircraft. The Heron was a four-engined transport. The power plant was four D.H.Gypsy Queen 30 in-line piston engines each producing 250 horsepower. It had a cruising speed of 183 m.p.h. at 8,000 ft. with a service ceiling of 18,500 ft. and a range of 915 miles. It proved to be a highly successful aircraft in its class with simplicity and reliability being very attractive features.

The assistant manager told me that in view of the large size of this contract the Company had sent out a young service engineer to be resident with Garuda in Jakarta for a year. Garuda had decided to set up their own overhaul and repair workshop for the de Havilland Heron Engines and the de Havilland resident representative was to advise on the operation, overhaul, and repair procedures. The key posts in Garuda were at that time still held by the Dutch with Indonesian understudies. It would appear that the de Havilland service engineer working with Garuda in Jakarta was inexperienced in dealing with overseas organisations. Furthermore he was somewhat opinionated and dictatorial and in consequence lacking in diplomacy. He was a very good engineer and certainly very well informed but due to this shortcoming in his character, he upset the Dutch engineers by insisting that they should do exactly as he advised. One day he discovered that the Dutch had done things differently to his advice and he lost his temper. Unfortunately he became somewhat personal, calling the Dutch engineers 'Bloody square heads'. Naturally the Dutch objected to this treatment and the outcome was that the Dutch Chief Engineer had cabled the de Havilland Engine Company requesting them to recall their service engineer. And this is where I came in! The Company wanted me to take over the Garuda Airways post and restore the good name of de Havillands by promoting peace and harmony as well as giving good technical advice and assistance to the Garuda technical staff. This was a somewhat daunting prospect but the Company gave me the opportunity to inform myself of the technicalities of the de Havilland Queen 30 series of engines fitted to the Heron aircraft. My department immediately applied to the Indonesian embassy in London for my visa and met with the delays which were usual with Communist countries. In the meanwhile I visited various manufacturers of the ancillary equipment fitted to the Heron engine such as Lucas etc. and spent a considerable amount of time in the de Havilland Engine Company factory studying various overhaul and testing procedures.

At this point an event occurred which changed my life forever. I had continued my membership of the London Linguists Club and often spent my Saturday afternoons visiting the club which was near Hyde Park Corner. As I was to reside in Indonesia for some time I decided to study the Indonesian language and hoped to find someone at the Club who might help me. I bought a 'Teach Yourself' book on the language and one Saturday afternoon went to the Club complete with this book and settled down to do a little studying. I was sitting in the company of several people and next to me was a young lady who could see the title of the book I was reading. She remarked to me that it was an unusual language I was studying. I agreed and explained my reasons for studying 'Bahasa Indonesia'. We continued our interesting conversation and finally I suggested that she might like to join me for a drink at a local pub. One could only obtain soft drinks and coffee at the Club. She agreed, and off we went, spending a pleasant couple of hours or so together until finally she said it was time for her to return home. I had my car parked at the Club so I offered her a lift home. She said she lived in Blackheath. I asked 'Which part of Blackheath?' She replied 'Kidbrook Park Road'. With a sudden inspiration I looked at her and said 'Did you walk across Blackheath common at midnight with an RAF officer three years ago?' By an amazing coincidence in a city of eight million people we had met again in entirely different circumstances. I was no longer in the RAF and Pam was no longer working at Harrods. In fact she was using her languages working for Cooks travel agency during the summer whilst filling in the winters doing supply teaching. The reason we did not immediately recognise each other was due to the fact that our midnight walk across Blackheath had been in total darkness. We thus could not see each other's faces clearly and after three years one's faint recollection of that passing moment tends to fade.

Needless to say, I was determined that this time I was not going to let this opportunity pass me by as I had done at our first meeting. I drove the young lady home and arranged a rendezvous the following day. From then on we saw each other quite frequently. My visa for Indonesia had still not come through and Easter was approaching. The Company asked me to do an urgent job for them in France whilst awaiting my visa. It appeared that the French nationalised airline was using de Havilland aircraft for internal schedules and had set up their own engine overhaul establishment near Rouen. They were experiencing problems on their engine bench testing for which they could not find a solution and so they sought our Company's advice. The Company asked me if I would go over there and sort out their problems for them. I told Pam I would be off to France for a short time after Easter. By another remarkable coincidence Pam told me that she had arranged with Erna Low Travel Agency to act as courier to a group of tourists, the majority of whom were elderly and female, visiting Paris over the long Easter week-end. I said in that case I could bring forward my departure for France to coincide with her timetable and we could meet up in Paris. The Company agreed to my earlier departure, before Easter instead of after, and off I went on my romantic trip with all expenses paid by de Havillands!

Pam and I met up in Paris and I spent my Easter weekend tagging along with the English tourist sightseers and of course in the constant company of the official guide – my charming girl friend. We organised Pam's tourist crowd so that they were finally dumped each evening in a suitable restaurant and, having carefully given them directions on how to get back to their hotel, we bade them 'Good night' and off we went for the start of our own nightly excursion, which was invariably to the Left Bank, to the Latin Quarter of the city or to Montmartre where we excitingly set out to 'paint the town red'. We first commenced operations by finding a suitable restaurant in Montmartre for an evening meal and from there on we hit the night spots, sometimes dancing in some low dive cellar and sometimes in a night club. One amusing incident occurred when we selected what appeared to us a very suitable restaurant for an evening meal. We opened the door of the restaurant and, on entering, were immediately greeted by a loud chorus of welcome from the other diners – in French of course. It was a new experience for us. We had unknowingly chosen what the Parisians call a 'chansonnier' restaurant. Here, with your meal, there is a continuous singsong accompanied by a live band. The French songs are well known, often of a local nature, and one condition for getting your supper is that you have to sing for it! And so the announcer went round with a microphone from table to table for each song until it was our turn. I had to perform! The compère explained to the diners that I was English and was unable to give them a French song but he said I could give them a song in English. I had never in my life sung in public and never to a French public audience but nevertheless there was no choice if we were to have any supper! Swallowing my embarrassment and hoping the orchestra was clever enough to follow my song I burst forth with 'Daisy, Daisy, give me your answer do'. I sung it in a kind of lilting manner with repetition so that the orchestra quickly picked up the tune and apparently the French diners seemed to have some knowledge of the English song so that very soon the whole restaurant was roaring out the tune with great gusto. We got our supper!

And then came the crunch moment on the final evening fling. We had both obviously enjoyed our Paris weekend and regretted that it was now coming to an end. We were seated 'tête a tête' in a pleasant quiet restaurant when 'out of the blue' I popped the question 'Will you marry me?' Somewhat shocked by this sudden, unexpected and startling situation Pam remained silent for a short time whilst she gathered her thoughts. Then, desperately seeking to consider this new turn of events, she told me that she would have to think this question over when she returned to England and, in any case, it would be something on which she would have to consult her parents. To me this was quite understandable for, during the course of the hectic evenings in Paris, I had given her a completely frank outline of my own background, including my previous marriage and divorce. It must be remembered that the class distinction of the old Victorian social order which I have mentioned previously in connection with my father's early life was still prevailing at this time. Certainly there was evidence of the dilution of these social barriers but the social revolution of the 'permissive society' had not yet arrived. Pam had indicated that her father was from a very ancient county family and her Scottish mother was the daughter of a minister of religion.

But not only was there the problem of social status which at that time mattered greatly, but also Pam had to take into account several other adverse factors which would certainly upset her parents and destroy their hopes and expectations for the future of their only child. One, of course, was the disparity of our ages, my being nearly 20 and a half years older than her. The other, equally serious, was the fact that I was a divorcee which was again considered a disqualification by the social standards of that time. And, to add a further unhappy factor to an already complicated situation this almost unknown and unsuitable man was suggesting that the marriage of their only child should take place in Indonesia with no friends or relatives in attendance on the other side of the world almost 9000 miles away and that she would be living in some primitive remote Communist country, to which they could never hope to travel. The prospect of their daughter travelling alone to the ends of the earth to rendezvous with a man of whom they had practically no knowledge and who would then have their daughter at his mercy, was a completely shattering blow giving rise to great misgivings as to the viability of such a plan.

Pam's father, Richard John Sacheverell Bateman, was the last of a line of an ancient Derbyshire county family who had been at one time wealthy landowners, many of them titled. Though somewhat impecunious and, having failed to achieve what would be expected of someone with his intelligence and educational background (Marlborough and Kings College, Cambridge), he was nevertheless extremely conscious of his social background and maintained a rigid Victorian attitude of class distinction. Her mother was a Scot, the youngest of thirteen children of Alexander Stewart, the minister of a Scottish kirk in Aberdeen. He had also acquired the title of Doctor of Medicine by virtue of a correspondence course with an American university. This gave him the credentials to set up a hydropathic establishment or sanatorium on Deeside which provided spa facilities including thermal spa baths for patients with or without diseases of various types. This was a fashionable custom in those times and still is on the Continent. As was usual in Scotland at that time his family was brought up in a severe puritanical atmosphere. Pam's grandfather had published several tomes on religious subjects and was very popular with his parishioners. The press reported that at his funeral the cortege was followed by over 200 carriages. Pam's mother, who always called herself Laurie although she had been christened Annie, was also very conscious of social status and this was considerably augmented by her pride in her husband's background pedigree although she was obviously disappointed by his lack of success in life.

Our exciting weekend of 'painting the town red' in Paris now came to an end. Pam had to shepherd her flock of tourists back to London whilst I had to journey to Rouen to sort out the problems of the French SNECMA aeronautical engineers. In Pam's case she had to handle the problem of her shocked parents. In my case I had to handle the problem of the disgruntled French engineers who could not obtain their desired output from their overhauled de Havilland aero engines. I soon found out that my problems were fairly simple compared with those of Pam. On my arrival at the SNECMA workshops near Rouen I was immediately informed by the French engineers that, in spite of their strict compliance with, and conscientious following of the de Havilland piston engine overhaul techniques, their engines failed to produce the correct power output on their engine test bench. It was soon apparent to me that their test-fan had not been correctly calibrated. The test-fan is a kind of coarse wide blade propeller fitted to the engine on test and designed to provide a standard aerodynamic load at standard engine revolutions. By this standard loading the power output of the engine can be measured accurately. With the French problem the answer was merely the setting up of a factory calibrated engine obtained from de

Havillands and then fitting the French test fan and calibrating this to provide a future 'bench-mark' or test standard by which they could measure the output of their overhauled engines. After three weeks work with the French and having successfully solved their problem I returned to England. It had been an interesting experience of living in a French village at that time. Everything closed down from 8 o'clock in the evening. Every house was shuttered and the village was dead. The only life in the village was in a couple of bars where the local village men gathered. No females were ever present. My French engineer colleagues often took me with them to the livelier evening life in the nearby city of Rouen.

Back at the de Havilland factory I arranged another visit to one of our factories near Chester and it was during my stay here that the Leavesden factory sent a message saying that my visa for Indonesia had come through. Returning rapidly to Leavesden I then met Pam and she told me that her problem had not yet been solved. She had no answer to my proposal. I told her my visa had come through and time was running out – not only for me, but for her also since the date for her summer contract with Cooks was due to start very soon. She was to go to Switzerland and reside there looking after Cooks' clients on package tours to Lugano. This job would last through the season till early October.

After another interval in which Pam and her parents went through an agonising period of discussions and crises my proposal of marriage was finally accepted. I was received by Pam's parents and had a formal meeting with her father to ask for his assent. At this meeting my own impecunious situation was laid bare and grudging permission was given subject to my 'waking up' to the future financial implications of my proposed married status. To cover this and provide at least some security I was required to take out a life insurance – a thing I had never bothered with up to that date. As may be imagined I very promptly complied with this condition.

From this moment onwards life was just a mad rush for both Pam and myself. So little time was left to make all the necessary arrangements for departure to our new jobs and so little time was available to announce and celebrate our engagement. As for our marriage plans to take place when Pam had completed her summer season's contract with Cooks in Switzerland, we could only agree that she would join me in Indonesia. Exactly how was in the lap of the Gods – the Far East Gods! Yet, when one looks back to those days, it was with amazing calm and 'sang froid' that we both accepted that we would meet up some 9000 miles away, some time during next November in some seven months time just as though we were arranging to meet up next week!

We met and rapidly chose and bought the engagement ring with only 48 hours remaining before Pam's departure for Switzerland. Thus our engagement party was the next day with just the two of us having a dinner dance at the Orchard Hotel in the area of Northolt. I was not to see her again for another eight months.

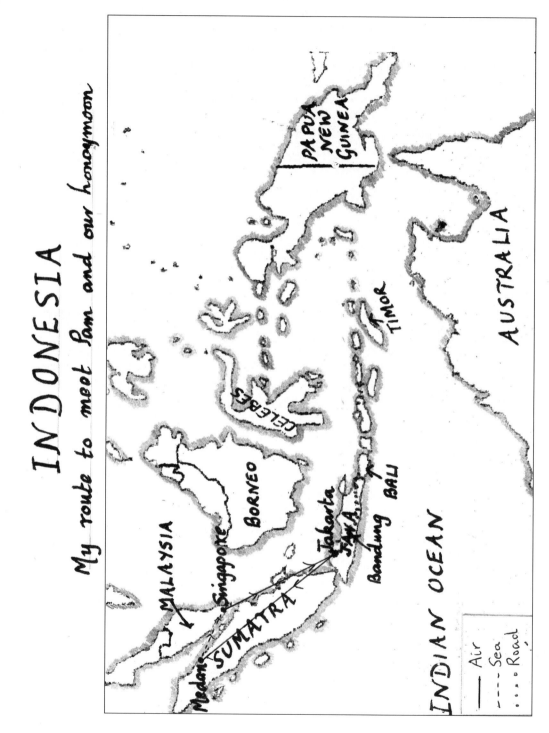

Chapter 20

Departure for Indonesia 1954
Garuda Airways in Jakarta

Indonesian de Havilland Heron Aircraft Operation

My own departure now occupied my attention and the Company arranged my air travel to Jakarta via Singapore. This flight was a comparatively slow business for commercial jet aircraft had not yet been introduced into general service. And so I progressed in a piston-engined 'thumper' with many intermediate calls for re-fuelling until we arrived at Karachi in newly created Pakistan. Here there was a night stop for we had been flying all day and everyone was exhausted. We took off again the next day, heading for Singapore. My neighbour in the next seat was a well-educated, intelligent young man in the diplomatic corps who was on the staff of the British Embassy in Singapore. He was returning from leave in England. We were very compatible travelling companions and enjoyed our long hours together so that time seemed to pass quickly. We were both French linguists and had similar interests. As my feelings warmed towards this fellow traveller I began to think of another extraordinary idea. I had received quite a number of warnings from people at the de Havilland factory concerning the precarious and dangerously weak situation of the Indonesian currency. I had been warned that, due to the poor leadership of the Indonesian Communist Government, the value of its currency had collapsed. If one took English pounds into the country the local law forced any exchange to be made at the official local rate which, in effect, would result in a loss of some two thirds of its sterling value. Furthermore any sterling taken into that country could never be taken out, even if one had to return to the U.K. unexpectedly. I had been advised that, if it were at all possible, it would be better to have my sterling banked in Singapore and thus beyond the clutches of the Communists in Indonesia. This I intended to do but unfortunately the night stop in Singapore was on a Sunday and the banks would be closed.

I was carrying some five or six hundred pounds in cash issued by my Company, to cover my initial expenses in Indonesia. In those days this was a considerable sum which in today's money would probably be worth £5000 or £6000 and, since boarding the flight, I had been puzzling on how to avoid taking it all into Indonesia. My extraordinary idea, which I have just mentioned, was to hand over this money to my travelling companion and ask him to open an account for me in a Singapore bank.

By common sense standards and conventional wisdom this idea of handing my money to a complete stranger was crazy but then I seemed to have entered into a new phase in my life where I was prepared to live dangerously and to accept risks which sane people would judge as being lunatic.

I broached my idea to this young man who certainly seemed rather surprised but, being in the Singapore British Embassy, he knew exactly the parlous state of Indonesia and of the Indonesian currency. He understood perfectly well my anxiety and my wish to establish a bank account in Singapore and not in Indonesia. Somehow I had complete confidence in this man and the fact that he was on the staff of the British Embassy for me was security enough. And it worked! I had to wait some three weeks after my arrival in Jakarta before I received his letter telling me he had deposited the money in the well-known Standard Chartered Bank in Singapore. I must admit that during the third week of waiting to hear from him I began to worry and was greatly concerned that I could possibly have made a monumental mistake! But all's well that ends well and from that time onwards I was in the happy position of getting value for my money. And I had no qualms about evading the Communists' stringent currency regulations for they made my life there extremely unpleasant and positively dangerous.

Indonesia at that time was emerging from centuries of cruel subjugation as a Dutch colony and in its new independence there was a nervous fear of a reactionary conspiracy by the white population seeking to regain control. There was also an element of revenge for their long suffering past. The majority of the native population lived in abject poverty in contrast to the rich Dutch colonials who owned the vast plantations of rubber, coffee, rice, bananas, sugar as well as the richest tobacco plantations in the world, the rare valuable leaves being in great demand world-wide. This leaf was used for making the casing of the most expensive cigars. Oil was a tremendous recent development in Sumatra. In consequence Communism had a strong appeal to the vast native population for it offered them a free share of this huge natural wealth. All they were advised to do was wrest it from the whites. They had nothing to lose since they had nothing anyway! They moved onto the plantations and became squatters. The President of Indonesia, Sukarno, was a great friend of the Chinese Communist leader, Chou En Lai, from whom he got all the necessary revolutionary guidance on how to wrest his country from the colonial Dutch. Peasant squatters moved in and took up residence in the rich rubber, tea, coffee etc. plantations. Their mud huts and squalid habitations destroyed the cultivation of the various crops and Indonesia's economy was slowly sinking. Hence the destruction of the international value of the Indonesian currency. Its vast national wealth was being slowly destroyed.

Furthermore Sukarno allowed the national infrastructure to run down, putting difficulties in front of all forms of commerce. When on a state visit to the U.S.A. he made a famous speech to Congress during which he was questioned as to why he had allowed his roads and railways to disintegrate. He replied that his peasant population did not own motor cars, only donkeys, so they did not need modern roads! He continued by saying that his people did not travel so they did not need railways! Life in Indonesia for the white population was extremely precarious. The native police would offer no protection if your skin was white and therefore one had to be very careful, especially at night-time. Murder and robbery of whites were everyday occurrences in Jakarta and often in the city at night there would be shooting by nationalists driving past hotels in cars and firing into the open ground floor of the leading hotels which were the favourite bars and gathering places for the white population. One never took a 'betja' (tricycle rickshaw) at night since there were many incidents of people being murdered by the driver who sat pedalling behind his client seated in the cane chair in front. The Indonesian driver could thus easily stab down on his unsuspecting passenger. It was always unwise to walk on the pavement

The author in a Japanese 'betja' (tricycle rickshaw) outside the Jakarta flat

in the city late at night since murderous thieves would lie in wait, concealed in shop doorways, and spring out on the unwary. If one had to walk anywhere at night in the city it was better to walk in the middle of the road.

Another difficulty of life in newly independent Indonesia under Communist rule was the egalitarian principle which was applied to every form of community service. This caused innumerable difficulties for everyday life in Jakarta. One such was the question of accommodation. When the Communists achieved independence and took control of the city the provincial country peasants descended en masse into the city for they had been taught that the streets were 'paved with gold.' And the Communists' promises ensured (they hoped) that they would all make their fortunes in no time at all. Consequently millions of people moved into the city. In a very short time the city population increased from one million to around four million, all seeking accommodation in a city originally housing less than one million. This problem was quickly solved by Communist egalitarian principle whereby a committee was set up and the existing accommodation was rationed to so many square feet per person, which became the law. If you happened to have more than your ration, then other people could have their ration in your flat. Likewise the municipal water system was not designed to provide for the overwhelming population increase so a Communist committee was set up which rationed the water and all other utilities. I very soon had personal experience of the power of this committee.

Garuda Airways being a government organisation had the privilege of being allocated its own employee accommodation. I was allocated a small flat in the native quarter of the city and my neighbours on all sides were Indonesians. My water supply was regulated by a meter located in a passageway to my flat. Each month an inspector would check the meter to ensure that one did not exceed one's ration. One month I received an ominous looking letter printed in red and in Indonesian, which I could not read. So I took it to Garuda the next day, and they, reading the thing, said that I was in serious trouble with the Authorities. It would appear that I had exceeded my water ration by a considerable amount and I had to appear in front of their Committee to explain my lack of respect for Indonesian water laws. A date was given for my appearance before the Committee. I investigated how this situation had developed, when I only used comparatively little water. I quickly discovered that a tap on my landing was being used by certain other Indonesian neighbours drawing off water through my meter when I was absent at work. On my appearance before the Committee I apologised and stated how I had been robbed by my neighbours. With a severe warning to control and improve my water system my case was dismissed.

I had a further instruction to appear before the Committee in connection with my electricity ration. I had bought a new refrigerator which was dual powered so that it could be run on a paraffin burner or plugged into an electrical supply. Naturally I took the easy way out and ran the thing on electricity. To my horror I received another of the red letters which again my Garuda Airways colleagues translated for me. It stated that I had exceeded my electricity ration and required me to appear and explain my misdeeds to the Committee. My colleagues, on my informing them of my recent purchase of the refrigerator, told me I had made a bad mistake in plugging into the electrical system since the official electricity ration for a small flat like mine would only be sufficient for three lights and one electric iron. They told me my ration would never permit the fridge to be operated on electricity and I should use only the paraffin burner system. Once again, I appeared in front of the Committee and apologised, pleading ignorance due to my short term of residence in the city. I was once again warned to organise better control of my water supply and to immediately stop stealing the electricity rations of good, honest Indonesian citizens.

Indonesia, formerly the Dutch East Indies, had been invaded by the Japanese in World War 2. Dutch control was destroyed and most of the Dutch colonials were confined in Japanese concentration camps where they were subjected to extreme cruelty and forced to exist at almost starvation level. I was told by Dutch colonial friends that the level of starvation was such that the camp regulations laid down that a rat was a luxury food which, if caught, had to be handed in to the sick quarters for the starving patients. An Australian who was one of the directors of the Jakarta import and export agency, Maclaine & Watson by name, which acted as agents for the sale of de Havilland aircraft to the Indonesian Government, told me of his own experiences in a Japanese concentration camp in Java. He had been an employee of this same agency in Jakarta when the Japanese invasion took place. He told me that he was a prisoner in a Japanese concentration camp and on the daily routine check parade which took place each morning, the guards, armed with rifles, would pick out a tall well-built prisoner and order him out in front of the assembled prisoners. They would then harangue him, accusing him of breaking camp regulations, and finally club him down to the ground with their rifle butts. They would then boast to the paraded prisoners that they had given a demonstration of how the small in stature Japanese people could easily overcome the Western physical superiority. Incidentally, the Australian's health was permanently ruined as he was unfortunately a big-framed man and consequently an obvious and frequent target for this treatment.

On the defeat of the Japanese, the Indonesians formed a guerrilla force located in hideouts in the mountains with the object of fighting the United Nations for their independence. Led by Sukarno they were successful in finally forcing the Allies to grant them independence from the resumed Dutch control. However, there was an extreme guerrilla group who disagreed with Sukarno's peace pact with the Dutch and persisted with their guerrilla operations. Periodically these guerrillas would descend from their mountain lairs at night and raid villages for food, destroying police posts. In the daytime they would often set up roadblocks, robbing travellers on the isolated mountain roads. Thus travelling outside the environs of the city was dangerous, particularly if one's journey was across the mountains into the interior of Java. I had some personal experience of this interior travelling which I will describe later in these memoirs.

My work and relationship with Garuda Airways proceeded very successfully and I quickly established an excellent rapport with the Dutch Chief Engineer and the Engineering section generally. The nationalised public services were all being taken over by Indonesians but the head of each department was Dutch with an Indonesian understudy who was being trained to take charge at a later date. Thus the head of the Technical organisation was a Dutchman (Mr. de Kok) who was a colonial. His family of tobacco farmers had been resident in Indonesia for some two or three hundred years. I soon found that Garuda was experiencing de Havilland engine bench testing problems similar to those experienced by the French, as recounted in my previous experience with SNECMA. But as we were nearly 9000 miles away from the D.H. factories it was not so easy to obtain the necessary equipment to solve this problem. However, eventually we did manage to get the required equipment and all problems were solved. The technical operation of Garuda was very efficient indeed and there were very commendable workshop organisations for the repair and overhaul of all their various engines (largely American) and aircraft. In fact it was the first time in Garuda's operations that a British aviation firm had succeeded in securing an entry into this airline, whose aircraft had been up to that time 100% American. This British intrusion was a cause of great disappointment to the Americans and they went to great lengths to denigrate the de Havilland Heron aircraft and its de Havilland Queen 30 engines..

But how the Dutch personnel of Garuda managed to operate the airline so efficiently was a source of constant wonder to me. This was because the Dutch colonial social system and way of life involved a drinking and dancing party almost every night. Jakarta being slap on the equator and surrounded by the sea was extremely hot and humid. Thus the Dutch evening parties did not start until about 10 o'clock at night and did not really get going until somewhere around midnight. The party would then go on until about three or even four in the morning. Yet the ground staff had to open up the hangars to service the aircraft at 5.30 a.m. with the first aircraft off usually around 6.30 a.m. But the aircraft always took off on time! Wonder of wonders!! They were certainly 'tough cookies' as the Americans say. Of course one reason this type of life was possible was that most work finished at around 2 p.m. owing to the intense heat and sticky humidity, so that a siesta in the afternoon and early evening was the normal daily routine. Humidity was nearly always hovering around 90 to 100% with ambient temperatures at midday around 100 degrees F. or more. The monsoon season would start around early summer and then rain would pour down in solid torrents for two or three hours every afternoon. This would continue for some three or four months. The people welcomed the rain and in fact the natives often stood in the rain deliberately getting soaked – within an hour of the rain ceasing the roasting sun would dry everything so that there was no indication that there had ever been any rain at all.

As previously mentioned my flat was in a native quarter of the city and was on the top floor of an elderly block of ancient construction. The crowded top floor was occupied by natives in the block each side of my flat, with an Indian sports shop on the ground floor. Being on the upper floor I had the disadvantage of the sun directly on my roof which was a flat area located between long normal sloping gable roofs on each side. There was no let-up of the heat in the evening or at night in the flat because the concrete walls were so thick they absorbed the heat during the day and passed it out to the flat occupants during the night. This unpleasant living condition began to concern me somewhat, not for myself, but for the possible adverse effect on my fiancée arriving from the U.K. in November. She had never travelled beyond Europe and had never experienced such climatic conditions nor such living conditions.

I was constantly thinking of this problem and what I could do to cool the place down. There was no such thing as air conditioning and a fan merely pushed the hot air from one side to the other. Finally I hit on an idea which seemed crazy but had possibilities. I would create a hanging roof garden like ancient Babylon!! My idea evolved from thinking that somehow I must provide some form of insulation on the rooftop. The thought struck me that a depth of earth thick enough to grow a lawn with flowerbeds over the whole surface of the flat roof would provide such insulation. Pursuing the idea further I visited a local horticultural nursery and the proprietor agreed that he could supply sufficient top soil which he was prepared to transport to my flat in straw panniers on the backs of donkeys controlled by young people who would carry it up to the roof of my flat on the upper floor.

However, searching around my block failed to produce any means of access to the roof. I then decided to overcome this problem by making my own roof access. I did this by knocking a hole through my own ceiling, which was 10 inch thick concrete and constructing a stairway to provide a method of mounting to the flat roof top. By

The Jakarta flat (the roof garden is between the two main roofs)

this time I realised that the work would necessitate my engaging some help if I was to complete the scheme and obtain some benefit before the arrival of Pam scheduled for November. I broached the subject to de Kok, the Garuda Chief Engineer, with whom I had developed a good friendship. He thought the idea very original but quite feasible and recommended an excellent Indonesian native handyman and his young son. With their chisels and hammers they enlarged my hole in the roof so that we had an aperture some two feet square which gave free access to the roof. Here we found filth and rats on my tarred flat rooftop which had never been visited since its original construction.

Now came the planning of this 'hanging roof garden'. I decided that the best idea was to construct four floor enclosures built with low concrete and brick surrounds approximately 18 inches deep and criss-crossed with four pathways. The enclosures would house the topsoil and cover a large area of the roof which measured about 30 by 50 feet. I planned to plant grass turf in the four enclosures. My plan left a sizeable free space in the centre between the enclosed lawns which I planned to be tiled and covered and would thus provide a sitting out area for entertaining and possibly for sleeping in the open air on the rooftop! This open-air room furnished eventually like a sitting room with a table and chairs became an evening relaxation area. Later I fitted up a small bar and a dartboard and so we had a miniature open-air pub in the sky to entertain my Dutch friends,

This work was successfully executed by my handyman and his son. Then began the operation of creating the lawns. I gave the go-ahead to the nurseryman to start the delivery of the top soil and soon the neighbourhood was amazed to see a constant train of donkeys, all laden with panniers of soil, who would park in the road outside my flat block. They beheld a constant trail of donkey men carrying the baskets of soil and ascending the stairs to my flat! The laying of the topsoil to a depth of some 18 inches was accomplished successfully. The grass turf was laid on top. In this climate, with daily watering, the rate of growth was astonishing. One could almost see the grass rising before one's eyes.

Constructing the roof garden in Jakarta

The author during construction of the Jakarta roof garden

My Roof Garden above my flat in Jakarta

In a further discussion, reporting the success of my idea to my friend de Kok, Chief Engineer of Garuda, he suggested another original idea to supplement what I had already accomplished. He suggested the construction of a secondary or auxiliary roof which should cover the whole of the tiled centre of the garden, thus providing further protection from the sun but open on all sides to give light and air for the garden. I thought this an excellent idea especially when he further suggested that the auxiliary roof structure could be constructed of light alloy metal (Duralumin) sections, held in Garuda stores, which they no longer needed. This material would be suitable for such a construction and he was willing to sell it to me at a nominal price. I immediately accepted his offer and, after much thought, designed a suitable structural scheme which would be strong enough to support this auxiliary roof in all climatic conditions. I worked out the quantity of material needed and bought the metal from Garuda's store. To ensure safety I got de Kok to vet my plans, which, with one minor change, he agreed were satisfactory.

With my handyman and his assistant we cut the structure members and drilled and bolted them together, forming the skeleton frame and roof structure which then needed a tile covering. We fitted the wooden tile battens and, with the advice of my Indonesian handyman, I found a good roof tiler who made a very fine tiled roof. This made an excellent shelter covering the whole centre tiled sitting out area. My garden lawns soon needed cutting which was done by hand. I abandoned the idea of borders and embellished the whole layout with miniature palm trees growing in tubs. The pathways between the lawn enclosures we tiled to make suitable walkways. As the scheme developed I became more ambitious and determined to use the roof area for entertaining my Garuda Dutch colleagues and so reciprocate their generous hospitality. My flat roof area was situated between conventional tiled gable roofs of adjoining flats and was open to the street with no railings or balustrades and I had visions of possibly inebriated guests falling from the roof to the street below. I therefore constructed low walling and safety railings to enclose the open ends and provided a gateway to give access to the front ledge which was the original roof level and looked down onto the street and to the canal flowing on the opposite side of the street.

This canal was one of many which threaded their way all over the city. This was a typical Dutch system providing basic utility services for a majority of the population. One could observe everyday natural human functions being performed in the waters and alongside the performer would often be a woman washing her family laundry, whilst just a little way along the bank of the canal would be another person doing their ablutions and cleaning their teeth! As Sukarno had told the American people, his people were not provided with luxuries!

I ran electric cables up through my ceiling aperture to provide lighting, and a power socket so that I was able to live, work and sleep on the rooftop. It was a joy to be able to escape the heat of the oven that existed between the walls of my flat below. Working in the evening writing my weekly reports to de Havillands in England my electric table light would attract all kinds of tropical flying insects, including huge moths with an unbelievably amazing wingspan, some of which were,

Indonesian domestic scene on a Jakarta canal

I'm sure, 12 inches or more across when in flight. Sometimes there were bats with an even greater wingspan. Visiting a beautiful horticultural garden near Jakarta, similar to Kew Gardens in London, I saw wonderful butterflies of a similar huge wingspan.

My illuminated 'hanging garden of Babylon' (Indonesia) attracted the curious interest of the local population and I soon became known as the mad Englishman who lived on the roof. However this notoriety attracted other interest for I received another of the dreaded red letters from the Municipality. Once again my Garuda friends translated the contents and informed me that I was in trouble with the Municipal Civil Engineer's department. The letter stated that I had constructed a building on my rooftop without applying for authority or the necessary municipal permit. In consequence I was to report to the Civil Engineer's department within a stated time limit to explain this breach of regulations. If I failed to obey this instruction my roof structure would be demolished by the Municipality.

Needless to say I took myself hot foot the next day to the relevant office of the Municipality, expecting to meet dour accusing officials full of threats to impose heavy penalties for my gross disregard of their stringent regulations. Instead I found disinterested Indonesian minor officials whose main interest seemed to be in the money they would charge me for the necessary forms I would need to purchase and submit for the required permit. There was no question of any inspection or examination of my structure and it appeared that all I had to do was complete the forms and the application would be approved automatically. There was only one serious 'fly in the ointment' and that was that they required that I should produce a letter from the owner of my flat sanctioning the alterations which I had made to the roof of his flat. This requirement proved to be a serious difficulty for I had thought that the flat belonged to Garuda, but I discovered that the flat was owned by an Arab from the South Yemen area around Aden. I sought out this Arab who spent most of his day sipping black coffee, smoking his bubbling hookah pipe and playing a peculiar chessboard game in a local café. I explained to him that I needed his letter approving the alterations I had made to his flat. He admitted that he had visited the flat and seen what had been done. He made no objections but quite calmly demanded the equivalent of £200 in local currency. He already knew from the Municipal Engineer's that I could not get the permit without his letter of sanction, so I was in a position where I was literally being blackmailed by the fat middle-aged Arab dressed in his galabiyah (night-shirt type of dress). For me £200 was a considerable amount of money and to find it to pay this Arab would cause me considerable difficulties. My arguments to the Arab that I had enriched and improved his miserable flat by adding the roof garden and virtually another room were brushed aside as of no consequence. It was my first experience of the social revolution in the new post-war world following the downfall of the British Empire. I suddenly realised that the white Raj omnipotence under which I had sheltered for a large part of my life overseas was at an end. No longer could I ignore the demands of this slothful Arab. I had to find a solution and that pretty urgently. I told him that I would be back with the money and the necessary letter for him to sign.

I decided to seek the advice of our Jakarta agents, Messrs. Maclaine and Watson, who were a very well-known rich international import and export agency with branches all over the Far East. They had organised, in liaison with the Indonesian Government, the contract for the sale of the 14 Heron aircraft. The Managing Director, after hearing my dismal story of the blackmailing Arab told me not to worry and said that, as a gesture of gratitude to me for the successful work I had done in re-establishing a good relationship with Garuda Airways Technical Department, his Company would pick up the bill and provide the required £200 for the Arab's letter. With tremendous relief and great joy I got my flat owner's authorising letter signed and accepted by the Municipal Authority. I felt extremely grateful to Messrs. Maclaine & Watson for their generous action. Had I known about it at the time my gratitude would probably have been tempered by the fact that, unknown to me, they were then negotiating another large profitable contract with de Havillands to provide the Indonesian Air Force with a squadron of expensive Vampire jet fighter aircraft. Perhaps they hoped that I would once again establish a similarly successful good relationship with the Indonesian Air Force as I had done with the civilian Garuda Airways. But more of that later in this story.

Chapter 21

My Marriage in Singapore

During this time, in anticipation of Pam's arrival in November, I had been making enquiries from the Civil Authorities in Jakarta town hall regarding the requirements for a registry office wedding. They reluctantly agreed that this was possible after giving me a gruelling inquisition as to who I was and what I was doing in Indonesia. Having satisfied themselves that I was legitimate they then presented me with a foolscap questionnaire for me to complete before reporting back to their office. This document required the names, dates of birth etc. of all my family including my maternal and paternal grandparents, which it took me some time to discover. When the questionnaire was finally completed I presented myself once again at the town hall. To my astonishment they presented me with another full-page questionnaire which again had to be completed and returned to them. The type of questions on this document was so stupid and so obviously political that I decided it would be unwise to attempt to get married under the Communist system in Indonesia. An example of the stupidity of the questionnaire was a demand to know what political clubs my grandfather and grandmother belonged to, and what were their hobbies.

I decided that the best and safest arrangement for my forthcoming marriage would be to go to the nearest British territory, which was Singapore, and have a proper British registry office wedding. By this time Pam had already left England and was on her way to Indonesia by sea. She was travelling on the Dutch line Rotterdam Lloyd aboard the 'Willem Ruys' which had called at Southampton to pick up its English passengers. Most people travelled by sea in those days because it was cheaper than by air and more comfortable. I knew the ship was due to call at Ceylon (now Sri Lanka), then, later, at Medan in Sumatra. After Medan the ship would call at Singapore on its way to Jakarta and Australia, its final destination. So I sent a cable addressed to Pam on the 'Willem Ruys' at Ceylon informing her of the change of plan and arranging to board her ship at Medan, from where we would go on to Singapore together and there get ourselves hitched up, I hoped!

It was now December (1954) and approaching Christmas and somehow I had to get myself to Medan on the coast of north west Sumatra some 1000 miles from Jakarta. Furthermore I had to get a ticket to travel with Pam on her ship to Singapore. I visited a Dutch travel agent in Jakarta and, to my surprise and great joy, found there was a plane from Jakarta to Medan. Although they could not give me a ticket for the sea voyage to Singapore they could, as agents for the shipping line, give me a piece of paper which I could exchange for a ticket at Medan. The plane (I forget the airline, probably KLM) left Jakarta on the morning of Christmas Eve and arrived at Medan in the early evening. Medan at that time was a very small 'one-eyed' little seaport town but was a great commercial centre for the tobacco and rubber industry of Indonesia. It seemed to have only one main street with the rest of the town sprawling widespread around it. Having booked into what seemed to be the only decent hotel in the place and had a meal, I wandered around this lifeless outpost of Sumatran civilisation trying to learn my local geography, but not achieving very much.

The next morning (Christmas Day), I was up and away early, determined to find the whereabouts of the Rotterdam Lloyd shipping office, so that I would be in good time the next day to get my ticket for the ship which would be due in that day. Walking down the main street, it seemed to me that I was the only white man in the whole place and, being Christmas Day, taxis did not appear to circulate so that I had no means of discovering the office of the shipping company. After I had walked some distance along the high street a car came charging along the road full of youngish white men, all in jovial mood. When they spotted me, a white stranger, they pulled up alongside and asked me what I was doing walking in such a place on Christmas Day. They were Dutch tobacco planters and spoke good English.

I told them my story that I was searching this one-eyed place for the location of the shipping office. They all burst out laughing and said 'Come with us. We are going to a Christmas party. Come on – jump in!' I declined the offer, saying it was very important that I located this shipping office. At that they all roared with laughter again and said 'Come with us and your problem is solved! The manager of the shipping office will also be at the party and he will take care of everything.' To commit myself to a load of foreign strangers in a car that was going I knew not where maybe would seem foolhardy but somehow I believed them and had confidence that they meant to help and extend hospitality to a stranger. This attitude was typical of the old colonial way of life where white men were always in a minority compared with the native population. There was a kind of international white brotherhood which would provide aid and hospitality, particularly in those remote parts of the world. I had another experience of this feature of white strangers' hospitality in the hills of the remote Northern Transvaal in South Africa, which I will recount later in this story of my life.

And so it came to pass that I found myself at a joyous Christmas party in the magnificent residence of a complete Dutch stranger where I was treated with most generous hospitality. On my unfolding my 'raison d'être' in this strange place I seemed to become a subject of great interest. The presence of an Englishman in their midst was a somewhat unique event in Medan, especially when he was there on the unusual errand of meeting his fiancée coming from London on a Dutch ship calling in at Medan. The planters who had picked me up in the high street were true to their word and introduced me to the shipping office manager who was present at the party. This Dutch gentleman was all attention and told me that I could relax and he would take care of everything. He said he would send a car to my hotel on the morrow which would take me to his office, where he would provide me with my ticket. He then told me I would need to hire a motor boat. I was astonished and asked, 'Why should I need a motor boat?' He replied that the 'Willem Ruys' was a ship of some 30,000 tons and so was far too large to enter the small harbour of Medan and so stood off outside the harbour. To board the ship one needed a motor boat which could be hired through his office. It proved to be a most enjoyable Christmas party and I received several invitations from these Dutch tobacco planters to be their guest on a conducted tour of their plantations the following day. Reluctantly I had to turn them down explaining that the 'Willem Ruys' was due in around midday and I had to get myself to the shipping office to collect my ticket and get organised with my own personal motor boat. And on the next day that is exactly what I did.

The shipping office manager was as good as his word and the next day a car arrived punctually at the hotel to take me to his office. Here the necessary paper work was done and I was in proud possession of my ticket for the ship and eventually of a delightful little motor boat whose crew headed the boat with me aboard out of the little harbour onto the high seas outside. There stood at anchor this towering mighty ship – or so it seemed to me down below in my little motor boat. As we neared the lowered landing stage I saw what seemed to be hundreds of people looking down from a great height, all mightily interested in this approaching small motor boat containing the solitary figure of a man, standing attired in an all white tropical suit staring upwards with anxious searching gaze. Somewhere in this crowd of faces looking down from a great height was the girl he had come to meet and to marry! Climbing the side of the ship and hoisting myself on deck I was soon plucked out of the crowd and greeted by the lady in question. Escorted to my cabin we had there a joyous reunion after being so long apart. The extraordinary circumstances whereby we had both travelled half way round the world for this belated rendezvous also added flavour to this unique occasion.

The next day passed swiftly, culminating in our disembarkation on the Singapore quayside. Here, with limited finances and knowing no one, we were as 'two babes in the wood', only it was a Singapore wood with no trees. I hailed a taxi, the driver of which was of course Chinese, and told him to take us to a reasonably priced decent hotel. He certainly took me at my word and we arrived at a Chinese hotel in a very Chinese quarter of Singapore. On inspection we found it quite satisfactory being clean, cheap and comfortable and the staff were very pleasant. So we stayed. We took separate rooms because the 'Permissive Society' of Western civilisation had not yet arrived and we behaved according to normal Christian conventions and, as a matter of fact, we still do! My next problem was to find out how one got married when newly arrived in Singapore. I had a vague idea that there was such a thing as a special licence obtainable when resident in England but what happens when one arrives unannounced in Singapore, complete with fiancée but without a friend of relative in the whole city?! I had one slender link to whom I might appeal for help. There was resident in Singapore a de Havilland Engine Company engineer, Len Jupp by name, in a Company position similar to myself, who covered the Singapore and Malayan area. I had never met him but I found his telephone number, rang him up and the conversation went something like this:-

My marriage in Singapore

Self: This is Fred Weston, the D.H. engineer in Java.

Len: Good God! What are you doing here? You're supposed to be in Jakarta!

Self: I know, but I've come to get married.

Len: Get married!! What do you mean? You must be crazy! Who are you going to marry?

Self: Well, as a matter of fact, I've got my fiancée with me now. She has just come out from London and we have arrived here together today. I was hoping perhaps you could help us as you know the place. My idea is perhaps we could get a special licence, get married in a Registry Office, and then I could return to Jakarta with my newly married bride.

Len: Good heavens! Certainly, I will help you as much as I can in your crazy set up. You can use my flat for the reception.

Self: What reception? I don't know anybody here!

Len: We'll soon fix that! I'll take you to Changi RAF station and we can invite, say, half a dozen married officers and their wives. And then I'll take you to the Royal Navy in the Singapore dockyard and we can invite half a dozen naval officers and their wives, and that will be your reception!

Self: Sounds a good idea to me. Let's get organised!

We went to the Singapore Town Hall Registry Office and arranged for a special 48-hour licence. Len Jupp and his good wife took care of us. They took care of everything including the 3-tiered wedding cake, champagne, cigars etc. Len escorted me to the RAF station at Changi and introduced me to the C.O. By good luck I knew the Chief Technical officer, now a Wing Commander, who agreed to be my best man. We issued invitations to half a dozen Changi married officers and their wives. Then we went to the Singapore dockyard where the Royal Navy operated and we issued invitations to half a dozen married naval Air Service officers and their wives. So we had our ready-made wedding party. We had the use of a splendid reception apartment free of charge, a huge wedding cake, loads of champagne and all the usual trimmings – all organised in a few days. All this was due to the wonderful friendship and camaraderie of the D.H. engineer, Len Jupp, and his charming wife.

The actual wedding ceremony took place in Singapore Town Hall and we were married on the morning of December 30th 1954 with the RAF Wing Commander, my best man, and his wife as witnesses and supported by Len Jupp and his wife. After the ceremony we all agreed to meet up at Len's flat for the famous reception party. In the meantime Pam and I went off back to our Chinese hotel to re-arrange our rooms. When we got to the hotel we saw the Chinese manager and the conversation went something like this:-

Self: Good Morning, May I ask a favour? Would you be so good as to move Miss Bateman's (Pam's maiden name) things from her room to mine?

Manager: Oh no! I'm sorry, but that's not allowed in this hotel. We cannot permit such a request.

Self: But we were married this morning in Singapore Town Hall Registry Office. So we are now man and wife.

Wedding day in Singapore with host Len Jupp and wife who were witnesses

Manager: Good heavens! Please forgive me! Why did you not tell me before and I would have had everything arranged for you?

Self: I apologise – but I did not think you would be interested.

Manager: On such a happy occasion we must be interested. Could you please give me a little time now and I will arrange for Miss Bateman's things to be moved as you wish? Would you please perhaps go for a coffee somewhere, say for about an hour, and I will have everything arranged.

We did as we were bid and found a pleasant Chinese pavement café nearby where we passed an hour or so watching the passing Chinese world, and then returned to our hotel. The receptionist gave me my room key, telling me that everything had been arranged as I requested and would I please check that all was correct. We went up to my room, opened the door and – lo and behold! – the whole room was full of lovely flesh flowers right to the ceiling. We gazed with astonishment and, turning round, we saw there behind us all the Chinese staff, to congratulate us and wish us great happiness in the future. It was a remarkably generous Chinese gesture to two foreign guests which will remain forevermore vivid in my memory. The two 'babes in the Singapore woods' had really found a kind and generous haven!

We passed a pleasant week in Singapore where, amongst other things, on New Year's Eve we paid a visit to the famous huge fun park called the Happy World. This is a huge fun fair area where all kinds of Chinese entertainment are on continuous offer. Several of these were open air dancing activities where live dance bands were playing. At one side of the dance floor was erected a stadium, or rising tiers of seats overlooking the dance floor. Seated on the various rising tiers were a large collection of young Chinese girls, sedately awaiting a partner. Chinese men entering this establishment bought tickets at the entrance, each ticket permitting him to go to the tiered stage, inspect the range of girls on show and choose a partner for his dance. The pair would enter the dance floor together but would not dance together in the Western style, instead they would face each other about three or four feet apart. Over this gap they conversed together but never touched each other. A sort of remote control type of dance. The music was a kind of rhythmic Westernised Chinese. There were a boxing booth, horror shows and all kinds of cafes and restaurants and, as evening approached, we decided to sample one of these restaurants. We entered the rather large marquee and found the place empty except for a group of Chinese businessmen in a far corner, gathered around a large table having an evening meal. We selected a table and, after studying the menu, gave our order to the Chinese waiter. After a few minutes the waiter returned and said that the group of Chinese gentlemen at the other table would like to offer us a Christian New Year's Eve drink. We were rather surprised at this extraordinary and unexpected welcome but felt that courtesy demanded that we should accept their kind offer. Imagine our embarrassment when, a few minutes later, the waiter returned and ceremoniously deposited a full bottle of Johnny Walker whisky and two glasses on our table. After opening the bottle he said that this was with the compliments of the Chinese gentlemen on the other table. We were greatly impressed with this overwhelming generosity and rather pleased that we should attract such unusual attention. Maybe it was because we seemed to be the only Europeans in this strange 'Happy World'. We returned the New Year toast to our Chinese friends, had our meal which was quite satisfactory and, not wishing to become further involved with the Chinese, we departed, leaving the bottle of whisky in situ for the benefit of the staff.

So the time approached for our return to Jakarta and to this end I went to the Garuda airline office in Singapore to arrange our return flight. I was pleasantly surprised to learn that the Garuda office had been advised by Jakarta that we should receive tickets free of charge for the flight from Singapore to Jakarta. But there were even more Garuda surprises in store for us on our return trip. Following a very pleasant flight we arrived at Jakarta around midday and, gathering our various belongings, we prepared to disembark to begin our newly married life in this remote Oriental city.

Chapter 22

Life in Jakarta, Indonesia
Afro-Asian Bandung Conference of Third
World Nations

As we descended from the aircraft at Jakarta, I saw to my amazement that there was a reception lane of Dutch Garuda staff and their wives extending from the aircraft steps to the airport restaurant. The Garuda Chief Engineer conducted me along this lane and I had the task of introducing Pam to each of the Dutch couples. I was told that everything was taken care of; I was not to bother about passport controls or customs inspection. We were conducted to the airport restaurant where, again to my surprise, half of the restaurant area had been roped off for a private welcoming luncheon party which had been organised in our honour. It would appear that the Singapore Garuda office had informed the Jakarta Garuda headquarters of the details of our return flight with the result that my Dutch colleagues had kindly prepared this reception. I felt greatly honoured. The meal continued throughout the afternoon and Pam had her first experience of Dutch Javanese 'Reistafel' which is a very spicy oriental rice meal consisting of numerous small dishes of many different foods often, to western tastes, of contrary flavours, such as fish with chicken, all served at the same time on numerous small dishes spread over an area covering the table in front of you, inviting you to take your pick. However, to the unaccustomed, this delicious food would soon develop a raging furnace in the throat which would need to be quenched with ice-cold beer. This was to be our staple diet in the months to come and this was how Pam, from the initial shock, learned to drink beer and enjoy it. I lived in Java on this native food for over eighteen months.

Finally, after some five hours, this remarkable reception and meal came to an end and at last we were driven to my humble flat complete with all our baggage. Pam, since meeting me in Sumatra, lived in never ceasing wonder as each day's new experiences unrolled. Now, arriving at my flat, she had another new experience in this peculiar abode of mine with its 'Babylonian' roof garden But this innovation proved to be such a blessing and was my salvation; it was to be our haven of rest and escape from the torrid heat and humidity which existed in the rooms below. At night we slept on the roof in the peaceful cool night air. By day from our roof garden we viewed the panorama of the street scene below with its unending stream of native life passing by with its constant traffic of cars and tricycle 'betjas' (rickshaws) with the pedestrian population in everlasting haste, with porters balancing their laden baskets at each end of an oscillating bamboo supported on their shoulders. As mentioned previously a canal flowed by on the other side of our street and one had an excellent view of the scenes I have previously described of the native domestic chores – the daily laundry, the washing and bathing and teeth cleaning operations conducted alongside the natural functions of ones neighbours. A gentle push of the water around the vicinity of the person performing his ablutions on the side of the canal was all that was considered necessary to achieve the desired sanitary standard.

My own domestic arrangements prior to Pam's arrival had developed along very satisfactory lines. I had inherited from the previous tenant of my flat a very reliable and capable Indonesian female 'general factotum' who did everything including the cleaning, shopping, cooking and laundry. I paid her possibly a little more than the local going rate in wages which, by our Westerns standards, were 'peanuts' and each day I gave her the equivalent of 2/6 (12$\frac{1}{2}$p in to-day's money) with which she would go to the market and buy everything necessary for the running of the flat and for my main meal of the day. This meal was my afternoon lunch which was always the Indonesian 'reistafel'. The beauty of the 'reistafel' is that you have a tremendous range of dishes, the selection from which can be changed to give the necessary variety of flavours etc. From my servant's excellent cooking I learned to love Indonesian food. After lunch came the inevitable siesta. In the evenings I went out and had an evening meal in one of a variety of different places or restaurants.

Pam's arrival fortunately did not necessitate any upset of these harmonious domestic arrangements for she immediately formed a good relationship with my Indonesian domestic and, equally fortunately, Pam accepted and enjoyed the Indonesian cooking. We varied our evening menu by a weekly visit to Chinatown in the Glodok riverside district of the city. Here we had a selection of wonderful Chinese dishes of such delicious flavours of which I have never tasted the like anywhere in the world. The Chinese environment in this area was, to say the least, strange, with many Chinese families living in crude houseboats somewhat similar to the poor quarters of Hong Kong. In the Chinese restaurant were living dozens of cats who, waiting for the finish of a meal and the departure of the customer, would all immediately leap on to the table and demolish the leftovers. It is in this Glodok district that there has unfortunately been serious rioting and deadly violent attacks on the Chinese and their properties in recent times. Conditions have calmed down since the resignation of Suharto, the former President, who followed Sukarno. However violent political and student riots persist against the ruling Authorities. Another new President B J Habibie has now apparently lost control of the Indonesian Army resulting in frightful massacres and destruction in East Timor. Here democratic government has been overtaken by murderous militia mobs shooting, looting, and torching the citizen's houses. The Indonesian Government and the United Nations seem powerless to restore order or to protect the people.

The day following our arrival from Singapore and the generous welcome we had experienced from my Garuda colleagues I set about arranging the continuation of our honeymoon. We had so far had just the one week in Singapore. I planned to extend this by a further two weeks, one of which we would spend travelling around Java, after which we would cross over the water to spend another week in Bali.

With this plan in view I visited the Indonesian passport control department in Jakarta in order to regularise Pam's position as my wife and register her change of name from Bateman to Weston. Looking back now with hindsight I realise I made a big mistake in going to the Indonesians. I should have gone to the British Embassy. Going to the Indonesians alerted their passport office that Pam had entered the country without going through passport control, which was to have dire consequences for us later. However the counter clerk, when he had heard my story and I had told him that I wished to continue my honeymoon with a trip round Java and over to Bali, was most co-operative and told me I could go off on the proposed trip, using just my passport for the two of us. He said the change of name in Pam's passport could be arranged when we came back.

We departed the next day in my rather ancient Wolseley ex-police car which I had brought out from England, at the Company's expense of course. It was nearing the end of its once strenuous life and really was in no fit condition to stand the stresses and strains of rural Indonesian roads which were notorious for their terrible run-down condition. They were almost one continuous chain of potholes and the only way to make any progress without the jarring bone-shaking jolts was to cruise at a fairly high speed which would enable the car to travel forward from the top of one rut to the top of the next rut without descending into the hole in between. This method of progress was of course quite tiring and uncomfortable and, after several

Honeymoon, night stop on journey across Java

days of such treatment, Pam begged to be released from this torture. In the meanwhile everything on the car that was detachable fell off. As I have previously related of my Iraq experiences, most things on the car were detachable, design and construction being based on a rigid strong steel girder frame with everything else attached to it. During our Java journey bits and pieces such as bumpers, lights etc. fell off, I would stop, go back and pick them up, throw them into the back of the car and press on. I could not be bothered with any idea of re-attaching the bits. I left that for the future when back to civilisation.

However, Pam's plea to stop her suffering brought an end to any further ideas of exploratory car travel in Java and we decided to dump the car and fly over to Bali by the nearest Garuda terminal. This we did and booked in at the Balinese rather touristy 'chromium plate' sole hotel on the island. This was not the type of hotel where we wanted to spend the rest of our honeymoon but to our delight we found that the hotel had a real down-to-earth native Balinese annex which was located on the island's sandy beach fronting the Pacific Ocean. The annex consisted of a typical crude bamboo construction situated on the sand in a sort of palm plantation, about a hundred yards or so from the water's edge and some two or three miles from the main hotel. For our hotel meals the arrangement was very convenient in that a waiter would arrive on a bicycle carrying our food in special containers. We had this heavenly world completely to ourselves for there were no other guests with our extraordinary ideas. High-speed aircraft with mass tourism had not yet arrived in Bali. We had miles of soft sandy beaches all to ourselves and we spent practically the

Shell Company petrol delivery to a Japanese village garage (1955)

Honeymoon in Bali

Honeymoon, Bali beach

whole of each day in swimsuit and trunks. We had of course to pay the price for our primitive surroundings which meant that the local crawly wildlife also claimed a share in our leafy habitation. I found a scorpion journeying up our hut wall – but these were minor penalties to pay for the joys of our exclusive beachcomber existence on the shores of the Pacific. We spent a considerable amount of time in the water which was delightfully warm and slowly progressed from shallows to the deeper waters some distance away. Here we had to be careful to avoid stinging jellyfish and nasty stingrays.

However, this idyll was shattered after four or five days when a hotel waiter appeared on the water's edge whilst we were bathing in the sea. He was waving a piece of paper and loudly calling us to come in. We were somewhat puzzled by the excited gesturing and yelling of this Indonesian and wondered whether we should ignore him but, in view of his obvious urgent pleading, we decided to investigate what was the cause of his agitation. When we finally waded into the shore where he was standing he handed me a cable which had just been received at the hotel. The

Balinese villagers bringing gifts to the temple prior to a temple dance

Balinese temple dance episode. The orchestra is seated at rear (right)

cable was from our agents, Maclaine & Watson, in Jakarta. It read that we must return immediately to Jakarta as the Indonesian Passport Control had issued an order that Pam was illegally in the country, and, if we did not report to the Jakarta Passport Control within the next 48 hours, she would be either imprisoned or expelled from the country. This was a shattering blow for it brought our idyll to an untimely end. Furthermore it was impossible to fly back to Java, pick up our car and return to Jakarta in 48 hours. However we packed up hurriedly and did our best to get back as rapidly as possible with horrible visions of Pam in prison as our driving incentive.

We finally arrived back a day after our 48 hour ultimatum had expired and I hurried to Maclaine & Watson's office in town to find out what had caused this furore. There I was accused by the Managing Director of Maclaine & Watson of placing their whole business in jeopardy by evading Indonesian passport control regulations in bringing Pam into the country without proper passport control authority. The Managing Director of Maclaine & Watson said that the Government had threatened him that that they would suspend his business licence for three months unless I wrote a letter of explanation of my conduct and apologised for my evil deeds. I explained to the M. D. what had happened in my reception by the Dutch and how I had been to the passport control office before leaving on our trip. I told him how they had given me permission to go off on the trip and had assured me that passport control would regularise Pam's passport during our absence. I said I saw no reason to apologise or admit to any misdeed since I had been given official permission by the Indonesian office. At that the M. D. flew into a rage and said that, in the right or in the wrong, I was to immediately write out my apology to the head of the Indonesian passport office. He insisted that he would dictate what he thought was necessary in my letter of apology. He said we were living under Communist masters where the only right was what they decided; justice did not enter into the matter. And further he said 'My entire business is threatened by them; any injustice you suffer is a minor matter compared with the total collapse of Maclaine & Watson.'

The M.D. then had my letter typed and when I had signed it we went together for an interview with the head of the Indonesian passport control section. There we were ushered into the sanctum of the passport control chief, a buxom lady in a khaki drill uniform with a nasty looking revolver strapped by a leather belt around her waist. She looked a somewhat fearsome female who would brook no nonsense. The M.D. introduced me as the accused and handed her my letter of apology and, with due humility (and to avoid being shot!) I said how abjectly desolated I was to have acted against the good laws of the great Indonesian nation and its worthy passport control section. This was translated by the M.D. and received with a sour look from the fearsome lady. She then led off in a tirade against Colonial peoples and against me in particular, finally ending with a dire warning that I had better behave or my wife and myself would be thrown out of the country. This in spite of the fact that I was there to help them operate their national airline. However we had escaped any serious penalty and on our dismissal the M.D. heaved a sigh of relief that the penalty on the operation of his business had been rescinded.

Prior to Pam's arrival, in the course of my conversations with Jerry Fowler, a representative of Maclaine & Watson in Jakarta, I had of course told him of the planned marriage and had described Pam's background with mention of her academic achievements and her Edinburgh University M.A. Honours degree. This information was apparently relayed via Steve Day, one of the directors of Maclaine & Watson, to the authorities of the International School in Jakarta, where his children were being educated. I was approached by one of the governors of this school, which was sponsored by the American Standard Oil Co. He said they had need of an English teacher with qualifications such as Pam's and asked me to help them to persuade her to accept a teaching post with the school as soon as possible after her arrival. As soon as we had returned from our honeymoon she had an interview with the school governors and very quickly joined the staff of the Jakarta International School. There were attending the school some eighteen different nationalities of children between the ages of 5 and 14 from countries ranging from the Far East such as Japan to the Far West such as America. In fact Pam soon found herself much more deeply involved in the school management than she had contemplated when first accepting the post. It would appear that, very soon after Pam started teaching there, the American headmistress had resigned, due to her returning home to the States, and Pam was pressed to take on the post. She was reluctant to accept such responsibility, having no previous experience at such a level, in fact very little experience of teaching at all. Nevertheless the urgent pleading of the powers that be finally persuaded her to accept. Thus within weeks of arriving for her first experience of the Far East, and having just married in the strangest circumstances a man she hardly knew, she now found herself head of a school of some eighteen different nationalities. In addition she was teaching a class of 12-14 year olds of about eight different nationalities. What was more, the organisation and curriculum had been set up on an American basis by the previous American headmistress. Pam was quite unfamiliar with such a system; she decided that the British system would be more appropriate, since at least she knew the structure of that system and would be able to contribute something to the running of the school.

As the newly married English couple we were the centre of much hospitable interest from the Garuda Airline staff and received many invitations from the Dutch personnel. One particularly amusing incident occurred during an invitation to dinner one evening at the house of a young Dutch couple. Pam suffers from hay fever and is allergic to a number of emissions including animal fur, particularly cats and dogs. Our Dutch hosts possessed a young furry kitten which jumped on to Pam's lap whilst the Dutch lady was in the kitchen and her husband was out of the room organising the preprandial drinks. Almost immediately Pam's eyes began watering and very quickly her eyes reddened with tears running down her face so that, when the husband returned with the drinks, he was horrified that this newly married man could be so cruel as to make his wife cry in this manner. Fortunately my reputation was restored when the blame was passed over to the moggy.

We had of course to take our part in the colonial Dutch way of life, meaning the nightly parties previously described. With the unaccustomed equatorial heat and humidity Pam's daily stock of energy was almost exhausted before the parties started and, by the time they came to life around midnight, she was falling asleep. However we did manage to 'show willing' by doing a little dancing but, when it came to serious conversation, poor Pam could hardly keep her eyes open. These parties were not our favourite activity.

I was a member of the Box Club, the Jakarta Cricket Club, which had tennis and squash courts, so that about twice a week we played tennis for a couple of hours after tea, followed sometimes by a game of squash. The Club also had occasional sessions of Scottish dancing in which we joined, dressed in the conventional Jakarta Scottish dancing attire of swimsuit and bath towel. It was the only way to last out the various reels. Incidentally the Box Club was later burned down during politically inspired rioting. One feature of life in Indonesia which I shall never forget was the most beautiful colourful sunsets which occurred every night without fail in Jakarta. As the sun went down, so would commence a most wonderful vivid live sky panorama of constantly changing colour, altering at a most unbelievable rate so that one had the impression of a great modern artist giving a live demonstration of his genius. The magnificent colours would last about half an hour, gradually fading into the semi-darkness of the early evening.

Life in Jakarta continued for me on a more pleasant vein having now my wife with me to share my pleasures and problems and, above all, to provide that pleasant companionship which had been so lacking in my first lonely nine months in Indonesia. However, whilst life for me on the personal level was much more pleasant, there existed always those continuous tensions and anxieties in the general condition of life for foreigners under the Communist regime in Indonesia. This tension in public life was very real in the foreign community and exhibited itself in all kinds of evidence and rumours in everyday life. Stories proliferated of the lack of judicial justice for a white man. For example, in the Jakarta heavy traffic, with the low standard of Indonesian driving skills, it was very easy to experience a car traffic accident. If the responsibility was obviously the fault of the Indonesian driver, the ensuing court case would be adjourned time after time over the course of years in the hope that the foreigner would have departed the country during that time. If a white man was attacked in the street by muggers or robbers and a policeman chanced on the scene during the event he would turn his back on the action and disappear rapidly round the nearest corner.

I well remember the gruesome murder of the Dunlop Tyre Company representative in Jakarta. Dunlops were celebrating some anniversary in their trading history in Indonesia and held a celebratory lunch for employees and guests in a well-known restaurant in town. The occasion was a great success and there was much laughter and obvious enjoyment at the table. At the conclusion of the lunch the Dunlop representative paid the bill and followed his guests out, walking down the aisle towards the exit. When he was halfway to the door an Indonesian who had been seated near the aisle suddenly sprang up and stabbed the surprised Dunlop man in the stomach. In horror his friends turned back and held the Indonesian until the police arrived. Meanwhile the unfortunate Dunlop man was carried out of the restaurant and laid on the pavement bleeding to death whilst friends phoned several hospitals who, on learning that the victim was a foreigner, refused to help. Finally help and an ambulance were provided by an American oil company hospital. The man died from loss of blood, his life's blood having oozed out on the Indonesian pavement.

When, during subsequent interrogation of the Indonesian murderer, police demanded to know what was the reason for his unprovoked attack on the Dunlop representative, the Indonesian replied that he resented the obvious light-hearted enjoyment of his country's hospitality by this bunch of foreigners whom he associated with his country's former Colonial masters. This attitude of mind was at that time typical of any Government official and of most of the native Indonesian public! If your skin was white then you were automatically relegated to the Dutch colonial oppressor class. It is interesting to note at this time, when the Indonesian University was established at Bandung in central Java, the Government stipulated that the recruitment of academic teaching staff must not include any member from a Colonial or ex-Colonial nation. Thus British, French, Dutch, Portuguese etc. could not be academic candidates, and the university was finally staffed with a considerable number of Austrian, German and American lecturers and professors.

Another factor which greatly increased this anti-white foreigner complex was the sensational International Afro-Asian Bandung Conference in April 1955 when 29 third world countries journeyed to Indonesia and, for the first time in world history, these widely differing third world peoples joined together to present a common front to their former European Colonial masters. Indonesia, as the host nation, in an endeavour to impress its visitors from far and wide made sure that its attention to security and the strict disciplining of its white population was very visible to their friends. The Government ordered the Army and the police to provide enormous numbers of patrolling guards at public communication centres etc. At the Jakarta airport one saw numerous patrolling soldiers carrying every type of warlike arms including hand-grenades attached to their waist belts. Fortunately these birth pangs of the newly emerging independent third world Indonesia in the 1950s have long since been overcome and the difficulties and angers I experienced are no longer evident in modern Indonesia. However, anti-foreigner resentment still exists, particularly against the Chinese population minority who have recently suffered murderous violence as I have previously mentioned. In the latest news from Indonesia there seems to be considerable political unrest in some of the islands with violent riotous uprisings against the Government especially amongst students and the young population.

Another interesting feature of the Indonesian Government's attitude to and policy of recruitment of specialists and advisers for their various projects was their preference for Indian nationals. In Indonesian official circles India was viewed as an advanced nation and worthy leader of the Asiatic world. If any Government project needed specialist guidance or advice which was not available from Indonesian sources, then India would be the preferred source of supply.

The subject of Indians brings me now to an extraordinary experience I had with the Indian owner of the sports shop which was on the ground floor at street level below my own flat. One day I called into this sports shop with the object of buying some tennis balls. The Indian owner was most affable and very friendly. He invited me to partake of a coffee with him, which of course is a typical oriental business man's approach before broaching any serious business discussion. Seated with my coffee at his office table at the rear of his shop we had a pleasant conversation relating to my unusual presence living in this native community. He remarked that he had observed and speculated upon the extraordinary activities that had been going on with the donkey train arriving outside his shop, bringing loads of earth which were then carted up to my flat roof. He asked me jokingly if I was building another Westminster Abbey upon my roof. Enlightening him on how it came about that I was living in such unlikely circumstances and briefing him on the unusual activities on my roof top, our conversation became quite intimate and he suddenly asked me 'How do you live?' This struck me as a very strange question so I replied that I could not understand what his question meant. So he then said 'From where do you get your money to live?' I explained that my salary was paid by de Havilland in England and I had an account in a Singapore bank into which the Company paid my expenses. He then came up with an amazing proposition. He offered to finance me completely on a monthly basis. I could draw cash from him to any amount at any time during the month and, at the end of each month, he would present me with a detailed account. He said he had a brother in Singapore who owned a sports shop similar to his own with a bank account with the Standard Chartered Bank in Singapore. To settle my account he suggested that I should write to my bank instructing them to transfer the agreed monthly balance to his brother's account, the details of which he would provide. To get my acceptance of his proposition he offered to convert my monthly bill into Sterling at a very favourable rate. This was an offer I could not refuse, as the modern adverts say, and in which I could not lose. I accepted and it gave me great satisfaction that I was defeating the malignant treatment I had received at the hands of the Communist Authorities in Jakarta. By this means my Sterling obtained its correct international value. An example of the local Indonesian robbery of foreigners' funds was in the price of a bottle of Johnny Walker whisky which cost £17 (in today's money around £170) at the standard Indonesian rate of exchange. I am happy to say that this financial arrangement with the Indian worked extremely well. We had complete trust in each other and in fact developed a great friendship. For me our conversations proved to be extremely interesting because, as time went by, the Indian began to tell me of his boyhood life in India. He told me intimate details of his attitude to and his fear of the white man – the Raj – in his Indian home town. This friendship and financial relationship continued during the whole of my stay in Indonesia, even after my work later on took me to Bandung in central Java, some 150 miles from Jakarta.

My move to Bandung was first broached to me by de Havilland when I received a letter from the Company informing me that, thanks to the efforts of our local Agent,

Maclaine & Watson, they had succeeded in finalising a military contract to sell to the Indonesian Government a squadron of de Havilland Vampire jet fighter aircraft which would be based at Bandung. Stan Sharp, the manager of the After Sales Service Department, suggested in his letter that as I had been so successful in establishing a good relationship with the Indonesian Garuda Airways I might like to consider extending my stay in Indonesia by covering the technical after sales aspects of this new contract. The letter also stated that I would in any case be recalled to the United Kingdom as the contractual period of the on-site after sales service for Garuda Airways was now completed. Although I had enjoyed my work with Garuda I had not enjoyed my stay in Jakarta due to the political hostility and antipathy always evident when dealing with the Indonesian authorities and I hated the general atmosphere of vulnerability and insecurity in which the white population lived. But I found the country itself beautiful and unusually attractive and, above all, thanks to my Indian friend, my Singapore bank balance was moving in a positive direction. I decided to risk a further stay and wrote back agreeing to accept the Vampire jet fighter job at Bandung.

The Company then confirmed my new appointment with instructions to wind up my work with Garuda and return to the U.K. for de-briefing on the Garuda job and training for the Vampire job. I was asked to call in at Rangoon on my return journey to spend two or three weeks with the Burmese Air Force who were operating de Havilland Vampire fighter aircraft, and then to fly to India and spend some time with the headquarters of the Indian Airways who were operating de Havilland Heron aircraft on their internal routes. The Company accepted liability for my wife's return passage to the U.K. but directed that she should return by sea which was cheaper! This of course involved our travelling separately, but we found on studying the time schedule of the Italian shipping line operating from Jakarta that, whilst Pam's ship was journeying westwards, I could complete my scheduled stops in Burma and India and then fly to Genoa terminal where Pam would disembark, and we could then travel overland together after spending a few days on the coast near Genoa.

Once again our audacious travel planning proved successful. I stayed in Burma living in the Burmese Officers mess, at their Air Force station just outside Rangoon city. This was quite an unusual experience and I much enjoyed the friendly hospitable attitude of the Burmese officers One witnessed everyday a remarkable transformation or metamorphosis of the Burmese Air Force officers. All day from breakfast to teatime the officers wore a European type of blue uniform similar to that of the RAF and the pilots flying their Vampire jet fighters looked no different to the general appearance of an RAF fighter pilot. But, returning to the mess from the hangar at tea-time, having finished flying for the day, they immediately changed into their Burmese native dress of sandals and a sort of skirt arrangement. One moment they were Western style air force officers flying modern jets and the next moment they were oriental native Burmese. However my stay was very pleasant and successful and the Burmese were most friendly and hospitable.

At that time three quarters of the country was controlled by Communist guerrillas and it was very dangerous to travel very far beyond the limits of Rangoon city. The officers mess bedrooms were on ground level and I was warned by the officers to secrete my valuables and even my clothing in my wardrobe because, at night, bandits armed with long bamboo canes fitted with hooks at the end would often tour past the bedrooms at night and would poke their long canes through any open window and hook out any visible clothing while the inmate slept. One could wake up in the morning to find ones clothing and valuables gone. Rangoon at that time was in the throes of a national strike by the refuse collectors who were all imported Indians of the untouchable caste of low grade manual workers. The Burmese were strict Buddhists and could not be recruited to do such work. In consequence, whilst I was there, the streets of Rangoon, had mountains of rubbish building up in the main thoroughfares. These refuse heaps were infested with and overrun by huge rats. Again the Buddhist religion forbids the killing of any living creature so the rats enjoyed a peaceful and satiated life among the refuse mountains.

However my future rendezvous in Genoa was enforcing a rigid time schedule to my stopovers and so I bade farewell to my Burmese Air Force friends. I continued my flight westwards to India with the object of calling in at Air India in Delhi. However the only airline available deposited me in Calcutta and I had to transfer the next day to an internal flight to Delhi. I spent the stopover night in Calcutta town centre in a very grand hotel, the name of which I have forgotten. After dinner at the hotel I went for an evening stroll in the city centre. Coming back I witnessed an amazing scene. All along the pavements of this city centre main street running past my luxurious hotel were long lines of Indians stretched out lying on sheets of newspaper, preparing to spend the night sleeping on the pavements. They were so numerous that to reach my hotel I had to gingerly step over their dormant bodies. This scene was a potent example of the depths of poverty almost shoulder to shoulder with the height of luxury, which is so typical of the way of life in India. The next day I flew on the internal Indian airline to Delhi where I spent a few days in liaison with the technical management of Air India. But my rendezvous date in Genoa was approaching fast and forbade me to linger too long in Delhi where I was again in a luxurious downtown hotel. Here the hotel waiters were dressed in beautiful, rich, colourful Indian costumes, a kind of livery with their hands ensconced in fitted pure white gloves so that no contact was made with plates or cutlery.

And so, onwards and westwards on my final lap to Genoa where I booked into a reasonable hotel and awaited the arrival of my wife's ship, which was due the following day. The ship duly arrived the next day complete with Pam as per schedule and, once again, our planned meeting took place after we had both travelled thousands of miles over several weeks pursuing completely different itineraries to make our rendezvous exactly on time. Was this pure luck or good management? Looking back to those days I begin to wonder at the audacity of such arrangements. Were we just plain lucky or plain stupid? Anyhow we were both delighted to see each other again after our travels and we decided to celebrate the occasion by indulging in a sightseeing break touring the beautiful Italian coastal resorts just a few miles south of Genoa. We spent two or three days visiting this delightful Italian coast, staying in Portofino and then Rapallo. Now came the crunch point – we ran out of money! In those days it often took weeks to transfer money from one's bank and this was a time when the British Government had applied rigid and extremely tight controls on money for foreign holidays. In fact you were only allowed a maximum of £50 for such a holiday. I had overspent the money I had collected in travellers cheques from my bank in Singapore and now there was no way we could obtain urgently needed funds except by declaring ourselves penniless at the British consulate and throwing ourselves on the benevolence of His Majesty's Government. This we did in Rapallo and they did not blink an eyelid! With the stringent currency regulations and the ridiculously limited sum of £50 only that one was allowed to take on holiday they must have received many supplicants such as ourselves. The Consulate allowed us to borrow £25 from the Government treasure chest after proving our eligibility and signing an undertaking that we would repay H.M. Treasury within three months. I had a feeling that I was a penniless tramp holding out a begging bowl. Having collected our life-saving cash we decided it was about time we turned our backs on the delights of Rapallo and headed back home to England. With our limited resources we bought train tickets, as that was the cheapest way back. Our non-stop journey through Switzerland, France and across the Channel, living on sandwiches, brought us home to dear old England. We made our home temporarily with Pam's parents in view of the fact that I should be returning to Indonesia shortly. As yet we had no home of our own. However we began searching for a suitable property in which we could establish our own home later when I returned. Obviously it would have to be located within reasonable distance of my work at Leavesden. Thus we spent a considerable time touring round the Watford and St. Albans area looking for a suitable property.

After reporting back to the de Havilland Engine Company at Leavesden near Watford I began an intensive study of the de Havilland Goblin jet engine which was the power plant fitted to the Vampire fighter aircraft. The particular marque of Goblin engine fitted to the Indonesian Vampire produced 3,350 lb. thrust. At that time one pound thrust could be approximated to one horsepower at sea level so that the Vampire type engine had approximately a 3,350 h.p. output. This power gave the Vampire a maximum speed of 548 m.p.h. at 30,000 feet with a service ceiling of 42,800 feet and a maximum range of 1,220 miles at 30,000 feet. It could carry 4 20-mm. guns in the nose and had provision for up to 2000lb of bombs or rockets under the wings.

I was informed that, due to lack of funds, the Indonesian Vampires would not be flown out to their destination but would be dismantled, crated and dispatched by sea. This of course would involve a considerable time spent en route to Indonesia and there would be the task of re-assembling the aircraft at Bandung in central Java. There would be no provision for a de Havilland specialist assembly team, so that the supervision and responsibility for the correct assembly of the aircraft by the Indonesians would fall on the two resident de Havilland engineers who would be in temporary residence in accordance with the sales contract. One engineer would be from the de Havilland Aircraft Company and would be responsible for overseeing the airframe work and the other would be myself from the D.H. Engine Company responsible for the power plants

Eventually I was notified that the crated aircraft had been embarked and had begun their long sea voyage. It was now time for me to return to Indonesia and get myself established in Bandung in preparation for the arrival of the Vampires. This I did, stopping in Singapore and this time ensuring I stayed long enough to deposit my funds into my Singapore bank account, keeping just enough cash to satisfy the Jakarta customs and immigration authorities. Pausing in Jakarta long enough to renew my contacts with my Garuda friends, with our agents Maclaine & Watson, and with my Indian friend of the sports shop 'Treasury', I collected from the docks a new Morris Oxford car which I had purchased in England under the special export scheme, and headed for Bandung in the interior of Java. There I found comfortable accommodation in a pleasant hotel in downtown Bandung where I discovered that quite a number of my fellow hotel guests were German or Austrian academic staff of the newly created Technical Faculty of the Bandung University. As I was the only Englishman around the place we soon became chummy and I learned from them some very intimate details of the character of these Austrian and German people and the bickering relationships they had with each other. I remember them telling me with some relish how they had brought about the downfall of a German professor who was the head of one of the University departments. Apparently they had carried out a private investigation of the credentials and the claimed qualifications of this professor. By referring back to Germany they had discovered that he had obtained his post by claiming false qualifications. The net result was that the professor was dismissed from his post much to the satisfaction of my German friends. The Germans seem to have difficulty in achieving good, open friendships with their neighbours and fellow colleagues. Michael Bloch's Biography of Ribbentrop, the Foreign Affairs Minister of Hitler's Nazi government, tells unbelievable stories of the vendettas and feuds between the various German Nazi Ministers and officials.

I was escorted by an Indonesian Air Force officer to their base and aerodrome which was just outside Bandung. Here I was fixed up with the necessary Air Force station entry pass and authority to operate in their military hangars. The crated aircraft duly arrived and there began one of the most comic and fraught operations I have ever witnessed in any Air Force I have visited around the world.

Balinese female temple dancer

Balinese male temple dancer

Chapter 23

The Indonesian Air Force at Bandung, Java
Indonesian Vampire Jet Fighter Aircraft
Operation
Return to England
Rebirth of the German Air Force

To appreciate the significance of the events in Java which I am about to describe it will perhaps help if I mention the background of local public interest excited at that time by the Indonesian national media which was fed by extravagant government propaganda boasting of the entry of Indonesia into the 20th century jet age. It must be remembered that Indonesia had only recently gained its independence after centuries of subjugation to their Dutch colonial masters and after the years of bondage to the Japanese invaders during World War 2. Thus the government was able to generate by propaganda a public euphoria by declaring the wonderful progress that independent Indonesia had made in such a short time. It proudly proclaimed that, having just taken the leadership of the Third World countries by hosting the successful Bandung Afro-Asian conference, it was now taking its place in world aviation as a modern up-to-date nation entering the new jet age. As a result of this national interest in the arrival of the Vampire aircraft the Indonesian Air Force leaders were extremely anxious that the aircraft should appear in the air at the earliest possible moment. Thus the personnel at the Bandung Air Force station were under great pressure during the events which followed the arrival of the aircraft. There was a kind of universal determination at the Bandung base that, by hook or by crook, they were going to get these aircraft into the air and show the world the progress they had made in their new freedom.

The first crates to arrive at the Bandung base were quickly opened up and the dis-assembled components moved out for re-assembly. The Bandung station did not have the technical resources which were available in Jakarta since there were no overhaul and repair workshops for the major overhaul and repair of engines or airframes. This was considered no handicap by the Indonesian Air Force at Bandung. The whole station personnel decided that their country was going to enter the jet age fast, regardless of any lack of technicians or tools – everyone, from cooks and butchers to the camp gate policemen were volunteers to help re-build these aircraft. To add to the confusion of hordes of unskilled personnel all clamouring for a part of

Indonesian Air Force Vampire fighter aircraft with the de Havilland team.
From the right: Self, Test Pilot George Errington, Jakarta Agent Steve Day,
Airframe Engineer

Test Pilot George Errington talking to Indonesian Air Force Commander prior to
demonstration air test

the action, it was found that the specialist tooling required for certain operations in the re-assembly of the aircraft had not been packed with the first deliveries and in consequence these aircraft had to be assembled with improvised tooling. One could almost say that they were assembled with knife, fork and spoon! Such were the technically dangerous conditions that were causing the De Havilland aircraft engineer and myself the greatest anxiety. The worry of what might happen in this unbelievably chaotic operation was giving both of us nightmares. We both rushed from aircraft to aircraft assembly teams, hoping to cover at least all the critical operations which would affect the safety of the aircraft. We wanted to be sure the wings would not drop off in the test flight or that the engines would not come adrift or fail in flight.

It is an incredible fact that all twelve aircraft were re-assembled successfully. As part of the Vampire sales contract de Havillands had agreed to provide one of their Company test pilots to air-test the aircraft in Indonesia after re-assembly. For this purpose George Errington turned up and proceeded to put the Vampires through their paces to check whether they would fall apart under the severe and violent air testing. I flew with him on one of the air tests and I can testify that this particular aeroplane was certainly subjected to maximum stresses. At around 10,000 feet during tight vertical bank turns at about 500 m.p.h. or more the G factor was too great for this elderly aviator and I blacked out for a minute or so.

By this time the Indonesian media had created a tremendous national interest by sensational reporting of the introduction of their very first national Air Force jet aircraft. The media seized on every detail connected with the operation of the aircraft, of which I remember one was George Errington's astonishing 'sang froid' in his air testing operations and his quiet unconcerned attitude to the air tests compared with the brash 'hoo-haa' and extrovert displays put on by the Americans in similar situations. I remember also how the press made a big story of how George flew on his air testing in ordinary sports shirt and light slacks wearing only a cotton cloth helmet compared with the Americans in their sophisticated flying suits and huge 'bone domes' which were their flying headgear..

It was finally decided by the Indonesian Government that there would be a ceremonial formal handing over, at which our Agents, Maclaine & Watson, would officially hand over the certificated documents for the completed aircraft to the Chief of the Indonesian Air Force. All the aircraft were lined up at the Bandung Air Force Station and made an imposing sight. The public were admitted to the ceremony and were permitted to view the spare jet engines which were housed in one of the hangars. My de Havilland colleague, George, and I gave interviews to the press which, incidentally, included Chinese newspaper correspondents. George gave a flying display which created a minor sensation.

For the following six months I made regular periodic trips in my car to Jakarta to brief Maclaine & Watson on the progress of the Vampire operations and, of course, to call on my Indian friend to replenish my financial resources. This cross-country journey I viewed with a mixture of delight and anxiety. The mountainous country one

Line up of Indonesian Air Force de Havilland Vampire Jet fighter aircraft

Open Day – Indonesian Air Force Bandung

The author giving interview to Chinese press journalists on the de Havilland Goblin Jet engine fitted to the Vampire fighter

had to transverse was so beautiful with lush greenery and forests but one knew that the rocky mountain tops concealed fanatic guerrilla bandits who would keep themselves in funds by the occasional road block in some remote spot. I always carried a loaded revolver with me – just in case! However it fortunately never happened to me. Whether I could have used my revolver to any effect in an emergency is debatable but knowing it was there gave me a little comfort.

When George Errington's mission of air testing was finished he accompanied me to Jakarta starting his return journey to the U.K. On the journey we both expressed our enjoyment and wonder at the beauty of the countryside in spite of the danger. We started at a very early hour in the morning so that we should arrive with enough of the working morning left to complete our business in Jakarta. In consequence we witnessed remarkable views of the huge layers of mist and clouds lying in the deep valleys, from which we would rise as we climbed to the higher mountainous regions to look down on these tremendous areas of cloud and mist rolling along the mountain sides and completely hiding the deep valleys. As the journey progressed and with the passing of time the mist and clouds lifted and revealed the exotic beauty of the lush vegetation and the magnificent forests. Half way on this journey was situated a very good class old Dutch mountain hotel which provided excellent food etc. and where there was an open air swimming pool. George and I stopped for breakfast here and

Mount Prahu active volcano near Bandung, Java

Angry Mount Prahu volcano boiling over (near Bandung, Java)

indulged in a refreshing swim. I parted company with George in Jakarta and sadly I learned a few years later that he had been killed in a car accident. He loved his TR sports car.

The longer one stayed and travelled in Indonesia the greater became the fascination for this extraordinary volcanic archipelago which extends over 4000 miles from East to West and comprises more than 13,000 islands. Many thousands of the islands are small and uninhabited but there are quite a number of very large islands such as Sumatra, Java, Borneo, New Guinea etc. For example Sumatra is 1150 miles in length and is the fifth largest island in the world. In fact Indonesia is the fourth most highly populated country in the world. The equator runs right though the centre of this archipelago and it can perhaps be viewed as the tops of one continuous chain of volcanic mountains which at some time in the distant past have risen above the surrounding sea areas. The mountain range Bukit Barisan extends 1050 miles throughout the length of Sumatra and continues under the sea across the narrow channel to rise again in Java where it continues for hundreds of miles. In the Sumatra chain there are 93 volcanoes with the highest peak of 12500 feet at the south eastern tip of the chain. Here is the site of the world famous volcano Krakatan which, after being dormant for 200 years, erupted in 1883 killing 36,000 people and its ash spread across the world reaching the U.S.A. As a result of this eruption a new small island rose from under the sea close to the tip of Sumatra. In the Java chain there are 100 volcanoes of which 15 are active. Quite close to Bandung is the Mount Prahu with an active volcano nearby which I visited during my stay. Passing through Lembang, a small town near the foothills of the mountain, the countryside gradually changes as one climbs until near the volcano mouth is the most eerie desolate environment I have ever experienced anywhere in the world. There was not the slightest sign of life, not a plant, nor a single bird, anywhere to be seen in the locality – just a deathly silence with a boiling cauldron down below in the huge pit tremendous in diameter, sending up occasional fountains of bubbling liquid lava.

It is interesting to note that Bandung gets some 80 inches of rain a year, probably twice the U.K. rate, which may account for the tremendous crops of rice and tea in the area. But Indonesia's main economy is based on oil with great contributions from rubber, tobacco, tea, coffee, palm oil, with gold, silver and coal deposits. At the time when I was there the total population was around 100 million with some 80% concentrated in the island of Java. In the 1990 census the population had increased to 181 million. It is now over 200 million with 100 million located on the island of Java. It was our experience in Java that one could never escape from people, even if one climbed to the remotest mountain peak, which we did, and to our dismay found signboards displaying the hammer and sickle, the symbol of the all-reaching Communist party. We turned with difficulty on the narrow mountain road and fled from the mounting crowd of children who suddenly appeared from nowhere.

I was mightily glad when finally my Company agreed that my tour of duty in Indonesia was completed and I returned to Jakarta once more to catch my plane for my return flight home. As the plane took off and mounted the skies over Jakarta I experienced such joy as I looked down. I felt what I should imagine would be the feelings of a convict as he passed out of the prison gates to freedom. Indonesia at that time was a Police State under its Communist regime but today that situation has changed and Communist dictatorship no longer exists. A form of autocracy has taken over. Or should we say a modified democracy existed with a dictator who had a policy of nepotism. But in spite of the restrictions of such a policy Indonesia has made astounding industrial advances and the Indonesia of today is unrecognisable from the country in which we lived over forty years ago. At the moment Indonesia, along with the rest of the Far East, is passing through difficult times economically but the concerned support of the Western international financial organisations is already reversing the situation and there is no doubt that Indonesia will eventually become a great and powerful force in the economic world.

In the three months interval with Pam in England prior to my return to Indonesia, as mentioned previously, Pam and I searched around Watford and St. Albans for a property in which to set up home. Actually we found a beautiful and ideal modern cottage with an 'oldy worldy' look in Radlett in a select area inhabited mainly by well-to-do professional people who commuted daily into London. But I considered the price was beyond my means at that time. I had visions of a millstone mortgage round my neck for the rest of my life! The price of the house was £4150 but my basic pay was only £13.80 a week – just £676 a year – so I resisted the idea and suggested we continue our search. This we did but always came back to the Radlett house for Pam had fallen in love with the place. Finally I wilted and gave in, praying that somehow I would find ways of paying the dreaded mortgage of £23 13s 9d each month. I quote these figures so the modern generation of today paying mortgages of hundreds of pounds can have a good laugh!

We bought the 5 bedroom cottage with the aid of a mortgage from the local municipal authority paying interest at $5^1/_4\%$. I had to return to Indonesia before we could take possession. This was due to a delay by the previous owner who regretted that he had sold at the price and was angry because we refused to release him from the sale contract. He refused to move out until the last minute. Pam finally took possession on her own with the vicious and vengeful occupier refusing to hand over the key, thus forcing her to do a 40 mile journey in fog to obtain a key from his solicitor. Pending my return from Indonesia she continued to live with her parents and let the house to tenants on a short-term lease. By so doing we discovered the tremendous letting potential of Watford and district – a veritable property developers' gold mine. This discovery was to be an important factor in our financial future. On my return we moved into the Radlett cottage and soon descended into debt as I had feared. Our daughter Anne was born soon after we moved in. But necessity is the mother of invention. We had five bedrooms of which 3 were really surplus to our requirements. Eureka! We would create a small furnished flat with the three surplus bedrooms and the letting thereof would help solve our financial problems – we hoped. And we did just that; using ingenuity to produce cooking arrangements and incorporating one of our two bathrooms into the arrangement we produced a self-contained flatlet. Inserting one advertisement in the local weekly Watford paper produced to our amazement about a hundred replies. We had to quickly learn how to be wise and kind landlords. We were lucky; our tenants were nice people, co-operative and appreciative of our efforts to provide them with a comfortable home.

Several months after my return from Indonesia de Havillands gave me an unusual assignment. In January 1957 I was asked to go to Bonn in Germany to represent the Company in the introduction of a Heron aircraft to the newly formed German Luftwaffe. This event had caused quite a stir in Germany for, although it was not a fighting aircraft, it was notable as the first aircraft permitted to the German Air Force by the Allies since their surrender at the end of World War 2. It was the first post-war aircraft to carry the livery and insignia of the newly arisen German Air Force. Actually it was the German Minister for Foreign Affairs who had ordered the aircraft as his personal official transport to be operated and maintained by the German Air Force. Herr Strauss had made quite a national feature of this event and on his first trip had invited a section of the German press to accompany him to witness how he had succeeded in securing the start of the re-birth of the German Air Force. So, with great advance media propaganda boasting of his new personal aeroplane which foreshadowed the rise of New Germany from its miserable guilty past, he took off from Bonn early one Saturday morning in February 1957, complete with his bevy of newspaper reporters accompanying him in the Heron cabin. The weather was not kind and already it was raining. As the aircraft climbed to cruising altitude the rain conditions intensified. The pilot decided to use his windscreen wipers but unfortunately this young man was an inexperienced officer of the Luftwaffe and he appears not to have learnt the fundamental law of always operating aircraft controls smoothly in a graduated manner. There were four stages for setting the windscreen wiper control from minimum to maximum power. He swept his control straight through the lot at one go. With the heavy rain load on the windscreen wiper motor, plus the sudden overload demand by the control setting, the electric motor began to overheat and gave off fumes. The fumes penetrated the flight deck and the pilot panicked. Thinking that the aeroplane was on fire he immediately put the aircraft into a violent steep nose dive, hoping to extinguish the supposed fire. However he gave no warning to his passengers to fasten their set belts and in consequence Herr Strauss was ejected from his seat rather rapidly and ascended towards the cabin roof! A clever press photographer in the cabin managed to capture a shot of the Minister at the height of his ascent to the roof. The aeroplane returned to Bonn. This picture was published in one of Germany's well known national periodicals, I think it was Das Bild, together with an article mocking Herr Strauss and making a denigratory criticism of the de Havilland aeroplane, accusing the Minister of having bought a pup.

This adverse propaganda by the German press caused considerable anxiety to the de Havilland hierarchy at home who were hoping to sell other military aircraft to

Germany, and in any case it was completely unfair. The Company decided to take the German periodical to court, claiming libel. They soon established positive evidence that the whole incident was the pilot's error and the German paper withdrew its statement and apologised. The pilot was relieved of his post as personal pilot to Herr Strauss. The Company took steps to ensure future pilots of the aircraft were fully briefed on its handling. After a further couple of months of trouble free operations I returned to England. Needless to say the windscreen wiper system was modified to ensure that such mishandling could not happen again.

Chapter 24

Air Tour of Northern Europe
The Pioneer Jet de Havilland Comet Disasters

On my return to Leavesden I was asked by the Company to form part of a Company team that would fly round Northern Europe visiting all those customers who were using de Havilland aircraft. The trip would be a sort of 'Flying the Company Flag' and would use a Company Dove aircraft to impress the operators in the various countries we would visit. The team consisted of a Company pilot from the sales demonstration department, myself representing the after sales engineering service and a navigator from our aerodrome traffic control section. Our first port of call was Copenhagen in Denmark where we spent several days visiting various operators and we were entertained most hospitably by a Danish millionaire. He was the local de Havilland Agent but his connection with aviation I have forgotten. However I do remember the excellent entertainment he kindly arranged for us. We visited the main tourist spots of Copenhagen including the wonderful Tivoli leisure gardens full of interest including the splendid puppet theatre. We then flew on eastwards to Finland where the Finnish Air Force was operating de Havilland aircraft. This again was most interesting because the Finns had created their capacious aircraft hangars by carving huge caves into a mountain rock face to give security from enemy attack. We spent some time in their engine overhaul workshops, giving advice on various technical questions which they raised with us. The Chief Engineer was most hospitable and actually invited us to spend the week-end with him in his holiday home where, like most Finns, he had a cellar fitted out to provide a full scale Sauna Bath. We witnessed the entire operation of setting up the Sauna which apparently is a universal feature of the Finns' way of life.

The Sauna room was a sort of cellar of a moderate size, probably about 12 ft x 10 ft. in their stone built house. This cellar room was bare of furniture but with staging built up at one end. This staging rose from the ground floor to the ceiling and provided seating for about a dozen people at various levels above the floor. The operational system in this room was a kind of old fashioned 'copper' or large metal container built into brickwork, beneath which was a tunnel fireplace to provide heating to the container. A collection of sizeable round granite-like stones similar to those large stones occasionally found on a stony beach was placed inside the metal container. The fire was lit fairly early in the morning and maintained at a lively condition all day until late afternoon when the stones were at a very high temperature and had elevated the general atmospheric temperature in the room to a very high level. It was at this point that the Finnish fun and games started. We were introduced into the room naked some time before the maximum temperature had been reached. The temperature of the room could be controlled by opening or closing the cover at the top of the container, which held the hot stones. We took our seats on the wooden staging and sampled the effects of the heated atmosphere. By mounting to the higher seating near the ceiling one could obtain higher temperatures due of course to the general heat rising. To accentuate the effect of the heat on our naked bodies we were provided with birch switches, with which we were instructed to indulge in gentle flagellation, which would stimulate the whole body blood system. As the temperature rose the effect on the inner linings of ones orifices such as nostrils, ears, etc. became very painful until, in my own case, I could no longer bear the pain and I had to descend from the staging seats and lie on the floor with my head resting on the stone floor to reach the lowest level and thus the lowest temperature. This permitted some small relief. After the prescribed duration of this boiling process we were conducted from this inferno into an adjoining bathroom to shower in cold water. No one with heart problems should ever undertake this kind of activity, for the shock is intense but marvellously stimulating. But a further shock was in store because the final phase was for us to leave the house and run across a footpath to plunge into a nearby mountain lake whose temperature seemed to be not much above freezing point. In my own case the initial shock was so intense that I seemed to lose all bodily feeling and had no sensation at all except a dumb mad desire to swim as fast as possible to get myself out of this freezing water. I provided a little amusement for my companions at this final phase because the way from the house to the lakeside staging, where we plunged in, crossed a public footpath. My colleagues discreetly covered their nakedness with a towel around their waists but I, not realising there were people on a public footpath, blindly ran stark naked in broad daylight across the footpath and plunged into the lake. The Finnish spectators on their Sunday afternoon lakeside stroll had the unusual experience of seeing a wildly fleeing naked Englishman crossing the public highway and madly plunging into the ice-cold water of the lake.

Following the lake plunge ordeal we were conducted, still naked, to the final and much more pleasant phase of the Finnish sauna. This was a kind of rewarding relaxation where we all gathered in another cellar room and sat in a circle around a typical continental circular heating stove which blazed out kindly heat to warm our frozen bodies. Here we were served beer and delicious sandwiches with cheese and biscuits and other delights by the ladies of the house who took not the slightest notice of our birthday suits and in fact joined us in the general convivial occasion.

After this pleasant week-end's intimate glimpse of Finnish family life we did some further work in the Air Force workshops, advising on problems of salvaging worn parts on aircraft engine overhaul etc After this the Chief Engineer suggested we might fly down south to Helsinki where we could have discussions with headquarters staff. This we did, and I shall never forget the extraordinary aerial view of Finland that we had that day as we flew at about ten thousand feet over this strange country which appears from the air to be mostly water. Finland consists of over 60,000 shallow lakes joined together with what seemed from the air to be narrow necks of land, and 17,000 small islands. Thus from the air the whole country appeared to be like a mighty lace-work of water joined together by threads of land. Further north there is more continuous land with the mountainous area we had just left rising to just over 4000 feet. With so many areas of inland water salmon fishing is an important industry. Salmon used to be so cheap in Finland that there existed a national law which stipulated that domestic servants living in must have in their employment contracts a mandatory clause stating that salmon must not be served for their meals more than twice a week.

Finland was once a huge low lying glacier plateau and a remarkable feature is that land is still rising from the sea at the rate of 2.7 square miles every year. However the land has produced extensive forestry and has generated considerable timber products, especially paper. At the time we were there in 1957 Finland was experiencing rapid economic growth, having by then recovered from her WW2 war experiences and defeat and subjugation by the Russian Communist regime led by Stalin. Thus agriculture and new industries had arisen, giving rise to exports in engineering, chemicals, and food processing, utilising a vast development of hydroelectric power in the mining of copper and iron ore. In fact, since those times Finland has become one of the world's largest manufacturers of electronic I.T. items, such as Nokia mobile phones. Its shipbuilding industry now produces mighty luxury liners for the United States of America.

A third of the country lies north of the Arctic Circle so that summer in Finland is a very short-lived period of the climatic year. In fact real summer by our standards, we were told, lasts for only about three weeks and mild weather which the Finns call summer lasts for about another four weeks. The rest of the year sees the majority of the people living behind closed and shuttered windows and doors, which probably explains why the average Finn is of rather pale complexion. However, although much of the country is in or adjacent to the Arctic Circle the proximity of the Baltic Sea has a warming effect with west winds bringing warm air currents, so alleviating the extremely cold Arctic conditions.

Our stay in Helsinki was interesting in that our hotel in the city centre had its own sauna bath system which we decided to try out to compare it with our previous experience. Of course there was no freezing lake to provide shock treatment after the boiling process but the general system was similar except that it was very public. In addition the final phase consisted of a most brutal massage administered by a female masseuse whilst one was stretched out naked on a contraption similar to the operating table in a hospital theatre.

As part of our entertainment we were conducted by our Finnish host to a Helsinki night club which had an interesting floorshow as part of its programme. After the show we decided to leave the night club at about 1 a.m. and together outside we called a taxi to return to our hotel. When the taxi driver discovered from our conversation that we were English he refused to take us in his taxi and drove off. I presume he was a Communist and one of the Finnish minority that rejoiced in

Central Helsinki, Finland

Helsinki Harbour, Finland

supporting Russia. Anyway he caused us to have another unusual experience because we then decided to walk back to the hotel. At two o'clock in the morning it was broad daylight as we took a route through a very pleasant park in the centre of Helsinki. It is another remarkable feature of Finland that the sun never sinks below the horizon for over 70 days during the so-called summer. Thus for those seventy days or more there is continuous daylight and no night-time. Night owls and night burglars should avoid Finland at this time of the year.

We finally decided to say farewell to our Finnish friends and to wend our aerial way westwards. We took off from Helsinki and crossed the Baltic Sea to Sweden where we landed at Stockholm. I have no great recollection of what we did in the short time we spent here except I do remember the enormous amount of government propaganda against drink driving and the emphasis on the severity of the penalties if you were caught breaking their laws against this evil. I was rather impressed by this Government action against this dangerous and anti-social activity because in England at that time our own attitude was rather lax.

We headed westwards again, to Norway where we put down at Stavanger on the west coast. The Norwegians were using our aircraft, Herons if I remember correctly, for fjord hopping in their internal airline. We visited their workshops and, as in Finland, gave advice on various engine overhaul problems including salvage schemes for worn parts. There was not, however, the same friendly informal relationship that we had experienced during our stay in Finland and so we did not tarry long with the Norwegians. Having accomplished our liaison visit we once again took off, heading westwards for home, landing at Leavesden airfield in good shape after a successful trip of many thousands of miles.

On my return my department manager, Stan Sharp and Thomson, his assistant, invited me for a lunch time pub session in a local near Leavesden during which I was offered promotion to take charge of one of the sections in the service engineers department. This meant relinquishing my world-wide travels and the relevant expense accounts which up to that time had proved of great financial help to my meagre salary. It was an accepted policy of the Company at that time that a service engineer posted abroad as their resident representative would have an expense account to cover his daily living, entertainment and hospitality to the customer, and all relevant expenses. He thus had no need to touch his basic salary whilst abroad on such a contract. This the Company paid into his U.K. bank. Needless to say I turned the offer down, explaining that it would mean I would be permanently at the Leavesden base and the loss of my expense account would adversely affect my financial position. I said that whilst I was gratified by their obvious confidence in my ability to lead the section I had doubts whether my basic salary would be adequate to maintain my standard of living. At this the manager became annoyed at my rejection of his offer and accused me of living beyond my means. I presume that he meant that I should not be living in such an expensive house in such an expensive neighbourhood. This was not very intelligent on his part for my reaction was immediately to finalise my determination to reject the offer. If he had offered a rise in my basic salary this might have caused me to reconsider my decision. As it was we agreed to differ and shortly after I was offered a very important and long term post resident in India.

The background to this offer was another strange chapter of events as was the case preceding my first post in Indonesia. The Indian Air Force had been equipped with a considerable number of Vampire jet fighters and had established a major engineering support establishment at Bangalore, capital of Karnataka province in southern India. In this former British military base they had located extensive workshops for the overhaul and repair of their aircraft, including large jet engine workshops and test house for the overhaul and bench testing of their de Havilland Goblin jet engines fitted in their Vampire aircraft.

In view of the importance of this contract for de Havillands an Engine Company engineer had been resident on contract in Bangalore for several years, working in close liaison with the Indian workshops. In fact I was given to understand that this engineer was on such good terms and had established such a close relationship with the Indian Air Force engineers that he had become more or less the permanent Superintendent of the jet engine workshops. He had literally become 'one of them' and more or less gone native. I understood he had tremendous influence and high standing with the Indian engineers, such that every engine overhauled was personally tested and approved by him. He lived as an Indian in Indian quarters. This was highly satisfactory to the de Havilland Engine Company for the first few years, but it would appear that recently this engineer had begun to assume a somewhat independent attitude to the Company. Possibly under Indian influence he began to ignore Company instructions and procedures. A visit by a senior Company representative produced an adverse report. The Company decided it was time for him to be relieved of his post and return home. He was given instructions to wind up his work at Bangalore and return to Leavesden. These instructions he completely ignored. After an interval the Company repeated their instructions to him to return home. Again he failed to follow the Company instructions. Finally the Company was able to concentrate his mind by cutting off his salary and expense account. This rapidly brought him back to the English earth at Leavesden. On his return his relationship with the English was in no way as harmonious as it had been with the Indians and he parted company with the de Havilland Engine Company.

This is where I came into the picture for the Company offer to me was obviously to take over the post at Bangalore just recently relinquished by the recalled rebellious engineer. The prospect was not enticing but nevertheless I accepted the offer and the Company immediately took steps to arrange a new contract with the Indian government. However it became evident from the long delaying Indian tactics that they were reluctant to sign a new contract. The Indian Air Force engineers were possibly annoyed that the Company had forcibly removed their former 'Anglo pro Indian' jet engine guide and mentor. With typical oriental reluctance to give a definite negative answer to the proposed new contract the long delays and difficult negotiations finally persuaded the Company that the Bangalore engineer's contract should be abandoned.

It was during this time that de Havillands, together, later, with the Government Department, R.A.E. Farnborough, had set up an intensive investigation to discover the cause, over the last two years, of a series of crashes of the pioneer de Havilland 'Comet' jet airliner. These crashes resulted in the 'Comet' being grounded world-wide. Major airlines who had previously used the 'Comet' suffered serious financial losses which led to many legal claims for loss of earnings and threatened court actions for damages and compensation. These financial difficulties brought de Havillands to the brink of bankruptcy. Obviously it was a matter of great urgency to find the answer to this problem. The D.H. Engine Company investigating team was from the Company Design and Development Department and I was loaned to this investigating team to assist the team pending the Indians making up their minds on my Bangalore contract.

Between 1952 and April 1954 there had been five 'Comet' incidents. The first two, one on 26th October 1952 on take-off at Rome Airport and the other on 3rd March 1953 on take-off at Karachi Airport in Pakistan, were the result of pilot error. The lift characteristics of the high speed jet airliner were very different to those of old piston engine aircraft and there was a tendency for inexperienced 'Comet' pilots to lift the nose of the aircraft too high too soon, causing a stalling condition. The first incident on stalled ground impact damaged the undercarriage, but with no fatalities. In the second incident the stalling aircraft struck a low wall and burned out, killing the ten crew and the pilot.

The third incident on 2nd May 1953 involved a B.O.A.C. 'Comet' taking off in monsoon conditions from Calcutta in India .Whilst climbing to cruise altitude, the aircraft suddenly dived steeply out of control and disintegrated. The six crew and thirty-seven passengers were all killed. Following the enquiry and a whole series of modifications the 'Comet' resumed service. On 10th January 1954 another 'Comet' taking off from Rome for London reached cruising height and then for no apparent reason exploded. The 'Comet' was grounded world-wide and the enquiry found that the cause of the accident was sudden decompression in the passenger cabin. Fifty modifications were introduced following the recommendations of the enquiry committee and the Comet once again resumed service.

Finally, on 5th April 1954, a B.O.A.C. 'Comet', again taking off from Rome with seven crew and fourteen passengers, reached cruising altitude, exploded and fell into the sea some ten miles or so south of Elba. At this point it may be appropriate to consider briefly the background of the Company of which I was a member. The de Havilland Aircraft and Engine Companies were founded in the 1920s by Geoffrey de Havilland. Geoffrey (1882-1965) was an early British aeronautical pioneer who worked on his first biplane in 1909. He was Chief Engineer of the early Royal Aircraft Factory and later, from 1911-14, of the former Aircraft Manufacturing Company. He designed and produced several World War I aircraft, notably the DH4 single engine light bomber and that most famous single engine biplane, the DH9A light bomber which remained in use by the RAF at home and overseas until 1931. Many other Air Forces world-wide were also equipped with the DH9A which was used for many years after World War I ended. In fact my own first flight as a boy apprentice at the age of 16 in 1924 was in the DH9A WW1 light bomber. The aircraft I flew in had a 400 h.p. Liberty engine designed by Rolls Royce but manufactured in America. There was an alternative power plant which was a Rolls Royce 360 h.p. Eagle engine. The Liberty engine version at that time had an evil reputation for being nose heavy. Inexperienced pilots when landing could tip onto their nose causing the engine to crush the petrol tank which brought about an almighty explosion and a raging fire from which the pilot had very little chance of escape. In my crash duties as a young airman I have ghastly recollections of picking out from the cockpit rudder control bar area a carbonised foot of the unfortunate pilot. The DH9A or 'NINE-ACK' as it was known in the service had a maximum speed of 114 m.p.h. and a ceiling of 16,500 feet but an endurance of $5^3/_4$ hours which was good for that time. When serving overseas it carried a spare wheel, complete with tyre, attached to one side of the engine bay on the outside of the nose nacelle. This was because the aviation tyres were so thin with no tread in order to reduce weight that they could be easily punctured by Egyptian desert camel thorn or rough landing ground in India. These aircraft were used extensively for patrolling the North West Frontier of India which in itself was quite a dangerous occupation, seeing that the maximum height obtainable by the DH9A was only 16,500 feet whereas the N.W. Frontier Himalayan mountains were 20,000 feet or more. Furthermore the mountainous nature of the countryside precluded any hope of a suitable forced landing spot if an emergency

The de Havilland 9A (Nineack) aircraft, originally a WWI design day bomber, which was used well into the 1930's. This type was also used at Wittering as a trainer aircraft

arose and actual landing grounds were few and far between in this hostile tribal area. This aeroplane proved to be a very long continuous factory production unit for de Havillands and altogether a total of 4000 DH9As were built.

In the post World War I years the de Havilland Company produced a considerable number of commercial passenger aircraft of wooden construction. One such was the 8 passenger DH18 which was used to provide a peacetime service between London and Paris. Production of a larger civil aircraft, the DH34, followed. This provided the cross channel passenger service from 1922 to 1926. The famous DH60 moth with a Cirrus engine eventually emerged from the de Havilland factory in 1925 and I was ground crew at the Central Flying School (Wittering) servicing a flight of these aircraft. This flight eventually gave an inverted formation display at the annual Hendon Air Display. An inverted auxiliary fuel supply system sited on the undercarriage had to be introduced to supplement the engine normal carburration system and so permit these inverted Moths to retain engine power. Later, in 1930, the DH Cirrus was replaced by the DH Gypsy engine which had been re-designed to operate with inverted in-line cylinders. This permitted a greatly improved streamlining of the Tiger Moth aircraft shape. The Tiger Moth was the RAF primary training aircraft right throughout World War 2 and has been used by flying clubs throughout the world for many years since the war. In fact, as I have previously recounted in this story, I took my own pilotsair test on a Tiger Moth aircraft in Egypt to obtain my private pilot's licence. Production of the DH Tiger Moth from all sources totalled more than 9000 machines. Another DH aircraft used by the RAF during World War 2 was the Dragon Rapide called the Dominie in the RAF This was used for primary multi-engine bomber training and radio operator training flying classrooms.

The Gypsy Major 4 cylinder engine became world famous and was employed in a number of light aircraft. Eventual engine development improved the power output to 150 h.p. The Gypsy Major was followed by the 6 cylinder Gypsy Queen and the Gypsy VI developing over 200 h.p. in its supercharged form. The invention of the jet engine by Whittle was enthusiastically developed by the de Havilland Engine Company in World War 2, resulting in the unique design of the centrifugal Goblin jet (1941) producing 3,500 lb. thrust.. A more powerful jet development was the Ghost producing 5000 lb. thrust which powered the tragic DH 'Comet' and the more successful Sea Vixen aircraft.

As can be seen from this short synopsis the de Havilland Companies were in the forefront of aircraft design and development from the very earliest days of aviation. This leadership in industry continued right up to the jet age when DH made the pioneering revolutionary first in the world pure jet-powered commercial airliner – the famous 'Comet'. Then followed, as previously mentioned, the series of fatal disasters. Prime Minister Winston Churchill had always taken a keen interest in British aviation development from its earliest days and especially after he became Secretary of State for War and Air from 1919-21. He followed closely de Havillands success in producing the Comet and was very proud that Britain was leading the

*A great day for de Havilland and British aviation: The Comet G-ALYP 'Yoke Peter' about
to fly to Johannesburg. It has already flown over 500 hours.*

world with this revolutionary jet airliner. He was greatly disappointed with the
unfortunate series of Comet disasters that ensued but remained optimistic that de
Havillands would find the cause of these crashes, and introduce curative
modifications to restore its pre-eminence as the world's first jet airliner. This search
by de Havillands for the cause of the failures continued over a very lengthy period
without results until Churchill became exasperated and issued an ultimatum that the
cause of these crashes must be found regardless of expense. He ordered that the
fatally crashed Comet aircraft which disintegrated off the Italian coast and fell into
the sea was to be completely salvaged by the Royal Navy and sent back to
Farnborough for an intensive investigation. The Royal Navy commenced their
salvaging operations on the 10th January 1954, working with diving experts to lift
the components of the smashed aircraft to the surface for despatch to Farnborough.
The object was to endeavour to rebuild the aircraft and engines and so find where the
failure had occurred. Fortunately for my own Company, the DH Engine Company,
the engines were found more or less intact. They were received back in the factory
and immediately an intense investigation of the engines was commenced. This is
where I came into the picture. I was loaned to the Design and Development
Department to assist the Engine Company investigating team. It is interesting to note
that the weather conditions during November 1954 had deteriorated to such an extent
that the Royal Navy divers reported conditions too risky to continue. The Admiralty
reported this to Churchill who was furious and issued orders that the diving and
salvaging operations were to continue regardless of the risk. This was most fortunate
for de Havillands for the R.N. was able to bring to the surface vital components of
the crashed aircraft which permitted mock assembly at Farnboroughand highlighted
the area and eventually the cause of the failure.

Meanwhile the Engine Company investigating team was desperate to determine
what happened to the engines at the moment of failure. This urgency was due
obviously to the desire to determine the cause of the crash but at the same time there
was an equal urgency to determine whether the engines were at fault. Because the de
Havilland Aircraft Company had been unable after lengthy investigation to find the

cause of the disasters there was a very strong rumour going the rounds all over the country that one of the DH Ghost jet engines had exploded in mid-air and part of the engine had blown a hole in the aircraft fuselage side adjacent to the engine. This, the rumour claimed, caused an explosive de-compression of the fuselage and the disintegration of the complete aircraft. The rumour even pinpointed the starboard side of the fuselage which had been penetrated by the exploding starboard engine.

The investigating team I was working with did an amazing and clever detective job worthy of Sherlock Holmes. The recovery of the starboard engine from the sea permitted our engineers to trace every scratch and fracture, permitting a complete picture of the direction of travel of engine parts before and during the emergency, and provided a measure of the intensity of the disintegration. It was firmly established beyond any doubt that the engines had nothing to do with the cause of the aircraft failure. However there was indeed strong evidence that the fuselage failure had occurred by fracture on the starboard side. Finally failure in the aircraft structure was established and metal fatigue in this fuselage area was proved which had resulted in the decompression and disintegration of the aircraft. Very little publicity has ever been given to this tragic story so perhaps some account of this sad train of events may be of interest to the general readership.

It should be realised that the modern passenger airliner fuselage is merely a large metal tube in which the passengers sit, with a compartment also in the tube, for their luggage. In the case of the Comet the flight deck or pilot's cockpit was a separate compartment attached to the front of the fuselage tube. This of course had a door for communication to the tube fuselage. In flight operation this tube was hoisted into the air by its wing structure and pushed to an altitude between 30,000 and 40,000 feet by its powerful jet engines. The reason it was operated at such a high altitude was that the air at this altitude was much less dense and so offered far less resistance, enabling the aircraft to travel much more economically than at ground level and at far greater speeds.

However the human beings inside the tube cannot survive at that kind of altitude due to the rarefied air containing less oxygen. It is neither economical nor practical to supply oxygen via a mask to each individual passenger so that the alternative is to make the atmosphere inside the tube as nearly as possible the same as at 7000 to 8000 ft. which is bearable to most people. This is done by pumping air under pressure into the tube to maintain an approximate atmospheric pressure as stated and so maintain the air density and thus the oxygen content. In the case of the Comet aircraft this required a continuous air pressure of some $8\frac{1}{4}$lbs. per sq. in. Thus, with the tremendous number of square inches inside the tube, in the aggregate the total internal pressure amounted to tons. The tube with its passengers is therefore travelling along like an inflated balloon which, with a small prick, will explode with a bang. And this is exactly what happened to the Comet. The small prick was caused by metal fatigue resulting in a crack adjacent to the junction of the tube to the flight deck compartment. The metal fatigue was caused by the repeated reversal of metal stress due to constant pressurisation and de-pressurisation on take-off and landing.

A factor in the failure sequence was an unfortunate error in the airframe design. The original prototype passenger tube was naturally tested for strength by simulating the total amount of take-offs and landings over a life of say ten years. This test proved satisfactory but no account was taken of the fact that for the simulation test the tube was bolted to a rigid frame on the ground whereas in flight conditions the tube was bolted to the much weaker flight deck compartment. The strength of the in-flight condition was obviously much less than the simulated flight test where it was bolted to a much stronger frame. Another unfortunate factor in the failure of one of the aircraft salvaged off the Italian coast was that in the area of the tube junction to the cockpit a small hole had been drilled in error by a construction operator in the wrong place. In aircraft construction if a small error such as this is made and reported the operator may be given a 'concession' providing the inspector decides that the error was too small to cause any structural weakness. The work then proceeds by blocking the incorrect hole and drilling a hole in the correct position. Unfortunately the metal fatigue caused by the take-off and landing stress reversal centred on the erroneously drilled hole. This stress raiser travelled to a nearby window aperture and caused a crack. At that time the window apertures were square in shape. The tons of pressure tore through the tube frame like a burst balloon. The force of the internal explosion blew a hole in the starboard side of the aircraft and the passengers and their seats and the total contents of the interior were blown through the hole. The force of their exit was like a hurricane. When the bodies of the passengers were recovered they were found mostly naked, stripped of their clothes and often minus their limbs. This showed the intensity of the explosion and the manner of their ejection from the interior of the aircraft cabin..

A development from the Comet disaster came from America where Boeings, one of America's largest aircraft manufacturers, was just in the process of designing and developing their own jet airliner. Naturally they were anxious to learn from the experiences of the de Havilland pioneers. They made an offer to de Havillands to pay for the whole cost of the investigation on condition that they would be permitted to have an observer attend the formal public enquiry proceedings. As mentioned previously de Havillands were on the point of bankruptcy and so gladly accepted this offer. The Boeing observer was supplied with all the technical information relating to the faulty design and its effects. This information supplied to Boeing was a gift from heaven and was their salvation for they had made a complete failure of their first attempt to design and operate a high altitude airliner. This original Boeing attempt was the famous Boeing 247 which first flew in February 1933, powered of course by piston engines. It was developed over a period of six years. After extensive air testing it was publicised as a commercial airliner and named 'Stratocruiser'. The K.L.M. Company showed interest and a demonstration flight was arranged at Seattle. Unfortunately for Boeing the 'Stratocruiser' stalled at altitude and disintegrated. The accident report stated that structural failure was due to faulty design for operation at high altitude. Boeing abandoned the design for high altitude operation and made no further attempt to solve this problem until some twenty years later. The invention by

Whittle of the jet engine plus the successful development of the de Havilland 'Comet' caused Boeing to resume their design studies for high altitude commercial aircraft.

Another feature of the aircraft failure from which Boeings was able to profit was the investigation into the causes of the metal fatigue. As stated previously the metal fatigue originated from the repeated reversal of stresses in the tube walls. De Havillands were pioneers in designing a pressurised passenger cabin to be operated at 30 to 40,000 ft. Never before had any pressurised airframe been designed for passenger flying at such altitude. Thus no study had ever been made of the scientific formulae relating to the pressurisation and de-pressurisation stresses resulting from the take-off and landing operation in such a revolutionary aircraft. The effect on the Comet metal tube walls can be likened to bending a piece of tin or thin duralumin backwards and forwards repeatedly. This effect is due to forces acting outwards during the pressurisation in the climb and cruise at altitude and releasing inwards of the thin walls in the descent to landing of the aircraft. Boeings were very fortunate that they were able to learn from de Havillands experience. It was confirmed that they certainly needed that guidance according to a Boeing test pilot whose lecture on the first Boeing jet airliner I attended later that year. This American test pilot said in his lecture that the original Boeing design was found to have many weaknesses requiring re-design. He said that the first prototype had its undercarriage collapse when they first pushed it out of the hangar. He also said that taxiing trials resulted in severe overheating in the brake system which Boeings had to re-design using the de Havilland system under licence.

Despite this sad story of how the original de Havilland Comet disasters were a great setback to this pioneer aircraft the Comet survived in the form of a modified and strengthened plane fitted with Rolls Royce Avon jet engines operated by the Royal Air Force. Further development with a 'stretched' fuselage finally resulted in a modified Comet aircraft. This was also fitted with Rolls Royce Avon engines producing 10,500 lb. thrust and carrying 81 passengers. This aircraft was used to commence a commercial service from London to New York in October 1958. It had a maximum speed of 550 m.p.h. and a range of 4000 miles. Further developments improved the aircraft to carry 102 passengers and it was bought and operated by a number of foreign airlines. Finally the basic Comet was re-designed and modified to provide the Nimrod RAF aircraft used for maritime patrols and is in use by the RAF even today and is likely to remain in service for some years yet.

Chapter 25

The German Army Helicopter Squadron Return to England

When it became evident that the Indians did not require a resident engineer in Bangalore I was asked to undertake a new post as resident Company engineer with the German army (Bundeswehr) at Celle near Hanover in northern Germany. The Germans had bought a squadron of Westland Skeeter helicopters. These were fitted with an engine designed and manufactured by the Blackburn Engine Company. Unfortunately, before this engine was fully developed, the company was the victim of the merger mania ('shot-gun marriages') forced on the aircraft industry by the British government. The de Havilland Engine Company itself was also merged into the Hawker Siddeley conglomerate. As an outcome of this merger policy Blackburns was closed down and the de Havilland Engine Company was ordered to take over Blackburns. Thus it found itself lumbered with an engine designed and built by another Company but not fully clear of its birth pains. In consequence the Westland helicopters operated by the Germans which were fitted with this engine experienced a variety of engine troubles including cracked induction manifolds and the frightful starting system which was based on cartridge firing design. In the severe cold of the northern German winter starting the engines was a very uncertain and fallible business. I remember one aircraft that took most of the very cold morning and the firing of innumerable cartridges before the engine would start up – though the engine had nothing wrong with it and was in good tune.

For a few weeks before my family joined me I lodged in the German Army Officers Mess. This was quite an interesting experience from my point of view. It was intriguing, for instance, that I had been, only a comparatively short time previously, doing my utmost in the RAF to help ensure that as many Germans as possible were killed or maimed. Now I was doing my utmost to help them to rebuild their Army. Another interesting aspect of this German Army squadron was that practically all the officers were ex-Nazis. This was inevitable since the only experienced military pilots and senior officer material at this time were all ex-Nazis and the Germans were anxious to have a national defence force once again. This situation often gave rise to some embarrassing moments during my stay in the German officers' mess.

It so happened that Celle airfield was located quite near the terrible Belsen WW2 Nazi concentration camp where the killer gas chambers and the gruesome ovens were plainly visible if one walked two or three miles along the road from Celle. Most of the German squadron officers when in my company had enough intelligence and sensitivity not to mention the subject of Belsen but one senior fanatical officer, a

Westland (Saunders Roe) Skeeter helicopter as supplied to the German Army and German Navy

German Navy pilots preparing for a Skeeter helicopter exercise. The Author on right

Major, made a point of expressly targeting me for propaganda conversation. The Germans were still operating the pre-war officers' etiquette so that one assembled in the mess for a pre-prandial drink prior to moving into the dining room for lunch. As soon as I entered the mess, the Major would descend on me, offer me a drink and then commence his Nazi propaganda. He declared that the Belsen story and all the published facts concerning the operation of the gas chambers and the extermination of the Jews were all American lies. He said he could prove it by mathematics, for if you counted the total number of gas chambers working twenty four hours a day and the quoted number of Jews exterminated you would find it a physical impossibility!

I don't think he believed he had convinced me for when flying with him he was not at all friendly. In fact he was furious when I accidentally trod on his gold braided cap which, unknown to me, he had placed under my co-pilot's seat alongside him in the cockpit during one of our flights to Southern Germany.

My family joined me after a few weeks and we had a most difficult time trying to find suitable accommodation. A large part of available accommodation was occupied by the Allied defence forces. Since I was no longer military personnel I had to take my chance as a civilian with the German civilian population in the quest for accommodation. The World War 2 Allied bombing campaign had destroyed a tremendous amount of housing and the German government policy at that time was similar to their previous ruthless war policy which of course was 'Guns before butter'. This time it was 'business buildings before housing' with the object of quickly re-incarnating their smashed economy. Thus the whole national building construction programme was focussed on the erection of office blocks and the creation of business premises. In consequence there were practically no efforts being made to construct houses for private accommodation. Due to the Allied bombing programme which destroyed whole cities millions of people had been made homeless and, at the time of which I write, not much had been done to change this situation.

The only accommodation we could find in Celle for ourselves and our two young children (for Pam had given birth to a second daughter, Christine, at our home in Radlett three months prevopusly) was a single large room in a very ancient large family house. It was on three floors which had been divided up into letting units with a wholesale wine merchants office on the ground floor. The wine merchant was the owner of the block. Celle, a picturesque town on the River Aller about 25 miles north-east of Hanover in Lower Saxony is fortunate in that it is one of the few towns in Germany to have escaped destruction in the Allied bombing campaign of World War 2. Its prolific 15th and 16th century buildings are in a fine state of preservation and are maintained in their original condition by an enlightened and strict local authority. Thus, at that time, walking down the main street of Celle, one could imagine that one was almost back in Shakespearean times.

The substantial town house in which we had the one room accommodation was situated in the main street and its 16/17th century elegant exterior contributed to the charming picture. Unfortunately the interior of the house was also 16/17th century so that living conditions there were not so charming. On our floor we had to share the kitchen with other occupants, including the owner, whose teenage son made a practice of being a looker-on when my wife was preparing a meal. It must be remembered that the German civil population had just passed through a terrible post-war situation where a large number of the people were almost starving and, even at that time, food was in short supply and very expensive. In fact the owner's family asked to have our used tea leaves for their own further use. We were fortunate that, although I was not permitted to live in British military personnel accommodation, I was allowed to use the British N.A.A.F.I. Thus our food supply was witnessed in the kitchen by the teenage son of the owner who, breathing down our necks, looked on optimistically It was a source of great wonder and envy by our German neighbours. Our room heating consisted of one old-fashioned typical continental cast iron tubular stove with a chimney ascending through the ceiling and burning wood or coal, around which we gathered to keep warm.

However our one room accommodation was a considerable inconvenience because our younger daughter was only three months old and therefore it was necessary to avoid disturbing her when she went off to sleep in the early evening. To entertain my German army colleagues in my accommodation was impossible so that, for entertainment we would take them out to a local restaurant for an evening meal. Our room would be the rendezvous where we would have to enjoin them to whisper so that the baby would not be awakened.

At that time Germany and its people still suffered from a guilty conscience and from world-wide condemnation. The people of Celle were acutely aware of the nearby presence of Belsen concentration camp. When one spoke to any of the residents of Celle, whilst they admitted that they now knew about the sordid and horrific activities that took place in Belsen, they always denied any awareness of these during the war years. This denial was in spite of the fact that, every Sunday in the War years, the main Celle railway station had been the scene of arriving crowds consisting of hundreds of miserable unfortunate broken Jewish people suffering from a cruel hellish journey disgorging from the cattle trucks. From there, harried by Nazi German military and S.S. overseers, they were forced to march the long road to their deaths.

Another peculiar feature of my association with my German army ex-Nazi colleagues was that every one that I had spoken with had served on the Eastern front but none apparently had ever served on the Western front. Whether such an unusual coincidence was in fact true or merely a polite avoidance of an embarrassing subject I was not able to discover. As I have mentioned previously, in aeronautical engineering there is a constant flow of mandatory official modifications to engines etc., some big and important, most small and not critical. The Commanding Officer of this Army Helicopter Squadron was one of the few ex-Nazis in this Squadron that I liked. He had the typical German super efficiency of working to the book and insisted that I should brief him on every modification, however small, before briefing the remainder of the squadron technical staff.

Thus it became an almost daily routine to cart drawings and documents to the C.O.'s office where we would go through the whole 'raison d'être' and procedures for embodiment of each modification. As I explained each step in the procedure he would exclaim 'Ach! Ja!' This expression became so embodied in my mind that I found myself exclaiming 'Ach! Ja!' to every friend or colleague when they made any statement. In addition to my commitment to the German Army I also liaised with the German Navy at Kiel. Here they were using the same helicopter for ship-borne operations and I found these young German naval ex-Nazis much more likeable. In fact on my recall to England they expressed to de Havillands their disappointment that I was no longer visiting their unit. It was this German Navy appreciative report to de Havillands that defeated the denigratory report from the German Army Westland team and restored my technical reputation.

On my return to England the Company decided to widen my expertise by involving me in a new field of power plant based on rocket power. A small rocket motor developing some 3000 lbs. thrust had been designed by the Company to be an auxiliary detachable power unit which could be used on the then existing Vee bombers to give temporary additional power for assisted take-off and thus carry a greater bomb load. The unit was designed to be detachable and jettisoned immediately after take-off. It would be fitted with an automatic parachute device which would permit the unit to be recoverable and re-usable. To me this was an interesting experience for I was introduced into the new field of rocket power. I regret to say that the power unit was not a success mainly due to the unreliability of helical spring operation in the control actuation of the unit and the unreliability of the parachute system on the release of the rocket power unit after take-off. I spent a short time at the Defence Evaluation and Research Agency (formerly A&AEE) Boscombe Down partaking in the testing of the power unit parachute system in flight trials. Almost always the release and landing was a failure. I also visited RAF Wittering where trials of the unit were taking place in a Vee bomber squadron located there. Here again the rocket assisted take-off unit was not enjoying much success.

It was whilst I was at Wittering that I was urgently recalled to Leavesden where, to my delight, I was informed that the German Navy at Kiel had expressly asked that my liaison visits should be resumed. This was especially pleasing to me because my recall to England from the German Army liaison post was, I found later, due to denigratory reports to my manager, Stan Sharp, by the Westland Company from their engineer at Celle. This engineer was a former naval rating and I think he had an inferiority complex which activated a desire to show that a retired commissioned officer could not possibly be a good service engineer.

However my reputation was re-established at Leavesden and at the Company's request I made a flying visit to the German Navy at Kiel. I stayed with them a short while to resume the good relationship that previously obtained and then returned to England where I was asked if I would consider a post in South Africa. This post was for a two-year contract as a specialist engineer on loan to the de Havilland subsidiary Company in Johannesburg. Responsibility for DH products would extend over the whole of southern Africa and include Kenya. Much to the surprise of my Company management I jumped at the offer. One of the reasons for their surprise was the fact that the political scenario in South Africa, as reported in the British media, was degenerating into an unstable and threatening situation. A second reason was that the Managing Director of the South African Company had a bad reputation in our department at Leavesden and was noted for adverse reports on British de Havilland engineers on loan to his Company. But, as I have described previously, I had handled such situations and I relished the prospect of a complete two years in a, for me, new country plus, of course, the prospect of adding capital to my diminishing bank balance. I think my Management was a little worried that I had made a hasty decision which I might regret later and possibly change my mind. It was suggested that I might leave immediately for home and discuss the matter with my wife. I replied that it was not necessary since I had made my decision and I would abide by it. 'In that case', said Stan Sharp, 'you should be ready to leave in about three weeks.'

I should mention here that, as I described earlier, Pam and I had discovered the property letting potential in the Watford area. To increase our income we had decided some months earlier to exploit this letting potential by investing in a suitably large old Victorian type of property that we could convert into bed-sits or studio flats. We had found just the type of property we wanted; a rundown 10 roomed 3-storey old property built at the beginning of the century and very conveniently sited in a residential area of Watford close to Bushey railway station and handy to the shopping area. It was ideally placed for letting for it would appeal both to locals and commuters. I had used up my available capital buying the Radlett property so I had to do a diplomatic persuasive job on my bank manger in Portsmouth to provide a 100% mortgage loan. He was somewhat taken aback when I said I wanted to buy the property as an investment and said he was not allowed to lend money for an investment property. He could only lend to private customers for property they were going to live in. I told him that was exactly what we intended to do; to let our Radlett house and live in the Watford property whilst we did a D.I.Y. job of converting it into flatlets. He smiled and said 'Start again; say you want to borrow money to buy a house to live in'. I did just that. He said 'How much do you want?' I said '100% – £3500 (actually the price of the property was £2,900). He replied 'Send me an established Watford surveyor's report confirming the property is worth the price and I'll give you the loan.' With hearty relief we soon got the surveyor's report posted to Portsmouth and 'Hey Presto!' I had become the proud owner of a second property.

Quickly letting our Radlett house we moved over, 'lock, stock and barrel', to Watford and set to work furiously on the job of rehabilitating the property and converting it into a sizeable ground floor flat and three small flatlets. For months we worked until midnight on most nights and we had almost completed the job when I came home with the news that I would be leaving for South Africa in about three weeks time and the family could follow me out there at their leisure. 'Leisure', said Pam, 'what leisure? There is the work to finish off and the letting (we had already let two flatlets) of the remainder of the house. Besides all the jobs I will have packing up as well as having two small children under three to look after. Not to mention arranging for an agent to take over responsibility for the property, rent collection etc.'

Of course what Pam had said in horror struck tones was all too true and I did my best in the short time available to me to take some of the load off her shoulders. With my own technical responsibilities to get myself briefed up on the Company aircraft and engines in operation in South Africa my time available was somewhat limited.

Chapter 26

South Africa

Sharpeville Massacre of Black Protesters

Westland Wasp Helicopter Operation

I flew out to Johannesburg by South African Airways on 1st January 1960. Settling in quite happily, helped by the friendly De Havilland engineer I was relieving, I found life at Baragwanath airfield, where the de Havilland technical offices were sited, quite peaceful and pleasant. That is, until all hell broke out a few weeks later when, on 21st March 1960, the Sharpeville massacre took place. Sharpeville is a small black African township just a few miles down the road from Baragwanath. The Sharpeville Blacks had staged a sizeable mass demonstration outside the local police station. The demonstration was protesting against the rigid Government 'pass laws' which required all non-whites to carry an identification paper to prove their legal right to reside and work in South Africa.

The demonstration consisted of a crowd chanting African freedom songs and circulating in native rhythmic dances in front of the police station in a square in central Sharpeville. Finally, in a gesture of defiance, the Black protesters threw their own passes onto a huge bonfire in the centre of the square. The police station rang through to Johannesburg for assistance fearing they would be attacked and overwhelmed by the violent crowd. A military type armoured Police car called a Saracen arrived with an armed combat Police crew. The armoured car drove into the centre of the square and was immediately surrounded by the chanting mob of several hundred Blacks. The white crew with their loaded guns mounted on the roof of the armoured car and the officer in charge ordered the mob to disperse. The Blacks took no notice and continued circling the armoured car, chanting defiance. The chanting increased and after some time the armoured car Police suddenly lost their nerve and their self-control and opened fire indiscriminately into the crowd. They claimed afterwards that they thought they were about to be attacked and that their lives were in danger. Sixty-nine Blacks were shot dead and 180 wounded. The dead and wounded were brought to Baragwanath native hospital which was close by the airfield.

This type of demonstration was organised nationally by the African National Congress (A.N.C.) who are now the ruling Government party in power. A rival party called the Pan-African Congress (P.A.C.) agreed to co-operate in this general national protest movement. The massacre was really the beginning of the end of Apartheid and of the end of the rule of the Afrikaner Nationalist Party. In fact it was the beginning of the end of white supremacy in South Africa and it signalled the birth of the future Black people's rule of South Africa.

When the Police fired on the crowd the people scattered but the news spread like wildfire world-wide. South Africa became internationally condemned and was left with hardly a friend in the world. The country became a hated pariah nation overnight. The world media seized on the news with relish. South Africa and 'Apartheid' provided almost continuous subjects for the world media for years to come. With blatant hypocrisy America, a country which had solved its racial problem by massacring the native Americans including women and children, conducted a virulent campaign of animosity and finally organised a world boycott. This they accomplished successfully in spite of the history of their shocking conduct in the solution of their own racial problem, which was, of course, the almost complete annihilation of their native population, the Red Indians. In this connection it is interesting to note that the American Congress did not recognise American natives as an ethnic race until 1972. At the time of which I write Blacks in America had only a few years previously emerged from practical slavery and were then only tolerated as second class citizens to be exploited in menial jobs. The Ku Klux Klan was a product of those times. Even in the 1960s black university students in the southern states were attacked and sometimes murdered for refusing to obey the segregation laws.

To return to my own particular situation following the Sharpeville massacre the proximity of the event caused shock and consternation among my South African colleagues. They feared the worst and all conversation was concentrated on this subject and the possible immediate outcome. My fellow engineer in the office at Baragwanath was a born and bred South African who had recently bought a house on a new estate quite near the Baragwanath airfield. The white male population of this estate immediately formed an armed vigilante patrol covering the estate day and night. It seemed to me that the entire white population of the country gradually moved into a state of fear and depression with a pessimistic outlook towards the future. Hordes of the white English-speaking people began to emigrate to countries like Australia, New Zealand, Canada and other places where a British way of life existed. The value of property in South Africa dropped at an enormous rate so that very soon one could buy magnificent villas with beautiful gardens and some four or five acres of land for about a quarter of their previous market value. When people discovered that I had only recently arrived from England, they told me that I was crazy to come to South Africa. The white Afrikaners declared they were Africans and would not be driven into the sea.

Prior to my family's arrival I had found a pleasant rustic villa with a thatched roof in a good residential district of Johannesburg. What is more, I had found, with the aid of kind friends, a native girl servant ready to start work as soon as Pam arrived from England. Her name was Dora. Dora stayed with us the whole ten years we lived in South Africa. In fact she became one of the family. She lived with us; her quarters were in our garden. My son who was born in South Africa was nursed by her and he regarded her as his second mother. She acted as a sort of matriarch to our family and did not hesitate to reprove me and tell me not to shout when I sometimes became angry over some domestic shortcoming.

South Africa (Johannesburg). Our native servant Dorah and native handyman William with out two daughters, Anne (on right) and Christine

But, however close and devoted to their white employers, the Black African had a dormant inherent antithesis to the white race. This antithesis could sometimes be subconscious but its rare expression would often be quite pacific and treated as a natural human reaction which possibly might require physical action sometime in the distant future. A good example of this came one day after Dora had been with us for a couple of years and we were all on very familiar terms with her. Following the Sharpeville massacre tension in the white community gradually increased until a possible black revolution became almost a daily topic of white conversation. We were talking together with Dora in the house when we seemed to be all one happy family. We spoke of the prevailing talk of a Black rising against the whites and I said to Dora 'Surely you would not want to cut our throats, Dora?' She replied calmly 'Oh no! – the black girl working next door would do that – and I would do the same for her white bosses!' We were shocked at this accepted idea of reciprocal service to our neighbours.

It soon became obvious, with my house on the other side of Johannesburg from my place of work, that I needed a car urgently. The Company did not provide one so that it became an urgent necessity that I bought one. This was the beginning of another unfortunate story. To avoid dealers' high charges I scanned the Jo'burg newspaper's small ads columns. At the same time I arranged a Company loan to avoid hire purchase charges. I found a very suitable almost new Opel estate type car advertised privately and phoned the owner. When he learned that I was at Baragwanath airfield he offered to bring it out to my office. He sounded very helpful and co-operative and when I saw the car it seemed to be a bargain and just what I needed. My colleagues viewed it with favour and I agreed to buy. The owner and I set out together to my bank, Barclays in Johannesburg, to draw the money in cash, and the owner invited me to his house to complete the paper work. It was a pleasant house in a respectable suburb of the city and his wife and children were quite an ordinary decent family. We completed the transaction; I paid over the money, got a receipt and the log-book and congratulated myself on having made a good 'buy' from a good honest citizen.

Three months later the Johannesburg C.I.D. police department rang me up at the office and told me that they suspected I had bought a stolen car. The phone call came in the afternoon when an Afrikaans voice said 'This is the police C.I.D., Johannesburg. Are you in possession of Opel car registration number so and so? On my replying 'Yes,' the voice said 'Could we please examine your car?' I agreed and the voice suggested that they would meet me in the city half way on my journey home. I also agreed to this arrangement although I thought it a little strange to meet such people in a public place in the street. I began to think I should be cautious in this matter. The meeting duly took place, as arranged, on my way home. Two burly great Afrikaners in civilian clothes came to my car and introduced themselves, asking permission to look round my car. Finally they asked to open the bonnet and began peering at the engine. They then asked me if I had had the car re-sprayed. I said that I had only bought the car three months previously and it was practically new. So there was no reason why I should have had the car re-sprayed. They said 'In that case you have definitely bought a stolen car and we are going to impound your car. We have caught the thief who has stolen seven cars. Your car will be exhibit evidence in the court case and we will hold it in our police compound. Please follow us to the police station.' Even then I was not convinced that this was not a gangster's trap but I agreed to follow them to the police station, at the same time telling myself to watch out for danger. They drove straight to a police station and, without bothering to glance in my direction, went straight inside. I knew then that they were the genuine article and that I had a problem. As soon as I walked in I was informed that I no longer possessed a car and that it would be locked away in the police compound which happened to be opposite the station. They told me it would probably reside there for about a year until the court case was finalised. I said 'How am I going to get to my home which is ten miles from here?' 'Don't worry,' was the answer, 'we'll give you a lift home and take a statement from you when we get there.' This they did and, to Pam's horror, I arrived, escorted by two policemen. However they were quite friendly and polite and appreciated the tea Pam served. Having taken the story of my car purchase they enlightened me with details of the ghastly trap into which I had fallen.

It appeared that the smooth talking helpful innocent looking-citizen in his pleasant house and his impressively respectable family was a professional thief who had a clever, almost perfect, system of catching suckers such as myself. He had a liaison with a salvage car breaker's yard owner who would inform him immediately he had an insurance company write-off car of recent vintage. The thief would buy this and take it to his own private garage. He would then search amongst the private cars parked in the vicinity of cinemas and other public entertainment areas at night time until he found the identical model which he would then steal. He would drive it to his private garage, exchange the engine from the insurance crashed car with that of the stolen car and re-spray the stolen car to the same colour as the insurance crashed car. The chassis number would be changed to that of the crashed car. The re-sprayed stolen car would then be taken to the motor tax registration office and offered up as the crashed car re-built. New registration and number plates would be requested. The tax officer inspector would pass the car, congratulating the thief on his excellent re-build work!

A year later I was informed by the police that the case was ended and the car released to its original owners prior to the theft. The original owners happened to be an insurance company who kindly allowed me the price of the engine, which of course was not theirs. I received about £100 for my original outlay of some £600. Meanwhile for the whole year I had been reduced to paying back my loan from my company and getting to work by public transport. Pam was not impressed with her first year in South Africa! We survived, however, although I must admit our life during that first year was extremely difficult. To give some idea of our experiences I should return to the moment of Pam's arrival from England. She landed at Cape Town after a tiring two weeks voyage with our two young daughters aged three and a half and almost two years old. I met her off the ship with my wonderful car and we drove back along the famous south coast 'Garden Route'. To my surprise and annoyance Pam was in no mood to appreciate the beauty of the passing countryside. All she seemed to wish for was to get home and settle and eventually we arrived at the pleasant thatch roof house which I described earlier.

Very soon we discovered that we were not the only residents of this attractive house. Rats paraded quite openly, running along the top of the walls joining the roof thatch, in addition to which we had a chorus from a small lizard-like creature called the 'Tokay' which is the cry it emits periodically during the evening. Although the house and garden were very attractive we objected to sharing with our unwelcome visitors so we very quickly moved out. This time we moved into 'Buckingham Palace' as we ironically named it because of the size of the house and its five-acre estate. As stated previously after the Sharpeville massacre the white South African public became extremely nervous and some panicked. Some tried to sell their properties at almost give-away prices and failed. The owners of our 'Buckingham Palace' had failed to sell but nevertheless were determined to leave the country regardless. We answered their small ads advert offering occupation of the property rent free provided the tenant maintained the place in good order and retained the four staff running it, two servants and two gardeners to look after a large cultivation of asparagus. We soon found that our outlay to cover the wages of our four employees plus the expenses of the property maintenance far exceeded the normal level of rent which we would pay for suitable accommodation.

We discovered that people going on overseas leave were happy to let their houses at a nominal rent so we took advantage of this by taking several short lets in different suburbs of Jo'burg, which had the advantage of permitting us to get to know the city quite well. Some Austrian friends, Hans and Maria Kaliba, were kind enough to lend us their house and their car while they went on leave. Hans worked for Siemens and the help he and his wife gave us came at a time when we most needed it. From there we moved to a grand but older house in Parktown, one of the longer established suburbs quite near the city. It belonged to a Mrs. Carleton Jones, an elderly widow

Matron of Marymount Convent Maternity Home preparing to exchange my new born son Richard for my signed cheque witnessed by my two young daughters

whose late husband had been a mining magnate at Carletonville, one of the towns on the Rand which had therefore been named after him. We had assured Mrs. Carleton Jones that we were experienced gardeners which was true but our experience of gardening was in England. We were now in Johannesburg in the winter, a season in which we wrongly imagined there was little to be done. But in Jo'burg there is no winter rain and on a visit of inspection Mrs. Carleton Jones was somewhat horrified to find that we had not done any watering. We had really blotted our copybook there. It was during our short stay here that our son Richard was born in September 1961, at the Marymount Nursing Home, run by Catholic nuns. An amusing incident took place at the nursing home on the last day of their stay when I came to collect them in our jalopy car. The Matron Sister escorted Pam out of the building carrying Richard in her arms but she would not hand him over until I had given her the signed cheque for the bill.

My Company work was interesting enough and moved at a slow peaceful pace except of course for the panic stricken atmosphere created by the Sharpeville massacre. Baragwanath was a green grass 'sports airfield' with no runways. It was the site of the Johannesburg Flying Club operating mostly de Havilland Tiger Moths, which was the reason why the Company technical offices were located there. The head office and administration was in the city centre and the Managing Director at the time of my arrival was an elderly South African pioneer who in the very early days had been a 'flying circus' pilot, going round the country selling local air trips at five shillings a go. He had a distinguished World War 2 record and retired from the Service as a senior officer. Very soon after my arrival he also retired from the Company and handed over the reins to the 'ogre' Davison whom I have previously mentioned. Davison was by profession an accountant and thought in terms of commission and balance sheets so that the direction of the Company changed dramatically under the leadership of the 'Tenpercenter'. Whereas previously the Company policy had seemed to be aimed at giving aid and assistance to all operators of de Havilland aircraft, now the emphasis was on aircraft sales with after sales service being relegated to a minor role. With this new policy in view the Baragwanath offices were closed down and the technical department moved into the city offices so that we were all under one roof. We were all directed to focus our efforts on sales – not after sales service.

During this time the aviation industry in England was undergoing revolutionary changes with contraction by mergers and 'shot-gun marriages' being forced on the industry by the government. In South Africa Davison lost his Company manager who was promoted to oversee the de Havilland merger taking place in New Zealand. In his place Davison recruited Air Vice Marshal Jacklin who had recently retired as Chief of Staff in the Rhodesian Air Force. He was a highly experienced military pilot with a keen interest in aviation and a great desire to promote South African aviation together with our own Company interests. But this was contrary to the policy of Davison, the 'Tenpercenter' and very soon we were all involved in sales work; in my own case one might say 'technical sales'.

Due to the precarious financial position of de Havilland in England resulting from the Comet disasters and the relentless aviation contraction policy of the British Government, the English D.H. Company became an easy target for take-over and merger bids. Very soon de Havilland found themselves a part of the Hawker Siddeley empire and this had a very considerable impact on the hitherto easy going slow moving existence of the South African D.H. subsidiary Company. Suddenly we were plunged into representation and sales of all kinds of diversionary commercial products completely unconnected with aeroplanes, of which our sales staff and management had not the slightest knowledge, nor the slightest ideas on marketing. These included Hawker products such as bulk steel and aluminium products, garage doors, automatic vending machines, ships' stabilisers, lawn mowers and steamrollers.

To add to these unforeseen and divergent commercial activities D.H., just prior to the merger, had themselves embarked on a highly adventurous manufacturing project. This was the purchase from the American space industry of a licence to manufacture and sell in Europe a high precision electronic flow meter called the Pottermeter after a Mr. Potter, an American engineer, who had invented it. This instrument was used in the American space industry rockets to give high precision control of fuel flow etc.   It had also been developed for commercial application where high precision liquid flow control was required, such as oil pipe line flow, especially where pipe lines crossed from one country to another, involving customs duties, taxes etc. Another extensive application was on road transport vehicles carrying liquids like milk, petrol etc. where accurate measurement was required. D.H. thought they saw a highly lucrative future for this licensed manufacturing diversion and we in South Africa were called upon to sell it as well as the odd Tiger Moth or Vampire fighter aircraft.

Our sales staff reading the electronic flowmeter brochures had difficulty in understanding them and were not frightfully interested. The M.D. handed over responsibility for selling the Pottermeter to me, at the same time elevating my status in the Company to Technical Manager. Much to the surprise of my own management and the D.H. empire the Pottermeter instrument sales in South Africa took off and soon exceeded sales in Great Britain and the rest of the D.H. empire.

By this time the aircraft industry mergers had taken place and Davison, the South African M.D., knowing my two-year contract was near completion, offered me a permanent position with the South African Company. My answer was that I would accept on two conditions, one being that my wife should be agreeable to live permanently in South Africa and other being the agreement of the parent D.H. Engine Company at Leavesden, England.

To my astonishment Pam said that she would be happy to remain in South Africa. Previous to South Africa Pam had always very much preferred to return to England rather than to remain in the various countries in which we had lived. My second condition was met when the Company back in England, in reply to my letter on the subject, said in effect 'If you have been offered a job, take it because we have no idea what will happen to us with all these mergers taking place.' And so I became a permanent member of a South African Company whose name was changed to Hawker de Havilland. The D.H. aeroplanes were now only a part of a greatly increased sales section of this new Company. In addition to our representation of de Havilland and Hawker products we found ourselves responsible for Westland helicopters for they were using D.H./Blackburn engines. The South African Navy had bought the Westland Wasp helicopter to equip their frigates, following the British Royal Navy system. The South African Navy Westland Wasps would be the cause of some remarkable experiences which I will relate later in this South African story.

In my new role of Technical Manager and Technical Sales I travelled far and wide throughout the Southern African continent. We developed a system whereby either my engineer colleague Bill Walsh or I would visit the countries in Southern Africa in turn, once a month if possible. These countries included Angola, South West Africa, Southern Rhodesia (later called Zimbabwe), Zaire, Tanzania, Mozambique, Zambia (formerly Northern Rhodesia), Malawi, and Botswana. I also once visited Kenya to supervise the re-assembly of a squadron of Westland Lysander aircraft received crated from the factory. Our technique was to visit each country's capital city and call on the British Embassy or Consul, if one existed. If not we would call on the native minister responsible for defence or national commerce, depending on any information we may have gleaned from the press or other sources. Our object, of course, was to gather as much information as possible on the aviation policy and future planning in both the military and civilian fields, which could involve requirements for new aircraft and, hopefully, Hawker de Havilland sales.

To some degree this strategy was successful in achieving some sales of both military and civil aircraft. The South African Air Force bought expensive Buccaneer jet aircraft for maritime reconnaissance and submarine detection over the southern seas on the Cape route. In spite of their successful operation, expansion of this service was prevented by the Labour Government in Britain led by Harold Wilson, who refused to sanction the purchase of further Buccaneers to form a second squadron of aircraft on the grounds that they could be used against the Black population. Thus two years further work for the Blackburn factory near Hull was lost due to politics. However I succeeded in establishing several million pounds of sales of new aircraft for Malawi.

A further extraordinary outcome from Harold Wilson's embargo was concerned with a South African Air Force Shackleton which was the antiquated maritime type performing the patrol duties over the Cape sea route prior to the acquisition of the Buccaneers. Due to the policy of the Labour Government refusing to permit further purchase of Buccaneers the South Africans were taking every care in preserving their elderly Shackleton fleet. One day the S.A.A.F. had an unfortunate Shackleton crash where under normal circumstances the aircraft would have been a write-off. The extensive damage sustained from this crash would have made it completely uneconomic to repair.

I made a technical survey of the crash but, in spite of my negative report, the South Africans asked that A.V. Roe, the manufacturers in England, should give an estimate of the possible repair costs. AVRO sent out a senior engineer to conduct a further survey for the basis of a salvage scheme and eventually came up with the astonishing estimate of at least one million pounds. In today's money this would probably be eight million. They said this huge sum was necessary because they would have to send out to South Africa a large working party of all trades for a job that would take some months. They would have to pay not only high wages but also the costs of accommodation and support in Cape Town. In addition they would have to provide daily transport from Cape Town to Ysterplatz, the S.A.A.F. station where the crashed aircraft was sited and which was some ten miles or so outside Cape Town. This of course would be additional to the cost of spares, replacements and technical requirements as well as the labour costs.

To our amazement the South African Government accepted the estimate, stating they had no alternative since they needed the maritime reconnaissance aircraft and Britain had refused to permit the purchase of replacements. The AVRO working party duly arrived to start the repair job. The AVRO senior engineer who had previously surveyed the crashed aircraft remained in Cape Town to supervise the work and I joined him to assist him with liaison with the S.A.A.F., with whom I had an excellent relationship, and to provide any help which might be needed locally. The working party arrived at the Ysterplatz hangar which housed the crashed Shackleton, deposited their toolboxes around the aeroplane but refused to commence work. They gave a typical British trade union example of belligerent exploitation of their power which at that time was rife in Britain and which the rest of Europe called the 'British Disease'. A spokesman had been elected for this party of probably fifteen tradesmen. This individual was possibly a shop floor trade union official. He asked for an interview with my friend, the AVRO engineer. At the interview the spokesman demanded an increase in their already specially increased wages on the grounds that, as they were 6000 miles away from England, they could no longer have the normal sexual intercourse services of their wives and thus would have to pay prostitutes in Cape Town for such services. My AVRO friend agreed to this demand. When he rejoined me and told me he had agreed to this demand I was horrified and said I would never have agreed to such an audacious low-grade attitude. He replied that my reaction was due to my inexperience of modern England. He had already had considerable experience in England dealing with trade union problems and here in Cape Town this AVRO labour force had a unique monopoly which he had to handle in the most diplomatic manner possible. I was completely 'shot down' and I presume these workers enjoyed their extra money. The work proceeded well and was completely successful. I had to admit that my friend certainly knew his subject. The aircraft was completely re-built and passed its air test with honours to rejoin the Shackleton fleet and extend its very long life, giving good service to the South African Government.

Another episode in South African aviation history was concerned with Westland 'Wasp' helicopters which the South African Government had bought to operate from their S.A. Navy frigates. These frigates, based at Simonstown, had been bought second-hand from the British Royal Navy. They had been modified to allow the operation of the 'Wasp' helicopter which was housed in a small hangar at the rear of the main deck. With this frigate-helicopter facility in mind the South African Government, being a member of the United Nations Organisation, volunteered to set up a weather station in the Antarctic as a contribution to the international 'Geographic Year Scheme' which the United Nations had inaugurated. The United Nations scheme was aimed at improving the world human condition by the development of geographic sites for various purposes. The S.A. Government offer to set up a weather station in the Antarctic was based on the need to provide regular reliable meteorological information from an area that was subject to violent, harsh and rapid changes in its weather conditions. It would assist world meteorological forecasting technique. In fact the S.A. offer was an extremely difficult exercise and a challenge in which previous attempts by South Africa to achieve this object had failed. This S.A. offer to the United Nations was motivated by the idea that the use of a helicopter operating from the deck of a frigate would overcome the difficulties previously experienced by conventional ships prior to the development of deck-landing helicopters. The difficulties of the project were the violent, almost continuous Antarctic gale force winds bringing dense impenetrable snowstorms causing 'white-outs' and the inhospitable rocky coastline of the only suitable site, which was a small island in the Antarctic. The coastline of this island was all rugged and jagged cliffs and submerged rocks, offering no safe harbour or anchorage for a ship. Thus for any operation on the island the ship had to stand off out to sea resulting in difficulties in communicating with the island..

The South African plan was to sail with a team of meteorological scientists in a specially prepared S.A. Navy frigate complete with its 'Wasp' helicopter. On arrival at the site, the frigate would anchor near the island and, since there was no suitable landing site, the helicopter would fly off the 'weathermen' and lower them by winch onto the island to set up their station. The helicopter, having deposited the scientists by winch, would return to the frigate. At a pre-arranged time the helicopter would fly back to the island and hope to winch up the scientists. If a snowstorm 'white-out' occurred the meteorologists would be in a precarious position for the helicopter would never be able to find them. The Westland 'Wasp' helicopter used by the S.A. Navy on their frigate at Simonstown was flown and operated by the S.A. Air Force at Ysterplatz. It was equipped with a Rolls Royce turbo-shaft 'Nimbus' power plant manufactured at Leavesden. This was a small specialised turbo jet operating the helicopter rotors through a gear box with some small propulsion from the jet efflux. Unfortunately the power plant suffered a serious defect, a basically destructive vibration causing failure of a weak body structure carrying the rotating drive shaft.

After a series of disasters due to engine failure on training flights, mostly over Cape Bay, causing the deaths of four South African Air Force crew members, the Minister of Aviation issued an order that the proposed Antarctic trip by frigate with a 'Wasp' helicopter would be cancelled unless the power plant was modified to a safe standard. The Minister stated that the helicopter engine was too unreliable to attempt such a dangerous mission. This, of course, was a disastrous turn of events for the Leavesden factory in England, and for Westlands, as well as for my own subsidiary Company. Davison, our Managing Director, asked me to go down to Cape Town and try to sort out the mess. As previously mentioned, I had an extremely good relationship with the S.A.A.F., especially with their technical staff who gave me every assistance in my investigation of the reasons for the engine failures and of what could be done to eliminate such failures. I was greatly assisted by the Hawker Agent in Cape Town who was Brigadier Wilmott, a retired former Chief of Staff of the S.A.A.F. He persuaded the senior S.A.A.F. staff to give me a chance to penetrate to the heart of this tragic failure and to give me a hearing of my proposals to remedy the situation. This was indeed a valuable help for, as one can imagine, there was a very strong undercurrent of antipathy in the S.A.A.F. against the Wasp helicopter, with the resulting ban by the Ministry. This antipathy was particularly strong as it seemed possible that the Antarctic mission would have to be called off and the good name of South Africa further injured internationally.

In the S.A.A.F. workshops at Ysterplatz we stripped down the crashed engines which had been salvaged from the waters of Cape Bay. Soon we found the evidence in the cracks in the weak structure housing the drive shaft. I prepared a technical report with recommendations for strengthening the structure. This report was cabled to the factory at Leavesden and most fortunately the matter was handled by a newly appointed Managing Director. This M.D. was a ball of fire who forced the issue to be given the highest priority with the whole of the staff concerned working day and night. The result was that the engine structure was re-designed almost overnight and a complete prototype engine built and put on test within days. The severe endurance testing proved successful and a production engine was again built and – believe it or not – flown out to the S.A.A.F. at Ysterplatz by express air freight.

The new engine was installed in a S.A.A.F. 'Wasp' helicopter and rigorously air tested for days on end until even the most pessimistic in the S.A.A.F. agreed that the aeroplane was safe. Brigadier Wilmott and I had a final meeting with the entire technical and senior staff at Ysterplatz where the whole story was thrashed out.

Finally we were asked whether we guaranteed the new power plant modification within the limits of normal military aviation practice. We gave the assurance and the matter was then referred to the Minister who had raised the embargo. The S.A.A.F. assured him they were satisfied with the 'Wasp' helicopter new power plant and that they had complete confidence that the 'Wasp' was now reliable and capable of carrying out the proposed frigate mission. The Minister of Aviation lifted his embargo and gave his assent to immediate preparations being made for the despatch of the S.A. frigate and helicopter. When the news reached the S.A.A.F. at Ysterplatz that the expedition was 'on' the jubilation was unbelievable. The night before the frigate was due to sail I was invited by my S.A.A.F. colleagues to a celebration party to be held at a night-club in Cape Town centre. After a number of brandies I must confess that I, together with some half dozen S.A.A.F. officers, gave a public exhibition team dance to the famous tune 'Zorba the Greek'. As the tempo of the band increased so did our efforts to keep up and I am proud to say that none of us collapsed upon the stage. That is the first and last time I have ever performed on the stage in public at a nightclub. The frigate sailed the next morning on time and with a hearty send-off. The expedition was a complete success and the weather station was set up. I was recently informed by a South African doctor from Stellenbosch University working in this country that the weather station has been modernised and is well established, giving continuous valuable meteorological information to the world.

Occasionally we had visitors from our Principals in England, sometimes aircraft sales teams, sometimes specialists in the various branches of the Company's activities. Following normal Company etiquette the visitors would be looked after and entertained by members of our Company concerned with the 'raison d'être' of the visit. If the specialist was an engineer visiting in connection with some technical matter, it fell to my lot to help with the entertaining.

One of my entertainment responsibilities for our engineering visitors was to arrange a weekend visit to the famous Kruger Park Game Reserve. What is not greatly appreciated by the people of Europe is the magnitude and colossal size of this unspoilt area of Africa with its protected natural habitat for possibly millions of African wild beasts. These animals live in wild freedom and can wander at will in any part of the park which is over two hundred miles long and up to fifty or more miles in width, covering 8,000 square miles. It was founded in 1898 by zealous British and Afrikaner wild life devotees supported by both the Transvaal Boer Government under Kruger and later by the British Governments following the Boer War.

I had made quite a number of visits over the years both privately and with visitors, so that I was fairly knowledgeable on the best sites in the Park for viewing lions, elephants etc. in their natural haunts. One such weekend trip with a visiting British engineer proved to be very different from the usual Game Reserve experience. Leaving one Friday afternoon in a Company car I drove some 150 miles or so to the vicinity of the Game Reserve where I had booked us into an excellent hotel on a hilltop just outside the Reserve. My plan was to drive into the Reserve in the early

My wife and her parents with our children in Kruger National Park Game Reserve.
Rondavel accommodation with thatched roof

morning and head some fifteen miles or so to a somewhat remote watering hole I knew where, just after dawn, hundreds of wild animals of all kinds congregated to drink before dispersing to their hideouts.

To achieve the plan it naturally involved getting up and departing very early, in fact as near as possible to dawn. We were late getting up and from then on it was a frantic rush to try to arrive before the drinking animals disappeared. The entrance to the Game Reserve was about five or six miles from our hotel on a bush highway with no speed limit. Once inside the Game Reserve there is a very strict low speed limit. As we were late I drove fast towards the Game Reserve entrance when suddenly a huge male springbok sprang high in the air out of the deep grass and undergrowth which lined each side of the road. The springbok was immediately in front of the car and there was no way that I could avoid him. He collided with the car in mid-air and was killed instantly. The car radiator was damaged and the water quickly began draining away. I managed to get within about half a mile of the entrance when I had to stop with the water boiling. My companion volunteered to walk to the entrance to get help. My Company was a member of the South African A.A. who had a rescue centre about 30 miles inside the Game Reserve.

As we had left the hotel in such a rush we had had no time to shave and so I took this opportunity to rectify this omission with my electric battery shaver whilst waiting for the return of my companion. Intent on this operation I suddenly became aware of interested spectators. They were several towering giraffes peering down at this, for them, unusual spectacle of a stationary motor car emitting a purring noise coming from my electric razor. They saw a seated human passing this purring machine over his face. I was somewhat astonished at their presence for I was under the impression that all the wild animals were inside the Game Reserve which was enclosed by a high barbed wire fence impossible for animals to bypass. I now had had two incidents which proved me wrong.

My engineer companion eventually returned and told me that the game warden on duty had telephoned the A.A. who had agreed to come to our rescue. The warden said he would take care of the dead springbok. Our rescuers finally appeared in their breakdown vehicle. They towed us into the Game Reserve and we were plodding along slowly and painfully at the end of the tow cable attached to the rescue vehicle when suddenly it stopped and an arm waved frantically by the A.A. driver indicating to us a whole pride of about half a dozen lions. They were only about a hundred yards away, all stretched out in the shade under a tree, some lying on their backs, others lying asleep, all obviously very content, probably having just had a very good meal, one presumes. On arriving at the A.A. centre which was in Skukuza, the main rest camp compound, we handed the car over with instructions to ship it back to Johannesburg. The camp consists of a collection of rondavels, which are round thatch covered huts with sleeping, washing and cooking facilities. The rondavels can be rented out similar to a hotel. In the centre of the camp is a restaurant, shop, reading room etc. We booked into a rondavel, ordered a hire car and spent the rest of the weekend sightseeing. Finally a taxi took us to the nearest railway station where we boarded a train for Johannesburg. My companion found our unusual Game Reserve trip very interesting and told me how much he had enjoyed the adventures. Needless to say I was not very popular with the Company chief.

As one might expect in such a huge area of the Kruger Game Reserve containing vast numbers of wild animals attracting many visitors throughout the year there are bound to be incidents and sometimes frightening experiences for people who do not take sufficient care of their own safety in such wild surroundings. One such incident was reported in the Johannesburg Star evening paper of 12th May 1965 where a German couple in their small Volkswagen car was sightseeing on the Lower Sabie Road about seven miles from Sabie Rest Camp which is towards the south-western corner of the Game Reserve.

Suddenly a bull elephant leading a 35 strong herd of cows and calves broke out of a plantation on one side of the road and began crossing over to the plantation on the other side of the road. The German couple stopped their car about twelve yards from the crossing herd but two calves wandered a little closer to the parked car. The bull elephant swung round and lumbered to the car. It stamped its leg and flipped its huge extended ears in a most threatening manner, bellowing loudly, but the stupid Germans did not reverse back out of danger. The angry bull elephant, losing its temper and then bending down, hooked its tusks under the car bumper, lifted the front of the car complete with passengers and threw it back about fifteen feet.

The two Germans sat terrified in the car, helpless like peas in a pod, convinced that the elephant was preparing for a vicious attack on their Volkswagen. But the elephant then merely lifted its huge front leg, stamped a mighty dent in the car bonnet and then turned and trundled off into the bush, snorting loudly. The elephant was of course reacting in a perfectly natural way, protecting the young when it thought their safety was endangered. Another remarkable incident occurred in the Skukuza area in the early days of the Game Reserve when there were no cars for wardens to patrol in. A Game Warden was on horseback patrolling the area when a lion sprang out of the bush, landed on the back of the horse and knocked its rider to the ground. The lion immediately leapt onto the man who feigned death by being completely motionless. The lion seized the warden by his shoulder and began to drag him towards his lair, probably to provide a meal for its young. Meanwhile the warden surreptitiously felt for his hunting-knife. Finding it, he suddenly plunged it into the lion's heart. The lion collapsed and, in spite of his wounds, the warden was able to make his way to the rest-camp where he received first aid and eventually his wounds were treated in the local hospital. The lion's skin with the knife hole is on public exhibition in Skukuza rest-camp restaurant.

Having paid off my Company loan for the stolen car which had languished in the Johannesburg police compound, I then managed to collect enough capital to once again enter the motor car market. This time, however, I had much less ambitious ideas. I finally bought a rather tired Morris Oxford but at least my bank balance was in the black. After some considerable D.I.Y. work on this jalopy I finally got it into a reasonably reliable condition and we began to make weekend excursions to the coast at Durban and various scenic spots located in the Transvaal area. As time went by my three weeks annual leave became due. We made an adventurous plan to hire a caravan and journey north to Rhodesia (now Zimbabwe) to visit one of Pam's school friends who was married to a tobacco farmer. His farm was near Sinoia, not terribly far from the Kariba Dam on Lake Kariba. With our hired caravan hitched up to the Morris Oxford and loaded with all our necessities, we set off. It was very unfair treatment to give our tired jalopy and it complained bitterly. However the first day we made it to a very well organised caravan park where we had an evening meal in the small park restaurant and so to our caravan beds, feeling very pleased with our first day on the road. The next morning we were up betimes, ready for our breakfast in the caravan and looking forward to another day heading northwards. We had a small Calor bottled gas heater similar to a Primus for cooking. Whilst Pam was preparing the foodstuff ready for cooking, I set up the gas cooker and held a match to the top to get it going. Suddenly there was a huge 'woof' and the whole gas burner was enveloped in flames with a huge tongue of flame under pressure shooting out from the screwed joint of the jet pipe. Pam and the two small girls rushed to the caravan exit for it was obvious that the whole place would be ablaze in seconds. I picked up the flaming gas burner and quickly ran to the exit. Pam and the girls were crowding the exit so I hurled the thing through the narrow gap between their heads and the top of the caravan doorway. The burner landed on the ground well clear of

My daughter Anne with my unfaithful jalopy Morris Oxford car in Johannesburg,
South Africa

the caravan. My hands were burned but the mightily dangerous situation was averted. What happened was, that before setting off, we had renewed the gas container at the local Calor gas supplier who had not tightened the jet pipe into the new gas container. When I picked up the gas burner to set it up for cooking I must have moved the loose jet pipe, allowing a pressurised gas leak at the joint. But 'all's well that ends well' and with the minor burns on my hand bandaged up we were soon on our way north again.

We made a halt at Pietersburg and again at Louis Trichardt. Crossing the River Limpopo at Beit Bridge we were now in Rhodesia, soon to be called Zimbabwe. Our two young daughters sitting in the back of the car did not appreciate the long hours and hours journeying through the featureless bush country. We did our best to entertain them by organising various guessing and quiz games etc. After a night stop we headed towards Bulawayo and finally arrived at Sinoia where we spent some time with our friends, Helen and Ralph Rea, on their tobacco farm. This was a most interesting experience, seeing the everyday life on an African tobacco farm. Ralph, Pam's friend's English husband, had literally clawed this prosperous farm by his own hands from a rock-strewn wilderness. As a boy he had accompanied his father to Rhodesia under an emigration scheme. When he became of age he applied and was accepted by the Rhodesian Government to be included in a national land development scheme. This scheme offered grants of wild undeveloped country for a period of seven years on condition that, during this period of time, a viable self-supporting farm was to be developed to the satisfaction of a Government standard laid down. If, on inspection at the end of the seven-year period, the Government department was satisfied that the conditions had been met, the land was ceded freehold to the farmer. This was no sinecure for there would be no further assistance financially or otherwise from the Government. When Ralph as a young bachelor took over his rock-strewn wilderness, he was miles from civilisation and with no accommodation, no water supply, no electricity and no visible means of support. Water had to be brought several miles from the nearest river which flowed into Lake Kariba. He recruited a small team of local natives and slowly and laboriously moved manually huge lumps of rock, sometimes weighing tons, until he had cleared an area of ground sufficient to provide a viable plantation and then commence planting the tobacco. With the aid of his blacks he built himself a farmhouse and constructed a pipeline to bring water to the area instead of transporting it manually. Furthermore he built huts for his black workers. His crops were successful and were marketed in Salisbury, (now named Harare). During our stay we visited Salisbury tobacco market auctions and witnessed the incredible speed and expertise used in disposing of the tobacco crops. Each year Ralph slowly extended his planting area until the official crunch seven-year Government inspection became due. This he passed with flying colours. He then became the proud owner of a few acres of viable farmland in the midst of a massive area of rock-strewn wilderness. On getting married he had to extend and improve his bachelor quarters. With the aid of his wife he developed a pleasant and comfortable farmstead. Ralph increased his workforce each year so that,

Victoria Falls (Zimbabwe) at Danger Point

Victoria Falls – View Point

when we visited, he had created literally a native village of some considerable number of natives, each of whom now had a regular job and was paid weekly. Before Ralph arrived these natives had lived at starvation level with no prospect whatever of improving their lot in this vast rock-bound wilderness.

We visited Kariba Dam and on the return journey our old Morris Oxford broke down in wild elephant country. A good Samaritan passer-by in this wild country offered us a lift to civilisation so we abandoned the jalopy and these kind people drove us all the way back to Ralph's farm. The next morning we accompanied Ralph in his jeep, complete with toolbox, to our abandoned car and he was able to get us mobile again.

At the conclusion of our visit to Ralph's farm we headed homewards but decided that we should not leave Rhodesia without seeing the Victoria Falls which were discovered by Livingstone in 1855. We thus took a diversionary route westwards and so arrived at Livingstone and the Victoria Falls on the Zambesi River. We camped the night here and, the next morning, trudging through the rain forest to visit the Falls, we had an alarming experience. On a narrow path running through the forest we met head on with a huge male gorilla and his lady friend. This huge creature was fortunately not aggressive and we were able to pass by safely whilst the male viewed us with some curiosity, perched on a throne of a fallen tree stump. The Victoria Falls are indeed an impressive sight. The Falls are awesome, being nearly a mile (5538feet) wide, broken by islands and rocks. The river plunges via five main falls which vary in depth from 200 to 354 feet. The Victoria Falls are both deeper and wider than the world famous Niagara Falls in the U.S.A. Standing nearby there is a continuous roar and one sees a perpetual spray rising like a huge cloud some hundreds of feet above the Falls. The Falls are on the border between Zimbabwe and Zambia but are actually in Zimbabwe. They face the town of Livingstone which is in Zambia.

Once again resuming our journey and heading south-east we passed through the Wankie National Park Game Reserve which is another huge area of wild African countryside full of protected dangerous wild animals. As we passed through we saw many herds of elephants. An amazing sight was a whole area of forest land of several acres which looked as though it had been bombed. The trees over the entire area had all been smashed to the ground. In fact, it had been the playground of elephant herds who, when in playful mood, would test their strength by pushing over every tree in sight. It would appear that wild elephants get themselves into this destructive mood by consuming large quantities of a certain tree foliage which has the effect of inebriating them and they then go on these drunken sprees.

Passing through Bulawayo once again we crossed the River Limpopo and the border back into South Africa at Beit Bridge. We decided to head south on a different cross-country, route in order to enter the Kruger Park Game Reserve at the northerly Pafuri Gate. We turned off the main road at Messina and took a little used road going south-east. It passed through delightful rolling countryside but was completely devoid of any civilisation except for the occasional isolated village. Considering the unreliability of our tired old Morris Oxford, choosing such a lonely primitive route was adventurous, to say the least, and the inevitable happened. We broke down midway across this hilly sparsely inhabited land. But we were so lucky that our breakdown occurred in one of the very few small townships that existed in this area. Lady Luck really smiled on us for there was a garage within easy reach of our breakdown spot. This little township was completely Afrikaans as was all the population but they were so hospitable, kind and helpful. The garage people immediately set to work on the car and quickly diagnosed big-end bearing failure. The garage owner regretted that he had no spares. His mechanic however said that he had a set of the Morris big-end bearings at his home and he volunteered to fetch them. This he did and in no time we were all working underneath the car, replacing the big-end bearings. Pam and the girls went off down the only street looking for a café to get a coffee and so pass away the waiting time.

After a time, whilst I was still under the car, my daughter Anne came to the garage and told me that she had been sent by her mother to conduct me to the house of a local lady who wished me to join them for some refreshment. As the job was now well under way I washed up and followed Anne to this stranger's house. This was another example of that camaraderie that I mentioned previously in describing my experience with the Dutch tobacco farmers on Christmas Day in Medan, Sumatra, in Indonesia. Pam and the two children had been walking down the street looking for a café when they were accosted by an Afrikaans lady who asked Pam if she could help. Pam explained that she was looking for somewhere to get a coffee and immediately this good lady said 'Come with me and you and the children will have refreshment at my house.' And the lady conducted them to her house where coffee and cold drinks were served.

When the good lady learned there was a husband underneath the broken down car at the local garage she insisted that I be brought to join the party. Hence the appearance at the garage of my daughter Anne and my being led to the stranger's house. We discovered in conversation that the lady was the wife of the local stationmaster. A railway had been built from Mozambique to Rhodesia which traversed this wild country and this little township was one of its en route stops. Following this encounter with the delightful, hospitable Afrikaners we were able to collect the car and caravan and once more resume our journey southwards, During the course of our conversation with the station master's wife we learned that the English author Rider Haggard, later Sir Henry Rider Haggard, wrote his famous classic novels 'She' and 'The Return of She' whilst resident in this area. At this time Rider Haggard was a civil servant in the employ of the South African Government. His name, of course, was originally made famous by his first novel 'King Solomon's Mines'. This area in which we were now travelling later became part of an independent small republic called Venda which lies in the Northern Transvaal area. It was created a republic in September 1979. It centres on the Soutspansberg mountains and its series of foothills and mountain ridges is the countryside which we were crossing to get to the Kruger Game Reserve. The native inhabitants of the

Venda country have mixed antecedents and one minority group is the Mbedzi, famous as rain-makers. These people are governed by a female chief, a Rain Queen. It is thought that Rider Haggard based his characterisation of his 'She' on the 'Rain Queen' who reigned in this wild area during his stay around here at this time.

We finally reached the northern entrance of the Kruger Park Game Reserve which is the Pafuri Gate and our weary overloaded Morris motor car heaved a sigh of relief that no longer did it have to labour, pulling its heavy caravan load, up steep gradients and could now trundle along at the low maximum speed limit permitted in the Park. We successfully meandered slowly some couple of hundred miles through the Game Reserve leaving by one of the southern exits, the Numbi Gate, near Komatipoort close to the Mozambique border on the Crocodile River. Here we joined the main road once again and headed south eastwards to Pretoria and finally home to Johannesburg. We had covered over two thousand miles through some of the wildest parts of the Southern African continent.

We had another experience of the kind generosity and hospitality of the Afrikaner towards strangers in trouble when, several years later, we did one of our weekend excursions, this time to Loskop Dam, about 150 miles north-east of Johannesburg. The Dam which at that time was a delightful green picnicking area with a few rondavels that one could rent for short stays. I believe the whole area has now been converted into a large game reserve. I was still running my unfaithful Morris Oxford which had even more grounds for complaint because, in order to induce a greater sparkle into its elderly life, I had ambitiously increased the engine compression ratio by machining off a slight amount of the cylinder head face and advancing the ignition timing to tune the engine to a more sporty standard with the hope of increasing its power output. In consequence the big-end bearings were suffering even higher loads and gave up trying when we were about 30 miles from Loskop Dam. We had once again broken down in desolate wild country with no civilisation for miles around. In fact the last elements of civilisation we had passed some twenty miles back. This was a little 'dorp' (the Afrikaans word for a primitive small village with very few amenities). Some twenty miles even further back from the 'dorp' was Witbank, a small Afrikaner town involved in the coal-mining industry.

Thus, stranded we were in the late afternoon, and there was nothing could be done except wait on this solitary roadside and hope that a good Samaritan would come along. And come along he did – in the shape of another Afrikaner who, after trying in vain to revive the engine, promised that he would organise aid for us. He was heading in the direction of the 'dorp' I have mentioned and said he knew a scrap yard man there who had a break down rescue outfit who would come to our aid in due course. He was indeed true to his word and our breakdown man, another Afrikaner by the name of van der Merwe, duly appeared after some hour or so patiently waiting. The original van der Merwe family were Dutch settlers of the 17th Century and, due to considerable inter-breeding, became famous in Afrikaner circles for lack of intelligence. In fact many national jokes were centred on the stupidity of the van der Merwes. Fortunately our van der Merwe rescuer was not in the traditional low intelligence class and in fact was highly intelligent and extremely helpful.

With Pam, the children and myself in his vehicle and the car stowed at the back he brought us back to his scrap-yard. By this time it was late in the evening so we just left our Morris Oxford in his yard and, following his directions, we sought accommodation at a small hotel in the village. But, alas, it was full. Our scrap-yard Afrikaner had foreseen this possibility and had invited us to return to his house in the scrap-yard if this proved to be the case. So return we did and, in this humble dwelling, the kind hearted Afrikaner family provided a room for all the family, sleeping on camp beds or mattresses on the floor. We passed a somewhat restless night for unwelcome guests in the shape of bugs came out of the woodwork or the wallpaper corners. However we survived with a number of red bites and next morning had an Afrikaner type working breakfast where food and drink were consumed standing round a central table.

Then came the question of getting our car running again. Van der Merwe said he unfortunately did not have spare big-end bearings but was willing to do the necessary work if we could obtain the spares from somewhere. I told him I had a spare new set at our house in Johannesburg which was some sixty miles or so away. To my astonishment he volunteered to drive me back to the house, using his huge 'gas-guzzling' American car. Naturally I accepted and off we went, he driving furiously. We collected my spares at the house and we were back in time to get the job well under way before lunchtime. Lunch we provided from our picnic resources and by this time Pam and the children had made a plan to go to a little local cinema in the 'dorp' whilst awaiting the completion of the car work. She very soon returned from the cinema which she found so hot and uncomfortable that she was forced to leave, preferring to wait in the scrap-yard. We finished the car work in the afternoon and, settling our account with Van der Merwe, we headed eastwards once more to Loskop dam. Arriving safely at last we spent the night in our rented rondavel and the next day enjoyed a brief few hours in this very pleasant riverside leisure area before making the return journey to Johannesburg.

By this time we had come to the conclusion that such trips were hazardous in our unreliable jalopy. We decided that by now our finances warranted a more reliable vehicle. From the sublime to the ridiculous is how one might describe the change we made – I bought a second-hand Mercedes 190 saloon car which was, by our past standards, an elegant limousine indeed. But it was not such a revolutionary unwarranted outlay for I had heard from my good South African neighbours that Barclays Bank had re-possessed this car from a client who had defaulted on his bank loan. It was an elderly Mercedes but in good running order and my meagre offer of £400 was accepted. Lo and behold! The Weston family in the splendour of their new-found magnificent motorcar. It was this car which I shipped aboard the s.s. Europa when we finally left South Africa for Spain.

Chapter 27

Apartheid and Housebuilding in South Africa

My Retirement

Being a member of the Royal Aeronautical Society I attended the monthly Society meetings which were held in the evening at Witwatersrand University, Johannesburg. I soon found myself elected as a member of the Southern Africa Division committee. The Division covered the Society aviation interests in all those countries in Southern Africa below the Equator which I mentioned previously in connection with the D.H. sales campaign. After some years on the Committee, in 1967-8 I was honoured by being elected President of the Southern African Division, a position one held for 12 months. This automatically made one a member for that year of the London Aeronautical Society Council which, at that time, included the Duke of Edinburgh. The Duke was Honorary President in 1966, the centenary year of our Society. The centenary journal of the Society brought home clearly how comparatively recent is man's conquest of the air, for in this magazine is a photograph of the Wright Brothers, Wilbur and Orville. In 1903 they were the American inventors of the first heavier than air aeroplane. They were entertained by the Society in London at a formal dinner in 1907, the year of my birth, and presented with the Society's gold medal. Wilbur's first flight was just a few yards whilst his brother Orville did better the next day with a flight lasting 53 seconds. Even in 1926, in my own young days at the Central Flying School, as I have previously mentioned, we were flying Avro 504s with no brakes, no instruments, no radio, no parachutes, no engine throttle control and no undercarriage shock absorbers except the rubber cords as previously described and a maximum speed all of 90 m.p.h. In less than 50 years from then we think nothing of aeroplanes flying at supersonic speeds and of huge passenger planes carrying 400 or 500 people at around 500 m.p.h. with take-off and landing speeds approaching 200 m.p.h. In my young days if we cruised at 80 m.p.h. we thought we were really travelling; and our take-off and landing speeds were around 45 m.p.h. Even that speed gave our elastic cord shock absorbers quite a stressful loading.

The Wright brothers certainly invented the aeroplane but it was Whittle, the British RAF apprentice, later cadet and junior officer, who revolutionised world air travel and so changed world society by promoting economic and rapid communication between nations. Whittle patented his gas turbine and jet aircraft designs five years before the Germans entered into this field. The Germans profited because Whittle could not afford to renew his patents resulting in a German design which certainly provided fighter aircraft in the later stages of World War 2. Hitler gave full support financially and materially whereas the British, struggling to survive in the early days, naturally devoted their full resources to their known weapons. Later, when the crisis had passed, the class-ridden Establishment   in the shape of high level Government scientific Agencies impeded the development of Whittle's efforts. This resulted in at least two years delay in the production of a British jet fighter craft. In the post war years the German design was found to be crude and inefficient and the Whittle technology developed by Rolls Royce became standard world-wide. The German jet fighter engine had a working life of only 9 to 10 hours and then had to be changed. During its 9 hour life it often suffered many technical problems including surging which is a phenomenon of uncontrolled acceleration due to poor fuel feed control.

Following my becoming a permanent member of the South African Company, we of course changed our plans for our housing requirements. Previously, we thought only of renting property, on the assumption that we would be returning to England at the end of my contractual two years. During this period, for a variety of reasons we moved house some half dozen times and eventually settled down in the suburb of Montroux, a part of Northcliff, which was at that time a good class residential area on the northern boundary of Johannesburg adjoining the open bush country between Johannesburg and Pretoria.

Montroux was a fairly recently developed area of expanding Johannesburg. It contained superior properties with mostly the English speaking type of residents who were in comfortable financial circumstances. One might describe them as English speaking South African middle class. My next door neighbour was a born and bred South African and, like all the English speaking element of the population, he had a tremendous respect and admiration for the Mother Country, i.e. Britain. In consequence we were very well received by all of our neighbours and particularly by my next door neighbour, Allan Austin. When Allan discovered that I was an aircraft engineer with a background of considerable experience in metalwork and that I was an enthusiastic D.I.Y. exponent he became extremely friendly. He invited me to view his private workshop which was an amazingly sophisticated collection of D.I.Y. machinery housed in his double garage. He was an electrical engineer employed by the South African State Railways.

Allan was a remarkable man, extremely intelligent, and with a tremendous fund of amateur knowledge and experience in many crafts and trades, both in woodwork and in metalwork. Furthermore he had a great knowledge of building construction and architecture. When I met him he had already built three houses. Each one he had lived in for a time, then sold, and with the profit built a better one. I developed my own private workshop in my garage and, with his guidance, I also invested in D.I.Y. machinery that enabled all types of woodwork and metalwork to be produced quickly. We thus became real D.I.Y. buddies and were always visiting each other's workshops discussing projects.

Just after Christmas, one weekend evening in 1965, some time after I had already become a permanent South African resident, I called round to his place to discuss a problem. There I found a hilarious party going on, which I was invited to join. I was told that the occasion of the party was Allan's purchase of a plot of land in the adjoining bush country where he proposed to build his fourth house. The plot was in a new development suburb which had been approved by the Jo'burg municipal authorities; a municipal road with water and electricity work was already under way. At that time in South Africa such works were carried out at lightning speed compared to the U.K. This young country did not have the hurdle of the bureaucratic red tape of Western European countries. At the party Allan suggested that I should also buy a plot in this newly planned expansion in the bush. He introduced me to the estate agent who was present at the party. I told them I had no ambition to own a part of South Africa since I planned eventually to return to the U.K. Allan said 'I know you want to buy an expensive lathe. If you buy this plot I guarantee that you will have your lathe with the profit you can make by buying it now and selling it in nine months' time.' After a few more brandies the estate agent began to work on me, telling me that this was the last plot in the same row and next to Allan's. He told me the price of the plot and this happened to coincide with my Christmas bonus. In my brandy haze I considered the risk was negligible. I thought 'What the hell! I've got nothing to lose except my Christmas bonus!' So I signed on the dotted line.

Immediately I had signed, the thought struck me, belatedly, through the brandy haze, that I had not consulted Pam nor informed her of this somewhat adventurous plunge into land ownership in South Africa. This was a rather disturbing thought and I hastened to make amends by getting Allan's permission to ring Pam next door and give her the 'good' news over the phone. In my best diplomatic manner I told her of the availability of the plot, its situation and price etc. I said that the estate agent was with me at the party and had told me that this was the last plot available. She said 'O.K. We can go and see it to-morrow and discuss it with Allan.' This was the crunch moment. I had to admit that I had already signed up for it, my excuse being that I did not want to lose the opportunity. Needless to say I was not very popular and I made my way back to the house in somewhat chastened mood. However, as I have said, the price (£120) was nothing to worry about and so we dropped the subject altogether.

A few weeks later I again called round to Allan's workshop and found him standing in front of a professional easel and drawing board, studiously drawing the plans of a very large luxurious villa. He explained to me that this was to be the house which he proposed to build on the plot he had recently bought. He said 'Why don't you build a house on your plot?' I was horrified and replied 'How could I ever build a house on my plot when I haven't got the slightest idea about house building? I don't even know the difference between a face brick and a stock brick.' He replied 'When these plans are finally approved by the City Council civil engineers department, which will take about three or four weeks, I will start building. I will make you an offer now. If you will be my assistant, I will take you right through the whole technique of house building from the planning, marking out the foundations and carrying out all the building operations plus organising the services such as plumbing, electricity etc. After completing my house you will be able to start on your own and have my guidance. You can start with me by holding one end of the string when I mark out the foundations. We can work together through the whole building process and in addition I will brief you on the

*Ready to start building our
South African house*

The house that I built in Johannesburg, South Africa

details of the building material suppliers, sanitary ware suppliers etc.' I thanked him for the kind offer and said I would discuss it with Pam, and let him know my answer in a day or two. My previous Post-Christmas Party experience and Pam's reaction had taught me to be more cautious!

Pam and I discussed this proposal for some time before we finally decided that it was a good idea and an opportunity not to be missed and I accepted to be Allan's assistant house builder. Our decision was certainly influenced by the fact that Allan's prediction of the appreciation of the value of the plot was already becoming evident for I had recently had several offers from people wishing to buy it. Their price offers were way above what I had originally paid. Thus, with more confidence, we plunged into this new world of bricks and mortar, sand and cement, bricklayers and plumbers and all the 'infinite' requirements of house-building, not least the administrative regulations appertaining to these activities. Because of my ignorance of house building I felt that writing up a diary with a detailed account of every day's activity would provide some safety reference, so that when the time arrived to build my own house, I would have a record to which I could refer if necessary.

We worked evenings, weekends and holidays and Alan's house shell was completed in six months. The building team consisted of 6 black labourers, 2 white Afrikaner bricklayers and sub-contract auxiliaries such as plumbers and electricians. Following on from the actual house construction there was of course the interior work such as cupboards, bathroom utilities, curtain supports, painting and decorating, all of which was time consuming. The newly designed house was a large villa type with four bedrooms on one floor and a double garage with two floors, the upper storey providing storage. Between the house and the garage was a considerable sized area which provided a tiled patio. An ornamental gated wall joined the house to the garage. The house roof was extended on pillar supports to cover half the patio area. Thus the patio was enclosed on three sides while the roof extension providing alternative all weather protection. The house wall on the patio side was entirely glass with sliding doors to the sitting room. When the sliding doors were open the patio became an extension of the sitting room, providing a considerable area for entertainment.

Whilst it was possible to complete the building of the house in the comparatively short time of six months, the completion of the interior work took much longer, since it was done entirely on a D.I.Y. basis to cut down costs. Obviously the length of time spent on interior completion depended on the desired level of interior luxury and finish. Allan estimated from his previous house building experience that it might take up to a year to complete his fourth house which would be to a much higher standard than his previous efforts. He had more money available from the profits he had made from selling his first three houses.

Indeed the shell of Allan's house was completed in six months. I had successfully completed my apprenticeship and I was eager to get on with building my own house. Allan agreed that he could proceed without my further assistance. So arrived the exciting moment when I was to put into practice all I had learnt from Allan in the preceding six months. The first problem was to find the money! Whilst I had amazing confidence that I could successfully build my own house (Allan seemed to have less confidence in that matter) I had severe doubts as to my prospects for raising a mortgage in South Africa. I knew that, at this time, in England it would have been impossible to raise a 100% mortgage on a house that did not exist. At my age of 59 it would have been impossible and it was especially difficult when one added the fact that it was a D.I.Y. project by someone with no building experience whatever.

By happy chance, Allan's wife, Doreen, who had an important Company Secretary's post in Johannesburg, was on very friendly terms with the manager of the Johannesburg Building Society, which had financed their previous projects. She knew my problem and promised me that, if I applied to her Building Society, she would persuade her manager friend to give me favourable consideration. I submitted my application as Doreen advised and I was called up for my interview with the manager. I was so anxious about the subject of my age that in my application I had falsified it to read 55 instead of 59. The manager asked if I had ever built a house before. When I replied in the negative he asked if I had had building work experience. Again a negative answer but I tempered it with an exaggerated description of my building work with Allan. I was informed that my application would go before the board at its next meeting. Imagine my joy when, three weeks later, I was informed that my 100% mortgage amounting to £9000 had been granted. There was only one fly in the ointment. The Building Society informed me that, due to my lack of experience, at every important stage in the construction, from the foundations to the completion, an Inspector from the Building Society would have to certify in writing that each building operation was satisfactory. Each stage was listed distinctly in the mortgage contract. But, more serious was a clause in the contract that not a penny would be released by the Society until the walls had been built up to roof height. I quickly estimated that I needed at least £3000 to achieve this. So I had another problem: where to find £3000. I had no such capital in my bank account, nor did I have any assets in South Africa to use as collateral. I took my problem to my (Barclays) bank manager in Jo'burg and told him the whole story, requesting a £3000 loan. He demanded to know how long it would take to get my house to roof height. I said 'Three months,' hoping and praying that my guess would be right. He replied 'O.K. I will give you a short-term loan of £3000 for three months only. I thanked him and departed, relieved, but from then on I lived in constant dread that I might fail to achieve the target date. I would then have had another problem. In addition I was constantly worried that my £3000 calculation might prove wrong and I would end up three months later with a shortfall in both time and money.

I am relating this building episode in rather more detail than one would normally bestow on such a mundane subject because it provides a vivid example of the stupidity of the 'apartheid' system that existed in South Africa at that time. A considerable amount of thought was given by Pam and myself to the design of the house we proposed to build. Obviously, with my limited experience in this field, I intended to follow as closely as possible, Allan's house construction, but Pam had very definite ideas, for example on what type of kitchen she wanted. Her ideas were very different from those of Doreen. Allan had no children whereas we had three so this again involved differences in layout. Another difference was that on my patio I had provided for a fish-pond with six fountains, one of which came out of the mouth of an ornamental King Neptune's head (spouting into the adjacent fish-pond) which I planned to build into the garage wall which would form one side of the patio. My ornamental Neptune's head complete with designed water spurting fountain I purchased from a Johannesburg firm that specialised in pre-cast statues etc.

Adjacent to our plot was a large, interesting natural pond surrounded, of course, by wild bush country. We sited the villa in our plans so that, from the sitting room and patio, one had a pleasant view of this attractive stretch of water. Surprisingly there were no mosquitoes in the area although there were plenty of grass snakes and other wild creatures so that one had to be careful when walking through the bush countryside. My young son used to catch the grass snakes in a glass jar and take them to school to frighten the girl pupils in his class. For my building team I recruited an Afrikaner bricklayer, a Mr. Myburgh, who had ambitions to set up as a master builder. He was pleased to take on the whole bricklaying contract at £1200 for the complete building, in order to gain wider experience. I instructed him on how to read the plans and mark out the foundations etc. He engaged a white assistant and six black labourers with building experience and occasionally used his son as a bricklaying assistant. We hired a bulldozer and driver to clear and level the whole plot which covered about half an acre. The plot was in a newly developed northern suburb of Jo'burg named Randburg and it was to Randburg municipality that one had to apply for the plan approval, water connection, and a copy of all the regulations appertaining to the employment of labour on the building site. This included the provision of amenities on the building site such as a W.C. etc. for blacks and a separate one for whites. The foundations were marked out and the trenches were dug. I hired a cement mixer and we were ready to start laying the concrete foundations having previously arranged a contract for the supply of sand, cement, stones (ballast) etc. Pam became a sort of clerk of the works and, with the aid of a trailer I had bought, she would rush to a supplier to provide any of the materials that were running short and causing a hold-up. As the school day ended at lunch time, her teaching job in a small private school which the children also attended, permitted her afternoons to be free to give whatever assistance of this kind might be needed.

Then the apartheid fun and games started. The whole team, including ourselves, was on site at 7.15 a.m. one Monday morning, ready to start laying the concrete foundations. We started the concrete mixer with the black labourers standing by ready to do the mixing and moving when suddenly all the blacks scattered in all directions and disappeared. I asked Myburgh what was happening and he, pointing in the distance to an approaching van, said 'Police'. The van, driving over the rough bush land, arrived at the site and two policemen got out, approached me, and asked if I was the owner. When I replied in the affirmative they informed me that they had seen my black labourers run away. They said this indicated that those workers were not in possession of passes or work permits. They questioned Myburgh who admitted that he had recruited the blacks without checking their legality. He was fined £10 (probably nearer £100 in today's money) on the spot and I was warned that I could be charged in court if I employed blacks without passes or permits. I said to them 'I need black labourers for this job – what do I do?' They replied 'You go to Randburg Town Hall and they will supply your black labourers.' They said they would not bother to chase my blacks because they would be sure to catch them eventually. They departed. I paid Myburgh's fine.

Following the police instruction I called at the Randburg Town Hall and to my disgust was informed by the Afrikaners of the native labour department that they would bring my required six labourers from some remote native village some hundreds of miles away. I was required to pay for their railway fares plus a fee for the town hall services. 'When I asked if these blacks would have had building site experience they replied that these villagers would have no building experience and it would be my responsibility to train them for the type of work I required.

What the native labour department failed to mention was that the labourers would be coming from some primitive African jungle area and that they would be completely unaware of the facts of city life. So that, in addition to training them to do the building jobs, they would also have to be educated in the simple knowledge that by turning a thing called a 'tap' water would come out of the wall, and by pressing a thing called a 'switch' light would also come out of the wall. In addition they had to be taught that, to cross the road, it would be fatal to step out into the path of those roaring monsters called 'motor cars'.

Thus the rigid 'apartheid' minds of the Afrikaner civil servants and the police robbed me of an experienced efficient team of labourers and turned them into criminals because they were not in possession of pieces of paper called 'passes'. In their place I was forced to accept and pay for the transportation of six 'country bumpkins'. I had another experience of the apartheid hypocrisy in the case of a young African I attempted to help. His name was William Mashaba. He came one evening when I was working in my garage workshop. I was preparing gable end 18 ft. long timbers for my new house roof. I heard a plaintive voice saying 'Sir, can you give me a job?' He was speaking pathetically from my open garage entrance. I turned round and saw a young African. I said that unfortunately I had no money to employ an assistant. He pleaded with me, saying that he had walked a thousand miles from his homeland and that he only needed food and shelter, and a very small wage. 'Besides,' he said 'I can see you need an assistant to help you whilst you are struggling with that huge beam of wood.' I was impressed with his sincerity, for indeed I did need an assistant, not least to ensure the security of my building site whilst I was at work. I thought for a moment 'To hell, I will find the money from somewhere.' It was a decision which I never regretted. William proved to be a most faithful and an intelligent worker. Of course he had no pass and no work permit. When he had demonstrated his worth I decided that I would endeavour to make him 'legal' by taking him personally to the authorities and speaking for him. We were passed from one Government department to another and the net result was refusal and rejection. By this time William had received local native advice on how to solve his problem – without my help. He asked for the day off to go to Pretoria, some thirty miles away. The next day he smilingly showed me his 'pass' and work permit. It had cost him money paid as bribes and in cash to Afrikaner civil servants in the Pretoria Government offices. He had borrowed the money from Dora's boy friend who had provided all the advice and know-how for solving such problems.

My six labourers duly arrived and, after a period of training them, we were able once again to start the building work. Myburgh quickly knocked the black labourers into shape and we made rapid progress. I shall never forget the huge joy and relief I experienced when the Building Society inspector signed his approval certificate at the 'roof height' stage. At last I would be permitted to make my first draw from the mortgage loan. I had succeeded in my task a good fortnight before the three months'

Barclays Bank deadline. I proudly paid the £3000 short term loan back to the manager, who was rather puzzled by my excited and happy mood. Little did he know of the anxieties of this amateur builder. After that episode we made excellent progress for Myburgh was an amazing bricklayer. He demonstrated to me that, provided he had a good team and all materials to hand, he could lay 2000 bricks in a working day. His normal pace was 1000 bricks a day. The British trade unions stipulate a maximum of 450 bricks a day. I completed the house building outer shell in five months and then began the inner work. This is where William came in really useful for I had by then taught him the elements of woodwork and turned him into a first class painter. Incidentally I used 52,000 bricks in the house shell construction. Some 5% of these were damaged by the tilt lorry method of delivery. These I used mainly for hardcore in foundations for building the garden walls etc.

The family moved in on 3rd June 1967, only eight months from the start of building. The inside work was almost completed. Then followed the creation of a garden from the terrible 'builder's yard' area that existed around the house. The garage was just a mass of tools and materials covering the floor but gradually order was established out of chaos. To relieve the pressure on the workshop, I built a carport and had the drive tarmacked. The driveway to the house was about 50 yards long and was lined with flowerbeds and rows of standard roses. With the aid of a bulldozer I landscaped the garden and Pam and William created lawns and flowerbeds. An enclosing decorative wall round the whole plot completed the project.

Allan Austin was quite impressed with my successful efforts for I had done the whole job without any help from him at all. As I said previously, in my impatience to get started, I had got going whilst he was very preoccupied with his interior fitting work. I continued my building work without troubling him in any way. Some year or so after the house was completed William asked me sheepishly if he could have three months leave. I was a little taken aback at such a request and asked him why he wanted such a long holiday. He explained that he proposed to travel back to his village in Mozambique. There he hoped to buy four cows with the money he had saved whilst working for me. With the four cows he could then purchase a new wife, set her up working his family land, and return to South Africa to resume his job with me. Naturally I agreed to his request and wished him good luck. Three months later he reappeared as he had promised. He had successfully accomplished his plan and told me he now had a team of wives working for him on his family plot. A few months after his return he again came to me and timidly asked me if I would object to his taking a very good job he had been offered as a fully qualified artisan painter. It would appear that my training and his experience on my house building had stood him in good stead and he was now recognised as a fully qualified industrial painter. I told him I would never stand in his way to such success and I gave him as a farewell gift one of my dark business suits which had got a little shiny but was in very good condition. It was a Harrods suit so that it was of good quality and had kept its cut and shape. I say this because, three weeks after his departure, one Sunday afternoon he visited me, proudly dressed in his Harrods suit, wearing a Trilby hat and carrying a walking stick. He looked very smart indeed. He informed me of his good progress in his new job and thanked me for the assistance I had given him in the past.

Pam and I revisited South Africa in 1992 and spent some time in Johannesburg finding our way round our old haunts. Among our nostalgic travels we revisited Site 12, Aldara Park, Randburg where to our joy we saw the villa which I had built. It was in excellent condition. In fact it looked exactly the same as when we had left it 25 years before. The present residents very kindly showed us over the house and I must admit that I was at that moment so proud that my work had stood the test of time so well that it looked as though we had only left it yesterday.

Wondering whether Allan Austin, after 25 years, was still in the land of the living, for we had lost touch many years ago, we anxiously rang his front door bell. After an interval a lady appeared, who, in answer to our enquiry, introduced herself as Allan's sister-in-law. She said he was at that moment at the local shops but would be returning shortly. Indeed he did. She had invited us to partake of a cup of tea in her bachelor flat which Allan had built for her in his garden. When Allan appeared and saw me he seemed to collapse to the floor with shock. On recovering he said that he was convinced I had died and could hardly believe his eyes when he saw me drinking a cup of tea with his sister-in-law. It transpired that his wife Doreen had died only six months previously and his sister-in-law had been widowed about the same time so they had joined forces and it had proved a very convenient arrangement for them both. We had several celebratory meals together before we continued on our travels to Cape Town.

Our stay in the Johannesburg area had been a revelation in the amazing development of these northern suburbs. In fact our original suburb of Randburg had been overwhelmed by a huge ' new town' called Sandton which had sprung up since our original departure. This place Sandton was now so vast that when we arrived on our second visit to South Africa we were completely lost in both senses of the word. On our arrival by air at Jo'burg airport we hired a car, confident that we knew our way to the northern suburb hotel where we had booked in. To our astonishment we found ourselves lost in this huge new township. We had not taken the precaution of buying a map at the airport and all the shops were closed so that we wandered round, literally lost, for some considerable time. Sandton itself had become vast, not only as a residential area, but because the whole of the Johannesburg business area originally located in the centre of the city had moved northwards out of the city into this Sandton township. This move had been forced on the business community including all the large department stores by the deteriorating political situation. After 5 p.m. the city centre became a 'no-go' area and it was dangerous for whites to walk in the streets. This deteriorating political situation was also reflected in the once upon a time beautiful garden city of northern Jo'burg. The former splendid open gardens and residences in these suburbs had now become barbed wire fortresses with prominent notices at their entrances stating that an armed patrol was situated just round the corner and would appear on pressing an emergency alarm button in the house. Our own Aldara Park of course still existed, but it was now part of a huge built-up complex with no longer any visible sign of its former surrounding bush country. Our delightful pond area remained, however, and in fact had been embellished and now formed part of a small park area. In fact the whole bush country of some 30 miles between Johannesburg and Pretoria had disappeared. It was now entirely a developed built up area lining each side of the whole route joining the two cities.

To return to the story of my experiences in South Africa twenty five years previously when working with the South African Hawker de Havilland Company, I found my new role of technical sales extremely interesting. It soon became evident to me that, if I was to be successful in selling for example the high precision Pottermeter flow meter, I would need to know in some detail the various applications in which its use might prove advantageous. I then began to study those industries that might be receptive to this innovation. These included the Rhodesian oil company pipeline transportation from Mozambique to Rhodesia, African Explosives (I.C.I.) fertiliser manufacture, S.A. Government steel foundry works (ISCOR), motor tyre factory manufacturing processes, diamond dredging ships operating off the South West African coast and many others. In some of these I was successful in establishing sales and the reputation of the Pottermeter as a valuable tool in industries where accurate measurement and precise control of liquid flows was an important required feature. This applied particularly in the systems where automation in various industrial processes was being introduced. My success as mentioned previously was greater than that of the sales force in the U.K. This success story must have reached the ears of the former South African D.H. Technical Manager now in New Zealand for I was asked by my own M.D. (Davison) to make a write-up for the benefit of the New Zealand M.D. on my methods and techniques in selling the Pottermeter in South Africa.

However it was all to no avail for, with the poor marketing in the U.K. and the merger of D.H. with Hawker Siddeley, the manufacture of the Pottermeter folded and the whole project, to my great regret, collapsed. My own M.D., being impressed with my Pottermeter sales record, decided that I should spend a long session in the U.K., studying the numerous Westland/Hawker Siddeley products for which our Company was responsible. Over three months in the U.K.I travelled from factory to factory, studying steamrollers, lawn mowers, automatic vending machines, ships' stabilisers, a mobile Westland industrial platform operating on the hovercraft principle, not to mention the updated aviation interests of the conglomerate. Little came from it, for a certain malaise seemed to have affected the South African Company. I think it was resulting from the unfortunate death of Jacklin, who had been elevated to M.D. while Davison became Chairman. Air Vice Marshal Jacklin died from stomach cancer and from that time things seemed to go downhill.

Finally I personally lost interest completely and asked for early retirement. This was agreed by the Chairman as it suited his new plans for the re-organisation of the Company. Furthermore Hawker had decided to demerge their industrial products from the aviation side. I had been considering retirement from the Company for some time and had given thought to alternative employment that would provide for my young family. My success with my building project had provided such potential profit that I seriously thought of throwing in my aviation profession and taking up building as a full time career. I estimated that the profit from the one house alone would provide an income greater than that of my aviation post as technical manager with my Company. Building two houses a year would be quite possible and would more than double my annual aviation salary. But it was a gamble and capital was required to purchase sites. It was a risk I finally decided not to take with my limited financial resources.

At weekends we received the English Sunday papers and I had become interested in the reported craze of U.K. people buying property in Spain. In fact there seemed to be a considerable interest in emigration to this Mediterranean country of sunshine, wine and cheap living. I followed up this interest by seeking more information about Spain. As I could not visit the place, being some 6000 miles away, I obtained my information by borrowing books on the subject from the Johannesburg library. The more I read, the keener I became on the idea of starting a new life in a country that would provide inexpensive opportunities to utilise my building skills and at the same time it would be possible to live in a warm, sunny environment similar to the existing conditions in South Africa. My reading seemed to indicate that on my limited retired income I could live at a similar standard to the one which I was enjoying at that moment in South Africa. What I did not realise, of course, was that the books I was reading were out of date and the living conditions in Spain were changing daily, so that no longer was it possible to buy cheap, luxurious villas for peanuts, have servants and live a life of ease on the level of my retired income.

Unaware of these changed conditions, I finally decided to take the plunge and leave South Africa, following my early retirement. This decision involved considerable changes in our way of life. For one thing the villa had to be sold and this we did quite quickly, making 100% profit. Selling the villa early meant we had to find rented accommodation for the short period prior to our final farewell to South Africa. There seemed to be little choice for short term letting so we ended up in a rundown uninviting villa much nearer the city but in a less pleasant and older suburb. All my expensive private workshop tools and machinery were moved to this rental house and we had a kind of car boot sale in the garden. I arranged for my family and my car to be embarked at Cape Town for Spain on the Lloyd Triestino Line S.S. Europa. We took the train to Cape Town a few days before the embarkation to give Pam and the children a chance to visit the Cape area.

Chapter 28.

Departure to Spain

On 31st December 1969 we set sail from Cape Town and waved a fond farewell to South Africa and to the beautiful setting of Cape Town with its Table Mountain backdrop. When we went to our cabin we found that my former Cape Town colleague Brigadier Wilmott had arranged a most kind farewell gesture in the shape of an exquisite bouquet of gorgeous flowers, which seemed to bring some joy to the sad occasion. It was the end of our ten-year stay in a country we had learned to love.

We sailed up the West Coast of Africa to our first port of call, which was Luanda in Angola. Here the ship was in port for most of the day, which gave us the opportunity of going ashore for a tour of the town. Whilst I had been to Luanda several times on business and I hated this filthy Portuguese African colonial town, Pam had never had this opportunity so I engaged a taxi at the dockside to spend the morning making an extended drive round the town. The taxi was a Mercedes car and our driver was Portuguese, a friendly affable type. I am always interested in cars, especially Mercedes, my own car on board with us was a Mercedes, so I expressed interest in his vehicle. To my astonishment he told me that his car had done a million kilometres. He saw that I had difficulty in accepting such a statement and, being obviously pleased to have an English family as passengers, he invited us to have coffee at his home where, he said, he could show me proof from the Mercedes factory supporting his claim. We naturally accepted his invitation and enjoyed meeting his wife and young family in their home, a pleasant villa located in a residential suburb of the town. He proudly showed me a certificate from Mercedes which officially declared that his vehicle had completed a million kilometres. He told me he had had several engine changes during this long period of service. After that interesting experience the driver took us on a most delightful tour of the town before returning us to our floating home on the S.S. Europa. This short pleasant view of Luanda experienced by my family was in direct contrast to my own bitter experience on my last business trip to Luanda some time previously when I caught some horrible tropical disease which no South African doctor could diagnose. My life was only saved by massive doses of penicillin over a period of a week or more.

Our next port of call was Las Palmas in the Canary Islands. Here again we had the opportunity to stretch our legs on shore and we purchased a few electrical goods which appeared to be very cheap compared with our South African experience. Then we were on our way again, following the Moroccan coast in towards the Straits of Gibraltar which we passed through during the night. When we woke next morning we were sailing in shore quite close to the Spanish coastline. We had a splendid view of the coastline of the country which was to be our future home – Spain. The ship's

Captain maintained this inshore viewing most of the way northwards until we finally arrived at our destination, Barcelona. Here we off-loaded our car and all the heavy luggage containing the remains of our former home in South Africa. This we passed to a transport agent with instructions to forward it to Alicante. Alicante on the Costa Blanca was to be our temporary home until we had sorted ourselves out and made a plan for our future in our new country of residence.

As previously mentioned I had been a keen reader of the English Sunday papers whilst in South Africa and had corresponded with one of the advertised London agents selling building plots in Spain close to Alicante. The price of these plots was so cheap that I bought two – once again without seeing them or having any information on their viability. But it gave us an address in Alicante, that of the local representative. This address was our eventual destination. Meanwhile, after spending a few days in the excellent city of Barcelona we began to meander southwards in our car towards Alicante which was about 200 miles away. Hugging the coast, we paused sometimes overnight at the coastal towns, studying the way of life in Spain. Pam knew a little of the Spanish language but the children and I had no Spanish whatever.

We finally arrived in Alicante and spent two or three days there. On the recommendation of the local representative of the London estate agents we rented a flat in Albufera, an outlying seaside suburb of Alicante. The representative lived with his French wife in the same block which was useful from the business point of view. We had already discovered since landing in Spain that the cost of living and the cost of property etc, bore no resemblance whatever to what one had read in the library books of Johannesburg. Our retirement plans concocted in South Africa were no longer viable in Spain and we had to make an urgent revision to find ways of bolstering our meagre capital which seemed to be disappearing at an alarming rate.

It became immediately obvious to us that we could no longer dream of being the proud owners of a magnificent villa with servants and a splendid high living standard with no financial worries. On the contrary we realised that, far from being able to relax in comparative opulence, we had to return to earth and earn some money to meet our commitments, not the least of which was to complete the education of our three young children. We journeyed to the building plots, which I had bought unseen whilst in South Africa, and found them situated high in the mountainous area inland from Alicante. The plots were on steep, rough, rocky gradients on which, it seemed to us, only goats could exist. The site had no visible civilisation in the locality and no services such as water or electricity. I quickly sold them back to the London agents at a small loss.

By this time we had gained enough depressing information and seen enough adverse features of the conditions and way of life in Spain to completely undermine the optimism which we had when we set out on our voyage of discovery. In its place was gloomy financial anxiety and disappointment. My popularity with my family had by now descended to sub-zero level, especially with the children. Anne, 13, Christine almost 12, and Richard, 8, all viewed me as a saboteur who had destroyed the happy life they had had in Johannesburg. They had lost all their many friends, lost the enjoyable open air life where they had such fun in their own and their friends gardens; they had lost the happy school life they enjoyed and, even worse, they could not even communicate since they could not speak the language of their neighbours. Even Pam, whilst saying little, showed a certain resentment at having lost her happy South African way of life and having it replaced by daunting uncertainty and continuous financial worry.

Before our marriage Pam had had experience in the tourist trade in Switzerland and she suggested perhaps we might exploit this experience by developing our own travel agency. We toured up and down the coast in the Alicante area searching for a suitable spot in which we might settle. We finally pitched up in Calpe which at that time was a small fishing village, about 40 miles from Alicante and 10 miles from Benidorm. Here we chanced on a friendly English resident who invited us to his villa and gave us tea and very helpful advice on the prospects of a travel agency in Calpe. He also directed us to a building developer who had just completed a block of flats with spaces on the ground floor for shop development. We bought one of these spaces with the idea of opening a travel agency, only to discover that the daughter of the Mayor of Calpe had already done the same thing, but in the main or high street of the village. This immediately put an end to any ambition we had in the travel business but, working on the principle 'If you cant beat them, join them' we approached the Mayor and suggested a partnership with his daughter. At the same time we decided to change our plans for our newly purchased shop from a travel agency to an embryo gift shop. The Mayor of Calpe was agreeable to our

Spain – our gift shop investment in Calpe village near Bendidorm

suggestion of a partnership providing his daughter was happy with such an arrangement. We soon found that his daughter was only too happy for us to do all the work whilst she read comics all day. This may sound somewhat exaggerated but it is a fact that this grown-up woman in her early twenties sat in the shop reading Spanish comics most of the day while we conducted what little business there was at that time.

What we had not realised at the time of undertaking this enterprise in Calpe was that this small Spanish fishing village was at that time a poverty stricken community which had no use for a travel agency seeing that they did not travel. At that time Calpe was a picturesque quaint fishing port and a centre of interest for tourists from other areas but had not yet sufficiently emerged from its ancient traditional role to reap the huge potential tourism harvest that was awaiting exploitation. In consequence our only customers in our partnership travel agency were foreign tourists requesting our free service to change their existing bookings. In addition to this unhappy situation we had searched all over Spain for suitable English speaking schools for the children and sadly found that we were ahead of the time when such schools would eventually be available. We tried some establishments locally but language difficulties made this unsuccessful. We travelled as far as Gibraltar which we thought would surely have an English school. It certainly did but we found that there was no possibility whatever of entry since the Royal Navy and Gibraltarians booked places for their children at birth.

Finally we came to the conclusion that the only solution to give the children a proper English education was to send them to England. The failure of the travel agency to produce a living also forced Pam to look elsewhere and we came to the conclusion that she could contribute much more to the diminishing exchequer by taking a teaching post in England. Teachers in Spain were very badly paid and again there was the question of language so, at the end of that summer season of 1970, Pam and the children departed on their journey back to England. I had taken on the task of developing our newly purchased premises into a gift shop and so I remained in Calpe, hoping to restore our fortunes with the rising tourist trade. This was no easy task since our shop was located in an area of Calpe that had not yet been fully developed. There was no road, no pavement and there were no customers. The wide open track which led past our shop front was a mere rocky unmade roadway. Tourists or potential customers would not choose this route since they could easily twist their ankles on the precarious terrain. The empty shop space adjoining our shop was the home of a rat family, and this also did not promote an attractive environment to encourage shoppers. We had invested in this unlikely site due, of course, to the fact that it was going very cheaply and therefore suited our limited financial resources. We hoped that eventual development of Calpe would bring prosperity and change our fortunes.

We had chosen to settle in Calpe at a time when that little fishing village was only just beginning to feel the birth pangs and the stirrings of foreign tourism which were already producing such overnight riches for Benidorm, only ten miles down the road.

Spain – our villa just outside Calpe consisted of three units – two small units on the ground floor and the main flat on the upper floor

The local Calpe community leaders eyed the wonders of Benidorm's tourism with envy and were determined to emulate their example. To achieve this ambition Spanish entrepreneurs and developers from knowledgeable centres such as Valencia were welcomed by the Mayor and given every assistance – provided, of course, that he received his cut in the various projects. Our newly purchased shop was located in such a new building development, called Garvimar. The developer was an arrogant, unprincipled Spaniard who was in partnership with a builder, both from Valencia. The builder owned large orange orchards in the Valencia area, and these had previously supplied his basic livelihood. The two partners had decided to exploit the potential of tourism in Calpe.

The builder of the Garvimar apartment block, by name Martinez, converted the ground floor open blank space we had purchased into some semblance of a small shop with a tiled floor, shop front and entrance, a washroom and toilet, and a plastered brick counter. My own D.I.Y. efforts had completed the necessary shelving etc., so that, just prior to Pam and the children departing, we tackled the problem of stocking the shop. Neither of us had ever been shopkeepers, neither of us had the slightest idea of where or how one bought gift stock wholesale in Spain, and neither of us spoke Spanish except the few words Pam knew. After a ludicrous and disastrous attempt to recruit the help of the Mayor Pam suggested, to my horror, that we should walk into a gift shop in Alicante town and ask the owner where he obtained his stock. We did just that and it proved successful. The owner of the shop was a true Spanish gentleman who treated us 'innocents' with courtesy and offered us every assistance. In fact, as it was near midday and time for the afternoon siesta, he closed his shop and personally conducted us to the wholesaler from whom he bought his own stock.

And so we had our first taste of Spanish business life. The reader of this autobiography may think it is an exaggeration when I write that this first experience was a revelation of how Spain in 1970 was only just beginning to enter the 20th century. The gift stock wholesaler to whom we had so kindly been conducted by the Alicante shop owner was in a private house in a residential area with no signs or advertisement whatever to indicate his presence. One had to be in the know to be able to find and deal with the wholesaler. Advertising was taboo and this incognito was deliberate for Spain was only just beginning to throw off the effects of centuries of the Spanish Inquisition. The Inquisition was a regime of terror and torture operated by the Roman Catholic Church for some 400 years. This tremendous and frightful power of the Catholic Church depended on the system of the informer denouncing or accusing others of a breach of the faith. If your neighbour disliked you or had for any reason developed a hatred of you then you had to be extremely careful not to let that person know anything of your way of life. One could be accused for the slightest deviation from the conventional. For instance we learned of an innocent person who was accused of being a heretic because he was using soap produced in Moslem Morocco. In fact, when we arrived, the Police in Calpe were even then using this denunciation system. It was the law at that time that, following a successful prosecution, a reward of one third of any fine imposed would be paid to the informer. In Calpe we knew a person who made a living by travelling around new building estates seeking contraventions by uninformed immigrants which he would then report to the police and later collect his reward.

Naturally, under such a regime communication between people was destroyed by fear and over hundreds of years it became a way of Spanish life to avoid all relationships with people other than one's own close family circle. We employed a part-time young married handyman who told us that the only time he was ever invited to his fiancée's house prior to their marriage was the day they were officially engaged. This lack of communication had a similar effect on business and commercial activities. Another example of business 'under cover' I experienced in Valencia where again I was conducted to a private apartment in a block of flats. Here a wholesaler of fashion jewellery had his stock in a room of his flat and the items were in cardboard shoeboxes on shelving fixed around the room walls. The wholesaler had a long table in the centre of the room, on one side of which he sat with the client, sitting opposite him, selecting his purchases as the contents of the cardboard boxes were passed along the table under his gaze. On my first visit I spent a couple of hours gazing at a flow of ladies fashion jewellery, the names of which I had difficulty with in the English language, let alone in the Spanish language. By the time I had completed my purchases my head was reeling. Fortunately the wholesaler was also a pleasant Spanish gentleman whose kindly patience and helpfulness greatly assisted me to complete a task for which I had no knowledge or experience. In this way I managed to stock my little shop.

Pam and the children having now departed for England, I set out to establish my potential gift emporium offering the ladies lavish ranges of necklaces, bangles, beads, rings and all kinds of pretty ornaments to embellish their beauty and improve my bank balance. In addition I had discovered a wholesale source in Benidorm where one could obtain supplies of English greeting cards. The display of these began to attract the rising number of English speaking immigrants who were forming 'ex pat' communities in the newly developed building estates of the area around Calpe. So in time the shop became a sort of English speaking social centre where I listened and learned of all the trials and tribulations of the English speaking settlers – and there were many sad stories of swindles and sharp practice endured by the unwary gullible English immigrants

My ladies fashion jewellery became popular with the young village 'señoritast but they were not impressed by the tongue-tied English 'ignoramus' who could not speak a word of their language. It very soon became evident that, if I were to establish my business with any degree of success, I had to learn Spanish rapidly. To run the shop, and the flat which we had rented above the shop, precluded the possibility of attending any conventional centre of language teaching, so it was necessary to solve the problem by my usual D.I.Y. methods. I searched around the area for an English based gramophone record course of the Spanish language but was unsuccessful. However I found a set of Spanish language course records for French speaking students. I spoke French quite well, so I bought that set and started my studies. I set my record player playing my French recorded Spanish lessons whilst I was cooking and eating my breakfast. Then, after clearing away the breakfast, I would endeavour to repeat what I had heard. Speaking French was a great help since both languages are Latin based and thus the vocabularies have similar roots. I plodded along, thinking rather pessimistically that I would never speak the language when, suddenly, after some 12 months of boring grind, I began speaking Spanish. It was a kind of hidden evolution which was unnoticed by me but was brought to my attention one morning when I saw an English acquaintance and passed the time of day in Spanish. He remarked 'You speak good Spanish now.' That seemed to jolt my self-confidence and from that time onwards I was no longer ashamed to speak in Spanish.

During this time Calpe was slowly developing from its backward fishing village condition where street lighting hardly existed, where everybody and everything closed down after 8 p.m. leaving only a couple of café-bars to form the village night life during the dark winter nights. A road began to be constructed in front of my shop and actual pavements appeared that might encourage visitors to venture into the area. Street lighting began to appear, and a minister from Madrid with a great fanfare of publicity opened a dual carriageway from the village to the port and beaches. This new dual carriageway linked the old village to the port and to the new seaside suburbs which were being developed at that time. The Mayor managed to raise a large capital sum by local taxation which provided for the construction of a pleasant sea-front promenade. This became a great tourist attraction for it provided a very pleasant seaside walk from the old village 'avenida' right to the port and the famous

Spain – Peñon de Ifach, Calpe's miniature Gibraltar

Spain – another view of the Peñon with reflexion

sky-soaring rock the 'Peñon de Ifach' and then along some mile or so of beautiful sandy beaches

Pam and the children were settled at various schools in England and, during the school holidays, they came out to join me in Calpe, much to my joy and relief at having some relaxation from interminable hours in the shop. The shop prospered slowly but never looked like making us into rich capitalists. It provided a modest living and did give us some relief from the financial anxiety of the earlier continuous daily depletion of our capital. After some two years or so of operation in Calpe I received a visit from Señor Martinez, the original builder of the Garvimar complex who made me an offer of a villa in one of the outlying newly developed suburbs. He knew that I had been looking around for a villa and had viewed and rejected his villa which he now offered to me at a substantial discount. I got the impression that he and his partner were in some sort of financial difficulty and were selling off marginal assets to raise money. The villa in question was in a run-down condition, having been through a period of neglect and in fact it had developed serious building defects It was a fairly large villa built on pillars to give a good 180 degree view to the sea and the magnificent Peñon de Ifach. This rock nearly a thousand feet high towers above the port like a miniature Rock of Gibraltar. It is an extremely impressive landmark on Calpe's coastline and is now a well known tourist attraction.

I again refused his offer and in seeming desperation he said 'Make me an offer – any offer'. I made a ludicrous offer but finally agreed to buy it for almost a gift price. I had thereby loaded myself with an almost perpetual workload which, year by year,

Spain – another view of our villa at Calpe

Spain – the author and family – from left, Anne, Christine, Pam, self and Richard

occupied my spare time. It did however provide a base and a more congenial home for the family, where one had more privacy and better neighbours. We developed a cosmopolitan circle of friends of a variety of nationalities including Swiss, German, French, and Dutch, mainly through our sporting activities in tennis and golf. Particularly in tennis we had formed a small private group which met every Sunday morning to play doubles on a communal court belonging to a block of flats in Calpe. On the ground floor of the block was a café-bar to which we usually adjourned after a couple of hours of tennis. Here we spent an hour or so imbibing to restore our energy and with fresh vigour we changed our location to a restaurant-bar on the sea front. Here with the aid of the famous Spanish 'tapas' we imbibed some further 'restoratives', finally adjourning for a late lunch.

I had one particularly close tennis friend, a Swiss chap, by the name of Adolf Gassmann (Addy for short), from Zurich. He had made a considerable fortune in Australia, originally in the building trades and finally in the hotel business. I had a great admiration for him for his pluck in arriving in Australia with literally nothing and, by sheer courage and intelligence, making good. We became great friends.

One day he called at our villa just after lunch to inform me of a change in a forthcoming tennis date. Knowing his partiality for a certain '103' brandy I offered him a tot. He took his tot saying he had promised his wife to return quickly. However he willingly accepted a further 'one for the road' and relaxed to enjoy further road 'assistance'. Came four o'clock and I told him it was time for me to leave to open the shop for the post siesta session. He volunteered to come with me but I warned him that, being winter time, there would be no customers and he would be bored. Nevertheless he insisted on following me in his open jeep car, As we got near the shop he disappeared and I thought he had changed his mind and gone home.

Ten minutes after I had opened the shop he reappeared with a magnum of '103' brandy! We had a friendly drink and then he complained that there were no customers and he was bored. He asked for a sheet of paper and wrote out a large notice which he stuck onto my shop window. It read 'FREE BRANDY DRINKS TO ALL CALPE LADIES, VIRGINS DOUBLE TOTS.' When nothing happened he went outside inviting in all passing females. In a short time we had half a dozen or so ladies sipping brandy at my shop counter when in walked my wife Pam and a gentleman who was one of her Spanish class pupils. Pam had brought him to the shop to meet me as a fellow DIY enthusiast. He happened to be a very straight-laced individual and, horrified by the alcoholic gathering at my counter, to Pam's great embarrassment, he promptly fled. The ladies also disappeared.

Addy collapsed on the shop floor hysterical with laughter and protested that we did not appreciate his efforts to popularise and advertise our business, He decided it was time he returned home and made efforts to do so but, being somewhat befuddled by his liberal intake from the '103' magnum, he had considerable difficulty in locating his car keys and starting his car. Seeing his difficulties it was obvious to me that he was in no condition to drive home for at that time he had a villa half way up a fairly steep mountain road with many severe S-bends to negotiate. I persuaded him to let me drive him home in my own van which offer he fortunately accepted. When we arrived at his villa his wife answered the door and, with a rather venomous look at me, took over the care of a collapsing and somewhat helpless inebriated Addy.

The next morning, having opened the shop, I looked into Addy's open jeep to investigate why he had had such difficulty in starting the car the previous evening. There, on the floor of the car by the driver's seat, was a bunch of keys which I presumed were his house keys, car keys etc, together with his wallet and a considerable sum of money in notes and coins spread over the car floor.

Around lunchtime an anxious looking Addy arrived at the shop in an abashed mood, Somewhat apprehensively he asked me if I had seen any keys or money in his car. Tremendously relieved when I restored his lost possessions to him he thanked me and beat a hasty retreat. Later he recovered his usual cheery self but he seemed to be dogged by ill-luck. Armed robbers attacked him and his wife in their villa, actually shooting at but fortunately missing them. This decided him to return to Switzerland. But in the meanwhile he had unfortunately become an alcoholic. I think he had retired too young and had nothing to exercise his high degree of intelligence or his considerable talents as an entrepreneur. A few years later while touring Europe Pam and I decided to call on him in Zurich but were shocked to learn that he had died some six months previously. Apparently he had developed cancer of the lungs through excessive cigar smoking.

Around this time we were pressurised by our children, who were now at boarding school in England, to establish a home in England. They complained to us that they could not reciprocate the hospitality of their school friends who for example invited them occasionally to spend weekends in their homes at half term holidays. We were able, at last, to remedy this situation by the generosity of Pam's mother who kindly provided the wherewithal to purchase a house in Shrewsbury which was convenient to both our daughters' and our son's schools. And so, dividing our lives between our two homes in Shrewsbury and Calpe, we have had a dual life, spending the winter months in Spain and the summer months in England. This became possible because we decided to rid ourselves of the hassle of running the shop. We sold it to a German businessman and we were at long last able to have some leisure time for ourselves.

In our advancing age we felt that we should have one more fling before it was too late. We planned an ambitious European tour of the Eastern European countries that we had never before visited. The reader of these memoirs will by now have gathered that my life has been perhaps somewhat unusual and often interesting, but rarely boring. Likewise my family life with Pam and the children has been coloured in a similar manner by an unconventional way of life. I have just previously stated that we had sold the shop and, for the first time in our lives we felt rich. Of course we were not rich. It was just a reaction from a lifetime of constant financial pressure; the everlasting necessity of having to have careful regard for every penny. This new feeling of freedom to spend was so delicious and so enjoyable that we decided to celebrate this remarkable event by buying a new car in Spain and planning an extensive tour of Europe. We decided to buy the car under a Spanish Government tax free export scheme. Under this scheme we were able to buy a Renault 21 Estate car from a local dealer at a considerable discount. We set off on our planned grand European tour, starting in Spain and ending, we hoped, in England.

Our plan was to travel eastwards along the south of France and into Italy, visiting Florence and the Leaning Tower of Pisa. Then, heading north east to Bologna we would call at Venice, then Trieste. From here, we would head south to what was at that time Yugoslavia. Going via Zagreb, Split and Belgrade we intended to cross into Hungary, visiting Budapest. Turning north east via Vienna in Austria we planned to visit our friends Hans and Maria Kaliba who had been so kind to us early in our stay in South Africa now at Erlangen, near Nuremberg in Germany. From there we would travel homewards via Luxembourg, Belgium and France.

Such was the plan, but the reality was totally different. We progressed merrily and happily in our new car through southern France, spending a couple of days in Arles in Provence. Going via Aix, skirting Cannes, Nice and Monte Carlo, we crossed the French frontier into Italy at Menton and headed for San Remo. Then we took the Autostrada towards Pisa, spending a night in a nearby village. Next day, having climbed the Leaning Tower, we went on to Florence but the torrential rain prevented us from appreciating the beauty of its ancient buildings. Then, bypassing Bologna, we drove on towards Venice, spending two nights just outside the city. But, again, the heavy rain destroyed our appreciation of its unique character. Next day we passed through Trieste, crossing the frontier into Yugoslavia at Kozina. We spent the night at Opatija, a seaside resort near Rijeka, where we found a small but comfortable hotel on the sea front.

The next day proved to be our day of drama, where another of my cat's nine lives was to be crossed off the balance sheet of my life. We left this pleasant little seaside resort around 9.45 a.m., taking the road south towards Split. This ancient coastal road, built by the Romans thousands of years ago, is the only road south. Forbidding and impassable mountains inland have prevented any serious development. The road runs precariously over mountainous terrain, closely following the coastline so that it winds in and out of the many bays, often high along cliffs above the sea with precipitous drops on the landward side. Travelling along the beautiful Dalmatian coastline we were crossing just such a mountainous neck with a drop of several hundreds of feet into the sea on our right and a precipitous drop of hundreds of feet on our left. We were so happy, with not a care in the world, when suddenly the bottom dropped out of this happy world. We were rounding a right-hand bend at a moderate speed when the car began to skid sideways, completely out of control. It had just rained very slightly and, unknown to us, the road surface was impregnated with oil from decades of lorry traffic. The slight rain was insufficient to clean the road surface but sufficient to mix with the oil to make a glass-like skid-pan on this bend.

The car, skidding sideways and forwards to the left side of the road where existed a precipitous drop, struck a small stone bollard, one of several placed at wide intervals along the side of the road. This was sufficient to take off most of our forward speed but the rear of the car swung over the edge of the precipice. Amazingly, we came to a stop, balancing with the front of the car about eighteen inches over the edge and the rear of the car about three feet down the side. The car was at a dangerous angle, probably 20 to 30 degrees to the horizontal. Being a continental left hand drive car I was on the precipice drop side and I remember looking down and thinking to myself, 'It's only about a hundred feet drop down there'. What I did not realise was that there was another hundred feet drop from the ledge I was looking at. Quite a tumble!! Looking to my right I saw Pam seeming to tower above me on the passenger seat side. However we were quite calm although it seemed that the car might topple over down the precipice at any moment. She asked me, 'Shall I get out?' meaning only too clearly that, if she moved her weight to the right to get out of the car, it might overbalance, turn over and career down into the precipice.

At that very moment, coming in the opposite direction around the next bend about two hundred yards ahead, there appeared an Italian tourist coach whose occupants had seen us skid over the side. The driver accelerated and stopped alongside us and twenty or thirty screaming Italian tourists rushed out of the coach and grabbed the roof-rack which was an integral built-in feature of our car. This prevented the car toppling over while Pam climbed out. With the Italians anchoring the car I edged myself sideways to the passenger seat and climbed out also. With a great feeling of relief I once again had my feet on 'terra firma'. By this time a Yugoslav lorry had pulled up behind the coach and the driver really knew how to handle this kind of situation. He had probably seen it all before! He called for a tow-rope and a German tourist, who had also just arrived on the scene, produced, with the usual German efficiency, just the type of tow-rope called for. The Yugoslav driver moved the coach and cars clear of our car, then hitched the tow-rope from the rear of our car to his own rear bumper. With another rope he himself carried he attached it to the front of our car and then organised a squad of Italian and German men to grab and pull on the front rope whilst he climbed into his lorry and edged it forward, pulling the rear of our car up to the road. The combined effort pulled the car back onto the road and the car was pushed onto a safe parking spot. The stone bollard had ripped the underside of the engine and damaged the radiator in addition to damaging the front of the car. Having done their job, our helpers and rescuers continued on their way after receiving our heartfelt grateful thanks. Once again I had eluded the clutches of the Reaper and once again I marvelled at our escape. The brave action of the screaming Italian tourists in hanging onto our car roof-rack and so anchoring the car over the precipice edge had undoubtedly saved our lives and the car as well.

The Yugoslav lorry driver then kindly volunteered to take Pam to the nearest little town on his route where she could probably organise some kind of assistance. I, of course, was left on the roadside with the damaged car. After some time, a Yugoslav police patrol came along and stopped to investigate. Fortunately one of the two police could speak English and I was able to inform them of what had happened. Having heard my story, they both chortled cheerfully and said this kind of thing happened frequently when there was light rain on the road. They questioned me on whether any person had been injured or whether any third party's property had been damaged in the accident. When I gave a negative to both questions, after checking my passport and driving licence, they very helpfully said that, to leave the country, I would need a police certified statement confirming my being clear of any liability. Giving me their station address, they said that, if I called on them there, they would provide the necessary document.

After another long wait Pam eventually turned up with a breakdown rescue outfit which took us to Starigrad, a small town on the road to Split. Here a garage did a temporary repair, fitting a secondhand radiator. This took a couple of days, after which we were mobile once again. We had not been on the road very long when the engine began to overheat. Stopping at a local garage, investigation showed that we needed a new radiator. Our car being that year's new Renault model, such a radiator was not available in Yugoslavia. In fact, very little in the way of car spares was available in Yugoslavia. Eventually, by dint of several laborious attempts at phoning Spain, we managed to persuade our insurers in Madrid to send us a radiator by air freight.

The radiator eventually arrived and we collected it from Split airport by taxi. By this time we had decided to abandon all ideas of continuing our trip and we investigated the quickest route back to England. We found that there was a ferry service across the Adriatic Sea from Split to Ancona in Italy. This port was more or less facing Split on the opposite side of the Adriatic. The ferry could carry cars and the crossing was scheduled as an overnight trip embarking at 11 p.m. and arriving the following morning at 8 a.m. This would avoid having to retrace our steps through Yugoslavia and would save a tremendous amount of time. In addition we would be travelling in better conditions where help would be available in the case of another breakdown in our damaged car. Our car looked an ugly mess of mangled metal at the front and attracted considerable attention as we progressed homewards.

Having booked our passage and a cabin on this ferry we drove on to Split, spending a couple of days viewing this beautiful and delightful ancient city. What it is like now after the vicious bombardment it has suffered in recent times, I cannot guess. At the ferry port we presented our official police certificate to vindicate our legality in spite of our ugly appearance and boarded this excellent Italian ferry to sail at 11 p.m. We had a very comfortable cabin and, after a restful night, we docked at 8 a.m. the next morning in Ancona and had breakfast in a local hotel on the sea-front. Checking our return route, there seemed to be a choice. If we went via Milan there was a railway service through to London which would also provide carriage for the car. The alternative was to drive the car through the Swiss tunnels into France and so home, at the risk of a breakdown en route. You may probably guess which way I favoured, but Pam seemed to have lost her urge for adventure and advanced very strong argument for the train at Milan.

We motored to Milan which was about 300 miles over some mountainous country and, to avoid an acrimonious dispute, I agreed to consider the train option when we arrived there, but the good performance of the car on this first stage gave me confidence. I decided to drive back all the way to the U.K. and avoid all the hassle of train journeys. We passed through Milan with Pam in fear and trepidation at what might happen in the Swiss Alps. By careful coaxing 'sparing the horses' (engine ones) I succeeded in getting the car back to Shrewsbury without further incident, a feat of which I was very proud.

Safely back at home in Shrewsbury, the car was repaired and restored to its almost new pristine condition by the clever re-conditioning garage at Hadley. We had several trips to Spain following this adventure. Eventually came my 80th birthday. To my amazement my two daughters combined together and presented me with a birthday present of two air tickets to go around the world over a period of one year. These tickets were open and so, six months later, Pam and I set off on our round the world trip. From London we flew to Delhi. Here we decided to make a trip up North to Kashmir which nestles in the foothills of the Himalaya Mountains. As it was already late in the year we thought it best to go there straight away before the weather became too cold. We flew on the local internal airline landing at Srinagar having caught a glimpse of the snow-capped foothills of the Himalayas during our approach to the landing at Srinagar. We were met at the airport by a car provided by the Company which owned the houseboat which was to be our home for the next few days. After quite a long drive through native villages we came to the noisy Asian city of Srinagar and so to the beautiful lake where our future houseboat home 'The Golden Lotus' was at anchor. The tranquillity and beauty of the lake are unbelievable. It is another world and here we lived in Paradise existing on a diet of curried goat cooked to perfection by our Indian houseboat chef.

Returning to Delhi we travelled to Bombay and left India for Thailand. We spent six weeks there travelling north and south over a large area of the country. From Thailand we flew on to Hong Kong where we were greatly impressed with the animated vivacious hustle and bustle of the daily life. From Hong Kong we took a short trip to Canton (Guanghou). Here we had an amusing incident. In the usual Chinese Government system, in order to oversee our movements, we were escorted by an official Government guide who proved to be a very congenial young man. He was a university graduate and was a fanatic devotee of World War 2 history and memorabilia. When he discovered that I was a WW2 veteran he never left my side. He was always at my elbow to help me descend the steps of the coach or climb the steps of the hotel. He had conducted us to Zhaoqing where we were put up in a typical showpiece Government tourist hotel which was of a very high standard. It so happened that we had arrived at the hotel on New Year's Eve (1988) and we naturally wanted to celebrate the occasion. We consulted our Chinese guide on the possibility of some suitable entertainment locally and he informed us that in the village there was nothing of this nature that he could recommend. He said that the only thing he could recommend was a disco which was held in the cellar beneath the hotel. He said that there was a live band and it was very popular with the Chinese visitors from Hong Kong. As there was no alternative and we felt that we should at least make an effort to celebrate the New Year, we agreed to attend the disco, escorted of course by our ever-present Chinese guide.

After dinner we duly descended into the disco cellar and, seated at our table, we ordered our drinks. The band commenced playing and I asked Pam if she would like to dance. Before Pam could reply our Chinese guide quickly said, 'I will dance with you'. To my embarrassment I had to agree. And so the three of us proceeded to the dance floor. Here we were dancing as a small group and our guide was really entering into the spirit of the thing with very athletic manoeuvres, to which I responded. To my amazement the remainder of the young Chinese dancers on the floor stopped dancing and formed a circle around us and I found myself giving a sort of exhibition dance to the enjoyment of our young spectators. Probably their excited interest was due to the peculiar sight of an English old fogey and his wife performing rather athletic dancing with a young Chinese and two Indians. I should have mentioned that our Hong Kong excursion group consisted of ourselves and an Indian father and son from London. Our official Chinese guide, with the unlikely name of Roland, completed our little group. The next day we set off in our small minibus for a place called Fashan which was beside a beautiful lake with rolling hills in the distance. Such exquisite scenery was almost like a living example of the artistic scenes on an old-fashioned expensive Chinese porcelain dinner service. After visiting various factories and temples we had lunch at the Fashan Hotel, wending our way through dense crowds of bicycles. There seemed to be thousands of Chinese riding bicycles and hundreds of bikes parked in serried rows.

After a pleasant Chinese lunch we set off for Guangzhou and the famous Chingping open air market. Here we really had a close-up view of the Chinese way of life, particularly for the peasant class. The market was set out in a narrow street in stalls similar to those in Europe and the place was teeming with people. But the objects for sale were extraordinary to say the least. On one stall we saw, laid out in rows, filleted rats about twelve inches long, cut open down the centre and skinned. Whilst we were looking at this amazing sight, a cry from the crowd behind us attracted our attention and, turning round, we beheld a man carrying on a bamboo shoulder yoke a huge basket in which was a large completely skinned Alsatian dog. On the next stall was a huge mass of dried snakes of every type one could think of. Another stall table nearby carried most peculiar objects such as bears' paws, tigers bones etc, which one could only suppose were some sort of medicinal charms or used to bring good fortune. In the butchery section there was very little meat on show but the Chinese could select their meal from the dozens of cages of live cats, dogs and rabbits. In stall after stall we saw bags of weird roots. After wandering though the congested crowds we returned to the China Hotel and here we had an excellent Chinese tea and cakes. Finally, having settled our account with Roland, he took us to the railway station where we caught a train back overland through the New Territories to Hong Kong. The journey took just under three hours but it was mostly overnight so we saw very little during our passage through this area of the New Territories.

Leaving Hong Kong, our next flight took us to Japan. Whilst we were spending a few days in Tokyo there occurred the sad event of the Emperor's death and from that moment Tokyo seemed to be overcome with grief so that the whole atmosphere was depressing and morbid. To make matters worse during our stay, I contracted a severe cold which affected my breathing and this rather limited our activities However, on the recommendation of an English speaking assistant in the travel agency of a department store, we did manage to visit one or two places of interest. We took the train from Tokyo to Kyoto. This service was the famous 'bullet train' which travelled at speeds up to 150 m.p.h. but was incredibly smooth and comfortable. For most of the journey we were passing through built-up areas with the majority of the houses built very close together without any gardens at all. At one point of the journey we had glimpse of Mount Fuji with its snow-capped peak.

Visiting temples etc. in Kyoto we then moved on to Hiroshima which was about a two-hour train journey. Here, of course, was the site of the first atomic bomb attack on Japan. The city has a population of about two million people and has been almost completely re-built since its destruction in 1945. We visited the Peace Memorial Park there which contains the A-Bomb Dome. This building has since been preserved in its ruined state on the spot where the bomb fell, to serve as a kind of witness to the tremendous destruction and carnage caused by the bomb. In a museum in this Peace Memorial Park there was shown a film on the subject of the bomb and the effects it had on the people who suffered from radiation. Our own reaction from this visit was the way the Japanese agonised on their suffering and criticised this attack on their country, but never was there any mention of the years of death and cruelty that their military inflicted on many other nations of the East and on America at Pearl Harbour and the ensuing conflicts.

From Japan we moved on again eastwards on our world-circulating journey. This time our next stop was Hawaii and we parked down on what is known as The Big Island. The weather was frightful, nothing but continuous cloud and rain which was not conducive to happy sightseeing excursions. However we managed to make our trip interesting though I personally was somewhat disappointed since I had the conventional idea that these lovely sandy beaches would be full of almost naked beautiful girls with garlands of highly perfumed flowers dancing exotically to the romantic music of Hawaiian guitars. In fact there were high-rise blocks, concrete galore, no semi-naked girls and everybody rushing around in a typical American rat race. We made the most of the foul weather and lack of entertaining excursions by driving our hired car to the volcano area where we visited the special Volcano Centre which provided a wealth of information on the volcano phenomenon. It was most interesting and we were able to drive close to an area where volcano lava streams were actually flowing into the sea. One very interesting sight which we viewed in this area was Pearl Harbour which saw the Japanese air attack which forced the Americans into WW2. This attack left the major part of their Pacific fleet under the Pearl Harbour waters, not to mention the destruction of their air bases in the vicinity.

Moving on again, we flew to San Francisco in California where our elder daughter, Anne, and her American husband, Peter Dawson, were living. He is a retired vice-president of the huge finance and insurance companies conglomerate Trans America. We spent almost three months in the States and for our travels we bought a large and elegant Ford at a bargain price. We made trips to Los Angeles, the Grand Canyon in Arizona and Las Vegas. When we arrived in Las Vegas with its multitude of hotels cum gambling dens we went straight to the Circus Circus Hotel following the recommendation given us by our son-in-law Pete. Here we were informed that every one of its 2800 rooms was full. They kindly recommended the Riviera Hotel opposite and as a small compensation gave us two of their luncheon vouchers for the price of one. We had two most excellent lunches for about £1.50. Booking into the Riviera Hotel we had an enormous room and spent most of our time on the hotel tennis courts resisting the blandishments of the tremendous areas of gaming tables and the thousands of one-armed bandit machines. Every hotel provides acres of gambling palaces on their ground floors along with an enormous variety of side-shows and theatre acts amongst their gaming tables. At the Circus Circus Hotel we witnessed marvellous circus acts – hence the hotel name.

Returning homewards we stayed a short while with some South African friends who were living in Denver. From there we flew eastwards to Orlando and decided to tour the East Coast in order to visit the great cities of Washington, Boston and New York. Near Boston was the American town of Portsmouth in New Hampshire. As I have written at the commencement of these memoirs I was born in Portsmouth, Hampshire – Old Hampshire? So I decided to visit the American imitation of the original. We found a pleasant city indeed, part of which was a plausible imitation of the ancient buildings of Old Portsmouth from which Nelson had sailed in 1805 on his warship the 'Victory' to his death at the Battle of Trafalgar. This victory destroyed the combined French and Spanish fleets and so dashed forever Napoleon's hopes of invading England.

And so to New York where we took our flight homewards to London. Our round the world trip had taken six months.

Our children now grown up, left home and established themselves very successfully in different parts of the world. Their initial move, after leaving school, was to London or the Home Counties and they did their best to persuade us to move again and follow them down South. But we had found a pleasant retirement niche in friendly Shrewsbury; we had a pleasant home and we had all we wanted almost on our doorstep including a most friendly and enjoyable tennis club, by name Woodfield, only five minutes walk away. So we resisted all their persuasive pressure and remained put. And we have never regretted our decision.

It is perhaps interesting that I, having portrayed my humble origins in some detail and with some frankness in these memoirs, should by sheer accident have moved into a part of the country where the family name Weston is the family name of much more illustrious people and their forbears. Weston Park, only a few miles down the road from Shrewsbury, is the ancestral home of the seventh Earl of Bradford. One day, when our children were still at school, we had collected the two girls, Anne and Christine, from their boarding school at Abbots Bromley. We were on our way back to Shrewsbury when, passing Weston Park, we decided on the spur of the moment to visit the house and park, which we had never bothered to do up to that time. Just inside the house, on a wall, was a huge genealogical tree showing the family descent of the Earls of Bradford. To my astonishment it showed that the Earl's family had descended from a branch of the Westons. On a later visit to the house and following the advice of Colonel Weston (coincidentally he bore the same name) who was the Earl of Bradford's Estate Agent, we went over to a little church close by the house which we found to be the parish church of a nearby village called Weston under Lizard. Going into this tiny but delightful little church we read a notice inside which proudly proclaimed that the tombs of two Crusader knights named Weston possibly of the 13th century were housed in this church. The notice informed us that in those early days the Westons had 'de' in front of their name. And sure enough at the back of the church were the two tombs with the traditional wooden effigies of the knights lying on top. Later, visiting Winchester, we saw a similar tomb with an effigy of a knight named Weston lying on top of his resting-place behind the choir and altar of the magnificent Winchester Cathedral. I became curious after learning of this surprising association with the name Weston and found that Weston Park was mentioned in the Domesday Book of William the Conqueror. I presume the de Weston knights accompanied William on his invasion of England and were rewarded with the seigniory of this land which became known as Weston Park. At the time of the Domesday Book it had passed into the hands of another Norman, one Rainald de

Backleuil, but later was held by the de Westons and, surprisingly, the Myttons. The Mytton name is famous in the county of Shropshire, It would appear that the Westons and Myttons were intermarried. One of the Mytton family was Elizabeth who married Sir Thomas Wilbraham in 1651. It was this lady who was responsible for the rebuilding of the present house in 1671. Elizabeth's third daughter inherited Weston Park and she married the second Earl of Bradford. Thus started the connection of the family of the Earl of Bradford with Weston Park.

Another interesting historical connection of the Weston name occurred in Henry VIII's reign when Sir Francis Weston was beheaded, accused of an affair with Anne Boleyn, Henry's second wife. Anne Boleyn had a great interest in music and poetry and had an intimate small group of four young knights of similar taste. Included in the circle was a professional musician who was Anne's music teacher. Cardinal Wolsey had a great dislike of Anne from the days before her marriage when she criticised him for delays in obtaining Henry's first divorce and thus delaying her own marriage. Wolsey eventually succeeded in accusing her of an affair with these four knights and the musician.

These people were arrested and thrown into the Tower of London where they were subjected to torture to extract confessions. The musician was the only one to succumb and his evidence was accepted as sufficient to dubiously prove the rest guilty. They were all executed in 1536 on the lawn facing the Tower, except the

*The Weston Family on the occasion of my 90th birthday – from left, Christine, Anne,
Richard, Pam and self.*

musician who was not considered a gentleman and therefore not entitled to the privilege of being beheaded on the lawn of the Tower. He was hung, drawn and quartered in the usual London's criminal site. Anne herself, accused by Wolsey, was executed shortly after, also at the Tower.

However, out of compassion (?!) for his second royal wife he agreed to the hiring of a French executioner noted for his skill with his axe. This executioner's sharp axe and his accurate unerring aim resulted in a swift clean decapitation thus avoiding the misery which sometimes followed mutilation caused by bungled attempts to complete the execution.

Whilst I have never been interested in genealogy nor curious concerning the ancestry of my own branch of the Weston family, my accidental discoveries of the connection of the name with such illustrious local people have led me to think to end this autobiography on a contrasting note to that with which I commenced. I trust the reader of these memoirs may find the tales of an unusual life make interesting reading.

The Author and his wife Pam at an RAF Club Dinner

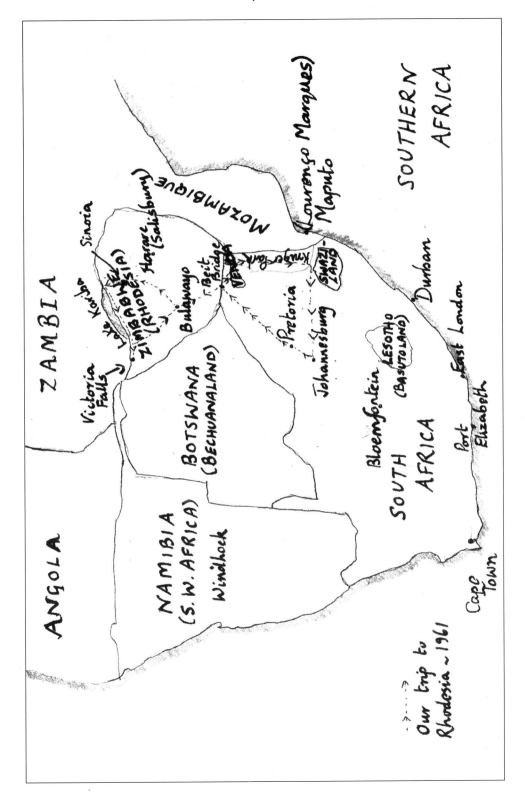

ANGOLA

ZAMBIA

Victoria Falls

Lake Kariba

Sinoia

MOZAMBIQUE

Lourenço Marques)
Maputo

SOUTHERN
AFRICA

ZIMBABWE
(RHODESIA)

Harare (Salisbury)

Bulawayo

Beit Bridge

Kruger Park

SWAZI-
LAND

Durban

BOTSWANA
(BECHUANALAND)

Pretoria

Johannesburg

LESOTHO
(BASUTOLAND)

Bloemfontein

SOUTH
AFRICA

East London

NAMIBIA
(S.W. AFRICA)
Windhoek

Port
Elizabeth

Cape
Town

> - - - >
Our trip to
Rhodesia ~ 1961

Index

List of Maps